CORPORATE FUTURES

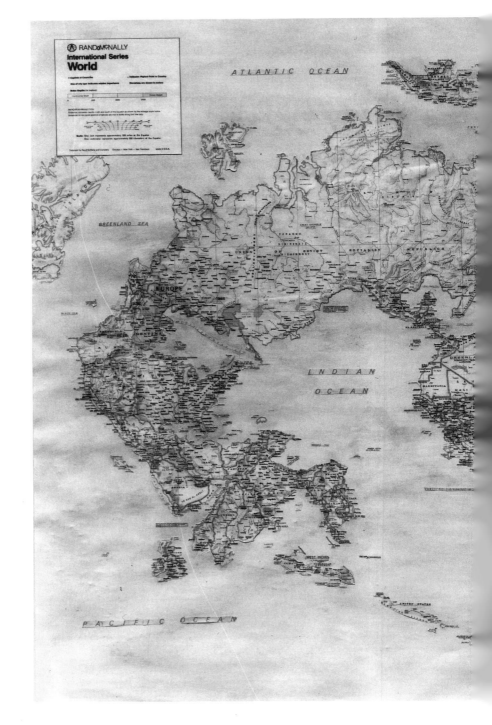

World Map 2, © 1989 by Nina Katchadourian

Late Editions

5

Cultural Studies for the End of the Century

CORPORATE FUTURES

THE DIFFUSION OF THE CULTURALLY SENSITIVE CORPORATE FORM

George E. Marcus, EDITOR

The University of Chicago Press
Chicago and London

George E. Marcus is professor of anthropology at Rice University. He is coauthor of *Anthropology as Cultural Critique* (University of Chicago Press, 1986) and was the inaugural editor of the journal *Cultural Anthropology*.

The University of Chicago Press, Chicago 60637
The University of Chicago Press, Ltd., London
© 1998 by The University of Chicago
All rights reserved. Published 1998
Printed in the United States of America
07 06 05 04 03 02 01 00 99 98   1 2 3 4 5

ISBN: 0-226-50453-0 (cloth)
ISBN: 0-226-50454-9 (paper)

ISSN: 1070-8987 (for Late Editions)

♾ The paper used in this publication meets the minimum requirements of the American National Standard for Information Sciences—Permanence of Paper for Printed Library Materials, ANSI Z39.48-1992.

CONTENTS

Introduction

And I'd actually like to do a book in which there is no metalanguage, no master discourse, where you wouldn't know which is strongest, the sociological theory or the documents or the interviews or literature or the fiction, where all these genres or regimes would be at the same level, each one interpreting the others without anybody being able to say which is judging what.

But that's impossible; and besides, it would be incredibly boring. And what good would it do?

Well, it would be good for training people like you. And it would be good for educating the public, for getting people to understand, getting them to love technologies. I'd like to turn the failure of Aramis into a success, so it won't have died in vain, so . . .

You're funny, Norbert. You want to reeducate the whole world and you want to produce a discourse that doesn't control anyone! Readers want a line, they want mass transit, not point-to-point, not personalized cabins. You want to know what I think? You are about to embark on another Aramis project, another wild-goose chase. As infeasible as the first one. Remember the lesson of Aramis: "Don't innovate in every respect at once." Your book is just one more rickety endeavor, ill-conceived from birth, a white elephant.

> (Concluding fictional dialogue between a sociologist of science and his student in *Aramis, or the Love of Technology,* by Bruno Latour)

This is the fifth volume in a series of annuals, lasting until the year 2000. Readers familiar with previous works in this series will be aware of the unusual combination of modesty and chutzpah by which this project is motivated. We take very seriously the critiques of standard modes of representation and exposition that have swept the academy as well as expert discourses over the last decade and more. As social scientists monitoring with keen self-consciousness vast social changes now in process, we are only too well aware of the inadequacy of our conceptual apparatus to capture—describe and explain—the full extent of what those who answer our questions and give us "data" are telling us about their situations. Indeed, we believe that those who become our subjects, situated as social and cultural actors in milieus of change that we want to analyze and interpret, are engaged in acts of reconceptualizing their circumstances that share some kinship with our own predicaments as distanced, professional analysts of changing contemporary social and cultural realities. This series has moved from the diverse perspectives in *Perilous States* (Late Editions 1) on being amid the ruins of civil societies following the upheavals of states in the late 1980s and early 1990s, to the predicaments of doing fin-de-siècle science in *Technoscientific Imaginaries* (Late Editions 2), to the remarkable shifts in forms of media and the shape of careers that document contemporary change as registered in *Connected Engagements with Media* and *Cultural Producers* (Late Editions 3 and 4), to the present volume's concern with the facts-and-figures-oriented corporation's turn toward its soft cultural underbelly, and to things cultural in general. Overall, we have been consistently interested in the form and content of ongoing reflective reassessments conducted as part of everyday life by variously situated social actors with a deep sense of real and imagined fin-de-siècle changes.

Indeed, in terms of their own highly specific idioms and purposes, the social actors who become, in conversation with us, our specific subjects of research may even provide more nuanced, deeper, and richer conceptualizations of contemporary change than the remade, distanced, and authoritative exposition typical of the social-scientist expert, cultural critic, or journalist commentator—or, at least, this is the founding wager and provocation of this series.

Building its contributions around a signature format of interview or conversation, these volumes place a premium on an exposure of situated discussions with social actors at selected sites of research, in preference to standard forms of exposition in which the voice of the analytic commentator, presenting arguments, offering interpretations, and making conclusions, is paramount. Instead, the art of the genre with which this series is experimenting depends on a skillful contextualizing of material by authorial framing and editing such that the sense of argument, theory, concept, or conclusion that a reader expects from conventional commentaries on contemporary society and culture resides instead in the presentation of material itself, evoked as interview or conversation.

The modesty of this enterprise, then, is in our sense of the limitations of distanced commentaries on contemporary events and processes in conveying an understanding of them commensurate with their complexity and ambiguity. In no sense is this series meant to be a substitute for such conventional ethnography or social science writing; it is meant as a distinctive, valuable, and some-times challenging supplement to them. The chutzpah of this project is in the alternative that we offer—in effect, a series of experiments with form—in which value is claimed for paying primary attention to the exposure of material that is usually masked and subordinated to more "finished" commentary, de-scription, and argument. Because of the conceptual work and rethinking that is done in many settings by social actors, we believe that emphasizing the expo-sure of eliciting conversations and embedded discourses provides equivalent and even more complex understandings of social processes and institutions undergoing fin-de-siècle transformation than authoritative, expert discourse on society and culture. Consequently, the resulting pieces of these volumes might seem more raw and messier than conventional academic scholarly papers in the material they present, and certainly, they require more in the way of indulgence and participation from the reader.

The volumes of this series are generated by a standard cycle of production. Two meetings are held annually and in conjunction with each other during the late spring at the Rice University anthropology department. One is a collective editorial meeting on the current year's project; the other is a separate stimulus meeting for the next volume, attended by the contributors to the current year's volume, to discuss possible covering themes and to suggest likely contributors. In succeeding months, I invite prospective participants, who in the past have been mostly scholars at various stages of career development, typically from anthropology, history, sociology, literary studies, or interdisciplinary fields. They are asked to propose contributions that will take them back to sites of past interest or to already collected material, but will require them to operate in an unconventional genre, built on the interview/dialogue format. In a sense, the pieces that are developed for the series represent negotiations between me as the editor and upholder of the rationale of the series and the contributors who have developed highly variant and always interesting accommodations to this rationale. Drafts of pieces are circulated prior to the collective editorial meeting held in late May.

At this meeting there are discussions about revisions for final drafts to be submitted in the fall. Most interestingly, a general sense of a particular vol-ume's ethos emerges through these discussions that focus on details, unsus-pected connections among pieces, and the variant forms that they take. The result always remains an assemblage that does not approximate, nor seeks to do so, the mostly elusive ideal of the neatly interlocking, comprehensive schol-arly collection as treatise. Still, our assemblages have managed to evidence consistencies and striking points of coherence.

Before proceeding with our present attention to the corporation's invest-ments in the culture concept, as well as with the spread of the corporate form itself into cultural sites, traditionally set in opposition to corporations, we should perhaps summarize as a reintroduction to the series major distinctive features of its pieces and volumes:

— Ideally, in this series, the necessary framing or contextualization of pieces should be embedded in the interviews and conversations themselves. In practice, such embedded framing is rarely sufficient, so that authorial voice is often present and gravitates between making an argument and scene-setting.

— Because so much emphasis is placed on edited conversations and the exposure of subjects' discourses, there is always more of that in pieces than might be of specific interest to or intended by authorial design. We consider this excess, or slippage, so to speak, in each piece to be more of a virtue than a flaw of the series since it often allows for connections and associations to be made by readers out of the control of the series' rationale.

— The emphasis of these pieces is not so much on the specific telling of highly individual stories or on the singular case, as might be supposed from the use of the subject-focused interview genre. Rather, what is special about most of these pieces is that they provide *perspective,* speak the general, from a situated actor's point of view, in which the latter's conditions, purposes, and idioms are highly visible, or at least the ambiguities of which are accessible to the reader. It is precisely this imputed heightened tendency at present of the social actor, self-conscious of great transformations and breaks with the past, to reassess and "size up" his or her milieu that fascinates and motivates this project, and suggests what it can offer that other more conventional "voiceover" modes of exposition cannot.

— While working within common themes like science, political change, media, and corporations, for each of which there exists extensive literatures, the volumes of this series, taking shape as somewhat opportunistic assemblages, often comprise unusual juxtapositions and inclusions that stretch the commonsensical boundaries of a particular theme. For example, in the present volume we move from looking at the corporate interest in culture to the cultural interest in the corporate form (see part 3, "Opposition, Inc."). Again this is a kind of slippage characteristic of this project that we consider, on balance, more a virtue than a vice.

The Corporate Interest in Culture

While the debate between human relations and scientific management in the modern American corporation is itself nearly a century old, it is clear that expertise concerned with scientific management, economistic modeling, human engineering, and formal thinking about the rational bases of organizational behavior, generally, have dominated both the rhetoric and practices of corporate leadership. It is only in the past two decades that there have been signs of

change in the valence of the discourse of human relations as regards the preferred language of social engineering in the ranks of corporate management.
Now with a particular value given to the notion of "corporate culture," human
relations seem no longer to be just the "soft" framework for the discourse of
liberal experts and social critics of corporations in relation to how they treat
labor, nor only the preserve of public relations departments and corporate philanthropy in the effort to present capitalism with an ethical, socially responsible
face. Rather, values, norms, collective ethos, authority in personal relations,
and participatory structures of groups now seem to be a salient and very serious
frame of thinking for corporate managers at all levels. What was once primarily
the intellectual capital of oppositional groups or critics of corporations now
seems to be appropriated by corporate leadership as an integral yet ambivalent
characteristic of their own thinking.

This, of course, does not mean that corporate managers have been thor-
oughly won over to "culture" as the frame in which all operations of the corporation must now be thought about. To the contrary, Christopher Newfield's
piece in this volume provides a fascinating and complex account of the ironic
course that human relations approaches have taken in recent years among corporate management, especially toward the use of the idiom of the corporation
as a culture, which has much in common with the standard anthropological
concept of a culture as a distinctive enduring human group, flexibly constructing itself through symbols, conventions, and rules.

In the early 1980s there appeared a slew of popular books that consolidated
the human relations approach and foretold the coming hegemony of alternative
management theories based on building corporations as cultures of more effective production and less hierarchical participation. Newfield notes (chapter 1,
this volume):

> By the early 1980s human relations seemed ready to rule. It had an
> optimistic—even democratic—view of the capacities of the ordinary
> employee. It said that history was emancipating the complex, multi-
> dimensional, flexible, contextually aware individual from the weight
> of a dying bureaucratic age. It had shored up its weak quantitative
> flank. It looked forward to a renaissance in nonquantitative thinking.
> All these together would have offered business quite an amazing jolt.
> Technological reason and bureaucratic rule would be put in their place
> *from the inside.* It was one thing for social critics like Herbert Mar-
> cuse to decry the subtle tyrannies of a society designed to create "one-
> dimensional man." It was another for business intellectuals to attempt
> not simply a shuffling of the org charts but the transformations of the
> corporation's basic *metabolism.*

Yet as Newfield then goes on to recount, "the human relations revolution
never took place. We got the Reagan Revolution instead. Finance was back.

Rational-choice theories ran economics. Spreadsheet warriors like David Stock-man ran social policy. The boardroom was in full charge of firms. The numbers were in charge of the boardroom. Wall Street was in charge of the economy. 'Participation' meant stock options, not a voice in running either the economy or the firm. In government, the economy, and the individual firm, the relation-ships people were routed by the creatures from Planet Finance."

But also just as remarkably, all the managerial talk about corporate culture did not wane—in fact, by the 1990s it has transmuted and even intensified. It has remained a trope that corporate managers still take seriously and through which they still try to think both realistically and ideologically about the orga-nizations that they govern in broader social environments and political arenas that they less confidently understand than they once thought they did. Just as the traditional anthropological concept of culture changed over the same short period (see, for example, Marcus and Fischer 1986), so has the notion of cul-ture in terms of which corporate managers—and the consultants and experts who train and advise them—think about their organizations.

In anthropology, the concept of culture has moved from the sense of a whole integrated, self-contained social group and way of life to a sense of an entity, that while still defining a coherent group or community, is highly mutable, flexible, open to shaping from many directions at once in its changing environ-ments, and most importantly, a result of constructions continuously debated and contested among its highly independent, even unruly membership. This mode of discourse about culture is an adaptation to complex changes in world-scale systems and emergent structures that have reshaped the conditions of everyday life of the peoples that anthropologists have traditionally studied. Likewise, the discourse about corporations as cultures now focuses on this sense of flexibility over solidity, multiplicity over standard models. This is the theoretical equivalent, in fact, of taking pleasure in diversity and risk, seen more as possibility than as threat, which characterizes the academic literature on postmodernism that has so influenced changes in the notion of culture in such fields as anthropology, sociology, history, and literary studies.

There is indeed a new wave of business advice books and human relation gurus (with some continuities from the earlier period, such as the fascinating case of Tom Peters, whose career Newfield reviews). The messages of this latter wave emphasize much more adaptations of the internal orders of corpo-rations in more sensitive response to changes in their own broader social envi-ronments than the use of culture as an organizational weapon to respond to competition from alien societies, notably the Japanese, with cultures that seem to "work" for business. In a globalizing world and economy, the stimulus chal-lenges in response to which thinking of corporations as cultures has an appeal is located much more at home and *within* than abroad and is more subtle than a looming competitor with a cultural advantage.

There is now, for instance, talk of diversity management, corporate citizenship, and democracy. The emphasis on organizational competitiveness is still there, but the discourse is inflected with concerns about values, corporate personhood, the relation of individuals to community—in general, those topics that might have been considered before as "soft" in relation to "means-ends" modifications of organizational practices with the bottom line of competitive enhancement always in sight. In a recent paper on doctrines and practices of diversity management in U.S. corporations, Avery Gordon (1995) exposes the darker side of this progressive movement of liberal regimes of social policy into the boardrooms of corporate governance.[1] As the internal governance of corporations as cultures has come to reflect concerns of the wider society, so at the same time the interest of corporations in external social conditions and their commitment to traditional participation as patrons and philanthropists, out of self-interest and a sense of responsibility, in a so-called public sphere are less motivated. New social contracts are being forged within private corporate cultures, according to Gordon, and less so with reference to a more unruly and fragmented public sphere. Corporate cultures monitor and reflect in their internal rhetorics and policies of governance the changes in U.S. society, but they also substantively desert their past role as interested "citizen" actively involved in shaping public policy.

A committed focus on defining corporate culture in effect allows corporations to negotiate broader social changes in arenas that they control. The move toward reproducing society's control over culture in liberal policymaking within the corporate culture seems to register a loss of confidence among corporate leadership in the capacity of political order, the nation-state apparatus, to manage society itself as an environment for business. So the interest in corporate culture represents both capitalism's effort to manage the uncertainties of social change within its own organizational boundaries and its retreat from such a task in the wider society, the current conditions of which defeat an attempt to formulate any clear, overall sense of society's basic structure and dynamics.[2]

Thus in terms of the specific agenda of the Late Editions series as well as the range of cases that this particular volume addresses, we believe that the developing interest of corporations in themselves as cultures defines one of those spaces of self-conscious reassessment that exposes how social actors, in this case caught up in the reordering of managerial capitalism, are rethinking their habits of thought in the face of inadequately understood conditions of deep transformation that challenges past modes for neglecting, taking for granted, or at least comfortably operating with a conception of how the broader social order functions.[3] As the papers included here show, this rethinking is never in the form of an academic exercise or a purely intellectual task. Strategies, corporate morale, ethics, and responsibility, justifying and protecting one's judgments and assessments out of self-interest for one's position, and also a pure intent just to figure things out as well, are all at stake, interwoven through every testimony, commentary, exchange, and reflection registered in this volume. Indeed, how these values and interests ebb and flow in the various pieces is a source of their fascination and primary contribution. Still, there is here a keen sort of affinity between *us*—the academic participants in these volumes—and *them,* our situated subjects of interviews. This particularly marked affinity arises in the migration of the culture concept from the academic world to the corporate world as a frame for this discourse of the moment, both self-promotional and deeply uncertain, in the shadow of a felt inadequacy to now understand what could be mostly taken for granted before. For anthropologists especially there will be a particular irony in this migration of their signature concept appropriated and transformed in a sphere of their own society quite foreign to them—that of business—and without any consultation or credit either.

This affinity between academics and corporate actors is at best ambiguous and certainly does not signal an obvious alignment of interests. But for academics and cultural critics, at least, who have defined themselves as outside and intellectually independent of the major institutions of capitalism, this affinity through the culture concept should be unsettling in that it deprives them of their most familiar traditional strategies of gaining critical distance and perspective on corporations.

As actors in both domains rethink concepts with which they approach complex and changing realities, they also have to rethink their relationship to each other as the frameworks of cultural analysis migrate in one direction and the increasing requirement of corporate organization moves in the other. Regarding the latter, the papers of part 3 illustrate the special predicaments of subjects who have defined themselves as constitutionally outside and "in opposition" to corporations and formal institutions of government now having to "incorporate" themselves in different ways, thus becoming part of or complicit with corporate capitalism in ways that they cannot ignore. And, conversely, the papers on corporate subjects reveal how corporate actors have appropriated many of the terms and strategies of thinking about culture in an academic frame. This of course makes the *differences* that remain between the critical scholar and the corporate manager all the more important to identify.

The sometimes ambivalent affinities that develop between academic authors and their subjects are interesting to consider in this regard. For instance, Newfield moves from being in an earlier work a distanced critic of Tom Peters (see Newfield 1995) to sympathetically trying to work through his proposals here. Or, in several pieces (for example, those by Constance Perin and Melissa Cefkin), the authors give up or negotiate constitutional stances of critical opposition to come to terms with the complex positionings and rethinkings of corporate actors. In some pieces (those of Robbie Davis-Floyd and Perin), the primary subjects are academics located within or tangential to corporate operations, and in these cases the migratory path of the intellectual frameworks at play is even more blurred.

In general, then, it is just very difficult in many of these pieces to establish the rhetorically distanced critical punchlines characteristic of much academic writing on corporations. These performed affinities do not entail strong alliances of interest between academics and corporate actors, or a loss of critical perspective, but they do expose fairly a struggle with the much more nuanced sense of how critical arguments must be formed when the boundary is blurred that normally creates the possibility of defining a position of social and cultural critique "outside" the domain of corporate capitalism.

But why is a discourse about culture—what a culture is, what having one is—an appropriate and attractive medium for a certain segment of corporate leadership to remake the basic terms in which they think about their organizations? To what predicament embedded in capitalism, and its current state, does thinking about corporate culture respond? Very relevant is a classic instance of truth-telling against conventional ways of thinking about business organizations and economic processes. This is Joseph Schumpeter's insight that capitalism entails a process of creative destruction, as both a premise about its normal operation and one that becomes even more obvious, however uncomfortably and self-consciously, in periods of rapid change and great structural transformation:

> The opening up of new markets, foreign or domestic, and the organizational development from the craft shop and factory to such concerns as U.S. Steel illustrate the same process of industrial maturation—if I may use that biological term—that incessantly revolutionizes the economic structure *from within,* incessantly destroying the old one, incessantly creating a new one. This process of Creative Destruction is the essential fact about capitalism. It is what capitalism consists in and what every capitalist concern has got to live in. . . .
>
> The usual theorist's paper and the usual government commission's report practically never try to see that behavior, on the one hand, as a result of a piece of past history and, on the other hand, as an attempt to deal with a situation that is sure to change presently—as an attempt by those firms to keep on their feet, on ground that is slipping away from under them. In other words, the problem that is usually being visualized is how capitalism administers existing structures, whereas the relevant problem is how it creates and destroys them. As long as this is not recognized, the investigator does a meaningless job. As soon as it is recognized, his outlook on capitalist practice and its social results changes considerably.

Creative destruction as a vision of corporate development seems to fly in the face of the affirmative, self-justifying task of building, sustaining, and managing organizations on firm foundations, which while allowing for a rhetoric of change has been dominated by one of stability, progress, and growth. Under what conditions and in what terms might "the usual theorist's paper" or "the usual government commmission report," or for that matter, corporate managerial cognition, address explicitly and in its assumptions the process of creative destruction as envisioned by Schumpeter? Obviously, it would take the sort of crisis of representation that we have been probing in this series, brought on by the perception among social actors variously situated within once relatively stable institutions of both seismic jolts as well as tremors of change felt in their everyday functions and habits of thought. In this sense, corporate culture discourse in all its varieties since the late 1970s is the medium whereby the needs of corporate ideology for a discourse of progress, stability, and control and the felt anxieties of change intersect.

The value of flexibility and a vision of continuous change embedded in newer conceptions of culture provide the necessary doctrines for corporations in uncertain times. The double-edged quality of the term *creative destruction* itself captures well the ideological and cognitive work that cultural discourse currently does for corporations: *creative* counterbalances and gives positive value to a process that is undeniably *destruction* with considerable human costs and displacements implied. The pieces of this volume, then, in what might be read into their contexts of elicitation and the voices they represent, can be seen as diverse soundings within corporate capitalism of a coming to terms with itself as preeminently a process of creative destruction.

It is important to ask just to whom does the concern with corporate culture apply? While there are diverse cases presented in this volume, its center of gravity is the U.S. corporation, and within this frame the current vulnerabilities, hopes, and predicaments of middle managers—a stratum the decline of which has been much addressed recently by journalists and scholars. Along with blue-collar workers, they find themselves, when laid off, as the victims of corporate culture ideology emphasizing flexibility, but they are often its ideologues and true believers while still employed.

The actual creators of corporate culture discourse have been those academics, experts, and consultants who have direct institutional ties to corporate personnel and have helped make it a self-conscious frame among them for articulating thinking about their situations. Several of the pieces here show the direct influence of this particular expert, "knowledge worker" industry. As noted, the most fervent consumers of the cultural perspective seem to be those most vulnerable in current displacements and reorganizations—middle management as well as the owners and managers of relatively small corporations and firms. Thinking about business organizations in cultural terms by those who feel most imperiled or have had their worlds shaken by dismissal is a way of dealing with change in despair or hope, a mode of combining wishful thinking with insight that might be too hard to take unadorned. For example, compare the messages delivered by Tom Peters, in Newfield's piece, with the elaborate spin of the visionary manager, in Cefkin's piece, who is a ravenous consumer of corporate culture theories, with the promotional presentation of enlightened planning methods of Shell, in Davis-Floyd's piece.

What remains unclear is whether the investment in corporate culture is present in the boardrooms of the highest rungs of corporate leadership, to the extent any management ideology or technology ever has been. But it is certainly the case in those pieces where there is some registering of the commitments of upper management that cultural factors are of profound influence, even when they are not articulated or labeled explicitly as an interest in culture (for example, in the strong commitment to scenarios in Shell planning, Davis-Floyd's piece).

I have organized this year's assemblage of papers according to two sets of topics. One set concerns internal operations and practices of corporations—governance (the pieces by Newfield and Cefkin, and the one by Villaveces-Izquierdo on a highly explicit, bizarre, yet successful effort in Colombia to create corporate culture on a model of Japanese culture), accounting (Perin's piece on the movement to nonfinancial measures of firm performance), and planning (Davis-Floyd's piece on Shell scenarios). The other set concerns corporate subjects oriented to the external environments in which they operate—a world of risks and speculations (the piece by Gudrun Klein on the lending practices of German bankers; and the piece by Michael Fortun on an entrepreneurial biomedical scientist). Compared to the embracing of cultural issues by the subjects of the first set of pieces—as a means of promoting doctrines of flexibility to reorient corporations in the midst of poorly understood conditions of change—the pieces of the second part show their subjects to be much less explicit about culture as a frame for thinking, but cultural factors are no less important to consider in the much more complex assessments of the external environments of business activity as the conditions of markets, the state of risk, and the perception of opportunity. Even when the cultural calculation is denied or minimized, as in the case of the German bankers in Klein's piece, it is done so uneasily and with considerable ambivalence, as if something is still not being said (this sense is especially well probed in Klein's interviews). Not in a long while has there been so much leakage of the fuzzy uncertainness associated with cultural factors into the sphere of the reliance on formal rationality as a rhetoric of discourse.

The third section, an unusual feature of this volume, deals with the movement of the corporate form or apparatus into the operation of groups that constitutionally define their functions outside it, and sometimes ideologically in opposition to it—the world of voluntary associations, nonprofits (the pieces by Michael and Kim Fortun and by Laurel George), and grassroots organizations (K. Fortun's piece). As noted, the pieces of this section pose the contemporary version of the long-standing predicament of cooptation, or more accurately, complicitly, for the social critic, the activist, or the artist. Part 3 concerns the strategies of response and structures of feelings of groups, self-conceived as outside formal institutional orders, that find themselves increasingly aware in the fin-de-siècle of their insideness as a condition of their very survival as oppositional or alternative organizations.

As a means of offering previews to the pieces included in this volume, we present brief personal "takes" by the authors collected at the beginning of sections. Rather than trying to thematize and integrate the pieces, which is really the work of the reader, these previews follow the fault line of the series that each of these pieces exemplifies, and are meant to highlight the settings that they evoke and the forms that they take. Indeed, the authors of these pieces, through various strategies of presentation and editing, display a keen sensitivity to the narrative frames in which their interlocutors are speaking and to what linguists refer to as the indexical and pragmatic dimension of speech acts. They invite the reader to pay attention to the ambiguities and nuances of inflection and story line as well as to the authors' own style of intervention and presence.

"Reading motivation" into these pieces is thus how we intend for the reader to become involved with the volume and to make more of it than a mere assemblage on a general topic. It is not so much the concepts that emerge from the pieces—clear solutions in the discourse of social actors to the analyst's contemporary problem of representation—as speculations about what motivates a particular narrative line that lead to valuable reflections on the irreducible ambiguities defining situated interpretations of any arena of institutional life. For those of us participating in this project the questions that these pieces raise as a result of paying close attention to the kinds of materials exposed in the manners presented are the only answers that are possible for those who want a documentary understanding of fin-de-siècle changes in progress.

Notes

1. The other papers on corporate culture published in the same issue of *Social Text* in which Gordon's is included are worth reading in conjunction with the arguments that she develops; see Livingston 1995, Moylan 1995, and Newfield 1995.

2. These points are consistent with Lash and Urry's analysis (1987) of post-Fordist modes of production as marking an end to organized capitalism, and Robert Reich's arguments (1991) about the disengagement of "symbolic analysts," including the managerial elite of contemporary corporations, from the fortunes of their societies defined by the nation-state apparatus.

3. The spirit of this concern is captured in an interesting and ambitious discussion among social theorists in the name of "reflexive modernization" (see Beck, Giddens, and Lash 1995).

References

Beck, Ulrich, Anthony Giddens, and Scott Lash. 1995. *Reflexive Modernization.* Stanford: Stanford University Press.

Gordon, Avery. 1995. "The Work of Corporate Culture: Diversity Management." *Social Text* 13 (3): 3–30.

Lash, Scott, and James Urry. 1987. *The End of Organized Capitalism.* Madison: University of Wisconsin Press.

Latour, Bruno. 1996. *Aramis, or the Love of Technology.* Cambridge: Harvard University Press.

Livingston, James. 1995. "Corporations and Cultural Studies." *Social Text* 13 (3): 61–68.

Marcus, George E., and Michael M. J. Fischer. 1986. *Anthropology as Cultural Critique: An Experimental Moment in the Human Sciences.* Chicago: University of Chicago Press.

Moylan, Tom. 1995. "Peoples or Markets: Some Thoughts on Culture and Corporations in the University of the Twenty-first Century." *Social Text* 13 (3): 45–60.

Newfield, Christopher. 1995. "Corporate Pleasures for a Corporate Planet." *Social Text* 13 (3): 31–44.

Reich, Robert. 1991. *The Work of Nations.* New York: Random House.

Schumpeter, Joseph A. 1950. *Capitalism, Socialism, and Democracy.* 3d ed. New York: Harper and Brothers.

GOVERNANCE, ACCOUNTING, PLANNING

Chris Newfield

A hundred and fifty years ago Matthew Arnold wrote a famous poem about a scholar-gypsy, which helped him forget that he himself was a poet-bureaucrat. Nobody was better at being one than he, the good poet and school superintendent and codifier of the social role of culture. But even Arnold couldn't create a visionary world and supervise this one simultaneously (that would require Wallace Stevens, poet-executive). Arnold did pass an awkward combination on to later cultural scholars, and it lay at the center of my own professional training. The available models of thinking and writing were the heroes of creative individuality that I studied (Shakespeare, Donne, Wordsworth, Emerson, Dickinson, Du Bois, Wharton, Hurston, Foucault, Derrida), while my everyday life was that of a lower-middle manager, based on evaluating, meeting, photocopying, reporting, and simultaneously supervising and being supervised. I wrote a book about the nineteenth-century cultural roots of the divided kind of person I called the "corporate individualist." This identity was the skeletal frame for the middle-class employee of the large organizations that grew up after the Civil War. It was equal parts originality and conformity, and its owner struggled for self-expression and freedom in ways that were strangely compatible with the highly regulated life of the white-collar administrator.

Producers of "culture" proper, like poets, novelists, and television writers, continue to imagine people finding or at least seeking freedom outside of large organizations. My own view, to the contrary, is that most people seek only the kind of freedom they can find *inside* organizations. Big bureaucracy pays the salary for most of the modern American middle class. Excess regulation conditions its pursuit of workplace independence. But who was writing about the cold war in the cubicles? Who was dramatizing the collision of forces too complex and pervasive to be taped before a live studio audience?

In some management writers I found an awareness, rather than a humanistic forgetting, of the conflicts between individualism and corporate order that con-

ditions the prospects of contemporary society. In the tradition that opposed
scientific management, I found something that surprised me more: proclama-
tions that business had entered a revolutionary stage. In most descriptions this
revolution involved the demise of hierarchical bureaucracy and of the submissive, rule-following middle manager, and their replacement by "horizontal"
groups and "empowered" employees.

I wanted to find out more about this. Was business undergoing an internal
revolution that was mostly invisible to outsiders? What would it mean for our
paralyzed politics and somewhat depressed society? At a historical moment in
which business seemed to be absorbing American culture, was culture revolutionizing American business?

Tom Peters was a natural person to ask. He's been one of a half dozen leading
figures in management theory since the publication of *In Search of Excellence*
(1982), and I think this owes a lot to his passionate defense of individual leeway
against every kind of company system. If anyone hated the immersion of work
in bureaucratic life, he did. Peters had direct experience of the phenomenon,
having worked for the Pentagon prior to service in Vietnam, and for the federal
Office of Management and Budget afterward. It was hard to imagine better
white-collar preparation for rage against the machine—if that's what it was.

I did some modest triangulation of Peters's positions with those of a number
of other people in the Tom Peters Group, three of whom appear here. I came to
think of Peters and Jim Kouzes, the CEO of the Learning Systems division of
TPG, as alter egos. Kouzes is a major management writer in his own right, and
is as community minded as Peters is anarchistic. I was interested to see how
well their apparently disparate ideas fit together. Government service is one
common denominator—Kouzes served in the Peace Corps and trained community leaders afterward—and a background in organizational sciences is
another. I've also included part of my discussions with Michelle Cottle, who
had a journalism background and edited the TPG newsletter, and Malati Shinazy, a trainer who has taught at nearly every level of lower and higher education and who came to TPG with an unusually strong background in gender and
race issues. Both women have since left the company, which sharpens my interest in the differences between the theorists and the practitioners in the same
operation.

The essay lays out and pushes on the ideas without attempting to settle some
big operational questions. Will existing American business allow itself to be
changed in the ways these "human relations" ideas predict? Are these ideas
too close to existing norms to make any behavioral difference? Are they rose-
colored glasses for looking at post–cold war capitalism's combination of flexibility, increased inequality, exploitation, and powerlessness?

The answers to these questions are yes and no. Their past doesn't predict
their future. What *can* be predicted is that, as Alain Lipietz has pointed out,
any alternative worldview will arrive in many versions, including an "em-

ployer's version." Some strands of management theory are at the very least an employer's version of what may turn into a genuine alternative to corporate culture as we know it.

Constance Perin

For the last decade or so I've been trying to unbox some of the cultural dimensions of industrialization as manifested in large profit-making organizations. I've been putting my crowbar into the work that professional and technical people do in diverse industries here and in Western Europe—manufacturers of computers and personal products, an engineering firm, the accounting division of an oil company, the research and development division of a telecommunications company. During this spate of "reengineering" and "downsizing," companies' financial rationales for these moves are organized by the drive to maximize productivity, innovation, and creativity, usually denoted by such outputs as the numbers of patents, products, and reports, all calibrated in terms of the speed with which they appear, then translated into financial balance sheets. To judge the probability of reaching these goals, managers largely rely on inputs—primarily the numbers of hours worked and "face time"—time and presence on the job. Just how the work gets done—on what social and cultural conditions do productivity, innovation, creativity depend?—engages them hardly at all. The credibility of "hard" measures of time and money is even further heightened by the illegitimacy attaching to such "soft" factors of production.

These observations made me even more intrigued with a turn to the soft that I'd been watching out of the corner of my eye. Invited to contribute to this volume, I took the opportunity to inform myself about the status of several critiques of money as the sole measure of value. My piece should be read as both traveler's report and ruminations to invite those of readers. At its center is an interview with an imaginative tour guide and tutor, Robert Elliott, a senior partner in a Big Eight accounting firm. We sat by a window in his office in an upper floor of a Manhattan skyscraper as if on the prow of a trading ship overlooking the sea of commerce, talking of redesigning the sextant for the passage to the next century.

Melissa Cefkin

Over the last several years many corporations have engaged in "interventions" of a spiritual, inspirational, or philosophical nature. Purporting to pave the way to greater satisfaction for the individual while improving the lot of the corporation itself, Catherine Casey has recently referred to the corporations that take these on as "designer corporations," [1] while a peer of mine has dubbed the interventions themselves "corporate fucking-with-your-head initiatives." M.

is a general manager of an office in a division of a major multinational corporation that had recently undertaken a "change" effort—change being the motif used commonly by consultants, corporations, and organizational development professionals to refer to such movements—and was one of the original designers of the effort.

I first met M. a year prior to this interview when I did three months of fieldwork in his office. I was a part of a team of researchers hired by M.'s corporation to do a systematic study of the context and state of the organization through the early stages of their change effort. I was thus a part, in whatever manner, of the kinds of interests M. addresses himself to in the interview. That I found myself caught in the many intricacies in doing "applied" research—the problems of engaging without antagonizing a sponsor of my work, negotiating the tensions between my own critical evaluations and hopes for positive change—is surely apparent in the interview.

My interest in M. is in his position, at once powerful and precarious, as a middle manager, as a corporate actor working at the cusp of the related but separate elements of strategic and operational management, and as a designer and proponent of the change effort. How he reconciles the actions he takes in his position with his own anxieties and visions for the future is what centrally concerns me in the interview.

The interview emerged rather indistinctly out of general conversation as M. began weaving stories of the histories of his own thinking together with his visions for the future. I chose to leave the almost stream-of-consciousness development of M.'s narrative in place and selected a minimalist framing to the conversation for its performance effect. Reading a transcript of our conversation later, M. claimed that he would not have ventured this far in his thinking and pushed his ideas to such an extreme, "sounded so far out," in his normal business environment. But in my observations of corporations grappling with change efforts and adopting new forms of organizational structures, to workers not in the position to decide on, select, and manage such efforts, many of these efforts themselves are as "far out" to them as this thinking may seem to M. from where he stands. And despite the intentions of architects of such movements, they are often "rolled out" in the same hierarchical manner they were supposedly trying to overcome. In this process workers do not have many opportunities to deeply, honestly, and regularly voice or act on their responses to the efforts, especially if their opinions are critical. I have experimented here with trying to create the same effect for the reader by leaving the recognition and realization of critical engagement unrealized in my response.

Note
1. See Catherine Casey, *Work, Self and Society After Industrialism* (London: Routledge Press, 1995).

Santiago Villaveces-Izquierdo

In 1960 Eduardo Caballero Calderón, a well-known Colombian writer and novelist, said, "For us everything that is strange and not ours has authority. That's why I say we are like that shrewd variety of crustaceans, the hermitage crabs of the island of San Andrés. Packed together in the sands of the beaches, these crabs wait until other crustaceans abandon their shells so they can take them over, similar to those who in a sudden flash take over the house of their neighbor. We take over and settle ourselves in the crusts of exotic ideas and systems that belong to other species of crustaceans who are capable of building them through their own means." [1]

The interpretations of Colombian identity building have long lingered in the minds of journalists, novelists, and academics, and more so since the 1980s with the surge of complex social formations that combine rapid fortune building and the exercise of violence with a profound influence over the configuration of social and political power.[2] Against this backdrop, many are the claims that urge the need to construct out of the Colombians more ethical and responsible individuals. Unexpectedly, while having an informal conversation with my father, a Colombian business consultant, he brought to my attention the intricacies that make of Foto Japón a quite remarkable site that presents itself as a mixture of the crafts of business as usual and a pedagogy for building up ethical subjects out of its employees.

After arranging the necessary interviews with the company's staff, I started a journey that plunged me into various layers that not just uncovered Foto Japón's own complexity but also echoed wider issues that point to the ways Calderón's crustacean metaphor works in the Colombia of the 1990s. This piece resembles my journey through the different layers and depths that configure a truly postmodern late-century organization where collage, mimicry, invention, and business all equally play a feature role in the creation and recreation of a global and local mix. An exploration of the rituals, sacralizations, and pedagogical models of Foto Japón is placed in dialogue with the unexpected dynamics created by the confluence of local realities and imaginaries with imported hopes, artifacts, and philosophies. Through this dialogue the tensions and paradoxes unleashed by simultaneously declaring a lack of cultural identity and by prescribing the need to adopt imported ethical and behavioral raw models are put forth. The piece as a whole revisits the composite existence of Calderón's Colombians, we hermit crabs.

Notes

1. Eduardo Caballero Calderón. 1963. "Historia Privada de los Colombianos." In Calderón *Obras,* p. 267. Medellín: Editorial Bedout.

2. For example the effects on ethical values and identity building that have taken place on behalf of the so-called drug subcultures.

Robbie E. Davis-Floyd

In chapter 5 you will find two interviews that I conducted with Betty Sue Flowers about her writing and editing of Shell International's 1992 and 1995 futures-planning scenarios. I first met Betty Sue at a men's conference (à la Robert Bly and the mythopoetic men's movement) in Austin, Texas, where she and I were two of only four women speakers, and the only two present the night we met. It took me a while to spot her in a huge ballroom filled with eight hundred men and two women—she sat in the back row wearing a businesslike gray dress with black buttons, and as a result (in spite of her shoulder-length blonde hair) was nearly invisible—by choice, I later found out. Standing out is not her style.

After the evening's presentations ended, I could hardly wait to find her, introduce myself, and ask her what she thought of the event. We headed for the hotel bar, where we found a cozy sofa and chatted late into the night, about Robert Bly and the men's movement, about women and men, about her work and mine. She was an English professor who had specialized in Victorian literature, I was an anthropologist who had specialized in cultural constructions of childbirth. We found common ground in our mutual fascination with myth. For me, myths are creation stories in which it is possible to read and identify a culture's fundamental assumptions about reality. I want to understand myth because I want to understand culture, and it is in myth that culture is encoded. To Betty Sue a myth is "a story that organizes experience through telling something explicitly about meaning—where we're going, where we came from, or who we are." When I asked her, "How did you get interested in myth in the first place?" she responded,

> There are a lot of ways to tell this story, but if you were going to be psychoanalytical about it, I would say that my parents were very different in how they saw the world. I observed my father making one story about the same event and my mother making another, and that it was her *story* that would cause her grief or discomfort, and that my father's story actually created smooth sailing for him. I realized that the difference lay not in what was happening to them, but in something very different in the way that they were *thinking about it*. And that taught me to be on the alert for the stories people were telling to interpret their experiences.

Thus Betty Sue is less interested in the culture encoded in myth and more interested in the power of the story to influence human thought and action—a focus she was able to convey (in a way that caught on with the culture) in the title she chose for Joseph Campbell's book, *The Power of Myth.*

It was therefore logical for her to be intrigued when Shell approached her about writing stories that would be explicitly designed to have this power in the business world. And it was logical for me, once she completed those stories, to be dying of curiosity about her experience of consciously creating living myths designed explicitly to make people think about the kind of future their culture—in this case, the culture of an international oil company, one of the largest in the world—would create. I was teaching at Rice University when George Marcus first spoke to me about the theme of Late Editions 5, and I knew right away what my contribution was going to be.

I interviewed Betty Sue twice. The first time (September 1993) she met me in her office in the English department on the University of Texas campus, where we talked for two hours about the process of her writing and editing of the 1992 Shell scenarios. Two years later I conducted a short follow-up interview with her about the aftermath of those first scenarios and about Shell's plans to bring her back to write a second set. This time, the tables were turned: Betty Sue had just finished interviewing me (about childbirth and cyborgs) for an episode of a television show she was hosting, "Conversations with Betty Sue Flowers." After we finished taping, we sojourned to the boardroom of the television station so I could once more interview her.

As you will see in these interviews, Betty Sue was bound by Shell not to reveal much about the content of the stories. But she told me in the second interview that the man who had hired her at Shell, Joe Jaworski, was in the process of writing a book (with Shell's permission) that does give the full text of the 1992 scenarios. That book, which Betty Sue edited, has since appeared under the title *Synchronicity* (Jaworski 1996).

There is no ending to this story. Throughout the fall and spring of 1996–97 Betty Sue made monthly trips to Geneva to write global scenarios for a group of fifty large multinational corporations concerned about the fate of the planet and its human inhabitants; they want to use these scenarios to help them imagine and then work to create a viable human future in which they can do business without destroying the environment in which we all must live. Such scenarios may become a nexus for the merging of myth and reality. In their creation I begin to glimpse the ephemeral possibility that the human myth of a better world may eventually result in the human reality of achieving it.

1

CORPORATE CULTURE WARS

ON A HUMAN RELATIONS GURU. *Aside from its valuable tracing, through the career of Tom Peters, of the recent fortunes of the human relations approach to corporations, what I found fascinating in this piece was the change it marked in Newfield as critic. In contrast to his earlier more distanced, conventionally critical piece on Peters (Newfield 1995), that operates as an ironic unmasking of a new kind of corporate ideology readable in Peters's discourse, here Newfield works himself into and through Peters's wisdom in ways that preserve the ethos of independent critique. As Newfield expressed this to me,*

The first half of the paper introduces Peters et al. but provides a context that motivates the need to think about changes in human relations for the 1990s. The second half organizes these changes into features that might hold up better intellectually against the scornful skeptics who see human relations as a kinder, gentler form of managerial manipulation (and with much reason). I've evolved since the Social Text *piece from seeing Peters as a very appealing radical conservative to seeing the ensemble of ideas surrounding him as a potential source of progressive change within corporations at the very moment when the corporate economy seems to be moving the other way.*

Newfield's piece is thus a fascinating example of how critique is positioned "inside" the material it first defined with more distance. The terms of alternative possibility arise from negotiating the affinities between the intellectual capital of particular varieties of initially embraced academic and opposed corporate discourse. – G. E. M.

* * *

I. Preparations and Reversals

1. Lead or Leave

"We are being hurt by the myth that leadership is something reserved for a few charismatic men and women. In fact, leadership is everyone's business."

I'm surprised to be hearing this. I thought that leadership by definition was for the few. My dictionary defines *leader* as "one in charge or in command of others." That sounds like *leader* means the *one* that stands out from and above the rest. My dictionary uses words like *principal, foremost,* and *head* to describe the leader's place. So isn't leadership for everyone a contradiction? And if authority were distributed to everyone, wouldn't this be too radical to be mentioned in passing?

Everyone a leader—the idea is made more striking by its source. It's not coming from a grassroots community activist but from a business management writer. I'm in the Palo Alto, California, offices of a prominent business education firm called the Tom Peters Group (TPG), and I'm talking to the CEO of the organization's learning systems division, Jim Kouzes, coauthor of *The Leadership Challenge* and *Credibility.* I keep having an odd thought while conducting these interviews. As democracy in society seems increasingly blocked by entrenched institutions, one of these entrenched institutions, the business corporation, may be increasingly interested in employee democracy.

"Everyone a leader" also seems the antithesis of the times. We're living in Gilded Age II, distinguished by warp-drive concentration of wealth and a peculiar lack of public resistance. But Tom Peters has been calling on the middling cadres to resist various forces of decline for ten or fifteen years. He exhorts them to break their chains. He asks them to take the plunge into leadership. In a recent book he recommends Reagan Pentagon analyst Richard Perle's view about hanging onto personal power in large organizations: "The question always arises as to what authority you have. The answer is you have to assume you have absolute authority until somebody tells you otherwise, until somebody stops you. Because if you try to derive your authority, your freedom of action, from any other source than yourself, you are not going to have any fun, and you are not going to get much done" (Peters 1994a, 110). It's odd to hear a hardline conservative like Perle so openly rejecting a law-and-order approach to institutional procedures in favor of a kind of Nietzschean vitalism. Elsewhere, Peters cites a very different part of the political spectrum offering the same message. Body Shop founder and outspoken business progressive Anita Roddick claims that only "anarchists" can save bosses from themselves. "It's clear, isn't it?" Peters concludes. "Pushing the needle all the way over, unabashedly championing revolution, and getting the company anarchists to the barricades"—this is how "doing something" and "taking action" need to be reconceived. Doing something involves knowing, in the words of former Xerox CEO David Kearns, that "we have to overthrow the old regime" (Peters 1994a, 274). The company revolution requires a revolution within each individual that allows him or her to be his or her own sovereign authority. And this agenda— you taking power—shows up on both the business right and the business left.

The starting point for Peters is simply to make the leap. "The real role that I perform," he tells me, "is to help nudge the five or ten percent of the people who are in my seminar audiences who almost have the nerve to step out and do something a little bit different to actually do it. You've got to be a total ego-maniac if you think you're going to influence the people who think you're a jerk or who really are terrified—that's far too much to imagine. So the real impact is people who are beginning to get it and to give 'em the will to fight on the good fight for another ninety days or to jump off the deep end if they're standing on the edge of the pool with fluttering toes."

Peters often makes seizing leadership sound like a question of holding leadership *attitudes*. He excels at conjuring the mood in which you *feel* that you are leadership material. He sometimes provides a kind of historical perspective that paints the suppression of frontline leadership as an ancient, monarchist hang-over that capitalism is still battling to expel:

> Britain's first Duke of Wellington . . . worried about the impact of rail transportation, which was just arriving on the scene. "My Lords," he proclaimed in a speech in the House of Lords, "these iron horses will enable the working classes to move about." Indeed, suspicion of the working class and the reduction of most jobs to insignificance (hyper-specialization) were the bedrock of the Industrial Revolution. The time has come (it's long overdue actually) to reverse all that. (Peters 1994a, 80)

Reversing all that—does that mean undoing management's control of labor? What then would be left of the standard industrial corporation? Let the chips fall, Peters says. It sounds like frontline people must *recognize consciously and systematically* that all *absences* of employee power and all *missing* frontline leadership are vestiges of a defunct industrial royalism. Anyway, "everything is changing" so there's nothing else to do but forge ahead. Peters tells us that "the dependent society is dying." He calls for new individuals—for "brand-new personalities." He calls on ordinary employees "to try most anything." He implies that the revolution takes shape through the act of plunging into it. He tells you not to "fret about making a fool of yourself. (After all the world is such a foolish place. Why not prance in the circus parade with gusto?) In short, powerless is a state of mind" (Peters 1994a, 111, 113, 111). *Your* state of mind. Mostly you think you are weak. You resent your impotence and yet you do nothing. So *do* something. *Try* it. Everybody has the power to lead. Which is lucky, since companies are telling more and more employees, "lead or leave."

2. The Sagging Middle and the Corporate Role

But what good will more leadership do? What is the crisis that leadership will address? What difference can more optimism and novelty make? Some histori-cal background will help make sense of these questions and of the TPG's responses to them. The most relevant crisis consists of the struggles of the American corporate system, now getting on into their third decade, and which long ago graduated from crisis in the ordinary sense to a semipermanent, anxious way of life that has been called the age of diminished expectations. The crisis now seems to be an epochal change, a change in the fundamental structure of the entire global economy. If corporate struggles are the result of fundamental structural change, what could ideas about employee attitudes possibly do about that?

I don't expect to settle the question here. But I'm going to go into some detail about both the background and the current state of ideas like Kouzes's and Peters's. I've come to see TPG and some similar management firms as speaking for and to consciously *middle-class* interests within the changing corporate world. These middle-class interests sometimes differ from those of upper management, and these differences are becoming more pervasive and acute. These management writers are analyzing—and encouraging—some type of movement beyond the *bureaucratic* form that's defined corporate life since the Civil War. In the process they may be partially reversing the priority of *structural* over *attitudinal* factors, of *financial* over *cultural* factors that control the current debate. They may also, intentionally or not, be pointing the way beyond the current binary choice between *entrepreneurial* and *participatory* ideals about relations among white-collar workers, and toward some new combination of them. And the move beyond this binary choice may, in turn, prophecy new forms of capitalist institutions, forms that lead beyond capitalism as we know it.

The standard starting point for our current rocky and unsettled period is 1973. That was the year of the first major leap in oil prices, and was the last year in which nonsupervisory wage workers saw their wage rise after adjusting for inflation. While we read descriptions of unprecedented upheaval in the press in the 1990s, it's easy for us to forget the very similar descriptions of enormous change that began to crop up around 1974 and that have not ceased since. By 1980 *Business Week* was warning ominously that "the U.S. economy must undergo a fundamental change if it is to retain a measure of economic viability let alone leadership in the remaining 20 years of this century" (quoted in Bluestone and Harrison 1982, 3). The symptoms of decline were legion. There were numerous plant closings and massive blue-collar layoffs on such a scale that many spoke of the wholesale "deindustrialization" of the American economy. Average annual growth in the gross national product fell from 4.1 percent in the 1960s to 2.9 percent in the 1970s. American products seemed unable to compete for market share with the products of formerly crippled economies like Germany's and Japan's. Capital investment moved from expanding and modernizing American productive capacity to financial transactions, including the purchase of existing American firms and investment in production abroad. The American standard of living fell from first to tenth, and there seemed little that the business community was either willing or able to do about it.[1]

Corporate lawyer Martin Lipton recently described that downturn as a turning point in the history of corporate capitalism:

> There's been a basic change in business philosophy. At the beginning of the century the purpose of corporations was to grow big, which led on to the creation of cartels worldwide. Then there was a shift of power to professional managers. Now there's disaggregation across the world, from AT&T to ICI.
>
> The basic reason is that big business has failed. The corporations haven't provided a steady increase in the standard of living, and corporate managers have fallen flat on their faces. In the seventies many of them lost their capacity for self-analysis and self-correction. Basically they've faced the same problem as the communist regimes in the East: the failure to perform. (quoted in Sampson 1995, 230)

Forget for a moment that the present-day AT&T is larger than the version that split off its Baby Bells. The baseline feeling remains one of a continuing economic decline, where large corporations are more the problem than the solution.

In the mid 1990s the numbers were up for corporate profits, GNP growth, and the rate of productivity increases. But national solace was dampened by a similar increase in the numbers for economic and social polarization. The concentration of wealth and managerial control had become major national issues. The gap between the top 20 percent of the population and the rest is now the highest it's been since World War II. The Clinton nineties have continued the Reagan eighties in undoing the wider distribution of wealth ushered in by postwar prosperity: "The Congressional Budget Office disclosed in 1992 that a staggering 77 percent of the before-tax income growth of U.S. families between 1977 and 1989 went to the top 1 percent" (Herman 1995, 46). The United States now has nearly the highest rate of child poverty and the most unequal distribution of income in the First World. Although we've historically seen ourselves as a paradise for the middle class, ours is the First World's smallest.[2] Most studies suggest that for the top 20 percent, things have been good or great for the past fifteen years, while fortunes have stagnated or declined for the rest. The United States may be becoming (at least) two nations economically, "segregated," in Robert Reich's phrase, by income (1991, 274).

Even some members of the financial community have been sounding warnings about the trend. Felix Rohatyn, senior partner at the Wall Street investment banking firm Lazard Frères, writes, "What is occurring is a huge transfer of wealth from lower-skilled, middle-class American workers to the owners of capital assets and to a new technological aristocracy with a large element of compensation tied to stock values." Chairman of the Federal Reserve Bank Alan Greenspan, not normally noted for his populist sympathies, "warned Congress in July 1995 that the growing inequality of income in the United States could become a 'major threat to our society.' " A governor of the Fed, Lawrence Lindsay, has pointed out that "the employee's share of increased income had fallen dramatically during the past ten years"—"from 52 to 38 percent." As Simon Head sums it up, "the central problem of the 1990s has been more the maldistribution of wealth than the failure to increase overall wealth" (Head 1996, 47, 50, 51).

The corporation has failed *socially* by failing to insulate its own people from this escalation in concentration and "winner-take-all." The concentration story is readily told with a brief blizzard of numbers. Jerry Buss, the owner of the National Basketball Association team the Los Angeles Lakers, is by 1997 paying his star center Shaquille O'Neal $1 million more each year than he paid in 1979 for the entire Laker team. But a focus on celebrity salaries obscures the even more elephantine proportions of salaries in business. O'Neal's $17 million per year (excluding another $17 million or so in endorsement and other income) is less than half of what Travelers Group chief executive officer Sanford Weill makes year in, year out (Springer 1996, A18). Weill's $50 million is a thousand times what my Ph.D. gets me, but it is only a quarter of the wealth Disney CEO Michael Eisner accumulates in some years, around $200 million. And that's less than half of what Michael Milken amassed in 1986.

Now it's true that not all mountains are as high as Everest. But switching to averages doesn't help much. To the contrary, averages suggest uncanny similarities between international contrasts of rich and poor and contrasts within the American corporation. "Globally, the top 20% of society has 150 times the wealth of the bottom 20%," according to a United Nations survey (Wright 1992, A37). This is almost exactly the ratio between CEO income and average employee income within the U.S.'s larger firms. Examining income in the 424 largest U.S. companies, compensation analyst Graef Crystal shows that for the three-year period 1992–94, the multiple moved from 145, to 170, and then to 187 (Crystal 1995, D2). The global gap has been on the move, having increased by a factor of five since the early 1960s, when the ratio between the top and bottom fifths stood at 30:1. The American gap between CEO and worker pay has matched the global gap almost step for step—it was about 40:1 in 1960, and was 42:1 as recently as 1980 (Byrne 1993, 56–57). The proportions of global inequality are beyond the dreams of the pharaohs—"The world now has more than 350 billionaires whose combined net worth equals the annual income of the poorest 45 percent of the world's population" (Korten 1996). Numbers like these prompt some authors to use phrases like "urban revolution worldwide" and "the coming anarchy." But what do we say about the large

American corporation, where income distribution is surprisingly similar? The corporation has not only succeeded in cutting its contribution to the larger society—in tax contributions, employment base, environmental costs, even charity—it has also seriously cut its contribution to its own insiders, first to its production workers and more recently to its loyal bureaucrats and middle managers.

By the late 1990s the corporation seems less the reliable fountainhead of American affluence than a machine for replicating Third World ratios of inequality within both blue-collar *and* white-collar America. These problems are structural and systemic; they seem way beyond the reach of employee empowerment attitudes.

3. The Grasp of Finance

Because economic troubles are systemic, the solutions have tried to be systemic as well. "Capital vs. Community" is the title of the introduction to Barry Bluestone and Bennett Harrison's book *The Deindustrialization of America* (1982), which appeared in the same year that *In Search of Excellence* was launching Tom Peters's speaking and writing career. The title describes the two major types of systemic response to economic decline—freeing up capital to seek the best potential profits, regardless of social effects like unemployment; and subordinating the use of capital to public definitions of the social good. Should profits be maximized? Or should they be distributed according to a community or nation's ideas of social justice or fairness? Sometimes this debate is summarized as "profits vs. people." The former argue that you can't help people anyway unless you're free to make real money. The latter say that without coercion, that money rarely comes back to the vast majority of people. This is a classical debate within capitalist democracies. Is capital best used for private interests? Or is capital part of the commonwealth best directed by the public and its representatives?

If you compared Peters and Robert Waterman to Bluestone and Harrison in 1982, you might assume they line up neatly on opposite sides. Peters and Waterman omitted public policy solutions to economic crisis and wrote as though economic conditions are given as facts of life. They concentrated on the care and maintenance of a firm's human resources, putting these in the service of improving the corporation's economic efficiency. Bluestone and Harrison regarded economic conditions as the direct result of deliberate boardroom investment strategies—moving manufacturing to lower-wage sites overseas or to nonunion regions of the U.S., buying unrelated businesses to get their established revenues on one's own balance sheets, and so on. Their most famous example was U.S. Steel. It closed fourteen mills, laid off thirteen thousand workers, took an $850 million tax break from the federal government, and then, instead of building high-tech steel plants, spent $6 billion to buy Marathon Oil. Bluestone and Harrison called for community control over decisions like these, which they regarded as wasteful and unnecessary. They advocated such forms of control as plant-closing legislation to cover some of the "social costs" of capital mobility.

It's tempting to set up the debate in this familiar way. What we get then is capital vs. community, the corporation vs. society, and profits vs. people. The *policy* debate feeds the binary contrast between the two sides. Corporations are equated with their executive decisions (with much reason, since that's all outsiders see). Communities are equated with economic naiveté and excessive solicitude for society's losers. In addition to its recent lopsidedness—the mobility of capital has been whipping the pants off the "common good"—the policy debate discourages investigating the corporation as a *heterogeneous culture,* rife with diversity and conflict, and possessed of domains of thought and action not represented by the boardroom.

When policy contrasts the corporation and the community, it identifies the corporation with its dominant form of governance—what sociologist Neil Fligstein calls the financial conception of control. Fligstein argues that the corporation came to be ruled by the finance conception of itself after the end of World War II. Its overall goal is simply to "increase assets and profits." To do this, it

> emphasizes control through the use of financial tools which measure performance according to profit rates. Product lines are evaluated on their short-run profitability and important management decisions are based on the potential profitability of each line. Firms are viewed as collections of assets earning differing rates of returns, not as producers of given goods. The firm is not seen as being a member of only one industry. Consequently if the prospect of an industry in which it participates declines, the firm disinvests. The problem for management from this perspective is to maximize short-run rates of return by altering product mix, thereby increasing shareholder equity and keeping the stock price high.
>
> The key strategies are: diversification through mergers and divestments (as opposed to internal expansion); financial ploys to increase the stock price, indebtedness, and ability to absorb other firms; and the use of financial controls to make decisions about the internal allocation of capital. (Fligstein 1990, 15)

The financial conception shifted power further toward financial people: "The financial controls that supported the multidivisional form [have become] the chief source of power in the large corporation over the past thirty years" (Fligstein 1990, 227).

In the 1980s financial control consolidated its grip on the corporation and the economy in general. Financial control had a plausible solution to the 1970s crisis—produce growth by cutting weak divisions and less profitable products and buying stronger ones. If the crisis consists of weak numbers, the solution is stronger numbers. "Firms who engage in mergers are able to expand their firm size instantly. Managers, who are confronted by shareholders and boards of directors, are under pressure to show that the firm is growing" (Fligstein, 292–93). Financiers also justified many a merger, leveraged buyout, and hostile takeover with a superficially "human relations" way of roasting mediocre upper management. The financial conception of control already had a constituency—the entire financial sector of the economy; top managers, including even the boardroom victims of takeovers; the disciplines of economics and related policy areas; a policy establishment whose ascent with Reagan's election merely consolidated their existing authority (recall Federal Reserve Chairman Paul Volker frosting the economy during the Carter administration); and the American public, since nearly all of us are cowed by numerical accounts of reality.

Whether or not it ever uses a phrase like "financial conception of control," most of the policy debate—the conservative vs. liberal debate—concedes the financial control of the corporation. Much of the liberal action consists of trying to add in some sense of social responsibility without challenging the rights of bottom-line calculators. A good example has been the Clinton administration's "corporate citizenship" campaign. Clinton and his labor secretary, Robert Reich, called on corporations to show voluntary consideration for employees, but did not elevate legal restrictions or employee demands to equal status with executive decisions. The details of these kinds of compromises are endlessly churned, but they all have one thing in common: the preservation of finance's priority to various social factors, even when those social factors are declared important.

Such compromises came up when I asked Kouzes and Peters questions about policy. Peters told me, "I think that we need a new social contract in which training, pensions, and health care are removed from the corporate world." I mentioned to Kouzes that Peters described himself to me as someone who "fell in love with the Great Society" and then bought most of the neoliberal critique of that. Kouzes replied that he himself was more of an FDR liberal. He defended NAFTA and free trade to me, and had a fairly low opinion of government's ability to do things right. But he also defended the role of government in personal terms: "My grandfather came over to the U.S. as a barrel maker, and then his son went on to be Deputy Assistant Secretary of Labor. That story took place in the era of Roosevelt. And understanding that, the importance of all of those policies, the difference they made in the life I lead today, makes me continue to understand the value of social intervention." Kouzes invoked FDR as a figure of inclusion rather than as a source of public supervision of financial decisions.

At one point in our conversation, I asked Peters, "So you don't worry about today's increase in mogul domination and centralization of power?"

"Well," he replied, "I don't worry about the increase in centralization of power. I'm not worried about concentration of power in that I think Bill Gates will be toppled by Bill Gates the Next in very short order. And so that part doesn't bother me. This is a period of great uncertainty. The world of the AT&Ts and the IBMs and the Sears Roebucks dominating anything is gone.

"But the wealth concentration, the entrepreneurial wealth concentration, I think is a matter of great concern. I think a smart Republican would figure out a way to give away or tax away a fair share of what they're earning, if he or she doesn't wish to be one of the first ones at the wall twenty-five years from now."

"Do you think there's a movement in the business community to get Republicans to do exactly that?" I asked.

"No. I read recently that Bob Allen, CEO of AT&T, was saying, 'I really am sorry that I had to lay another forty thousand people off at AT&T, but my $2.3 million salary is no more than average for people who do the kind of thing I do for a living.' I mean, get a life, Sport. But no, I don't see a movement in that direction."

"I'm just wondering if the people at the top are going to be outnumbered."

"Yeah, maybe so," Peters says. "It would be nice if, in his last few years, Warren Buffett, who remains a registered Democrat, would speak sense to some of these people that he deals with."

All of the Peters associates with whom I spoke dislike the punitive drift of policy these days. They are living proof that you can't lump business writers together with the conservatism of Jack Kemp or Newt Gingrich or Bob Dole. But they don't fire away at conservative theory, either. On *policy* issues they're closer to the Clintonesque center—maintain the deregulation of the market and financial decisions without causing *excessive* misery or unfairness. Accept a lot of inequity as the way the market works, accept, in liberal author Mickey Kaus's phrase, "the end of equality." Clinton retains some ideals from the Great Society, downsizes them (Henry Louis Gates Jr.'s Pretty Good Society?), and then seeks them through the relatively unrestricted private sector that the Great Society had found wanting in the first place. The liberal center offers no systematic and persistent linkage of the financial conception to social or economic decline. Liberals are less likely than ever to fire up the old hog for a night raid on corporate America.

The highway of management thinking is littered with the wrecks of those who tried to find this kind of "third way" in the middle. The Peters group is part of a third way, known as the "human relations" approach within management theory. On *policy* questions the entire approach sounds a lot like the Clinton center. It is for capital *and* for the worker, for financial controls *and* for employee control of their jobs and fates.

But the human relations approach doesn't do its main work in policy. It's on

its own ground when it talks about matters inside the corporation. It's there—
on the inside—that groups like Tom Peters's have their only real chance to
work out something better than Clinton's compromises. I'm piecing together
this "third way" from a variety of signs and symptoms coming from *inside* the
corporation. It does not uphold Bluestone and Harrison's idea of community
control over financial decisions. But neither does it line up with the standard
binary alternative—private control of finance capital governed only by "the
market." As I suggest at the end of this essay, a transformative human relations
will need to challenge *systematically* the finance conception of control over the
corporation itself.

4. Conflict in Human Relations

Human relations can mean nearly any focus on "the human side of enterprise"—one that puts people and their relationships at the center of the analysis, and pushes corporate structure, strategic planning, specific functions like
marketing, various kinds of design and engineering, and above all, financial
issues, at least partly to one side. It is over seventy-five years old, and early
exponents like Mary Parker Follett and Elton Mayo were reacting against scientific management, which they thought was fixated on the power of technical,
mechanical, and financial solutions at the expense of the psychological and
social. Human relations holds a few truths to be self-evident: "workers [are]
not only motivated by economic incentives. Workers . . . [are not] interchange-
able or disposable productive elements but . . . part of the community of the
firm. . . . There [is] a need to integrate them fully, to harmonize interests and
behavior, to develop a sense of belonging" (Guillén 1994, 59). "On-the-job
decisions will be made faster and better when the employees directly involved
are making them. People who have a say in their company's affairs will be
happier and more productive than people who are always carrying out somebody else's orders" (Case 1995, 86). The 1920s and the 1990s versions agree
that treating people right makes both ethical *and* economic sense. Financial
performance hinges on the very complicated, delicate, powerful human factor.
Economics, in other words, should be seen as a subset of corporate cultural
studies. The fundamental and unchanging idea is that you catch more flies with
honey.

   The human relations approach traces much of the last twenty-odd years of
economic difficulty to the stifling of employee initiative by inflexible and even
authoritarian corporate hierarchies. Rosabeth Moss Kanter began her influential book *The Change-Masters* (1983) like this:

> In my travels around corporate America, . . . I have been struck by an
> ever-louder echo of the same question, how to stimulate more inno-
> vation, enterprise, and initiative from their people.

> In every sector, old and new, I hear a renewed recognition of the importance of people, and of the talents and contributions of individuals, to a company's success. People seem to matter in direct proportion to an awareness of corporate crisis. (Kanter 1983, 17)

Wherever corporations struggle with their overall numbers, human relations is there to tell them they should struggle more with how they treat their people.

There's one big problem. Human relations can mean almost *any* focus on the human side. This can range from employee ownership and socialist workplace democracy to reengineering through the "empowerment" of overwork. It can mean self-management and it can mean the white-collar equivalent of piecework. It can mean autonomy on the job, or new degrees of bondage to finicky customers. It can mean a *participatory management* that is explicitly anti-authoritarian. As John Case puts it, "the dominant business paradigm in the twentieth century was always the . . . bureaucratic chain of command, with do-as-you're-told jobs and tight supervision of the ranks. But participatory management was like a backwater, always there, never quite disappearing, even as the mainstream of history seemed to pass it by. It would turn up in one company here and another company there. It would catch on, fade, then reappear somewhere else" (Case 1995, 86). Human relations can mean participatory management, but it can also mean new ways of sweating the higher ranks as well as the low. As the skeptical Tom Frank puts it, "the true [corporate] revolutionary may talk about 'teams,' but he lives to make himself an *uber* company man, a hyperintense competitor." Is the new corporate world one of self-determination or simply of "total competition?" (1996, 12).

I couldn't help noticing that nobody used the word *team* in the Peters offices. Nor did they use the term *participation. Involvement* came up a bit more, but I had hoped for a clear language about individuals defeating hierarchical authority that didn't materialize. I was impressed by the priority TPG placed on the *practice of relationships,* but this didn't necessarily point to participatory management. Nor did it mean that they singled out *sham* participatory thinkers, like some of the reengineering crowd, to denounce their thinly veiled devotion to outmoded financial conceptions of management. Sometimes I tried to get Peters and his associates to generalize about their place on embattled management terrain, especially when it seemed to me that their work rejected some major conventional wisdom, some defining American beliefs like the universal value of individual competition. But the Peters organization abstained from oppositional talk. The on-site trainers were focused on case-by-case intervention and specific institutional problems that varied from one firm to the next. But even the authors—the theorists—stuck to solving specific problems by producing change through the repair of impaired group dynamics.

So I did what comes naturally: after my time in the TPG offices I read a lot more books. Some of them led me back to the 1950s. I was trying to get a sense of whether they were taking human relations approaches in a new direction. I was trying to see if there was a fatal ambiguity in human relations that would keep it from cutting much of a figure outside the consulting world, if there was a history of predicting changes that never came to pass, or if there was a history of significant reforms. To help figure out where the human relations approach is now, I put together an evolutionary tale, and three moments of it are important here.

5. Human Relations Prepares to Rule

Using the artificial starting point of 1960 I noticed some big books arriving at ten year intervals. An industrial psychologist at the Massachusetts Institute of Technology, Douglas McGregor, published a remarkable work, *The Human Side of Enterprise,* that boiled down existing American corporate management to a coercive, hierarchical view of human nature he labeled Theory X, and that he claimed could and should be replaced with its near opposite, Theory Y. In 1970 an obscure journalist named Alvin Toffler wrote a blockbuster prophecy called *Future Shock,* which used Warren Bennis and other management writers to argue for the coming "collapse of hierarchy." Nineteen-eighty marked the appearance of the concept of "corporate culture," which helped condense the constellation of human relations concerns into a coherent intellectual field analogous to "corporate finance." An influential article of that year, "Managing Our Way to Economic Decline," attributed economic decline to a decline in relationships—in "intimate hands-on knowledge of the company's technologies, customers, and suppliers" (Hayes and Abernathy 1980, 67). Various writers were hard at work at the research and analysis that yielded the landmark business books of the following few years: William Ouchi's *Theory Z* (1981), Peters and Waterman's *In Search of Excellence* (1982), and Kanter's *The Change-Masters* (1983). These books and many others espoused and redefined McGregor's human side (see Waring 1991, chaps. 6–7).

Peters and Waterman invoke McGregor as a founding father of "what was to become the 'human relations' school of management." McGregor, they note, "termed Theory X 'the assumption of the mediocrity of the masses.'" The masses "need to be coerced, controlled, directed, and threatened with punishment to get them to put forward adequate effort," McGregor wrote. Theory Y, by contrast, assumes

> (1) that the expenditure of physical and mental effort in work is as natural as in play or rest—the typical human doesn't inherently dislike work; (2) external control and threat of punishment are not the only means for bringing about effort toward a company's ends; (3) commitment to objectives is a function of the rewards associated with their achievement . . . ; (4) the average human being learns, under

the right conditions, not only to accept but to seek responsibility; and
(5) *the capacity to exercise a relatively high degree of imagination,
ingenuity, and creativity in the solution of organizational problems is
widely, not narrowly, distributed in the population.* (quoted in Peters
and Waterman 1982, 95)

McGregor used X and Y to avoid reductive labeling, but it's fairly clear that X
and Y mark the spots of a reigning authoritarian and an insurgent democratic
theory of so-called economic man. Theory Y asserts that self-managed and
relatively egalitarian groups will be as productive as coerced and hierarchical
ones. Command-and-control management should not justify itself by invoking
the findings of the behavioral sciences.

Peters and Waterman display a common human relations embarrassment
about 1960s *applications* of Theory Y "that went off the deep end on T-groups,
bottom-up planning, democratic management, and other forms of a 'make
everyone happy' work environment" (1982, 96).[3] But they also display an un-
common honesty about Theory Y's importance to human relations thinking.
For McGregor justified much flatter and more open organizations on the fundamental level of human nature itself.

Moving on to 1970 we find Alvin Toffler already articulating most of what
has seemed stunningly new about the "new economy" of the 1990s. One of
his claims was that hierarchical bureaucracies were gradually being extin-
guished less by left-wing social movements than by internal changes in modern
economies. Technology in general and information technology in particular
were revolutionizing social systems and individual lives; the result was not only
revolutionary change but the revolutionizing of the pace of change beyond anything in previous human experience.

> As machines take over routine tasks and the accelerative thrust in-
> creases the amount of novelty in the environment, more and more of
> the energy of society (and its organizations) must turn toward the so-
> lution of non-routine problems. This requires a degree of imagination
> and creativity that bureaucracy, with its man-in-a-slot organization, its
> permanent structures, and its hierarchies, it not well equipped to pro-
> vide. Thus it is not surprising to find that wherever organizations to-
> day are caught up in the stream of technological or social change,
> wherever research and development is important, wherever men must
> cope with first-time problems, the decline of bureaucratic forms is
> most pronounced. In these frontier organizations a new system of hu-
> man relations is springing up. (Toffler 1970, 134–35)

Toffler condenses some ideas that in the 1990s would still consume tracts of
forest in the explaining. The slot filler would molt into creative maturity, would
"assume decision-making responsibility," would become empowered and creative. The decline of bureaucracy would mean the massive "humanization" of

rational planning (Toffler 1970, 135, 408). If McGregor supplied the empow-
erable human raw material, Toffler provided a roaring machinery of world-
historical change that was bulldozing bureaucracy.

Ten years later, the books of the early 1980s consolidated the human relations approach. William Ouchi offered as "Theory Z" the proposition "that
involved workers are the key to increased productivity." How do you involve
workers in the right way? Well, you start by not assuming, in business's usual
Theory X way, that they are lazy or incompetent. "Productivity, I believe, is a
problem of social organization or, in business terms, managerial organization.
Productivity is a problem that can be worked out through coordinating individual efforts . . . [and through] taking a cooperative, long-range view" (Ouchi
1981, 4–5). The two general lessons of Theory Z, Ouchi declared, are the need
for "trust" in colleagues and "subtlety" in information, especially the *inex-
plicit* or informal information that often makes the difference between success
and failure. Trust and subtlety require clear, continually revised understandings
of the complex relationships that comprise the firm. They require *intimacy*
(Ouchi 1981, 5–7). Productivity, Ouchi claimed, hinges on better—more intimate, more complex, more supported—group psychology. It hinges on increasing mutual involvement. It does not hinge on increasing the control or
punishment of individuals.

Peters and Waterman claimed that excellent management is part of an in-
digenous American tradition and need not be an exotic import. Its fundamentals are straightforward:

> There is good news from America. Good management practice today
> is not resident only in Japan. But, more important, the good news
> comes from treating people decently and asking them to shine, and
> from producing things that work. Scale efficiencies give way to small
> units with turned-on people. Precisely planned R & D efforts aimed
> at big bang products are replaced by armies of dedicated champions.
> A numbing focus on cost gives way to an enhancing focus on quality.
> Hierarchy and three-piece suits give way to first names, shirtsleeves,
> hoopla, and project-based flexibility. Working according to fat rule
> books is replaced by everyone's contributing. (Peters and Waterman
> 1982, xxiii)

Peters's *Liberation Management* (1992) was incipient in these lines: by liberating employee passions from the dim-witted yoke of hierarchical authority,
corporations will liberate themselves.

Ouchi, Peters, Waterman, and Kanter boosted human relations' basic participatory insights by intensifying two major features of the tradition. First, in
different ways they all stressed their *financial* evidence of the superiority of
involved workers. *In Search of Excellence* and *The Change-Masters* rested on
significant samples in which companies known for progressive human relations

policies had their numbers compared to those of a relatively traditional group. Kanter studied forty-seven pairs of companies. Peters and Waterman had a database of sixty-two American companies which they evaluated according to six measures of long-term financial performance. Having selected "excellent" companies on financial grounds, they then tried to itemize the common features of the group's excellent corporate culture.[4] Ouchi could back up his argument by pointing to the superior 1970s performance of all of Japanese industry. These writers added to a growing body of research that supported them when they said that "employee involvement and empowerment aren't only nice ideas, but will fix your lousy numbers" (for other examples, see Waring 1991, 156–59).

These writers also offered a point-blank targeting of "rational actor" theory that dominated management thinking, economics, and most of the social sciences. Rational actor theory supported the "paraphernalia of modern information and accounting systems, formal planning, management by objectives, and all of the other formal, explicit mechanisms of control characterizing" the conventional firm (Ouchi 1981, 61). It assumed that the best decisions are made on the basis of quantitative measurement, operations research, impersonal distance, routinized procedures, and other familiar practices of large bureaucracies. "Western management," writes Ouchi, thinks that "rational is better than non-rational, objective is more nearly rational than subjective, quantitative is more objective than non-quantitative, and thus quantitative analysis is preferred over judgments based on wisdom, experience, and subtlety." Though the human relations authors granted that quantitative knowledge has an important role to play, they hated its absolute rule. They hated its power to demote and dismiss the "human side"—the relationships, intimacy, subtlety, trust, and other informal and qualitative stuff on which real knowledge depends. As Peters explained to me, "relative to the dominant B-school paradigm, what Waterman and I were researching and writing about sixteen, seventeen years ago was an attack on structural solutions as the *only* type; we were trying to bring humanity into enterprise."

Ouchi wrote that Z companies retain the financial apparatus, and use it "for their information, but [it] rarely dominates in major decisions . . . the explicit and the implicit seem to exist in a state of balance." Peters and Waterman were even more uncompromising about the limits of business rationality. They declared that rational-actor views of firms belong to a defunct earlier period of organizational thinking. Everyone used to assume that "clear purposes and objectives for organizations exist, and that these can be determined straightforwardly," usually through financial objectives. Everyone used to assume that firms were "closed systems" in which little outside the organization need be considered. Those ideas, wrote Peters and Waterman, should be hauled to the boneyard. They announced a new phase in management thinking as of

1970, one based on *open* systems and *social* actors: "The social view supposes that decisions about objectives are value choices, not mechanical ones. Such choices are made not so much by clear-headed thinking as by social coalition, past habit patterns, and other dynamics that affect people working in groups" (Peters and Waterman 1982, 92). Toffler weighed in with a similar emphasis on social and interpersonal factors in his 1980 book. The new corporation, he wrote, will "combine economic and trans-economic objectives. It will have multiple bottom lines" (Toffler 1980, 260).

By the early 1980s human relations seemed ready to rule. It had an optimistic—even democratic—view of the capacities of the ordinary employee. It said that history was emancipating the complex, multidimensional, flexible, contextually aware individual from the weight of a dying bureaucratic age. It had shored up its weak quantitative flank. It looked forward to a renaissance in nonquantitative thinking. All these together would have offered business quite an amazing jolt. Technological reason and bureaucratic rule would be put in their place *from the inside.* It was one thing for social critics like Herbert Marcuse to decry the subtle tyrannies of a society designed to create "one-dimensional man." It was another for business intellectuals to attempt not simply a shuffling of the org charts but the transformation of the corporation's internal metabolism. "Attitude" and "structure" would change together, at the *molecular* level. In my rearview mirror, it looks like everything was ready for some role reversals in corporate America, some trading places: human relations would switch with financial rationality, *participation* with calculation, empowerment with control.

6. Fall and Rise?

But the human relations revolution never took place. We got the Reagan Revolution instead. Finance was back. Rational-choice theories ran economics. Spreadsheet warriors like David Stockman ran social policy. The boardroom was in full charge of firms. The numbers were in charge of the boardroom. Wall Street was in charge of the economy. "Participation" meant passive investment in stock funds, not a voice in running the economy or the firm. In government, the economy, and the individual enterprise, the relationships people were routed by the creatures from Planet Finance.

What happened? There are a thousand stories of the 1980s, but one is particularly relevant here. Most human relations writers, even wild spirits like Peters, conceded the *economic* argument to the finance people. Human relations may have sought metabolic change, but on the conceptual level it stuck with the belief that cultural and personnel issues could *supplement* financial assumptions without *replacing* or *changing* them. Human relations didn't say, Look, putting the creative individual and her relationships first means a different *role* for finance—a reduced one—and maybe a different *kind* of finance as well. It didn't confront the conservative market theory that justified the subordination of human relations to the financial picture. Dissent was fragmentary: in *The Third Wave* Toffler had suggested that "societal accounting" should replace simple cost accounting, but he let the idea drop (Toffler 1980, 259). Human relations didn't successfully distinguish itself from those empowerment techniques that were ready tools for dismantling the *cultural* position of the corporate middle class.

In trying to win over the middle manager and frontline worker in the late 1990s, TPG and their allies face a serious uphill battle. My own interviews with relatively young and low-level frontliners turned up a whopping distrust—even contempt—for consultants. None of them discriminated between different consultant brands. Though they work at high-concept places like Nordstroms and Electronic Data Systems, these frontliners have never seen a business idea that wasn't about controlling them. Most believe that management gurus are con artists who siphon off the potential bonus pool by giving the corner offices "expert" reasons to get rid of people. The only business theorist to really pass muster is the hilarious but deeply cynical cartoonist Scott Adams, who captures the drift with an installment devoted to a report by the "Dogbert Consulting Company":

> *Consultant:* Here's my final consulting report on your company.
> I've listed all the deadweight employees who should be fired.
> *Manager:* This is the company directory.
> *Consultant:* Finding that was a huge time-saver.

Lots of luck to management writers trying to get past images like these. Their ideas need to seem like *alternatives* to the job-cutting and overworking that, in Dilbert's world, any fool can make the big bucks by suggesting.

The uphill battle doesn't depend on the ideas alone. No one at TPG admitted to just doing ideas, or even to being a consultant in the first place. They called themselves business educators, writers, trainers, researchers, and seminar leaders—all roles that link concepts to practice and action. The concept of *training* was a crucial part of their strategy for getting past employee skepticism about management *ideas.*

One of the most frequently mentioned trainers at TPG was, at the time of her employment there, Malati Shinazy, who confronted skepticism as a central part of her job. I asked her what kind of issues she was dealing with.

"Cynicism. In the organization I'm working with, the senior folks went through the training first, then they encouraged it to go to the next level and the next level and now we're about three levels down. And the folks three levels down are looking up and saying, 'Wait a minute, our bosses and their bosses and their bosses made commitments to increase their leadership practices and shift their behaviors, and we haven't seen it.'

"Cynicism sets in on two levels," she continued. "One ignores that cultural change takes a while. It doesn't happen overnight. Changing any kind of behavior tends to be an incremental process even if you're fully committed. The system always tries to pull you back to where you were. That's one level of cynicism. The other level of cynicism says, 'I'm just an individual contributor, this has nothing to do with me. I'll just wait around and wait for somebody to tell me what to do.' That's the kind of stuff that pisses Tom off. Essentially what they're saying is, 'I'm powerless, and I don't need to do anything except wait.' And sure enough, they are. If that's what they're doing, they *are* powerless. I have a fairly low tolerance for that, too, so I have to manage my own response when I hear that."

For Shinazy, cynicism—impatience and learned helplessness—should be treated less through ideas in themselves than through training: through learning, unlearning, continuous effort, and constant reinforcement over very long periods of time. "For any real change," she said, "you need to get a significant number of people together. You need critical mass. For that you need to look at the long view. I'm thinking in terms of organizational diversity, which I've looked at and engaged in professionally for twenty years now. If you look at diversity over a twenty- or thirty-year span you can start to see small changes. If you look at anything shorter than that it doesn't look like any change at all. But cultural change takes at least a generation. Organizational cultures take the same time."

"Do you feel like changing people's attitudes is enough?" I asked. "Or do you see that just as a start? Do you feel like they have to go on to make serious structural change?"

"My sense," Shinazy said, "is you change their attitudes and then their behavior and that structural changes follow. The old structures become confining. People start shaking the cages. Actually, I've seen it. They no longer want to be anesthetized. They keep awake and they keep pushing. And they keep changing."

It's finally up to trainers like Shinazy to make the ideas work, and much of the power of human relations ideas derives from exactly this understanding of change: people really do want it, but they need to teach themselves and be taught how to get it, and it takes a shockingly long time. Organizational freedom is a practice that involves continuous improvement rather than an intellectual eureka. The practice is finally more important than the concept.

But human relations *ideas* remain critical to its chances for a broader practice. These ideas will need to move more completely *beyond the earlier participatory models* that remained a "backwater" in management thinking. Human relations will need to make it easier for the frontline user to believe that its solutions are really different from all the other new-wave ways of squeezing the middle and squashing the bottom. Converts are best made through the actual experience of shaking one's cage. But human relations writers need to keep shaking the ideas too. They're still ambiguous on some crucial points, and this weakens their application.

I doubt human relations will suddenly stand out by addressing finance and rationalist thinking on the level of *policy*. I have yet to read a sustained human relations attack on the intellectual base or the formal authority of financial control. Kouzes and Peters do decry the cult of the CEO, what Kouzes calls the "*People* magazine approach" to business reporting, as do Henry Mintzberg and other kindred writers (Mintzberg 1996, 64). But I think they will keep their policy hand tied behind their back. Sooner or later they're going to have to untie it. In the meantime, the other hand is doing something interesting. The other hand is working on a still unstable transformation of the conventional features of group life. It is not in policy or business politics but in business group psychology, in business *culture* that human relations is most likely to revive itself during our current reign of finance.

As I see it, the key to the ascendancy of a renewed human relations approach is its ability to synthesize a number of apparently contradictory features. The most interesting overall direction is toward overcoming the age-old but in fact superficial opposition between individual *entrepreneurship* and collaborative *participation*. Six aspects of the link between these came up in my conversations with the Tom Peters Group. The presence of more or less *all* these aspects at once, and the relationships among them, are even more important than any of the individual principles.

II. Transforming the Human Relations Approach

1. Radical Individualism for Company Man

New human relations thinkers recognize that they are dealing with company woman and organization man. The corporate middle class has long gotten ahead not by challenging superiors but by deferring to them. Sociologist C. Wright Mills was particularly eloquent on the middle-class propensity for submission. In his 1951 classic, *White Collar,* he wrote, "The twentieth-century white-collar man has never been independent as the farmer used to be, nor as hopeful of the main chance as the businessman. He is always somebody's man, the corporation's, the government's, the army's; and he is seen as the man who does not rise. The decline of the free entrepreneur and the rise of the dependent employee on the American scene has paralleled the decline of the independent individual and the rise of the little man in the American mind." Mills rightly identified the central feature of this middle-class citizen as dependence, and he devoted much of his book to detailing the new society to which dependence is wonderfully adapted: "What must be grasped is the picture of society as a great salesroom, an enormous file, an incorporated brain, a new universe of management and manipulation" (Mills 1951, xii, xv). The submissive individualist had become the ideal creature of bureaucracies both private and public, and thrived in the hive.

No wonder, then, that the boardroom would triumph in the 1980s. Frontliners and middle managers lacked a strong cultural tradition in which to see themselves as the source of transformative magic. Magic came from above; the middling ones served as its instruments. It was hard for the cadres to imagine new human relations as an alchemical power because *they* did not see alchemy in themselves. Some of my conversations at TPG addressed this sag in the corporate middle.

TPG publishes a monthly newsletter, once called *On Achieving Excellence* and now revamped as *Fast Forward.* It's not just any newsletter, but "the monthly newsletter that dares managers to break the rules." Michelle Cottle is its editor, and at twentysomething is the youngest person I spoke to in the organization. She's also the one to whom traditional images of the corporation seem least relevant.

Cottle thinks about frontliners generationally. We were talking about her background as a college English major and then short-term staffer at *Mother Jones.*

"A lot of people think everybody will soon be a contractor," she says. "Everybody will be self-employed. You'll contract out your services. You won't have any particular loyalty and it will be pure ability that decides whether you continue on or not."

"Would this be a big change for you?" I ask.

"It's already like that. Now with my colleagues, if you stay very long, *that's* a bad sign. There is never any security in journalism," Cottle continues. "I knew that when I chose the field, so it's not like I thought, 'Oh, great. I'll get a good job with the company and stay there forever,' and now I'm going, 'Oh, my god.' I'll never have any job security. This is clear. Nobody I've ever worked with figures that they'll be at their job more than two, three years."

Cottle sees this as a basic shift from the outlook of her parents' generation. The TPG target audience are older managers, "mostly middle age, mostly male, mostly white," whose attitude change still lies ahead. "The *Wall Street Journal*'s mission is the free market. Ours is innovation and risk taking. It's basically get up and do something." This is a message worth varying and expanding month after month because it's foreign to the way older employees think. Cottle agrees with other TPG people that resistance to employee liberation comes as much from traditional employees as from their bosses.

"If you spent most of your business life in a situation where you weren't forced to make decisions or you weren't forced to be responsible for anything except this particular little whatever, you don't want to have to suddenly have all this responsibility put on top of you. You're frightened by a lot of things. It's not just the chiefs commanding and controlling. Not all troops want to see the value of being given all this freedom, so that's as much a problem as anything. People have to be shown the value of this and they have to get used to it if they weren't raised to think along those lines. Otherwise it's 'Geez, what'll I do?"

Post–baby boom workers often note the absence of the job security their parents expected. But they also expect something in return for their continuous adaptation to change: greater autonomy and independence. If management doesn't provide security and upward mobility, then management doesn't get so much supervisory control. Peters sees this as a blessing in disguise. Cottle sees it as the way things are.

TPG has some kindred spirits in the world of management writing. Among the most advanced of these is Peter Senge, whose 1990 bestseller, *The Fifth Discipline: The Art and Practice of the Learning Organization,* insists that successful corporations are those that devote themselves to their employee's "personal mastery." "Traditionally," he writes, "organizations have supported people's development instrumentally—if people grew and developed, then the organization would be more effective. [Hanover Insurance CEO William] O'Brien goes one step further: 'In the type of organization we seek to build, the fullest development of people is on an equal plane with financial success" (Senge 1990, 143). Nineteen-nineties human relations is intensifying its long-standing insistence on the financial *and* the existential necessity of supporting individual fulfillment for its own employees.[5]

But this time around Senge, Peters, and others are hammering on the attitudes of the governed and not just of the governors. "The great irony of the age," Peters tells me, "is that the greatest resistance [to empowerment] comes from the best and the brightest. And I chide them about that directly and in person whenever I give a seminar. Gardeners and house painters understand this. $73,218-a-year senior purchasing officers and professionals with two degrees don't get it. *They* think they signed on at General Motors or General Mills for a lifetime. A lifetime in my dad's day really meant hustle pretty hard from age twenty-one, if you graduated from a university, to, say, thirty-five. Use the skills you picked up in the first fifteen years with some wisdom from age thirty-five to forty-five. Then, if you weren't going to be one of the five guys who ran the firm, coast from age forty-five to sixty-five, at which point you got the gold watch and a hundred bucks a month pension, whether you needed it or not. And you know, they were our most talented folks.

"If education made a difference," Peters continues, "the drug dealer and the gardener and the house painter ought to be resistant to [change] and the man or woman with two degrees ought to be responsive to it, but it doesn't seem to work out that way. Drug dealers understand; master's degree holders don't. That's a smart-ass remark, but I think there's a fair degree of truth to it."

There's a crucial insight in all of this. In resisting inflexible management, the employee's task is not simply to resist management but to resist himself, and his passivity in particular. Those frontliners who lack the college-boy protections of middle and upper corporate hierarchy are already more active. So are the post–baby boom workers that Cottle describes. Peters and Cottle both reverse the usual middle-class belief that they and the higher-ups are independent innovators while the lower-downs just follow rules. It's actually the middle that has thrived on rules.

Demanding activism, especially in the middle levels, does not necessarily mean blaming the victims of boardroom decisions. Peters ties submission and passivity to relative corporate privilege. It's the passivity of the fortunate that he targets. By itself, the call to liberate yourself from conformity can sound like a chest-beating excuse for firing some and flogging the rest. But radical individualism is a response to a genuine problem: company man's devotion to a hierarchy he claims to hate. Change in hierarchical *structure* requires a change in *attitude*—it means a willingness to give up what hierarchy has given.

2. War on Hierarchy

Radical individualism fits well with a second feature of radicalized participation. Peters and Kouzes are particularly good at calling for battle with hierarchy. Hierarchy keeps leadership from appearing everywhere in the organization. In my conversations with him, Kouzes made it crystal clear that he's bent on divorcing leadership from superiority of position.

"*Hierarchical* means master, priest, or holy. 'Hiros' literally was the priest. A hierarchy is an organization run by priests. Managers are the modern-day priests. Secular priests. And so no wonder managers make policies. Managers make commandments. Managers come down from the mountain and pass the commandments down to the flock. Hierarchy's just a word, but it's the origin of that word and what it means that's creating this whole mythology about what leadership is. Now I'm chief executive officer, I'm a priest. People come for sacraments. I bless them. They come for penance and they come to be forgiven. What an absurd idea."

"You take their offerings," I chime in, "and you turn this whole loft into your office."

"That's right. You know, there are altars with your effigy, founders' photographs, and people go pray at them. It's personally offensive to me. I just pulled out this quotation today for an interview I was doing myself. It's Walt Whitman and it says, 'This is what you should do. Love the earth and the sun and the animals, despise riches, give alms to everyone that asks, stand up for the stupid and crazy, devote your income to others, hate tyrants, argue not concerning God, have patience and indulgence towards the people, take off your hat to nothing known or unknown, or to any man or any number of men, etc.' I love that. It says, take your hat off to nothing or no one.

"The minute we start to venerate holy men and pay homage to them—"

"I'm looking at that picture of Alan Greenspan over there on your floor," I exclaim.

"—and create a whole mythology around the importance of these people, we subordinate ourselves and we disable ourselves."

Real leadership, Kouzes is saying, doesn't flow from the top of a hierarchy. Real leadership depends on getting around hierarchy. And our own gullible tendency to submit helps keep hierarchy in place.

Thus it shouldn't be a big surprise that the longest section of *Liberation Management* is called "Beyond Hierarchy." Peters writes,

> There's no liberation when much more than a semblance of the super-structures remains.
> "Reduce layers"? "Flatten the pyramid"? No. Go to your local sta-tioner's. Buy [a] clean sheet of paper. . . . And, then, rip. R-I-P. Rip, shred, tear, mutilate, destroy that hierarchy. (Peters 1992, 131)

Whenever the target is hierarchy, Peters stresses the cathartic pleasure of its destruction. The pleasure of destruction must arise from the frontliners' own analyses and actions. If they help reduce management because management tells them to, they've missed the whole point—leadership begins with the end of management by superior position.

Senge also argues that hierarchy is a key source of helplessness. "Helpless-ness, the belief that we cannot influence the circumstances under which we live, undermines the incentive to learn, as does the belief that someone somewhere else dictates our actions. . . . This is why learning organizations will, increas-ingly, be 'localized' organizations, extending the maximum degree of author-ity and power as far from the 'top' or corporate center as possible" (Senge 1990, 287).

For all these writers, it makes sense to ask the cubicles to lead only if hier-archy is being pushed aside.

3. The Primacy of Groups

So frontliners should stand up in the corporate world. And they should live by Captain Ahab's question, "Who's over me?"

At this point, it might look like these two principles of latter-day human relations boil down to an all-American rugged individualism. Most of us as-sume that though we may stray from it and compromise it at work and at home, individualism remains our baseline ideal. The U.S. has always defined itself as the individualist republic. For example, the National Security Council's land-mark document 68, written in 1950, defined the fundamental goal of postwar foreign policy as assuring "the integrity and vitality of our free society, which is founded upon the dignity and worth of the individual" (quoted in Bellah et al. 1991, 223). Americans generally assume that group formations and collective planning conflict with individualism because they block the pursuit of private self-interest. Politicians and policymakers have been backed up by a large majority of social scientists who believed that organizations, though of course indispensable to modern social life, were at war with the individual.[6] When 1980s-style laissez-faire revivalism demanded the liberation of individual entrepreneurship in a free enterprise system, it did so by charging the victimization of economic individualism by overdone obligations to groups. And the ongoing attacks on race-conscious policy, be it affirmative action in university admissions or "minority majority" congressional districts, win converts by claiming that such policies rest on group identities that hurt individual opportunity.

In spite of this powerful cultural tradition the Peters group routinely *ties individual performance to organizational behavior*—to a life of teams, collaboration, and relationships. Kouzes offered me an example that led me back to an interesting passage in the book he coauthored with Barry Posner, *The Leadership Challenge:*

> Early in our research, we asked Bill Flanagan, vice president of operations for Amdahl Corporation, to describe his personal best. After a few moments, Flanagan said that he couldn't do it. Startled, we asked him why. Flanagan replied, "Because it wasn't *my* personal best. It was *our* personal best. It wasn't *me*. It was *us*."
>
> In the more than 550 original cases that we studied, we didn't encounter a single example of extraordinary achievement that occurred without the active involvement and support of many people. . . . In thousands of additional stories, from all professions and from around the globe, people continue to tell us, "You can't do it alone. It's a team effort." . . . People passionately promoted teamwork as the interpersonal route to success. . . . The increasing emphasis on reengineering, world-class quality, knowledge work, and electronic communication, along with the surging number of global alliances and local partnerships, is testimony to the fact that in a more complex, wired world, the winning strategies will be based upon the *"we* not *I"* philosophy. (Kouzes and Posner 1995, 151–52)

I'm not completely surprised when Kouzes says to me, "I often joke with my seminar participants and say, 'I know what I've just said makes me sound like a Communist. But, in fact, it's based on the literature.' "

Call them what you want, but thinkers like Kouzes, Peters, and Posner *deny* the analytical distinction between individualism and group life that's been the bedrock of American conservatism *and* American liberalism for a century and a half. They contest our core identity, one that political theorist C. B. Mac-Pherson called "possessive individualism," in which personal identity and freedom hinge on private, individual accumulation and power. Though in public *policy* they often support the free market, in human relations they substitute conscious group behavior for Adam Smith's "invisible hand."

You might ask why the organization's metabolism should be continually influenced, negotiated, and reconstructed in the corporation but left alone in the general economy. A major reason is that while the TPG folks have little faith in the state, they have great faith in everyday employees. These employees do not intervene at a distance from their organization. They *are* their organization. Their "intervention" in it is nothing more than their everyday activity on the job. Their *individual performance* cannot be analytically or functionally separated from the quality of their working *groups.*

We're talking here about something like *group individualism,* in which individuality is enhanced by group experience. I didn't try out this term in any of my TPG conversations. But it has an utterly pivotal role to play in the TPG visions of corporate change. In *Liberation Management* Peters describes "self-contained work teams" as one of the "basic organizational building blocks" of the new corporation. He praises Quinn Mills's idea of "the cluster organization." A cluster is "a group of people drawn from different disciplines who work together on a semipermanent basis." The cluster has two dominant features. It "handles many administrative functions, thereby divorcing itself from an extensive managerial hierarchy." And "a cluster develops its own expertise" (quoted in Peters 1992, 245). Learning makes bossing less necessary. Groups make layers a little foolish. Building groups, in TPG theory, will not mean a war on so much as a bypass of managerial hierarchy.

Most advocates of teams see them as a breakthrough not just in efficiency but in governance. Peters says that groups and clusters go "miles beyond decentralization, even as practiced by progressive firms." He describes a reorganization in the Danish firm Oticon that did "a lot more than cede some precious authority to the hinterlands." It "put the hinterlands in charge." He cites Charles Handy's idea of corporate federalism, in which "the outlying units (reluctantly) yield power to the center" and not the other way around (Peters 1994a, 30). "In the traditional authoritarian organization, the dogma was managing, organizing, and controlling," says Hanover's CEO Bill O'Brien. "In the learning organization, the new 'dogma' will be vision, values, and mental models. The healthy corporations will be ones which can systematize ways to bring people together" around learned visions (Senge 1990, 181). Clusters, teams, groups (but for some reason, never committees). The team, according a blurb on the back of Senge's book, is "a true alternative to authoritarian hierarchy." The group, within the right kind of corporate arrangement, becomes hierarchy's functional replacement.

These writers imply the need for a fundamental rethinking of group psychology. The danger remains, of course, that it can become a facade for business or for cutbacks as usual. Advocates like Jon Katzenback and Douglas Smith, authors of the best-seller *The Wisdom of Teams,* say that teams break down hierarchical interaction and yet are wholly compatible with hierarchy. "Those who see teams as a replacement for hierarchy are missing the true potential of teams" (Katzenbach and Smith 1993, 5). My colleague Alan Liu argues that the "postindustrial teamwork or learning organization . . . is the knowledge entity that devalues the [individual] by systematically stripping it of both its traditional support groups and that over-identity that had first organized and universalized groups, class" (Liu 1996, 28). Clearly, there's some disagreement about the direction of teams. Many rightly worry that corporate groups will become an updated version of David Reisman's "lonely crowd," where everyone feels alone, and everyone has relationships only by obeying authority.

Are groups a replacement for authoritarian management or its cunning extension? The answer depends on the features that the groups have. One can't simply promote the idea of groups or say, "We need some groups in here." Groups are elaborate *practices* that require careful construction, training, ongoing development, and everyday work.

As I continue, I'll list some further features that can help make groups *alternatives* to traditional hierarchy. The two previous features are fundamental—groups need to foster autonomous individuals *and* to produce enough equality to permit autonomy *inside* the group. The crucial point here is that TPG and its allies show utter hostility toward *any devaluation of the individual.* Senge states in any number of ways that "team learning is the process of aligning and developing the capacity of a team to create the results its members truly desire" (Senge 1990, 236). The point of the group is to *enlarge* the individual's sphere and not diminish it. The individualism of Peters's writing is especially pervasive and unwavering. Once again, its group context conflicts with our time-honored belief in a war between individuals and groups, for it claims that group life has to figure out how to support the individual's passionate desires and reduce the individual's dependency.

Saying this obviously doesn't make it so. Nor does it mean Peters or anyone else has a foolproof path to group individualism. It doesn't mean a general formula will ever be in the offing. But it does signal a conceptual framework for the group as alternative to hierarchy. The individual must be as powerful as the group. There must be a meeting between individual and group, an interaction. The interaction must take place on a terrain of *equality* between the two. If a group drains the self like hierarchy does, then kill the group with a stake through its heart.

4. From Competition to Cooperation

One of the nasty things about groups is the way they can rapidly divide everyone into leaders and followers, the sheep and the dogs. It doesn't take a human relations specialist to see this danger. Even if the group has genuine autonomy from the boardroom, it can become stratified itself, so that a few people come to control the rest. How can a group flatten the larger structure if it can't even flatten itself?

I was reminded of the problem during one of my lectures not long ago. I'd been soliloquizing about people left, right, and center who'd been rejecting mythical kinds of rugged individualism in favor of a group individualism they actually found more liberating. A woman in the back of the hall raised her hand and said the discussion sections of my own course called my lecture into question. "The TA breaks up into groups all the time," she said. "Nothing happens. Most of the group doesn't know anything. The same few people do all the talking. Each time, the same people speak for the group to the TA. It's like each group has its own junior TAs. Everyone else just sits there." I expected her classmates to be insulted, but mostly they, well, just sat there. Some nodded their heads in agreement.

I explained that egalitarian group work is so hard not because it's unnatural but because we have so little experience. We're habituated to hierarchical contexts; we've adapted, and now we have to adapt back. What I said was, "This lecture is yet another structure that makes successful groups difficult, helping to prove yet again that authority must come from above. Given this experience, people prefer lectures where they sit there passively absorbing, and so we have more lectures, and turn out more people who want to sit passively listening to lectures." What I thought was, "Oh, great, you said your own method undermines the new idea you just presented. A nice way to help them take it seriously." How do I really *respond* to the student's criticism, I wondered—how *could* I change my own discussion sections so they avoid reproducing the hierarchies in which they invariably exist?

TPG has some interesting things to say about why groups go bad. One major reason came up a number of times: people sink to the bottom of even small groups because the group offers no *cooperative support*. Peters quotes Senge on this point: "Where we see that *to learn* we must be willing to look foolish, to let another teach us, learning doesn't always look so good anymore. . . . Only with the support, insight, and fellowship of a community can we face the dangers of learning meaningful things" (Peters 1994b, 260).

Kouzes is particularly vehement about giving individuals what they need before asking them to perform. "If you listen to the political debate," he tells me, "it's all about, We got to do this, and we got to do that, we gotta cut this, and we gotta increase that. We gotta be more competitive. We've gotta try harder, we've gotta do more. Well, it's all about the gottas. What about people's education level? What about their tools? What are we going to provide to them in the way of resources?"

The same sink-or-swim attitude pervades business as well, Kouzes observed. "The new employee contract people are talking about—it's not a contract, it's a one-way declaration. It's a unilateral declaration. Take it or leave it. What are corporations saying to their employees? 'We're not going to promise you employment for life.' What a wonderful thing to be able to say today. 'We're not going to promise you anything,' as if they ever did. 'You're accountable for your own success, so we're going to judge you by your performance and we're only going to give you pay increases equal to or a little bit above inflation. The rest you're going to have to earn in bonuses and oh, by the way, managers will get more, a higher percentage than you do, and they make more money.' And you go down the list and say, 'And you're responsible for your own education. We're not going to take responsibility for that. Now sign this contract.' If somebody offered me that deal, I wouldn't take it. Corporations and governments are making these unilateral declarations about how people ought to behave without providing any kind of support or any kind of capacity building. And so the public response to these declarations is to say, 'Look, we got to chain you up.' Well, we in business have got to change our behavior."

This *would* be a big change, since the business ultimatum Kouzes rejects has become the standard way firms squeeze out costs. There's a long list of major companies that have slashed salaries, benefits, health plans, and pensions by making them the employee's responsibility. This is one form of empowerment that a lot of people don't need and that a lot of people continue to get. Large companies often hire "temporary" workers through labor contractors, or "consultants" through agencies, for jobs they at one time would have filled with their own full-time, fully insured people. Companies have increased the subcontracting of parts of their production to lower-wage, lower-benefit, less-regulated firms.

I recently read about the version of this strategy used by a large British construction firm. The firm, called Contrac by the article's author, hired most of its frontline workers from a labor agency. The agency did not actually employ the workers but merely brokered the contract with them. The workers were technically self-employed, meaning that they had no employer to pay insurance, social security, or taxes. The author discovered that the labor agency was in fact wholly owned by Contrac through three or four layers of front companies. Contrac hired workers from itself without actually hiring them, and avoided liability for the usual worker protections and benefits (Anonymous 1996). The basic idea is to outsource everything except the cappuccino machine. It has been a major bottom-line strategy for U.S. firms, and it will not be relinquished willingly.

To make matters worse, TPG can develop the ideal of *cooperation* only in the teeth of the huge ideological power of the concept of *competition,* which lies at the heart of the American Way. Many observers explain the economic dislocation of the past twenty years as a bracing effect of competition. Ronald Reagan turned a 1987 visit to a recovering Harley Davidson factory into a standard parable of competition's virtues. He saw workers and managers using "team" collaboration to cope with major sales declines. Reagan remarked:

> In different ways, much of American industry underwent a simi-
> lar transformation during the 1980s. Faced with new competition and
> responding to forces in the free market, our companies went out and
> made better products and became more efficient at doing it. . . .
> Adversity made us tougher. New competition made us work harder.
> (Reagan 1990, 348).

This is your captain on autopilot, but it's an autopilot that most Americans feel obliged to respect.

Facing the sacred status of competition, Kouzes and Posner reviewed mass quantities of empirical research and conclude, "*cooperate* to succeed!" In one survey of 581 studies of "the effects of cooperation versus competition on productivity and achievement, 60 percent [of the findings] favored cooperation, 8 percent favored competition, and 32 percent found no difference" (Kouzes and Posner 1995, 154). Describing the "550 original cases" they examined themselves, Kouzes and Posner conclude that "in no one's personal-best narrative was creating competition between group members described as a way to achieve high performance" (Kouzes and Posner 1995, 151-52). "Competition almost never results in the best performance," write Kouzes and Posner; "pursuing excellence is a collaborators' game." They cite the research of competition critic Alfie Kohn, who writes, "The simplest way to understand why competition generally does not promote excellence is to realize that trying *to do well and trying to beat others are two different things.*" Kouzes and Posner elaborate: "One is about accomplishing the superior; the other, about making someone else inferior. One is about achievement; the other, about subordination" (Kouzes and Posner 1995, 152). Competition leads to subordination, and subordination hamstrings good performance.

This doesn't mean competition should disappear. All of the Peters personnel express a default approval of competition as a tonic, as smelling salts, a stimulant, an inspiration, a goad, and a bearer of urgent news. This goes double for Peters himself, who sees competitive defeat as the world's best wake-up call. But even Peters said to me, "The enjoyment will go up a hell of a lot if we are capable of inventing some new bases of security. I acknowledge the basic psychological proposition that people are desperate pursuers of stimuli and desperate pursuers of security simultaneously." The point could be made this way: competition should be used to provide information about one's relative performance. When competition goes beyond conveying performance information into defining relationships, it hurts people and profits alike. It should not be used to structure group relations. Competition and cooperation can be used together, as long as they're confined to distinctive roles. Competition is a source of good information and of bad social relations. It requires wasted capacity, hoarded knowledge, increased ignorance and reduced learning, more replicated effort and more short-term decision making.

A huge portion of *The Leadership Challenge* attempts to define future-oriented leadership as support for group collaboration. Kouzes insisted with me that financial results back him up. One of his most important examples is a famous turnaround case, a company called SRC:

> Take the Springfield Remanufacturing Corporation, Springfield, Missouri, run by a right-wing Republican by the name of Jack Stack. And Jack is a free enterprise capitalist—he's as Adam Smith as you can get. But he faced a crisis in 1983 when he managed the plant. He was ordered by International Harvester to sell the factory or shut it down. So he got a group of people of average education or below to get together with him and buy the company and turn it around.
>
> The problem was that Stack had the highest leveraged buyout in corporate history. He raised $100,000 from employees and borrowed $8.9 million. He had eighty-nine parts debt to one part equity. As it turned out, it's a tremendous success story. They went from a loss to making a profit within four years of the buyout. They've had an increase of 23,000 percent in corporate stock values. They went from about 190 to 800 employees. They've had sales growth exceeding 30 percent a year.
>
> Stack started by saying to himself, "The only way I'm going to make this happen is if I give these employees the skills, tools, and capability to do this. We need to give everybody in the company a voice in running the company and a stake in the financial outcome." He taught everyone, including people who sweep the floor, how to read a balance sheet, how to read an income statement, how to read a financial statement. Weekly he gives them a report on how well they are doing in their area. It's called open-book management. It's been one of the revolutions in business. The whole assumption that underlies open-book management is that the skills of finance, which we think only somebody with an MBA can manage to comprehend, are skills that everyone can learn.

Stack also wrote a book, *The Great Game of Business,* in which he stresses both the financial and the personal benefit of open books. "The more people know about a company, the better that company will perform. This is an iron-clad rule. You will *always* be more successful in business by sharing information with the people you work with than by keeping them in the dark." He adds a bit later, "Numbers can give meaning to your job, show you exactly where you fit in, why you're important" (Stack 1992, 71, 74). Information—about financial results, about processes, about personnel—is the crucial element of Stacks' support for his company's collaborative, cooperative efforts.

Sharing information partially counteracts hierarchies that are based on confidential information. Information makes and maintains the large, heterogeneous group of SRC employees involved in very different ways in the overall operation. The information allows for the drastic expansion of decision-making power in the company. "Without education," Stack writes, "you don't have democracy. All you have is manipulation. . . . The better educated people are, the more democratic you can be, and the better it will work." The result, he claims, is that "there has never been a really important decision in this company that hasn't been by acclamation, if not unanimous. Every major decision is talked through in advance" (Stack 1992, 226, 225). Open information is the key form of cooperation and the backbone of SRC's form of participatory management.

5. Diversity and Conflict

Another frequent curse of group experience is conformity. Nothing is more galling than being asked to agree with everything in order to sign on. If you believe, you can participate. If you dissent, you'll be ignored. Say something nice or don't say anything at all, etc., etc.

Many human relations writers reject an unchallengeable "common culture" valued by the cultural conservatism we wrongly equate with all business thought. It's true that TPG associates a strong corporate culture with a shared sense of purpose. Kouzes and Posner claim that one of the five major principles of leadership is "inspiring a shared vision." Some sense of collective mission is an attibute of just about everybody's idea of a functioning team. And yet, TPG likes teams and groups and shared visions without demanding unified agreement. The reason is pretty simple: though common values have an important role in defining the boundaries and the purpose of a group, common values can destroy a group's internal chemistry. Open negotiation, disputation, and conflict come first. Common purpose should be allowed to emerge only from that activity. Common values should *not* predetermine the outcome, even if they establish the initial conditions. Shared vision is like competition—useful, but only in its place.

Groups in fact go nowhere without internal differences. When I asked his opinion of "diversity management," Peters replied, "the Webster's definition of creativity and anybody else's definition of creativity is things that don't fit bouncing against each other. What better example of that than blacks, whites, Hispanics, Native Americans, Asians, men, women, young, old, etc., all screwed up as we sometimes see here in the Silicon Valley, all doing interesting things."

As a general rule, nothing inspires calls for common standards like racial difference. It's a rule that Peters breaks. "Diversity," he said, "to me, just makes plain, cold, hard, narrow-minded, capitalist pig, right-wing sense. Even if it weren't on the side of the angels, which I roughly think it is." "It seems obvious to me," he writes in *The Pursuit of Wow!*, "that Cacophony, Inc., a wild mixture of colors, sexes, styles, and ages will almost automatically generate and pursue more interesting ideas than Homogeneity, Inc." (Peters 1994b, 20). Peters is not so much talking about race or racism in America as about the necessarily disjointed and unsynthesized interior of any good group.

Peter Senge claims that groups depend not just on difference but on out-and-out conflict:

> Contrary to popular myth, great teams are not characterized by an absence of conflict. On the contrary, in my experience, one of the most reliable indicators of a team that is continually learning is the visible conflict of ideas. In great teams conflict becomes productive. . . . The free flow of conflicting ideas is critical for creative thinking, for discovering new solutions no one individual would have come to on his own. Conflict becomes, in effect, part of the ongoing dialogue.
>
> On the other hand, in mediocre teams, one of two conditions usually surrounds conflict. Either, there is an appearance of no conflict on the surface, or there is rigid polarization. In the "smooth surface" teams, members believe that they must suppress their conflicting views in order to maintain the team—if each person spoke her or his mind, the team would be torn apart by irreconcilable differences. (Senge 1990, 249)

Commonality and consensus don't govern group processes. Conflict does.

This is a big step beyond the fretful, controlling communitarianism that represents a dominant catch-all in today's policy debates. Whenever someone in mainstream policy says we need more stress on values, they mean we need more conformity in our groups.

Francis Fukuyama's book *Trust* offers a nice example of the usual stopping point. Like TPG, he sees a building trend in the best corporations toward "face-to-face, egalitarian, and intimate" groups (Fukuyama 1995, 221). The outcome of corporate evolution in high-trust cultures will be a "more communally-oriented workplace" (233).

Fukuyama has big social ambitions for his communal corporation. For once these structures are developed, a society can leave behind today's limited alternatives: *market relations,* dominated by "agreement between completely independent actors," and *hierarchical relations,* dominated by unequal exchanges between "related actors." New corporate society would achieve a third route to prosperity that subsumes markets and bureaucracy through *network relations,* where the actors are both free and connected, independent and co-operative. "In a network organization, there is no overall source of authority" (205). Actors can and must resolve their differences on their own. The power of groups derives from their *replacement of authoritarianism with participation* (which he never calls "democracy"). Participation is meaningful only if its outcomes can survive opposition from above. At that point, it really does undermine managerial authoritarianism.

This is a nice idea, the network, but it never actually leaves the "overall source of authority" behind. Fukuyama's thinking is torn between two views that wrack communitarians in general. He celebrates the active participation of all members in their small groups, where things are "face-to-face, egalitarian, and intimate." On the other hand, he insists on the presence of "commonly shared norms." The principle of governance is not the *participation* of all individuals, but their *unity,* their *homogeneity.*

The real test comes when Fukuyama is faced with difference and conflict in his own society, which for him means the unfathomable problem of African Americans. He traces economic weakness in African-American communities to their lack of "social cohesiveness." He warns that diversity is better sipped than gulped. He disparages a miscellany of social changes that challenge the unity of "older moral communities of shared value" (303, 305–6). He offers the Mormon church as a positive alternative model of community. And he concludes, "As this book has documented, a people's ability to maintain a shared 'language of good and evil' is critical to the creation of trust, social capital, and all the other positive economic consequences that flow from these attributes" (270). Face-to-face is good, as long as it's governed by the unity and conformity of Homogeneity, Inc.

This is the preformatted kind of participation that Peters and others are trying to rethink. On questions of ethnicity and race they have a long way to go, as one of Peters's own trainers put it to me. I slight these questions here, except to note that the Peters group won't have a fully convincing endorsement of conflict and difference until they can systematically address not just the diversity but also the conflicts surrounding gender and race. Corporate America lags behind a remarkably balky American society in achieving the basic racial integration demanded by the civil rights movements of thirty, forty, and fifty years ago. Business's dealings with gender and especially race do more than nearly anything else to discredit its claim to outstrip politics in creating positive social change. But the Peters group is in a position to help for one reason: they don't see conflict as a reason to call in the law.

6. Capture the Numbers

Another stupid thing about groups is their diversionary potential. They often feel like the corporative equivalent of eating off plastic plates at the children's table while the adults carve roast in the dining room. Jack Stack offers a parable on the subject:

> I knew a company that prided itself on its humanistic approach to business. The people were always going on whitewater rafting trips or mountain-climbing expeditions, and they set aside a part of every day for self-improvement sessions. The CEO played motivational tapes and threw regular Friday-afternoon beer busts to tell people how great

they were doing: a terrific corporate culture. But they forgot one thing: you have to make money to stay in business. After a brief but glorious run, the company folded, and the people all lost their jobs.

I am second to none in believing that business ought to be people-oriented. But no company serves its people well by elevating emotions over numbers. That's one of the things I like most about open-book management: it takes the emotions out of the business, or at least out of the decision-making process. Emotions can cloud the brain, but the numbers don't lie. . . . Don't get me wrong. I think emotions have a legitimate role to play in business. I'm all in favor of pompoms and celebrations and inspirational messages. I just don't think they should replace solid information about the condition of the company. (Stack 1992, 75)

This at first sounds like the rational-choice view that Ouchi, Peters, and Waterman had so directly attacked: emotions are a distracting luxury rather than "subtle" knowledge, so let the numbers run things along with the people who know them. But it's actually one of those knotty junctures in human relations writing where clashing ideas and idioms exist side by side. For Stack is also sending another, nearly opposite message: frontliners should seize the numbers. They shouldn't settle for a cut of the training budget but must share power over financial decisions.

What forms will frontliner finance take? My discussion with Michelle Cottle suggested one of them. Talking about her job as newsletter editor, she said to me, "I want the employees' perspective. I think it's a little more realistic than all this 'we're all going to go out and get to know each other and hug a tree and employ some new management practice and it's gonna work out better for everyone.' I'm a lot more interested in what the employees are saying. They're hard to get to, though. It's almost impossible to get to frontliners for interviews. For one, if you use their name, they lose their job."

"If you were to talk to frontline people," I asked, "what would you expect to hear from them?"

"The corporate mission statement only works for the first three levels in most companies," Cottle replied. "The guys down on the front line have no clue what their company's grand goal is because they're meeting quotas and working for compensation."

"What would they tell you?" I pressed. "Our mission statement is bullshit?"

"Well, they won't say that. I don't think you'd get cynicism about the official dogma. I just don't think it would come up. What the upper management would be very, very worried about is not affecting frontliners a lot."

"But you don't see them having a whole different perspective on how to run a company that you could generalize about?" I wondered.

"I think they have issues. But a lot of times they're more practical in terms of a problem they have in their department. 'This is the problem.' It has very little to do with upper management. It's the business equivalent of that political debate, 'Does the federal government know what's better for your local area, or does the state government?' It's not necessarily a different perspective on how to run the company, but maybe on how to run their department or division. Some people are completely clueless about what goes on beyond their department and others could turn your company around like this," she says, snapping her fingers.

I take this to mean that frontliners are much more inclined to distance themselves from the boardroom than they are inclined to attack it. They won't trash the mission statement or write their own; they will simply ignore it. On the matter of increased financial control, frontliners will tend to use decentralizing policies like open-book management to augment the independence of their own units. They will achieve some real independence in the process of making concrete local decisions. Their knowledge will be local, and will thus involve all the soft, subtle, emotional, *social* elements known to people on site. Decisions will be made by social actors in a relatively open system. Human relations elements will shape financial decisions in the units.

At the same time, human relations input into financial decisions can't only be local. Too many frontliners have seen their supposedly decentralized units ruled by a distant boardroom to jump for joy over local control. Any given unit needs to know the overall financial picture and work on general issues in direct contact with the rest of the firm. This is the founding idea of open-book management. The unit must be independent and *networked*. It can't revel in its own culture; it must also influence the top.

The corporation already has the infrastructure to combine local independence with networks in which power flows in every direction. Mostly it uses its infrastructure to sustain the hierarchical and fixed positions of conventional bureaucracy. One silver lining in the downsizing of the Bush-Clinton era has been the proof that corporate bureaucracies are easier to change than we used to assume. The daily functioning of frontliners in their own departments moves this transformation along. In the medium term, human relations—corporate *culture*—will need to stop serving as a *supplement* to financial decisions and become inseparable from them. Cultural perspectives—relationships, emotions, the whole participatory alchemy—will need to develop more technical competence with financial decisions. The cubicle's newly proprietary attitude toward and practice of finance would reduce the *structural* distance between the cubicle and the boardroom.

7. The Cultural Future

Toward the end of our conversation I said to Cottle, "Soon there will be three corporations in the country. Rupert Murdoch will own one of them."

"But only two percent of the population will work with him."

I laughed and said, "It's going to be strange."

And it will be. But it's crucial to remember that the strangeness of new human relations thought takes very specific forms that reflect its significant limits. It primarily reflects the perspectives of the corporation's white middle class. It is vulnerable to the middle-class sense that for various reasons of education, skill, and work ethic it deserves special treatment, come what may to the less favored. Human relations is weak on the big historical picture and the large social forces; it doesn't offer its followers "people-oriented" critiques of the global market or the World Bank. It has only occasional, reactive interest in rethinking government or reviving its power to represent the public interest. As speakers for the common good, it trails the pack.

Human relations is nonetheless much more impressive than outsiders have reason to expect. The 1990s version I've described through the lens of the Tom Peters Group looks very different from the boardroom face of business we see on CNN and in *Business Week*. It is redefining at least six fundamental issues of organizational life away from the conventional wisdom that control public discourse. New human relations insists on genuine individualism. It imagines a range of ways to shred or at least erode bureaucratic hierarchy. It argues that individualist leeway depends on intimate and equitable group life. Human relations has elaborately researched the superiority of cooperation to competition in the making of creative (and profitable) employees. But it also underscores the necessity of conflict and diversity in group life. Finally, it puts the social actor and the cultural factor back into corporate finance. Taken together, these six features point toward a *postbureaucratic* kind of economic institution.

I've put together all these features of new human relations because one or another of them by itself is usually ineffectual. Some writers talk about the new corporation as a team or network or "web of enterprise" without describing the autonomy of the individual in the web. Other writers define the empowered individual as a permanent high-wire act of endless entrepreneurship without specifying any means of support. These one-stop solutions deserve the skepticism they abundantly reap. For example, in response to some such fans of empowerment, embodied in a new magazine for "business revolutionaries," Tom Frank writes:

> For all its excesses, *Fast Company* gets at a basic truth of the corporate order: workplace democracy is exactly what we need most desperately in this age of rising economic desperation. But it's superstition of the first rank to believe that the market is going to correct the problems that the market has caused, that total competition is somehow going to rescue us from the destruction wreaked by total competition, that new management theories are the solution to old management theories. What the businessman's republic requires to keep it fair and honest is not greater power for business but some sort of power that confronts business. (Frank 1996, 12)[7]

This is quite right about the management theory that is all about competition and not about workplace democracy. Human relations will make a difference only if it puts the different pieces together. Human relations will reinforce a kinder, gentler corporate feudalism unless it can really synthesize its entrepreneurial and participatory wings.

Human relations in the 1990s doesn't try to put economics back in the hands of government, politics, or the people. It doesn't say that the state should regulate various markets. It doesn't repoliticize economics generally, or restore business to community control. And yet it does things very much like these *inside* the firm. It submits economics to cultural practices, ones based less in the political reregulation of finance than in the everyday density, complexity, and enmeshing "subtlety" of relationships. Human relations doesn't seek the social control of capital in general. But it does imagine the practical cultural control of a firm's financial decisions.

Could this involve a change in a firm's style of capitalism?[8] Could a firm replace profit maximization with some other priorities? Could we have capitalism without the corporation? Could the market—so often treated as an iron law of nature—be replaced by networks and matrices governed by new kinds of participation? Could we see multiple capitalisms as we move from firm to firm, and multiple bottom lines? Could the corporation be socialized? Could it resocialize society? Could the new corporation lead beyond capitalism itself?

Maybe. There are some signs of strange days ahead: A dwindling faith in the future among the richest firms. A divide between company man and company plan. An abundance of business heresy.[9] An incremental "revolt of the guards" (Zinn 1980, chap. 21). A stranger who calls, and whose call comes from inside the house.

Notes

1. This overview relies in part on Bluestone and Harrison 1982, chap. 1.

2. These results come from the Luxembourg Income Study, as reported in Bradsher 1995 and Henwood 1995.

3. They claim that Theory X and Theory Y are not really opposed, that to contrast the authoritarian and the democratic is misleading since most managers—like good parents—are both.

4. One of Peters's recent cracks suggests he's still irked, twelve years later, to have given this much credit to the numbers crowd. "In *In Search of Excellence,* Bob Waterman and I defined and measured excellence in terms of long-term financial health. Truth is, we could hardly have cared less. But we knew we needed to go through the drill to be taken seriously by the 5,000 conformists we hoped would buy the book." Peters is not one to be shy about biting the hand. He continues, "Nothing wrong with financial measures, mind you. Can't live without them. But they're far from the whole picture" (1994a, 219).

5. It's beyond my scope here to compare business reformers to social reformers. But

Senge's phrase resonates with a famous one—"the free development of each is the condition for the free development of all"—in Marx and Engel's description of postcapitalist "association" in the *Communist Manifesto.* Senge and TPG are pro- and not postcapitalist. But the expanded version of this essay will need to consider a common thread of middle-class dissent that runs from Marx through Peters: a rejection of the restraints on individual liberty required by existing capitalist institutions.

6. For an excellent historical survey and analysis of the issue, see Alford 1994.

7. For other entertaining and astute criticisms, see the essays by Boisvert, Frank, and others in *The Baffler,* no. 6 (1995).

8. For a range of examples of changes in firms' financial cultures, see Case 1995, chap. 9–13.

9. For a history of unorthodox business thought, see Kleiner 1996. This very interesting book appeared too late for me to make use of it here.

References

Alford, C. Fred. 1994. *Group Psychology and Political Theory.* New Haven, Conn.: Yale University Press.

Anonymous. 1996. "Paul T—Investigates." *New Left Review* 217 (May-June): 85–102.

Bellah, Robert, et al. 1991. *The Good Society.* New York: Knopf.

Bluestone, Barry, and Bennett Harrison. 1982. *The Deindustrialization of America.* New York: Basic Books.

Bradsher, Keith. 1995. "Poor Children in U.S. Are Among Worst Off in Study of 18 Industrialized Countries." *New York Times,* 14 Aug. A7.

Byrne, John A. 1993. "Executive Pay: The Party Ain't Over Yet." *Business Week,* 26 Apr., 56–64.

Case, John. 1995. *Open-Book Management: The Coming Business Revolution.* New York: Harper Business.

Crystal, Graef. 1995. "Growing the Pay Gap." *Los Angeles Times,* 23 July, D2.

Fligstein, Neil. 1990. *The Transformation of Corporate Control.* Cambridge, Mass.: Harvard University Press.

Frank, Tom. 1996. "Revolution, Inc." *Chicago Reader,* 12 July, 10–12.

Fukuyama, Francis. 1995. *Trust: The Social Virtues and the Creation of Prosperity.* New York: The Free Press.

Guillén, Mauro F. 1994. *Models of Management: Work, Authority, and Organization in a Comparative Perspective.* Chicago: University of Chicago Press.

Hayes, Robert H., and William J. Abernathy. 1980. "Managing Our Way to Economic Decline." *Harvard Business Review* (July-Aug.): 67–77.

Head, Simon. 1996. "The New, Ruthless Economy." *New York Review of Books,* 29 Feb., 47–52.

Henwood, Doug. 1995. *Left Business Observer* 71:4–5.

Herman, Edward S. 1995. "Immiserating Growth: The First World." *Z Magazine* (Jan.), 44–48.

Kanter, Rosabeth Moss. 1983. *The Change-Masters: Innovation for Productivity in the American Corporation.* New York: Simon and Schuster.

Kleiner, Art. 1996. *The Age of Heretics: Heroes, Outlaws, and the Forerunners of Corporate Change.* New York: Currency-Doubleday.

Korten, David C. 1996. "The Limits of the Earth." *The Nation* 15/22 July.

Kouzes, James M., and Barry Z. Posner. 1995. *The Leadership Challenge: How to Keep Getting Extraordinary Things Done in Organizations.* 2d ed. San Francisco: Jossey Bass.

Liu, Alan Y. 1996. "Literature on the Line." Unpub.

Mills, C. Wright. 1951. *White Collar: The American Middle Class.* New York: Oxford University Press.

Mintzberg, Henry. 1996. "Musings on Management." *Harvard Business Review* 96 (July-Aug.): 61–67.

Ouchi, William G. 1981. *Theory Z: How American Business Can Meet the Japanese Challenge.* Reading, Mass.: Addison-Wesley.

Peters, Tom. 1992. *Liberation Management: Necessary Disorganization for the Nano-second Nineties.* New York: Knopf.

———. 1994a. *Crazy Times Call For Crazy Organizations.* New York: Random House-Vintage.

———. 1994b. *The Pursuit of Wow!: Every Person's Guide to Topsy-Turvy Times.* New York: Random House.

Peters, Thomas J., and Robert H. Waterman Jr. 1982. *In Search of Excellence: Lessons from America's Best-Run Companies.* New York: Harper and Row.

Reagan, Ronald. 1990. *An American Life: The Autobiography.* New York: Simon and Schuster.

Reich, Robert. 1991. *The Work of Nations.* New York: Vintage.

Sampson, Anthony. 1995. *Company Man: The Rise and Fall of Corporate Life.* New York: Times Business-Random House.

Senge, Peter M. 1990. *The Fifth Discipline: The Art and Practice of the Learning Organization.* New York: Currency-Doubleday.

Springer, Steve. 1996. "Shaq-zaam! He's a $120-Million Laker." *Los Angeles Times,* 19 July, A1, A18.

Stack, Jack, with Bo Burlingham. 1992. *The Great Game of Business.* New York: Currency-Doubleday.

Toffler, Alvin. 1970. *Future Shock.* New York: Random House.

———. 1980. *The Third Wave.* New York: William Morrow.

Waring, Stephen P. 1991. *Taylorism Transformed: Scientific Management Theory Since 1945.* Chapel Hill: University of North Carolina Press.

Wright, Robin. 1992. "L.A. Riots Called Symptom of Worldwide Urban Trend." *Los Angeles Times,* 25 May, A1, A36–37.

Zinn, Howard. 1980. *A People's History of the United States.* New York: Harper and Row.

MAKING MORE MATTER AT THE BOTTOM LINE

ON A NEO-ACCOUNTANT. *How to insinuate messy nonfinancial measures into accounting while still being true to the function of delivering bottom lines is, as this piece elegantly exposes and argues, eminently a question of the sensitivity to authoritative rhetorics in business and the need to preserve and change them at the very same time. Moving from changes in modes of accounting to issues of corporate work and governance, Perin's discussion is in dialogue with Newfield's piece, which precedes hers, and Cefkin's, which follows.* – G. E. M.

* * *

To traders in financial markets, "the firm" is a commodity packaged in the carapace of its price per share. To a scattering of investors, managers, accountants, and scholars, "the firm" is a living creature embedded in a global ecology. For them, its cost per share can mask its influence in shaping other values worthy of notice, if not of pricing: the extent to which it is a source of environmental ills and social woes, a credit to the community, a good place to work, and not least among other features, a competitive and reliable source of income to its employees, shareholders, and investors. Some managers, for example, want to augment "traditional financial measures of corporate performance" with nonfinancial measures that acknowledge firms' "investments in vital 'intangibles,' such as intellectual capital and processes to improve quality and customer satisfaction" (Conference Board 1995, 9). The quality of output, customer satisfaction and retention, employee turnover, employee training, research and development investments, new product development, market growth and success, and environmental compliance are some of the nonfinancial measures of a firm's value that, these managers and others say, need to be part of the stock pricing process. Some accountants and investors speculate that knowing about such subjects would make firms more "transparent" and thereby change the grounds of capital competition. Idealistic critics believe that by going further to reconsider the categories of neoclassical economics (market, capital, labor, output), private firms and public organizations will become more democratic.

What is remarkable about these voices is that they are being raised to support the migration of previously unconvincing "soft" factors of production into the "hard" frame of "nonfinancial *measures.*" While these speak to the core concerns of the "human relations" and "sociotechnical" schools of managerialism, never before have they claimed a seat in capital markets. The claim may get teeth in the United States at any rate: writing in the business pages of a Sunday *New York Times,* Steven Wallman, then a commissioner of the Securities and Exchange Commission, said that more appropriate pricing is in the interests of "the continued success and vitality of our system of capital formation into the next century," making it increasingly important to revise the subjects that financial statements cover. If this does not occur, securities will be "harder jto price" and "both overpricing and underpricing will be more prevalent"—a sure route to increased volatility:

> When volatility increases, so does the perceived risk, and that causes investors to demand a higher return. A higher demanded return means a higher cost of capital for companies. A higher cost of capital means fewer jobs, lower shareholder returns over the long term and higher cost products and services. And that results in a less competitive corporate sector and a lowering of our standard of living. That's why we should care—it's critical to our society. (Wallman 1995)

Redefining the sources of value profoundly affects conventional understandings of "the economy." Speaking of environmental or "green accounting," Robert Solow proposes that it "would be a real achievement if it were to become a commonplace that capital assets, natural assets, and environmental assets were equally 'real' and subject to the same scale of values, indeed the same bookkeeping conventions. Deeper ways of thinking might be affected. . . . It is absolutely vital that 'capital' be interpreted in the broadest sense to include everything, tangible and intangible, in which the economy can invest or disinvest, including knowledge" (Solow 1992, 13, 17). Even the World Bank has come lately to this table carrying a groundbreaking accounting system for tracking the costs of environmental degradation and changes in national wealth—it makes room for "a catchall category for wealth embodied in human skills, health and social organization" (Passell 1995, 12).

Of several approaches to the question of how and why it's important to make more matter at the bottom line, I sketch three: at length, those of a senior partner in a Big Eight accounting firm, and more briefly, those of an economic sociologist and of a collective composed of corporate elites and those who study and advise them (for example, AT&T, Chase Manhattan Bank, PepsiCo., Pfizer, Polaroid, the Times Mirror Company, California Public Employees' Retirement System, the states of Connecticut, New Jersey, and Pennsylvania, the Putnam Funds, the World Bank, and the U.S. Department of Labor). The accountant, who spoke with me for about three hours, is Robert Elliott, senior partner and assistant to the president KPMG Peat Marwick LLP; the academic is Fred Block, professor of sociology at the University of California, Davis, through his book *Postindustrial Possibilities: A Critique of Economic Discourse* (1990); the collective is the Conference Board's International Working Group on Key Measures of Corporate Performance, through its 1995 report, "New Corporate Performance Measures: A Research Report," and, as well, interviews with two managers in a member company participating in that study. The Conference Board describes itself as a nonprofit and "nonadvocacy" group founded in 1916 to "improve the business enterprise system and to enhance the contribution of business to society" by providing forums for research and discussion on management issues.

In this turn to the soft, three skeins seem to be braiding. One grows out of environmental and ethical reawakenings. Public understandings of environmental and social consequences of investment, trade, and production have been heightened in this century by Rachel Carson (1962), Buckminster Fuller ("spaceship earth"), Earth Day (1970), the Stockholm Conference on the Environment (1972), and, of late, by the human and environmental disasters and near-disasters of Bhopal, the Exxon Valdez, Three Mile Island, and Chernobyl. The occasion of Solow's comments quoted earlier was the fortieth anniversary of Resources for the Future (RFF), a nonprofit research institute founded by the Ford and Rockefeller Foundations (and where I was invited to write *Everything in Its Place: Social Order and Land Use in America*). RFF's approaches to microeconomic and institutional analyses became precursors to a widespread cost/benefit technology, "green accounting," "quality of life" indicators, and all that has followed institutionally and politically (for example, the U.S. Environmental Protection Agency together with its institutionalized supporters and detractors). Currently being integrated into a gross national product/System of National Accounts and elaborated as ethical matters, these concerns are also the subject of congressional proposals for a "Best Practices Code of Conduct" for multinational corporations. Mutual funds investing only in firms meeting criteria for social responsibility are now among the choices consumers can make.

A second strand is shaped from the new necessity for firms to document their internal processes in order to stay on top of and adapt to volatile market conditions, as well as to comply with new social initiatives—for example, providing data on the environmental consequences of their production processes, documenting product quality, attesting to affirmative action progress, reporting their patterns of industrial safety, and assessing their fairness in dealing with consumers, customers, employees, and suppliers. At the same moment, the worldwide recession as either cause or excuse is leading firms to reduce labor costs by tracking production efficiency in a neo-Taylorist frame (benchmarking technology, "reengineering" programs). Firms are having to count what they previously may have regarded as uncountable and to make public what they may previously have regarded as nobody else's business.

Joining those is a third thread of investors who are coming to grips with their responsibilities for corporate governance—a bundle of issues such as executive compensation and institutional practices (for example, brokers' "churning" stocks). Public and private pension funds with unprecedentedly vast holdings have taken the lead in exercising their new clout and finding new culprits for unexpected declines in firm fortunes, such as short-term criteria for (over) rewarding executives and the consequences of multimillion dollar settlements in cases where firms have been found to violate nondiscrimination laws, expensive as well in reputation and employee morale. Owning both debt and equity, investors have begun to define it as their fiduciary duty to be informed about the nonpriced characteristics of firms. By making nonfinancial measures salient, the market will, they hope, come to value long-term business strategies and relieve firms of day-to-day market-driven pressures.

How each of these three lines of concern understands what it is promoting and what consequences it expects is part of the story I try to tell. I see their aspirations and images of a different future themselves as cultural mirrors and catalysts of what work itself has come to mean. In aiming to make capitalism more efficient, they are also trying to come to terms with the moral consequences of knowing the price of everything and the value of all too little.

A Neo-Accounting Perspective

Investors, regulators, and economists depend largely on the self-representations of firms' financial statements. These attest to the character of their assets, revenues, expenses, and liabilities. They are fundamental sources of social trust and loyalty in primary financial markets where parties are exchanging resources and cooperating at a distance. Trust maintains credibility with investors, suppliers, potential employees, customers, creditors, the state, and the public; loyalty lowers the costs of seeking new relationships. This legal and cultural technology rests largely with public accountants, so certified by the state and by professional bodies that also establish data categories and standards of evidence and analysis. Seeking out an accountant who could gloss the significance of nonfinancial measures, I found Robert Elliott. I asked him to talk with me about any and all issues it raises for investors, accountants, managers, economists. Elliott provides below a tour of issues whose nexus is accounting, beginning with the soft-hard myth and ending with an open question about whether global markets will drive the multiplicity of cultures and their accounting practices to uniformity.

"Sharp Pictures of Fuzzy Objects"

Accounting is really a social science. Accounting information measures behavior and therefore influences behavior. But the connection between behavior and the types of information that you collect, the frequency with which you collect it, how you summarize and report it, and who gets it is very soft. People tend to think in terms of accounting being hard because financial statements and other types of accounting reports are usually full of numbers that have lots of digits in them. But almost every number in a set of financial statements is an estimate. Even the number for cash most likely has soft spots in it. For example, some of that money is overseas, and it's been translated into dollars at some currency exchange rate, which may or may not be the rate that you're going to get when you bring it home. And it may be in countries with blocked currencies, where you may or may not ever be able to get it back. And of course it includes checks that have been deposited and may not clear, and on and on. So, even a number like cash is a little soft.

Inventory is more obviously soft. What if it's obsolete? What if it hasn't yet become obsolete but two days from now a competitor introduces a product that drops the value to salvage? Or take the liability on an insurance company's balance sheet for claims payable. This can include the amount to be paid when an automobile insurance policyholder is being sued for an accident, though the actual amount that they're going to have to pay will be determined—based on the glacial pace of our judicial system—between five and ten years from now. The case may be dismissed, or it may be settled for a million dollars, or a jury may award damages of $10 million and tack on $400 million in punitive damages. The insurance company has no choice but to make a guess, and all its guesses are added up and reported as a number with a lot of what appear to be significant digits, but only one or two digits may have any significance.

Joe Grundfest, a former SEC commissioner, has said, "You accountants bring litigation risk on yourselves by creating a misleading impression of precision. You can't take a sharp picture of a fuzzy object." An enterprise in motion snapped at a point in time in a set of financial statements is an extremely complex and fuzzy thing—fuzzy in the sense that where it's going depends not only on its trajectory at this time, but on what influences are brought to bear on it thereafter, and management's intent on how they manage it, and so forth. That is indeed a very fuzzy object. If our accounting products—financial statements—look like sharp pictures, it's an illusion.

Institutional investors are the high-volume investors. CalPERS, the New York State Retirement Fund, TIAA-CREF, Fidelity Funds—these large institutional investors do know more about the limitations on accounting information, and they do apply a fudge factor, as you suggest. But they also try to triangulate on the value of the company by getting lots of other kinds of information besides financial statement information. They look at economic and industry factors; they speak to company management and try to form their own view about where the company is going. They often build mathematical models to test the sensitivity of their estimate of value to changes in their key assumptions. Then they try to zero in on the major drivers in the business, and they monitor them closely. Accounting information is a subset of the total information these sophisticated investors use.

Short-termism

The problem is not the short cycle of reporting, namely quarterly. It's that what's reported doesn't reflect reality very well. Managers sometimes make business decisions to influence the quarterly reports, even though they know that's the wrong thing to do. Then other people conclude we shouldn't have quarterly reporting. "They don't have it overseas, and look how much better they're doing." As if the frequency of reporting were the only variable. What's interesting about this is that sophisticated investors understand when decisions are made solely to influence the accounting reports and penalize the company for it. Research shows when managers make uneconomic decisions just to window-dress the financial statements, their stock price falls relative to companies that didn't do that kind of thing. The idea here is called "market efficiency."

Impounded Information

Researchers in finance, and later in accounting, over many years formulated a hypothesis that the market very rapidly impounds information into securities prices; this is known as market efficiency. Prices are set in an auction market, and the people in the auction are presumably self-interested in getting the best price, whether they're on the buy side or the sell side. It's in their interests to capture every piece of information in the marketplace, even if it doesn't apply directly or explicitly to a particular company. The president just said he's going to do this and that, the Federal Reserve raised interest rates, or there's an embargo on magnesium. What does that imply about the price of a particular security, and how can I take advantage of that? With hundreds of thousands of buyers and sellers trying to get the slightest edge, they impound this information into prices very quickly. There are three flavors of the efficient markets hypothesis. The "weak" form says only that prices impound the entire history of their prior prices. That is, knowing where prices have been in the past does not enable you to predict where they're going in the future. The "semistrong" form is that all publicly available information is impounded into market prices. And the "strong" form says that all information is impounded, whether or not public.

Testing these three hypotheses, researchers found the market is efficient in the weak and semistrong forms, but not in the strong form, which means that bans on insider trading must work to some extent; otherwise insiders would be capitalizing their private information and market prices would reflect inside information, which they tend not to do. This means that when sophisticated investors see through managers' attempts to cook the books, the perception is impounded. Sophisticated investors think a management that's doing such things is incompetent, and they discount the price of the security because the company is ill managed. There's plenty of evidence that that happens. And it doesn't have to be misstated financial statements. Managers can try to fool the market by timing announcements in order to juice the stock price, like "We just perfected our disk drive," or whatever.

Imperfect Information: Price vs. Worth

Business people face the necessity to make important decisions, and they have to make them fast. They use the information they have. Their accounting systems are well developed; they produce reliable data and report in an orderly manner; but they're legacies from the dark past. The were originally developed generations ago—when companies were basically making and selling physical things—in order to run the company and to prepare financial statements for banks, investors, the IRS, and the SEC. But the world has gone off in a different direction. Today's companies are basically creating and processing information, but the financial reporting systems are still based on tracking *things,* not *ideas.*

Another problem is that lots of really relevant information is not available at all. For example, if I'm trying to make a business decision about whether to pursue an opportunity, I'd like to know what my competitors are thinking about. If we're both going after the same market, we'll both get less than we thought. On the other hand, if I can pursue this opportunity ahead of my competitors, I'll get the whole market, at least initially. I'd also like to know what the government in Washington is going to do to me next week, but I can't find that out. And I'd like to know what the Japanese are going to invent. So all kinds of market information, competitive information, macroeconomic information, most of it about the future, is not available. I get the best I can, and I decide to invest or not to invest.

Besides external information about markets and competitors and macroeconomic data, what else is unavailable to me as a decision maker or available in a form that's not very helpful? Within the firm I'm probably working with imperfect information on lots of important things. For example, I don't know as much as I ought to know about my customers and their loyalty and degree of satisfaction, and how much slack they're going to cut me if I try to convert them to a new product line, and so forth. And I don't really keep track of cv̇ - tomer *relationships* as much as I keep track of customer *transactions*. Another class of deficient information is about my employees. I don't know if they're all sick of working here and about to bail out; I don't know the extent to which they're refreshing their intellectual capital; and I don't know how they compare with the people down the street.

Then there's the quality of my processes, my inbound logistics, my production processes, my engineering, my marketing processes, my service, my outbound logistics. They're working, but where are the opportunities for improvement? What things are we doing that add no value? I have little information on that within the firm, and there are some theoretical problems that almost prevent me from getting the information I'd really like to know about value-adding capacity. All I can observe about the value of what I'm doing is the price my finished goods or services get in the marketplace. I can't allocate that value back across the things I did to create it to find out what I'm doing that really makes my customers better off, and where I'm just incurring deadweight costs. That's a really theoretically difficult problem. Accountants spend all their time allocating cost. They can tell you minutely what the components of a product cost. What they can't tell you is what they're worth.

Incommensurables and Interests

One of the very nice things about accounting information is that, to the extent it works, all the measures are in the same dimension, namely, monetary units. There aren't very many things in life that are so simple, where you can add up the good and the bad, the benefits and the sacrifices, in the same measurement unit—dollars or lire or yen—and come down to a "bottom line." That phrase comes from accounting, and it means the net income line on the income statement—that's the bottom line, the results for this year.

Nonaccountants have appropriated the term *bottom line:* "The bottom line on the State of the Union was this," or "the bottom line on the Contract with America is that." But the problem is that in those domains the inputs are in dollars but the outputs are in services and welfare, for example, wellness or national security. So, there is no bottom line. It doesn't come down to so many units of output. But if you consider business solely from the standpoint of suppliers of capital—investors or lenders—they put in cash now and they want to get out more cash later. The inputs and the outputs are in cash. All of the measures in accounting are in cash. If I put in a dollar today and get back two dollars in a year, that's a certain rate of return. I can measure the dollar in and the two dollars out later with reasonable precision.

However, that's an impoverished perspective, because it's only the perspective of the investor or creditor, who's putting in dollars and getting out dollars. But other people also have stakes in the enterprise. There are employees, who are putting in labor and getting back dollars, a career, job satisfaction, and growth in capabilities. That transaction is not straight dollars in, dollars out. That's at least labor in and dollars and knowledge out.

The other stakeholders have more complex transactions too. Customers are putting in dollars and getting out products and services. The community is putting in fresh air, water, and space and getting out jobs and pollution. These other perspectives are not as simple as dollars in, dollars out. When you look at the enterprise from any perspective other than investors and creditors, you don't get a clean bottom line expressed in dollars.

But the management of the enterprise has to accommodate the investors and lenders—because if they don't, they'll be fired—that is, they have to produce more dollars than they consumed. At the same time, though, they have to keep the employees, the suppliers, the customers, and the community satisfied. They have to pay taxes. They have to behave according to the law. The management of the enterprise can't ignore all these other interests, in addition to the financial interests. They must balance them.

There are potential penalties for ignoring other interests. By being rapacious with their employees, or the environment, or something like that, they might create more short-run dollars for investors. But these other people have a way of enforcing their demands. They can pass a law, or they can picket the plant, or they can do other things. So management has to consider them, even though they're not reflected in the financial statements.

But in making the decisions needed to keep the company alive by satisfying all these constituencies they have impoverished information. They also have impoverished information for deciding whether they should stay in this community or move, deal with this particular set of customers or not, put their production overseas or not. There are many things that have social or economic dimensions not readily translatable into dollars.

Narrow vs. Elaborate Stories

Of course, the advantage of having the accounting information that's all denominated in dollars is that you can collapse all this information into a bottom line, and while it's a narrow story, it's a comprehensive story along that dimension. Whereas these other stories tend to become very elaborate, because there's no way of combining information, it's just so many details that can't be combined into a single metric. If we could convert all this information, by the way, into a single unit, for example, "utils," measures of utility, we could say, a dollar has so many utils and keeping a homeless person with a roof over her head has so many utils so we'll translate everything into utils and add it up and get a bottom line. Of course, that can't be done. It's impossible. It's chimerical. There are a number of very simple but deep reasons for that, and Kenneth Arrow got a Nobel Prize for explaining them.

People's utility scales differ, and individuals do not apply the same scale in all cases. For example, I would pay you fifty cents for a lottery ticket with a 50 percent probability of paying a dollar, because its expected value is fifty cents. But I would pay you less than $1 million for a lottery ticket with a 50 percent chance of returning $2 million, because I am risk averse at that level. But you and I don't have the same utilities and risk preferences. I might have a preference for defense and you a preference for education, for example. For these types of reasons we can't summarize diverse matters in the same metrics. Therefore, the story becomes very long and elaborate.

Think about it in terms of a map. Reality is reality, and a map is an abstraction of reality. You can put enough information in a map to approach reality, but then it's unreadable. So you say, "What's the purpose of the map?" That will tell you what information to put in. If the purpose is to see who governs, you develop a political map. If the purpose is to navigate from here to there in a ship, you draw a marine navigation map. If the purpose is to drive there, you draw a road map. Each of these maps has a relationship to reality but is a very coarse abstraction. So these stories that you want to tell, in order for them to be rich enough, they're going to have to be so elaborate and time consuming that they're going to be a map too detailed to read. The larger features of interest will be obscured.

New Conversations

That's the balanced scorecard—putting more topics into the scorecard, building a matrix of measurements. Let me back up. The behavioral effect of measuring and reporting information is that it tends to motivate people to perform along that measurement line. What we don't measure and report creates no such incentive. Say you're an employee, and we don't want you slacking. So we measure the time that you get to work and the time you leave. You punch in and out. And we pay you for that. Naturally you would spend more hours at work. But you spend most of it sleeping on a palette in a storeroom. So, we say, we've got her present on this measurement, but we'd better add a measurement of productivity. Now we're going to count the things that you did while you were here, because we caught you cheating against that other measure. You may try to figure out how to cheat on the second measure, which will lead to a third, and so forth.

The idea is that a well-designed set of interlocking measures will reveal whether the employee cheats. If you had only financial measures, rather than the balanced scorecard, you could get the classic case of wearing out the workers, showing better profit in the short run, but jeopardizing the next period, when the workers are all going to quit, and then there'll be worse profit. But by then I will have moved on to my next job and I'll be doing this till I retire, and it'll never catch up to me—that's my hope as a manager anyway. Financial measures can encourage dysfunctional behaviors. But if the balanced scorecard is well designed, if it's really cleverly designed, it should be very difficult to solve for the dysfunctional solution.

What you measure is what people perform against. We must, in introducing a balanced scorecard, want to change outcomes in some way. Otherwise we wouldn't do it. Changing outcomes is going to change the distribution of power and income within the firm. It's going to create winners and losers. They're probably not randomly distributed in the organization. The losers are more likely to be the big shots who've built up their hand under the old rules. And the winners are likely to be the people who have been disadvantaged.

Weighting vs. Metrics

Weighting is very difficult. Imagine yourself a fly on the wall when the executive committee of the firm gets together; one of the people in the meeting is the human resources vice president, and that person is arguing for people. The head of sales is arguing for customers. You can go all the way around and get all these different perspectives. The chairman says, "Well, what weight should we put on this?" And the human resource person says, "Mine is the most important, it should have the heaviest weight." The head of research and development says, "That's fine, but if we don't have new technologies, we're out of business. Mine is the most important." It goes all the way around the table, and everybody's is the most important. The chairman knows that if they compromise on these weights, everyone will be dissatisfied. So weighting is a difficult problem.

The implications of not being able to combine utilities across individuals means that there's no rational, scientific way to make social welfare choices. I mentioned that Arrow got the Nobel Prize. It was for his impossibility theorem. He listed five simple fairness axioms necessary to make social welfare choices and demonstrated that they're inconsistent. Therefore, there's no way to make such choices through a rational, scientific system. One implication is that social welfare choices can't be made by some accounting system that expresses all the inputs and outputs in common units, adds them up, and says, "This is the best outcome."

The data certainly help, but the process has to involve bringing together the people with different views, having them bargain politically, and supplying leadership or arbitration so that disappointments are accepted. The participating parties have to accept the decision-making process, whether because they had their say, because they think it's relatively fair, or because of its authority—typically a combination of these.

Why Now?

[The move to nonfinancial measures and the balanced scoreboard] is a natural product of the maturation of the information technology age. The first commercial computer was introduced as recently as 1955 and all it did was payrolls. In other words, it replaced clerks in the back room multiplying hours times rates less taxes equals net pay. Then gradually, as the price of computing came down, computers got deployed to do more and more in the enterprise, and made it possible to reorient the enterprise to focus on meeting customer needs. The historical strategy from the Industrial Revolution was mass production to bring costs down. The more you could do that, the more people could afford things. That strategy of cost reduction was good for about a century. But now we're in a new strategy empowered by technology, which is meeting customer requirements.

Think about a customer who experiences a need at a point in space-time x, y, z, t. And here is a vendor that can meet that need at x_1, y_1, z_1, t_1. Holding quality constant, the vendor that can minimze the space-time gap between when the need emerges and when the vendor can fulfill it will be the successful vendor. Minimizing space-time gaps is the name of the competitive game. But think about what information technology does. Computers do things blindingly fast. Things that took weeks or months now take fractions of a second. Computers crunch time. Communications networks permit people to deal with each other instantaneously around the globe. They crunch space.

This collapse of time and space enabled by information technology is the basis of postindustrial competition. In the industrial era, Henry Ford produced millions of Model Ts at $500 apiece. Consumers benefited because for only $500 they were on wheels, but they had no choice. Today, the consumer can select from literally quadrillions of permutations of automobiles and have one made to order just for herself. Her range is still limited, of course. She can't yet call for a three-wheel car with wings—but that's coming—to the point that the consumer will actually design the product and it will be promptly delivered, and the space-time gap is minimized.

Information technology changes the basic strategic thrust of all industry from cost reduction to meeting individual customer needs better, quicker, cheaper. But the infrastructures of business are largely still on the old model, the industrial, cost-reduction model. Accounting is about costs: allocating costs, reducing costs. Now we must rotate this whole system to face the customer rather than the producer and satisfy the customer's needs, but all the infrastructure is still about cost accounting, cost allocation, cost reduction.

The new infrastructures must focus on creating value. In some industries this has already emerged, but in others it hasn't, such as higher education. In automobiles, it's now twenty years old; in other industries, ten years old. In terms of the grand sweep of history it's an eye blink, and it's happening now.

But we accountants don't have a new value-oriented paradigm to replace the old, industrial accounting paradigm focused on cost-reduction. Instead we're groping, we're sticking Band-Aids on the old model. We're saying, Well, what if we add a measure of customer satisfaction to our balanced scoreboard, and what if we also added a measure of cycle-time reduction—it's a bunch of ad hoc responses.

You say, Why now? I say it's a result of the ubiquitous computer and its deployment into uses other than just cost reduction. Originally we got rid of those payroll clerks and replaced them with a Univac, but now we've figured out how to use the Univac's successors to actually listen to the customer and design something that meets the customer's needs on the fly. That's why it would be amazing if it *weren't* happening at this time. It's inevitable; it's happening as a result of this technology-induced transformation of the basic business paradigm.

Centralizing vs. Devolving

They talk about the use of technology to centralize control of organizations—I don't think that's the macrotrend. They talk about empowerment, which doesn't mean anything anymore, but the underlying idea is that in order to get maximum use of the knowledge workers in an enterprise, to get the maximum speed of adaptation in an enterprise, and to best serve the customers, you have to take advantage of all the knowledge workers, all the human assets. The only way to do that is through the devolution of power, and that devolution is facilitated by the technology.

Formerly, the principal users of accounting information were managers. But with the devolution of power in enterprises, line workers are now important users of the information. Under the old systems of command and control—the [General Motors president and CEO Alfred P.] Sloan hierarchical model—there's a boss upstairs who determines what is to be done, sends orders down through the hierarchy, and measures results with accounting data. The boss then said, "Okay, I sent this signal and got that result; let me tune it because that's not the result I wanted." That's command and control.

Under a devolved structure, what I want to do as a manager is to set strategy and structure and infrastructure, and then I want the organization to run itself. I'm going to sit upstairs and tinker with the structure, not with the individual commands. In order for the line workers to be able to act like managers and to optimize for themselves, dealing directly with customers, they need much richer sources of information than they ever had in the past. So the information systems of the firm become reoriented. Instead of being used by top management to control the bottom layers of the firm, they become the method by which the lower levels can act as self-initiating, self-motivating, self-directed employees. That's more than just hot air. That's the direction things have to go, because organizations that can do that will be more nimble; they'll be more responsive. And if the top manager is spending his time issuing orders and looking at results, he's not going to be competitive with the company down the street whose top manager spends her time developing a better strategy and tuning the organization's structure to carry out that strategy. So firm A, which is not empowered, which is hierarchical, is going to die out in competition with firm B, which has figured out how to take advantage of all the brain power in the organization, through the use of information technology. Using technology for control and centralization is an obsolete idea.

Bob Kaplan wrote a wonderful case study at the Harvard Business School on a department of Eastman Chemicals down in Texas. This department had more measures than you could shake a stick at—gazillions of measures. They measured every aspect of process, outcome, input, and output and fed it up to top management, who got these bales of reports every month. But nothing was going right. To make a long story short, what they did was, they took the information and instead of a monthly cycle they went to a daily cycle, and instead of giving it to management they gave it to the shopfloor workers. And they also gave the workers a simple incentive structure. They turned the measurements into a profit-and-loss statement for this department, and they said that if the results improved by a certain amount, there would be a payoff, which happened to be they would give these employees a new kitchen in their work area. The result was that the profitability of the department improved very dramatically, when the workers (a) had an incentive, (b) had the information, and (c) had the power to use the information. Not only did the profits improve, but the quality of the product improved dramatically. The point is the devolution of power and information from the top to the bottom.

These ideas of empowerment, reengineering, and TQM [total quality management] have a powerful underlying idea, even if some of it is packaged faddishness. Corporate managers say, "Well, we need some of that. Give me two parts of empowerment and one part of reengineering and roll them in, and we're off"—without really internalizing the ideas and what it means for the way the organization runs and the way the CEO functions. Then you hear stories that TQM doesn't work, because in 70 percent of the cases where they tried it nothing happened. Well, they didn't really try it. They didn't do anything. They rolled in a TQM guy; he said do this, this, and this. They did it and nothing happened. Because they never absorbed the notion that they're not managing change—they're managing rate of change. It requires a whole different mind-set and a whole different infrastructure to do that.

Practically everybody who's a CEO today was trained in the industrial paradigm. CEOs—in their fifties and sixties, generally speaking, except for Bill Gates—went to school in the forties and fifties. It was a different world. Like the generals fighting the last war, again.

Accounting for the Ties That Bind

The relationships between companies and their suppliers change very much from an arm's-length-low-bidder-wins, cost-reduction mentality emblematic of the second wave paradigm. The relationship becomes almost like that in a *keiretsu*. A cooperative network of firms emerges.

A lot depends upon the importance of the relationships. For example, let's take a supplier relationship. If I am supplying you with paper clips, and that represents 10 to the minus sixth percent of your purchases, I don't have much bargaining power, and you're probably going to buy the lowest-cost paper clips that don't rust. But if I'm supplying you with flat screens for your laptop computer line, and there are only two flat screen makers in the world to speak of, one of which is in Kobe and has just been flattened by an earthquake, my bargaining power against you is very different. We have an investment in each other. I'm a very important supplier of yours; you're out of business without me. On the other hand, you're a very important customer of mine. So the relationship becomes much less arm's length, and we start sharing a tremendous amount of information.

My firm, for example, KPMG Peat Marwick, was the first major purchaser of the Apple Macintosh, and for quite a few years was the largest Macintosh buyer in the world. When we were trying to figure out what to buy, we went to Apple and said, "We think we'll be a big buyer; where are you headed with the technology; what are you going to do?" Then we went to IBM and asked the same question. IBM said to us, "Our PCs are in the stores. If you want them, buy them. If you don't want them, don't buy them." Apple said, "Come out to Cupertino, sign a nondisclosure agreement, and you can talk to the scientists and go around the labs. You can see where we're headed, what the technology's going to be two, four, and six years out. Furthermore, we'll give you some prototype machines to work with." We did work with the machines, and we fed back to Apple our suggestions for improvement. They responded to us, and we had a relationship like that for quite a few years. This is a typical cooperative relationship, where you share a lot of what would otherwise be very confidential information.

In many cases suppliers and companies get linked through electronic data interchange, look at each other's information in real time, at a depth that would have been unheard of ten years ago. These companies become virtually partners, and that gives rise to new accountability issues. A basic requirement for traditional accounting measurement is that transactions be bargained at arm's length. Such independent bargaining assures that the price in a transaction reflects the market's view of the worth of the goods or services. When "partners" agree on prices, such prices may reflect what's mutually advantageous to the parties rather than the values the market might assess. If I buy a widget from you for a dollar, what tells the accountants and the world in general that the widget is worth a dollar is that, in an arm's-length trade, it's sold for a dollar. In cooperative or partnership relationships, factors other than the true market value of the widget may dominate the price, rendering the accounting measures irrelevant.

So we have new accountability requirements emerging at the same time our basic technology for measuring accountabilities is deteriorating. I could tell the same story from the employee perspective, the customer perspective, even the investor perspective. They're no longer satisfied with getting a quarterly financial statement. They want to know what your strategy is and your capacity to execute. In these relationships, wherever the bargaining power is sufficient, the investors, customers, suppliers, and employees are demanding a much enriched information flow.

When my firm dealt with Apple under a nondisclosure agreement, they had to trust us, and we had to trust them. That gives rise to an accountability, too. "Did you meet your obligation not to reveal the information?" So one of the questions in this information world that we're entering is how transparent do institutions become and, conversely, how much are they able to sequester information? It's an interesting question.

Transparency and Competition

One of the questions that I've asked, but nobody's answered for me yet, is, "What would be the effect on competition if there were a perfect transparency of information?" I don't know the answer. It might change the basis of competition. I doubt that it would place all firms on an equal footing. Firms with a better management and better strategy, even completely exposed to the world, would probably still prosper. But I don't know. It's an interesting question.

In the meantime you have this macrotrend toward accountability, fundamentally propelled by increasing world population and consumption of nonrenewable resources, and the continuing demands of the have-nots, who are multiplying at quicker rates, for a bigger piece of the pie. Demands for accountability are building, and there's much more expectation on the part of individuals that institutions will tell more. At the same time, information technology makes greater accountability possible at reasonable cost. It therefore seems like a risk-free prediction that organizations will be operating more and more in a fish bowl. That's the transparency hypothesis. On the other side is the opaqueness hypothesis, which says that less accountability is a condition for companies to have an incentive to compete. I don't know how that plays out, but it's a set of tensions in the accountability world that we will have to monitor for another twenty or thirty years.

New Problems and Old Paradigms

We have a set of codes that we use in accounting. They're inculcated as part of the educational process, and then through the experience of being an accountant. There's probably some recursiveness to the relationship of the codes that we use and the codes that we therefore can't use. We can't refer to concepts we don't have codes for. The typical accountant sees the world from a set of perspectives as limited as accounting. The question is, is the code narrow because the accountant is narrow, or is the accountant narrow because the code is narrow? What is the relationship?

To some extent it's reinforced by the selection of individuals. For example, suppose I'm a college student and I'm considering a field in which to major. Should I major in anthropology, chemistry, physics, accounting, or what? I begin to compare myself with people. If I have low tolerance for ambiguity and a left-brain cognitive style, I see myself looking like an accountant or an engineer or something like that. I don't see myself looking like an artist or a psychologist. There's a self-selection, which in times of a low rate of change is probably beneficial. It means that talent sorts itself in a reasonably appropriate manner. But in times of rapid change it means that disciplines may be repopulating themselves under the old model and haven't changed over to the new one.

That's certainly the case in accounting. For five hundred years there's been no benefit to creativity in accounting. Application of the existing paradigm got the answer that we needed. All of a sudden we need thinkers and conceptualists, and we haven't attracted them—they're not there. But I'd venture to guess that you could unplug the word *accounting* and plug in a lot of other fields there.

Culture-specific Accounting

There are many cultural differences in accounting systems. For example, France has a very centrally planned economy, even though it's not socialist. Therefore, in Paris they tell you how to keep the books and how to classify every transaction and every asset and liability. When all French companies follow this standard chart of accounts it means they can add up all the companies and get a grand total in Paris, know what they have, and use it to manipulate the economy. So their accounting system reflects their cultural preferences for centralization.

American accounting systems are much more heterogeneous because there's much less planning from Washington. Then you get to the old Soviet Union. The communist idea was that what's important is labor. Their accounting systems were heavily biased toward labor. They didn't pay as much attention to cost of materials. So you wound up with things made out of titanium, which is more expensive than gold, because that's only material—the important thing is labor.

Then you get to Germany, where the way in which capital flows is not through public stock markets, the way it is in England and here, but through the banks. The accounting that the public sees in Germany is very obscure, because they want to keep the employees in the dark as much as possible because employees have considerable power. But the banks, which are actually supplying the capital, get whatever information they want. So accounting in Germany is transparent to the banks but opaque to the employees and the public. You can't fire employees, and the board of directors has labor representatives by law. The system is biased toward workers. They have ninety-nine holidays a year and work three hours a day. It dramatically affects the productivity of the economy. In Japan, where you have the *keiretsus* and firms are interdependent, they don't sink or swim on their own. They're in this big club, and Japanese accounting is quite different. Again, there's a large cultural aspect to accounting.

The question is, Will globalization of business and capital markets homogenize these cultures, and following that, their accounting? The dominant current expectation is that will happen—a trend toward uniformity and away from heterogeneity. We'll see whether the American model for accounting and allocating capital prevails. A lot of people think it's the wrong model. They think there are extremely dysfunctional aspects to public trading of securities and high liquidity, because it means there's no loyalty on the part of owners. They can bail out at a minute's notice and only pay a quarter-point transaction cost. That means you have no ownership continuity. In places where the owners are in for the long haul, the argument goes, there's more of an incentive to hold management accountable, etc. I don't know. It's a testable hypothesis.

Pragmatist and Idealists Converge

Several themes that Robert Elliott's illuminating tutorial and critique highlights are central to the pragmatic views of the Conference Board collective and the idealistic aspirations of Fred Block's *Postindustrial Possibilities: A Critique of Economic Discourse.* These two perspectives converge, surprisingly, on two goals: deeper disclosure and corporate self-awareness.

The Conference Board finds that traditional measures derived from accounting conventions are overly historical, not designed for prediction, provide incentives for unwanted behavior, consider inputs more than outputs, and do not capture intangible resources such as "intellectual capital." Nor do traditional financial measures sufficiently capture corporate investments in intellectual capital and processes to improve quality and customer satisfaction. By basing stock prices on quarterly financial reports the market not only ignores firm fundamentals but discourages long-term corporate strategies. At public hearings of the U.S. Competitiveness Policy Council established by Congress, many executives testified that they believe that financial markets are efficient and that they are unconcerned about short-termism or their capacity to raise "patient capital" for long-term plans. Yet privately "many executives expressed concern that U.S. markets did not provide 'patient capital' or fully appreciate the value managers were working so hard to create" (certainly by contrast to German and Japanese capital markets, which maintain a long-term focus; Conference Board 1995, 9).

The value of "new performance measures," some managers, executives, and accountants believe, is that they "could be used to provide a common language for improving communications on performance issues between managements, boards of directors, and receptive long-term investors" (Conference Board 1995, 11). Issues of particular concern are executive compensation criteria, patient capital, and disclosure of information to competitors. They see certain "performance issues" as being "keys" to a firm's growth, increased value, and longevity. These are to be "measured" judgmentally: each firm has first to define these in terms of its production system, markets, suppliers, and potential investors, and then assign "outcome measures" that capture their firm's performance. For example, the Whirlpool Corporation, manufacturer and distributor of major home appliances, developed these financial and non-financial categories:

Financial: economic value added, return on equity.

Customer satisfaction: market share, customer satisfaction survey, brand loyalty, satisfaction with service, trade-partner satisfaction, product availability.

Total quality: worldwide excellence (quality) score, defect levels, cycle time, service incidence rates.

People commitment: employee commitment survey.

Growth and innovation: percent new product sales. (Conference Board 1995, 54; see table for more examples from other companies)

The hitch is that even for the originators of this method (the balanced score-card that Elliott refers to), such measures do not "translate easily to the investment community . . . and [require] several years of experimentation within companies before it becomes a systematic part of reporting to external constituencies" (Kaplan and Norton 1993, 141). There are two other obstacles. Even when financial analysts say that they want more such information, they are, according to a Harvard Business School study, hard put to evaluate non-monetized information when making buy-sell decisions. Billionaire Warren Buffett's claim to fame as an American entrepreneur is that he has made a historic fortune not only by considering the qualitative details of firm's internal practices—their "fundamentals"—but by making these as important to his risk strategies as financial reports. He is unusual because most investors and lenders are likely to base their decisions on prices that, they believe, speak for themselves; they trust "impounding." Any nonmonetized or nonpriced information investors have to speak for, and like Buffett, they have to find and interpret it themselves. So, the move to deeper disclosure of "intangibles" would give them more pause than Wall Street has time for.

The second difficulty is that even when companies develop and use non-financial measures for management purposes they can't vouch for direct links to their bottom lines of various in-house programs, such as skills training, employee stock-ownership plans, team building, family leave policies. Although the firms see them as being "just good business," they have little confidence that their firm's ticker price reflects any reward for these good practices; 58 percent of corporate managers "believe their share price is either slightly or significantly undervalued" (Conference Board 1995, 52).

How do the various constituencies compare in their response to deeper information? Table 1 suggests they have different if not incompatible priorities. Notice that corporate managers—those nearest to the actual work of production—share similar priorities with financial analysts and portfolio managers and investors on only about nine out of nineteen performance measures. On six they diverge widely, and on the remaining measures they diverge by about two points. Another study of audiences for bottom-line stories made up of corporate managers, financial analysts, and portfolio managers and investors

Table 1. Relative Importance of Measures of Performance

1 = very valuable   *19 = of limited value*

	Corporate Managers	Financial Analysts	Portfolio & Investors
Earnings	1	1	2
Costs	5	8	4
Cash flow	2	2	2
Customer satisfaction	3	13	11
Segment performance	4	4	7
Market share	12	5	5
Employee turnover	18	15	15
Employee satisfaction	17	17	17
Employee training expenditures	19	18	16
R & D investments	11	9	8
R & D productivity	12	12	9
Product and process quality	7	14	14
New product development	6	10	3
Market growth	10	3	1
Capital expenditures	14	7	5
Corporate ethics statements	16	19	19
Environmental compliance	15	16	18
Statements of strategic goals	8	11	10
Measures of strategic achievement	9	10	12

Source: Conference Board 1995, 53; based on study by Ernst and Young Center for Business Innovation, 1994.

finds them unanimous that quarterly earnings are decisive for capital markets. Beyond that there are interesting differences signaling varying priorities if not worldviews. Fifty-eight percent of corporate managers believe their firm's share price is undervalued; financial analysts and portfolio managers want to know more than others do about firm strategies and particular nonfinancial measures; firms and analysts agree that information about employee satisfaction, turnover, and training is of little interest to investors. Standing apart are the largest institutional investors, such as public pension funds, which "behave very differently from . . . and do not want to be treated like analysts or portfolio managers" (Conference Board 1995, 52; reporting study by Eccles and Mavrinac 1994).

Even as the audiences for firm-performance stories are listening for different things, the vocabulary of capital markets perforce remains their lingua franca. Aiming to change the vocabulary is one thing, and, as the table dramatizes, realizing it is another. In suggesting that another representational paradigm needs to be explored—a move the Conference Board study does not begin to make—Elliott takes the discussion closer to its logical and cultural conclusion.

Idealists have no such difficulty. Scrutinizing neoclassical economics' methods and categories, Fred Block's critique unseals them to insert the social dynamics, contexts, and multiple rationalities they are designed to deny. Claiming to develop an "economic sociology," Block's essays show how accounting conventions rehearse economists' categories of "the market," "labor," "capital," and "output" as though they have "transparent meaning in a complex economy" and shape "seemingly objective economic facts of contemporary life" (1990, 32). He argues that to represent the activities undergirding the economy, these need to be replaced with categories that reflect the sources of productive capacity.

Yes, he agrees, these important activities are hard to measure: firms' policies for, investments in, and practices relating to pay scales, employment security, career tracks ("internal labor markets"), training, product quality versus schedule pressures, internal inventory and reporting systems, software and computer quality, safety, as well as structural resilience and flexibility for meeting changing market conditions. They are especially important, however, because they are the very dimensions now critical in a services economy. They deserve theoretical and technical attention from statisticians, accountants, and economists. Disappointingly, however, Block does not offer a sociological analysis of the translation problem, but merely restates it: "New ways will have to be devised to assess and measure the different components of organizational effectiveness, and these variables can then be introduced into complex econometric models" (132).

To revise "capital" and "labor" and the accounting schemes they foster implies revising institutions. In a scenario of alternatives, some of which are incipient in today's practices, Block reinterprets "the socialist tradition to place primary emphasis on expanding democracy. The central question becomes not capitalism or socialism, but how a society can create [public as well as private] economic institutions that give maximum scope to democratic participation" in economic decision-making (194). An example is quality circles, at-work discussions where employees identify production issues and "facilitate both individual and collective problem-solving." Beyond them, however, there is not now "a structure of governance . . . that assures that employees' views will be taken seriously and protects them from the arbitrary exercise of management power. It is futile to expect employees to speak out in a context where they feel powerless or think they might be punished for doing so." Employees need some "power to influence takeovers" and in other ways gain "a greater stake in the firm" and its managerial effectiveness (202–3).

Elaborating his category critique into an argument for "an economy organized around qualitative growth" Block recognizes the social embeddedness of production and consumption and privileges the importance of "the development of human capacities" alongside technological development (195). The

Conference Board pragmatists who want to measure "intellectual capital" and "knowledge" seem to be on the same wavelength. But do they know what these imply for the ways that their employees spend their days on the job?

New Work at Work

The move to nonfinancial measures is intrinsically significant for challenging economic thought and financial practices, and it is just as significant in the local, daily worlds where people earn their livings. For employees find that there's now another kind of work expected at work: Putting in time considering if, as, and how what they and others do affects their employer's bottom line, and more directly than ever before, their own. Self-awareness is the goal of this metawork—awareness of the resources they can count on to get their job done, the skills they have and need, the rewards they can expect, the cooperation they depend on, the information they require, the influence they have. Often coming under the aegis of human resources staff members who specialize in "organizational development" or "organizational learning," their new work asks them to participate in "quality-improvement" programs, team-building and sensitivity exercises, "reengineering" studies for streamlining work, and benchmarking analyses that compare industrywide practices with those of their firm. Employees are now paid to work and to think and talk about it, critically.

Employers have adopted such programs as their chief strategies for increasing efficiency and the return on investment, and, in some cases, assuring survival. Through these million-dollar campaigns, firms are reprogramming expectations if they are not at the same time taking away jobs and doubling those of employees lucky enough to remain. Executives themselves are going to retreats and workshops and learning "scenario building" for imagining and "visioning." In the corporate version of "participatory management," executives fervently enroll their captive audiences in their strategies, philosophies, and productivity goals.

During these bumpy years I've been doing field studies of the ways that work is conceived and carried out in a variety of industries. I'm usually asking engineers, computer scientists, biologists, managers, marketers, and lawyers about what they do, why their work is organized the way it is, and what, if any, changes are being considered and why. Unprompted, they often convert these queries into catalysts for telling stories about their careers and those of partners and spouses, about their company's history and recent changes, and, not least, about their own frustrations, disappointments, worries, and hopes. The expectations and disappointments of this cadre are especially noteworthy culturally (Perin 1988). Its members have acted out the American dream: stay in school, learn a specialty, experience some autonomy and influence at work, and be rewarded with earnings sufficient for a family house in the suburbs. As they're drafted into self-Taylorizing and arbitrarily conscripted into self-realization or complicity in career stasis, I've heard these middle-class exemplars talk cynically *and* earnestly. Clarifying the nature of their work and its relation to that of others, they begin to understand its possibilities, often with pleasure, and at the same time seeing its limitations more clearly than ever before, often with resignation.

Liberating at first glance, their self-awareness confronts an intimidating economy and a permanently uncertain organizational future. Living inside this paradox, millions in an increasingly disappointed middle class are also self-demystifying their relationship to the economy. But not, by all accounts, their political relationships: in the new conversations they are having about work I hear no mention of unionization or of other kinds of collective response, via professional associations, for example.

To the contrary, Charles Heckscher finds in a study of 250 middle-managers who have survived layoff and streamlining programs in fourteen organizational units in eight large industrial companies. They have pursued no relationships with professional or outside associations or groups, and indeed, "loyalty to the company remained very strong . . . even after substantial downsizing and, in some cases, rather brutal layoffs." But where this loyalty was strongest, the units the managers worked in were "neither the happiest nor the most effective," whereas in the few that were doing better, managers had largely "rejected traditional loyalty" (Heckscher, 1995, 11). Of the fourteen units, in three "managers manifested almost universal anger, bitterness, confusion, and pessimism about the future; in four, they were mixed, with some being angry and others more hopeful; in three, hope outweighed pessimism, and anger was nearly absent; and in four, feelings about both personal and organizational futures were widely positive." In these, managers were "resigned" yet "fairly optimistic," a state they achieved "by blocking out evidence of competitive problems, and by withdrawing into an ever-narrower focus on their own particular job." " 'My situation is fine, but the business is in terrible shape' " (10, 11). Several testified in similar terms about their experiences: " 'The layoff has scarred me. I used to speak out, but now I come and do my job and go home, and probably I'll come back tomorrow. I still love this company, but it has scarred me' " (41).

As many conversations as this new work requires, they are taking place mainly between people of equal influence, often equally powerless or unheard. "Speaking out" is increasingly dangerous, yet employees are being *expected* to discuss, analyze, criticize, improve, measure. In companies where I've done research, managers and other professionals will sometimes try to enlist me as their messenger up the ladder: "If you tell them that this isn't working and why, maybe they'll listen. We can't get their ear."

For all the downheartedness of managers and employees, I notice eagerness for conversations about how to understand and resolve the contradictions they live inside of, about how to achieve values and norms that are more consonant and less confused. But those cultural consultants most ready to engage with them tend to feed individualism rather than mend the torn communal fabric. There is often no one else in the newspapers, magazines, and television they spend time with, and so they take whoever is: New Age gurus, managerial mantra makers, and books by the yard advising them on going along to get along. Their responses to alienating and isolating communities of work in private corporations appear now to be expressed mainly against government—a displacement guaranteed at least not to cost them their jobs.

A senior executive of one of the companies participating in the Conference Board study, after discussing nonfinancial measures with me for about an hour, sounded weary and discouraged that his company's "way of life" of "doing right by the community, customers, and employees" is irrelevant to the investment community. The reason that financial analysts are suspicious of nonfinancial measures, he said, is that "they think that firms are trying to create company value by camouflaging its real erosion." "My hunch," he went on, "is that coming up with new understandings about how to make soft data harder is best worked on by academics—there's no return for the bankers to be working on this." Nor for the firms themselves: their intentions are, as Elliott points out, to make more money, not to tell richer stories.

For that, the call to academics sounds right—to philosophers, ethicists, poets, too, I might hope. One alchemizing soft into harder is Martha Nussbaum, professor of law and ethics and an advocate of retheorizing "cruder forms of economic utilitarianism and cost-benefit analysis" (Nussbaum 1995, 3). In *Poetic Justice: The Literary Imagination and Public Life* she seeks to foster "a humanistic and multivalued conception of public rationality . . . powerfully exemplified in the common-law tradition" by fleshing out dry formalisms with literary understandings of "the interaction between shared human aspirations and concrete social circumstances" (Nussbaum 1995, xv, 92–93). The novel does this work: "storytelling and literary imagining are not opposed to rational argument, but can provide essential ingredients in a rational argument" (xiii).

So does the economy produce thousands of stories about what's been left out of the bottom line that employees and former employees are ready to tell, with no one to tell them to. Perhaps, as Nussbaum suggests, we might imagine that the "judicious spectator" is listening—a figure that Adam Smith postulates, "whose judgment and responses" and empathetic detachment (as an absence of self-concern) are emblematic of an ideal of public reasoning. The judicious spectator is expected to feel fully "compassion and sympathy . . . [and] also fear, grief, anger, hope, and . . . love" because these are part and parcel of rational judgment (73, 74). For making more matter at the bottom line, a new kind of broker belongs on Wall Street, a judicious spectator to help negotiate and arbitrate the disparate values and priorities of those whose lifeworlds *are* firms and those whose lifework is to trade in firms.

Redemption and redeeming works are not incompatible with capitalism— at least that is a profound wish these reformative voices express. Toward the end of our discussion I mentioned to Bob Elliott that I'd found in the journal *Accounting, Organizations, and Society* articles documenting variations in the accountant stereotype in the popular media (fussy, boring bean counters or complicitous in cosmetic financial statements). He said, "At least one researcher claims the image is getting decidedly better . . . Like Itzhak Stern in *Schindler's List*. The one who saves them all is really the accountant who runs the factory."

References

Beard, Victoria. 1994. "Popular Culture and Professional Identity: Accountants in the Movies." *Accounting, Organizations, and Society* 19 (3): 303–18.

Block, Fred. 1990. *Postindustrial Possibilities: A Critique of Economic Discourse.* Berkeley: University of California Press.

Bougen, Philip D. 1994. "Joking Apart: The Serious Side to the Accountant Stereotype." *Accounting, Organizations, and Society* 19 (3): 319–35.

The Conference Board. 1995. *New Corporate Performance Measures: A Research Report.* New York: The Conference Board.

Eccles, Robert G., and Sarah C. Mavrinac. 1994. "Improving the Corporate Disclosure Process." Harvard Graduate School of Business Administration working paper 94-061.

Heckscher, Charles. 1995. *White-Collar Blues: Management Loyalties in an Age of Corporate Restructuring.* New York: Basic Books.

Kaplan, Robert S., and David P. Norton. 1993. "Putting the Balanced Scorecard to Work." *Harvard Business Review* (71) 5: 134–47.

Nussbaum, Martha C. 1995. *Poetic Justice: The Literary Imagination and Public Life.* Boston: Beacon Press.

Passell, Peter. 1995. "The Wealth of Nations: A 'Greener' Approach Turns List Upside Down." *New York Times,* 19 Sept., C1, 12.

Perin, Constance. 1977. *Everything in Its Place: Social Order and Land Use in America.* Princeton, N.J.: Princeton University Press.

————. 1988. *Belonging in America: Reading Between the Lines.* Madison: University of Wisconsin Press.

Solow, Robert. 1992. *An Almost Practical Step Toward Sustainability.* Washington, D.C.: Resources for the Future.

Wallman, Steven M. H. 1955. "Updating Disclosure for a New Century." *New York Times,* 24 Sept., F14.

3

Toward a Higher-Order Merger:
A Middle Manager's Story

ON A VISIONARY MIDDLE MANAGER. *In this piece the qualities of the current middle manager's cultural discourse is expertly elicited by Cefkin. She skillfully meshes her own questions and comments with the tone and tempo of M.'s enthusiastic responses. Though flush with his own success, M. pulls the content and form of his narrative from various, familiar sources in academic thought, popular therapeutic-advice literature, and the consultant industry: the attraction of chaos theory, the evolutionary frame of the narrative (without, however, much sense of the specific history of business), sloganish remarks on empowerment and participation, a retention of commitment to individualistic striving, achievement, and success within the hierarchical corporation. This discourse is thus revealing and exemplary in its blatant trendiness, but it is also quite specifically informative about what changing corporate practices and representations promise the sort of social and cultural transformations that M. envisions.* – G. E. M.

* * *

This is an era teeming with ideas about the nature, purpose, and status of the organization. Business organizations are making efforts to transform—restructure, reengineer, flatten the hierarchy, downsize (or yet more euphemistically, rightsize), go virtual, decentralize—according to these ideas. The Taylorist focus on labor as the locus of efficiency, productivity, and the consequent survival of the business has refocused on the form of the organization itself. To speculate on, explore, and imagine the future of business organizations invites a reimagination of institutional formations more broadly.

To M.—a highly regarded and successful manager in a profitable business division of a Fortune 500 company—this space of the imaginary seems fertile with possibilities. The management position in general, and M.'s action in it in

particular, must not be overlooked in its strategic positioning: given his organizational status, M.'s concerns are by definition both strategy, the visionary
elements of moving the organization forward, and operations, the mundane and
practical concerns of what must be done to keep a business functioning. In the
discourse that follows, M. shares some of his thoughts on business and institutions.[1] Motivated by my own interest in the many wide-ranging ideas, theories, and principles that have been engaged by 1990s business management
discourses, I encouraged M. to share his views on current business trends and
to speculate about their relationships to broader societal issues. I was particularly interested in gleaning how someone such as M., as an agent active in
the processes generating the new institutional formations he describes, viewed
these trends. Based on the two years of fieldwork I had done in corporate settings, three months of that time in M.'s office, I reckoned that M. would offer a
lively view on these matters. His particular willingness to play with new ideas,
to make far-reaching connections to the business at hand, was apparent.

I introduce M.'s narrative by way of my own understanding of some of the
broader contexts framing M.'s remarks. In addition, I intercept M.'s narrative
below (marked by indented paragraphs) both to offer clarifying information
and as a means to interject hints at my own further interpretations and questions
invited by M.'s statements.

The Present Context

The present that provides the context of M.'s narrative is one dominated by
an ethos of participation and ideals of empowerment reflected in such diverse
business trends as the seemingly more scientistic process reengineering movement[2] and the more spiritually informed empowerment movements. Empowerment, in particular, acts as an intensely value-laden symbol around which
future corporate formations are imagined. Suggestive of liberation and of the
gaining of political rights, it evokes notions of control, power, and authority.
Workplace empowerment movements evidence especially strong rhetoric of
social and communitarian objectives, including such specific strategies as operating through self-directed work groups, disseminating information more
broadly among workers, and decreasing the number of hierarchical layers of an
organization.[3] Despite these socially oriented objectives, workplace empowerment movements tend to be built on extremely individualistic underlying assumptions, calling on personal motivation and relying on individual responsibility as ways past the barriers of established unproductive structures. More
than just the application of political correctness to business, such empowerment movements are more importantly seen as ways to engender more efficient
and more productive business practices[4] by eliminating unnecessary tasks, dis-
tributing resources and decision making more equitably, and increasing effi-

ciency through more local control, all for the optimization of resources and business results.

Together with the threats and realities of downsizing, the possibilities embodied by these notions contribute to the now commonly acknowledged sense of destabilization among workers, especially middle management. Together with these current ideologies, which overwhelmingly support increased local control and the democratization of the workplace, new information technologies are expected to ease and expand workers' access to needed information and in turn to allow for an increase in their span of responsibility. At the same time, global economic shifts are creating new demands for greater flexibility and "just in time" (JIT) products. All these developments lead to the call for fewer cogs in the wheel, making precarious the middle manager's position.

It is in dialogue with this range of conditions that M.'s story may be best understood. I read M.'s narrative less as a statement of his ideological stance than as one marking out a discursive space in which he is positioning himself in response to the possible future being set up in this era of empowerment and downsizing. M.'s story seems to express less about the anxiety of the present than about the possibilities of the future.

The story that M. tells is yet more interesting in that it does not emerge out of tales of the success of the past. Tales of scientific and commercial successes, professional developments, organizational growth, and entrepreneurial innovations—several of which can be found in the pages of this volume—are commonly told from a historic standpoint. Whether talking to a biogeneticist about the invention of a drug or a former chief executive officer about his company's salvation from ruin through the adoption of total quality management (Kearns 1992), narratives relayed through a historical perspective tend to form a cohesive story and through it reveal something of a promotional aspect: people are in the right place at the right time, struggle and hardship produce transformative effects, chance leads to success, experts are there when you need them, and everything works out in the end.

In speculating on the meaning of the present and in imagining the future, M. can but be suggestive of the possibilities of success, something that as a manager he is employed to be concerned with. Whereas a more typical business success story might describe a future filled with satisfied customers, quality products, productive workers, and growing markets, M. does not constrain his story to a narrow focus on business success, but rather speaks about the nature of organization, community, and society more broadly. His thoughts are dotted with references from a broad range of sources. He mixes strains of social contract theory with hints of communitarianism. He calls on existential philosophy, on a Nietzschean will to power, and on developmental psychology to illustrate his views. Primarily, however, M. calls on the foundational scientific theories of evolution and chaos to substantiate and illustrate his thinking.

By calling on evolution and chaos theory M. would seem to ground his thinking, and with it the future, in the natural order that derives out of natural systems. By doing so M. implicitly constructs and attends to, in a way consistent with capitalism, the problem of social order. I do not mean to reduce M. and his views to a simple explanatory frame. Indeed, as M.'s narrative unfolds it would seem that his desire is to be more generative than limiting. Yet it is perhaps precisely this tension in M.'s own thinking—between his interest in being generative and his reliance on foundational frames of thinking—that best reflects the broader tension of the era. M.'s narrative can be read as exemplary of deeply embedded tensions, tensions raised by the ethos of participation within the context of the institutional basis of capitalistic business enterprise.

M.

M. is the senior manager of an office of a business division of a Fortune 500 company (here, Docuco) whose core business is office technology. M.'s division (here, Docubis) sells copying, mailroom service, and other business services related to document production and management, and is marketed through outsourcing. Docubis is organized by a headquarters, regional management offices, and approximately forty central offices (both managerial and operational) around the United States, as well as offices internationally. Each central office, in turn, operates a large number of its own outsourced locations (sites where the business services are offered through Docubis, but at a customer's location), known as facilities management, or FM.

Docubis is currently a highly successful and profitable part of Docuco. While Docuco continues to see gains in profit, it has thinned its ranks through a series of downsizing measures. Docubis itself was relatively untouched by these efforts, however, and indeed in both numbers of employees and in revenue, it continues to grow at a substantial rate. Nonetheless, as a service provider, the market niche of Docubis is volatile, hence its stated reason for operating through extensive use of contract labor, particularly at the front lines.

M. has been with Docuco for over twenty years. He is a white man in his forties, married to a successful financial advisor, and the father of two children in public primary schools.

M. oversees a (geographically extensive) local operation. The net revenue of M.'s operation in 1994 was approximately $17.5 million; Docubis as a whole had a revenue of roughly $800 million. Within the local organization, M. is the senior manager. In the total scheme of the organization, he is a middle manager. He reports to a manager at a regional level who reports to a vice president at headquarters. In contrast, there are three levels of hierarchy below M.: frontline workers (the largest single position of employment in the division) report to supervisors who report to managers who report to M.

Known as something of a maverick, M. has a reputation as a visionary thinker among some members of Docuco. His office was chosen as one of three sites in which Docubis launched its divisionwide change (empowerment) strategy in 1994. M. himself was a member of the task force that helped to define and design the strategy. The strategy, headed by a manager of quality at headquarters, involves a several-year effort with simultaneous top-down and bottom-up efforts to promote new ways of doing business, to create a more trusting, collaborative, and open work environment, and to work in ways that improve productivity.

The change effort, a rather dynamic and amorphous ensemble of strategies and ideologies, has been influenced by a range of perspectives. Dominant in the development of the strategy were ideas of self-directed workgroups,[5] social theories of learning,[6] Peter Senge's popularization of systems thinking and mental models,[7] chaos theory,[8] and Stephen Covey's principled centered leadership.[9] Before the strategy was widely disseminated throughout the organization, the upper management of the division (headquarters managers, as well as the senior managers from a select number of the division offices, including M. and his direct reports) participated in a four-day seminar led by Senge's group. Some time later, as one of three initial launch sites for the division more broadly, those in local management positions (both senior managers and supervisors) in M.'s operation attended a weeklong seminar in Utah with Covey. A series of workshops were then held to introduce and initiate new ways of thinking and working throughout all ranks of M.'s operation.

In addition to this activity, one that potentially placed M. and his operation at the forefront of significant organizational transformations, in 1994 M.'s office landed a huge business deal, largely, in M.'s and others' views, as a result of the deal's basis in these new kinds of visionary and strategic ways of thinking. The hallmark of the deal, as it is commonly described, was that Docubis was selected by the customer not based on price but because of Docubis' principles and approach. This deal, worth as much as $120 million over ten years, received companywide attention. A videotape was made to document the deal and was showcased on the occasion of the CEO's annual report simulcast to 130 locations internationally. The tape focused on M. and others who participated in the deal, including other members of his office and customers. Most remarkably, the telling of this story was interspersed with video clips of an interview with the business consultant Margaret Wheatley from her peaceful, snow-laden mountain home in Utah, describing her view of business organizations as self-organizing natural systems that would be better supported if understood through chaos theory.

Finally, M. received one of twenty-five highly coveted awards handed out by the CEO annually.

M.'s Story

The "Corp" of the Corporation?

M.: There are some changes going on here with the structure and the direction from headquarters—"headquarters," I keep using this phrase.
CEFKIN: Why shouldn't you?
M.: Well, it's so, it's so—hierarchical.
CEFKIN: Yes, but what else is it?
M.: I don't know [*With a chuckle*]. It's a group of people.

> The traditional organization chart is shaped something like a pyramid, with a treelike structure of branching units moving downward. The unit of relationship is the reporting hierarchy—who supervises whom, who reports to whom, who can fire whom, and so forth. The CEO or president is at the top, and managers are above their reports.
> Attentive to the symbolic impact of designating the corporate structure by a top-down image, M. has redesigned the organization chart for his office. While placing org charts from left to right is not uncommon, M. attempted to displace the senior figure, that is, himself, from either the top or the beginning (the left side). On the new chart M.'s position is placed just after the first quarter of the lefthand side of the chart where he is surrounded by his reports but is symbolically closer to the organization's support staff, who commonly have less status in traditional business organizations.

M.: The org chart has changed. It's more than vision, mission, and that kind of thing, but it's our purpose, our overriding purpose. It's an open hand, five fingers and a palm. Your eyes probably always go to the fingers as being the most interesting normally. But really the strength of the hand is in the palm. It's a service organization. So how do you represent it as service? It's an open hand willing to help. This is our organization, an open hand willing to help. So it's open environment, it's sharing, it's helping each other and the organization.

In this case the entire organization is focused on the palm, or the real strength of the organization, and that is the account teams, made up of operators, supervisors, and sales reps, who are focused on their customers.

This is a change of an organization with an attempt to eliminate as much as possible, as is reasonable, hierarchy. Instead of a top-down, bottom-up kind of organization, it's left to right, with the focus on the frontline organization. The people who make a difference are the people who are in front of the customer.

In this organization we've gone from five "direct reports" to eight. We've restructured those eight, separated out the group from "senior staff" (I don't know what else to call it, as of yet), but those people who carry the plan, who are accountable for results and work with teams. And another group of people who are really like support staff. And these individuals—a [systems] analyst, a training and development person, the controller who provides administrative and financial services and also information to the organization, and a learning coach—these are people who are focused more on quadrant 2 activities than the immediate rush of the business.

> The reference to "quadrant 2 activities" comes from the work of Covey. Quadrant 2 refers to a matrix of activities along an important/unimportant, and urgent/nonurgent continuum. Quadrant 2 activities are important and nonurgent.
>
> In my research I have found that people (managers in particular) in corporate settings tend to be voracious consumers of ideas, especially those forwarded by business consultants. Language change is one of the most visible aspects of this. In Docuco, many people "speak" Covey (that is, "be proactive," "begin with the end in mind"), a sign, in some people's view, of who really counts as an insider.

M.: And their function is to think in those terms and to support the organization and the senior staff and the teams as well as be available to individuals as personal coaches in their expertise areas.

So we have a purpose and we have an organization structure that's going to go about making a difference. Part of it is eliminating or minimizing hierarchy and treating these people as if they were extended members of the team. They're very highly empowered individuals, they work in concert with each other, and in this case I'm in the center of it, kind of conducting it all like an orchestra, keeping it going and feeding information and ideas back and forth and influencing and supporting those people to support the account team.

Connections

M.: In the support staff we identified eight things that we are doing right away, right now, that are projects to literally make a difference. For instance, if information is power and you want to give power to account teams to be empowered, what information do they need? In chaos theory, if you're trying to make things happen, you need to network dumb elements. You don't have to have a lot of smart elements, you just have to have a lot of elements, they can all be dumb, and connect them. If you connect dumb elements you have a brain, because that's all that a brain is, is millions of dumb little cells that are connected.

So the whole concept behind chaos theory is to connect things so things can happen, encourage chaos to happen, encourage people to bump up against each other, information to flow, and debates to be created. So how do you network our extended business? One idea (and we're not there yet) is PCs, and then how do you network them? You could have a literal network or you can tap them into the Internet and we can all be part of each other's network that way in the broader world. Well, that's three to five years from now before most of us will have the skills to do that.

So how do you that? Well, what we're planning on doing is providing a voice mailbox system for all the FMs.

> The FMs managed out of this office span several states. Currently they can be reached either by a direct telephone link, by mail, or by visiting. M. carries on here to describe further how voice mail will help connect people, and touches on some of the potential problems of the system, such as the question of privacy in a system where all employees at an FM will share a single voice mailbox, concluding:

M.: We don't know if this is even going to work, but at least it's the beginning of things starting to happen and communicating.

> Businesses exploit the presumed liberating feature of technology, both for the reason that automation frees people up from mundane work and for its enabling of more democratic communication. It is precisely this feature of presumed uncontrolled access to information and diversion that worries many managers and creates a hesitation in adopting new technological systems. Still, the position explicitly supported by most is along the lines of the following:
> "Better technology, better processes, and fewer, better workers. The ideal: Technology that actually helps workers make decisions, in organizations that encourage them to do so. That's the promise of computers, just now starting to be realized. Free access to information across an organization eliminates the need for hierarchical management systems that existed before," says James Sims, CEO of consultant Cambridge Technology Partners, Inc. "People can think for themselves. Decisions can be made faster, by those closest to the customer" (Hammonds, Kelly, and Thurston 1994, 81).

CEFKIN: You say you don't know if it's going to work, and when you ask the question yourself of how to make these connections and networking happen, the answers were all about technology. You either use PCs or telephones. Is there anything else that has to happen for the connection to happen? Is technology enough to make connections happen?

M.: No, but that is an exciting new idea because of how everyone can be involved immediately. The speed of communication is one way out. It allows immediate feedback and the quality of communication would improve dramatically. So that's the exciting part of it.

The other part of it is, we're trying to establish senses of communities. So in my mind it's shaping up as communities and there's a desire to have them recognize each other as part of a community and to do something about it.

From Single Cells to Groups

A kickoff is the annual all-employee business meeting and party used as a communication meeting, serving both to launch new strategies and initiatives and to generate momentum. They hold one in each of the major geographical centers in the areas that M.'s office does business.

M.: This year I purposely made a point of arranging all the kickoff meetings so my schedule would allow me to be there. There have been times where, in my own thinking I might have said the [nameless city] community is too small. I mean, you, [naming the sales manager for that area], and you, [naming the supervisor for that area], are empowered to create an event. I don't need to be there to make it a meaningful event. I was really going down that path for a long time.

But along the way my thinking has changed and I said, No, I've really got to get out there because I'm on the front edge of a lot of ideas even beyond any of the people who work with me because of some of the connections I've made. I am particularly capable at synthesizing a lot of off-the-wall ideas or concepts that at first blush wouldn't seem related. I seem to relate them all somehow. I do that, and I'm unique at that. Then in addition to that I'm a good spokesperson and I'm a different kind of leader. So people really enjoy, even though I have this limited relationship with these people at a distance, they literally enjoy having me around and I work at that. So we're missing huge opportunities if I don't get around socializing and stirring up people's juices to do the right thing.

So we made that happen, and I was at each of the meetings. I found that the [nameless city] group was so [*Hesitating to find the right word*] unsophisticated that my presentation had to be completely truncated to the simplest of statements and ideas. I had to take out most of the slides, I used the hand slide, I used the organization structure, but even there, it was like [*Speaking as a Docubis employee in nameless city*], "Who are these people and these managers? We don't know any of these people."

CEFKIN: So, when you say *unsophisticated* it's really that they lack the actual knowledge about—

M.: Both. It's also a very rural community. People's attitudes and values and level of sophistication about the world and world of ideas is limited.

M. explains further how one of the supervisors in the area helped him redesign his presentation, encouraging him to eliminate the graphs and charts.

M.: I kept one graph and I challenged them and his comment back later was they all started falling asleep immediately. I needed to know where they were, but I also needed to challenge them and move them forward, so I had to do a very different approach there.

What's interesting is the learning of how, just like this biological view of the world, that organizations are organisms. The reality is that it's like an amoeba and the [nameless city] group is a very different part of the amoeba than the others. Not better or worse, but just as you're managing individuals you've got to manage each area differently, the language you use, the ideas, how you bring those ideas together, the questions you ask, how you draw a team forward from where they are in their level of development or maturity, is very important.

> Having naturalized groups as organisms and amoeba, M. is comfortably within a metaphorical arena that allows him to both evaluate and yet support the nature of the group as is. First he identifies a matter of objection:

M.: The leaders, the managers, are all at the front of the room and they are the ones that are walking and talking and everyone else is sitting passively waiting for them to come by. Which is what I had to share with those people, what I saw and I didn't like, and I thought was inappropriate.

> Then, using the same metaphorical reasoning, he is able to explain it for himself.

M.: So, the beauty is to recognize that they're all unique. Even though you have an organization, each group is unique.

Art and the Bottom Line

M.: That was pretty fascinating. I mean we were at a brew and burger restaurant and we're in this room in the back. It's a large room and there was a brown-shaded plastic kind of folding wall partition that separated our room from another room, where there's another business group. And they were loud and obnoxious and laughing and we could sometimes hardly hear because of the noise in the room right next to us! I'm sitting there, I'm just grated. All this is grating against me. There's a long U-shaped table and the room wasn't quite big enough, so to get out of your chair you were bumping against this partition as you try to get up to talk to someone or go to the rest room or whatever it may be. So everything about it was funky and it yet it had elements of good stuff.

For instance, a team of [frontline workers] put this meeting together. This was the first business meeting they'd ever had as a community, their kickoff. Four or five people got together and organized it, and there were banners on the wall, the streamers and balloons and stuff and was kind of cute, but it was very hokey. And one of the [frontline workers] apparently is some kind of an artist and drew like a cartoon character and it was, I guess, we got confused about what the theme was. It was either a cowboy theme or football theme. [*Laughter*]

CEFKIN: You mean you couldn't tell?

M. No, I couldn't tell because people wore cowboy boots. Maybe it was a mixed metaphor and I didn't get it [*More laughter*]. I think it got confused in this presentation. After some time I started noticing that ladies and guys were wearing football jerseys, but also some people were wearing jeans and cowboy boots and stuff and at least one person had a bandanna. They weren't mixed, they weren't wearing a football jersey with a bandanna. I think they screwed up their message. Of course, the beauty of it, no one told me anything, so I was dressed in a suit. And I had to quickly throw on the only casual clothes I'd brought. So they insisted that I change and I was still more formally dressed in my casual outfit than everyone else.

So we stumbled, it was a major stumbling event, but it was the beginning of a business. And I said to [the supervisor] at one point, I said, "I don't know if I can stand this, no, not stand this, I don't know if I can relate? I wonder if I'm too far gone to relate to this group, and I'm pretty good at relating to all kinds of people in situations, but this is bizarre to me." It took me some time to soak up the spirit in the group and really change the level of which I interacted, and then to appreciate it as a result. It was like a different form of art, one that was jarring or challenging or not even pretty. But if you just hung around a while and stuck with it and looked at it you could see the beauty underneath.

So anyway, what this one person did is, he is an artist and he drew a football player with a torn shirt. And the shirt had, I guess, Docubis on it. And on the jersey are competitors' names, [*Naming several competitors.*] So here is this person, shredding, and it's this giant of a person. The shirt was shredded, and there were rippling stomach muscles [*Laughing*]. So it was like a cartoon character, and I'm revolted by this [*Laughing*], by this very macho looking thing! My first reaction is that I am revolted. And I saw some other things, it was a very male-dominated culture, which I didn't like at all. And this was just another example to me. And this was our placemat. This was a document that was colored, color copied, and laminated, and it was not real pretty, but that was your placemat.

So that was an interesting, creative approach. But like I said, at first I didn't like it and I was getting all these masculine symbols thrown at me, the football or the cowboy theme, whichever it was. The three guys at the front of the room, chatting and buddying up with each other. And they were the leaders. By the way, we worked very hard for a long time to find a woman supervisor, and after eight months of failure we just moved ahead and found a male. But here I am, looking at the culture we created. And they are three males and they are buddying up with each other. They were relaxed, they were kidding each other. They were kind of nervous, because it was their meeting, but they were kind of the center of attention, and everyone else doesn't know what is going on and what their role is, and I didn't like any of that.

So I'm just sitting there awkward and wondering what's going on. And then there is this picture. But at least, I realized, there was some business related to it, it was Docubis and competition. It was woven in the work element of it. And then the other thing I realized is, this is their first attempt. Someone went out on a limb and shared with everyone a skill they had. And they were proud of it. And I made a point of saying that was really good. I complimented them on their art and thanked them for their contribution to the meeting. I personally didn't like it, but I recognized, no matter how hokey or misplaced it was, it was the beginning of someone making a contribution.

It was very immature—not immature, it was very unsophisticated, and their first attempt. So its okay. It's natural. And let it go and encourage it. And the only thing I came away with was, instead of it taking them ten years to get sophisticated, we would like to get them to do that in five years. Our goals would be to nurture them faster than we were able to grow independently.

> As a point of contrast, M. described the kickoff in another of the cities that his office does business where they used such sophisticated techniques as surround-sound audio and video displays.

CEFKIN: What's the relationship to you, in terms of looking at the art and the technology and the way it was used as a measure of the sophistication. *How* does that relate to their conceptual thinking or their sophistication in terms of business?

M.: That's a good question. This goes back to the idea of how you measure a group. I was talking about the language, the words, the symbols, the dynamics of how those things flow through a group. This is another kind of a question like that.

I will refer back to a model I just recently learned of from the Chaos Club.

Putting Chaos into Practice

> A number of professional business consultants use chaos theory as the basis for their offerings. Together with a local consultant, M. helped initiate a monthly gathering of individuals—other consultants, businesspeople, and professors—to discuss chaos theory as

it applies to organizations. The purpose of the "Chaos Club" is to learn about "putting chaos into practice."

One of the tendencies that fascinates me in this trend is the tendency to put purpose and intent into supposed "natural systems" (as the organization itself is cast). Consider this phrase presented on an overhead slide at a meeting where chaos theory was being discussed: "The primary goal of the universe. . . ." Wheatley similarly presumes a hidden universe of meaning in suggesting that the "correct patterns" of principles, values, and guiding assumptions can generate complexity.

M.: That is her main objective, pulling together interesting people to talk about chaos and how it relates to organizations.

She had a triangle. The bottom of the triangle is theory, the left side of the triangle is model, and the right side of the triangle is practice. Her concept is that we all have practices and we all do things. We all get dressed in the morning, either putting the left shoe on the left foot first or right foot. There's an approach to hygiene and everything you do. We all have these individual practices. Any business has its individual practices. But a megapractice is one that is based on theoretical principles, that has a model that is tested and explored, a structure, an image of those principles in a way within practices that occur within that model. She talked about individuals. Some people are more theoretical, for instance, some people are more modelers and some people are more practitioners and they don't really care about the theory piece. So a megapractice, one that is integrated and successful, has to include all three. This is the long introduction to the answer to your question, which was, How does the technology and so on and the style of the presentation and all that matter?

The kickoff itself, is it based on principles? What are the principles of this kickoff? What are the messages that are being shared? Is it a football player with rippling stomach muscles, which is one kind of message that we could all relate to, but maybe not the most sophisticated way of viewing the world. Or, is it in [another city], a photograph of Stephen Covey on the wall with artwork and concepts from [the change strategy] and all the other symbols that have been thrown around at us. What are the principles that are being shared, what are the messages that are coming out, and how is it being done? Not only principles, but it was models as well that were being shared.

And then, how well did they do it? Did they do it flawlessly? The model that was being used, was it the most important person in [another city] who led the meeting and was that person a manager? Or was it a [frontline worker]? The moderator was an employee who wanted to do it and wanted to try and wanted to grow and wanted to take a risk. So that's a good model; it was not the old model, it's the new model.

CEFKIN: Can I push you on that a little? The way you described the [another city] kickoff is that they took all the new things that are going on—

technology, picture of Covey, the change strategy, all this kind of stuff—and they were able to appropriate and use the new symbols. Does that really reflect, or *how* does that really reflect a deeper or broader level of thinking rather than it just being that they've had more introductions to and are able to take the language and icons from something new and apply it? How does that actually reflect the change in thinking?

M.: That's a great question because my reaction to the [another city] meeting, was "Oh my God, they've been conditioned!" [*Laughter*] There's a better word than that, but that was my reaction to that. And what I neglected to share with you was, there was a picture of Covey every five feet! [*Laughter*] So your question is a beautiful question.

Yes, the risk with the [another city] group was they had what I believe and what experience and what research tells us are effective principles. They are effective principles, they're contemporary. And to realize, of course, that we're experimenting with these as we're really trying to find the truth. They were working with effective principles, they had internalized it, which is their job, to a large extent, and they had been creative with it. They had expressed out of themselves their own approach to those principles and that model. The risk was very clear: tell them what's important and they will be good at internalizing it and implementing it. But "Are they able to think for themselves?" was a major question that I came into that meeting with and left with.

The challenge of the leader is to be sensitive to all those messages and then to draw them out. And if you think about an organization, an individual, or a team or a community being on a continuum of maturity, sophistication, taking on responsibility for their environment and making it a great environment for themselves and all the stakeholders, the customers, and the owners, etc., etc. We're all at different levels. To realize where that group is and to celebrate with them. [To tell them] that you're okay, you're doing great, it's a wonderful journey you're on. Then to nudge them to the next level of sophistication—

> M.'s reference to the "continuum of maturity" is again a reference to Covey. Covey proposes that the seven habits are something to be practiced as a lifelong effort that is part of a maturity continuum in which people move from an attitude of dependence, to one of independence, and finally to interdependence.

M.: —But really, my job is to assess where they are, and to spark them to grow and develop and try to get to the next level of sophistication.

"It's Simply a Matter of Survival"

M.: Now, what is the next level of sophistication? What is this hierarchy of stuff? What is the endpoint here that we're trying to accomplish? I think what we're trying to accomplish is that everyone is treated as an adult. That they are given the freedom to act independently, and that they know that. And that they eagerly take it on. And that they literally make a difference in the world they find themselves in. And that they, you, go beyond doing that by working with other adults that leverage their own value that they bring. Their own unique skills, capabilities, perspectives, etc., and combine it with others, to connect with others and find a greater—Now what is greater? A greater success, where a bunch of individuals, adults, working in concert together accomplish more of their shared goals than they could if they worked independently. And that's the idea of working in a team, working within a community, and sharing resources and capabilities for a shared goal.

My last thought was, imagine war breaking out in [nameless city]. Those people would be highly empowered. They would empower themselves, they would find resources. They would live on next to nothing. When you read about the community in Russia that's being bombarded by the Russian troops, the will to live, and there are some very basic fundamental principles that we live our life by. Like continuing life, and the will to live is perhaps genetically embedded in us. But then a shared will to live, not only is that a very fundamental thing we all have, but when we do it as a group, we can have miraculous accomplishments given next to zero resources against all odds.

CEFKIN: This is interesting. So, on the one hand, what comes out of teamwork is the sharing of being able to accomplish goals together, but on the other hand, in the example you gave of war breaking out, there's the personal thing, perhaps in nature, of the will to live. In terms of working together, if war broke out in [nameless city], are you suggesting that they would be better off, they would be further ahead now, having worked with Docuco and learning concepts of teamwork and some of that kind of stuff

M.: No.

CEFKIN: —than they would have, that they wouldn't figure that out on their own?

M.: Yes, yes.

CEFKIN: Or do they have to be taught that?

M.: No.

CEFKIN: Or do they have to learn that?

M.: Yes. No.

CEFKIN: Okay, all those. Yes and no, maybe! [*Laughter*]

M.: Absolutely, no. Absolutely, that's a great refinement of this idea.

> That M. summarizes the above exchange as a "refinement of an idea" is reminiscent of a common communication pattern in Docuco, and possibly other organizations strongly influenced by total quality management (TQM). A form of corporate politeness, there is

a value placed on responding positively to another's statements. For instance, one states that she would like to "build on" another's comment, even if in fact she is disagreeing, and a manager may "share" something with a report, rather than "tell" him. "Problems" are reconceptualized as "opportunities."

M.: The reality is that people are adults, they are fully prepared in most cases, fully prepared human beings, ready to take on responsibilities for their lives; that they have very fundamental things that drive them; that over two-thousand-plus years have proven that human beings can survive the worst scenarios; that the race can survive. So empowerment, or the change strategy, or organizational management, using various different principles like chaos, is intended to bring out that natural inherent ability to make a huge difference in one's own life and to the greater good of the community they found themselves in. And so empowerment doesn't teach them those things. Empowerment, or some of the change strategy conversations and information, is intended to have us all begin thinking about the situation we find ourselves in to question whether in fact we are acting like true adults, and to find ways to eliminate the things that have stopped us from being the natural-born leaders we all were at the age of two years old. We're born leaders and learners.

Among the factors contributing to the loss of our natural-born leadership abilities, M. notes the conditioning and fear of risk built into earlier mechanistic models of organization.

M.: So the question is, How do you eliminate the barriers of freedom to act and do the right things, however that's defined for whatever group you're in? How do you provide the freedom to people to act so you can tap the power of the individuals and still be "in control"? Or, how do you still deliver the output that may not be intrinsically interesting to begin with? How do you give more power to the system to be more productive without it falling apart? How do you share power without losing power? How do you encourage chaos and get order? And there's a whole series of questions around that and that's, I think, what we're trying to accomplish.

CEFKIN: What is the relationship of this kind of thinking around empowerment and teamwork and sharing of productive powers to achieve goals, to business? Why should all this be going on in business? I mean, why is Covey, for example, so popular among businesses? Why should a business be concerned about creating community? If people are finding community in other parts of their lives, why should they also have to find it in business?

M.: Well, it's simply a matter of survival. It's really an evolution of organizations, as they are becoming more effective, and they are in an environment of the free market system, of pure competition, organizations are groping their way through and finding ways of being more effective and winning against other organizations who are aiming for the same things. Market share, customer loyalty, whatever it may be.

> M. continues here to elaborate an optimistic scenario of the increase in global competition in all areas of society, suggesting that with this rapid movement, barriers are breaking down and resources are going for the highest use.

M.: The nature of the environment is, it's becoming more competitive. There are these various organisms, instead of going from the original design of animals, from, you know, single-cell organisms to ultimately apes and man, competing for resources and survival, now we human beings have bonded together and created organizations that have created more "results." Like a spaceship to the moon, that kind of result. And so the power of this species, the human species—this is way off Docubis, which is what you wanted, right?

CEFKIN: Yup [*Joking*]. I want the truth from you on the power of human species. That's why I came here.

M.: Well, no! We're finding it together.

So, it's just really the evolution of this species, of controlling their environment. And its gone from tilling the soil and killing each other, and surviving by mutilation and death, to cooperating with each other to get basic stuff done. And as we've gone from the farming communities of the Greek era to the modern era, with science and technology and coming along in our knowledge and understanding and principles and theories of the world evolving and balancing against each other, we're getting more sophisticated. As a result, we're getting more done. We're still competing, but we're competing from organizations now. We have these artificial things called organizations with structures and stuff, and those organizations are competing with each other.

Organizational Woman

CEFKIN: You were very interested and very concerned, I think, when you were first bringing on a new [manager] as a woman, into your office. Concerned in a good way, but you were giving it some attention. The fact of her being a woman—

M.: Committed to doing it, yeah.

CEFKIN: Right. I remember you gave me an article that you had given the rest of the senior staff about women, health concerns that women were facing. And you told me that you'd given it to them because you wanted them to be aware of what it means in a broader sense to be a woman in today's world. And that was a curious artifact for me in thinking what it was about that that sparked you to think about this.

M.: I'm influenced by thinking and ideas that are being shared around. I love ideas, I'm searching for ideas that work, that are meaningful to me, that make sense and that have implications. So, one of the ideas that's out there is diversity as an important thing in and of itself. As I thought about that, listened to it, and thought about it and internalized it—diversity is critical to our success. But I quickly went from diversity being minorities and women to diversity of thoughts, diversity of perspectives, diversity of backgrounds, and that's why I get such a kick out of such strange people like you and your associates from IRL. [*Laughter*]

CEFKIN: Thank you, I'll take that as a compliment. I don't think I'm being strange enough for you today.

M.: No you're not.

And of course, I'm married to a woman so I am sensitive to and I'm learning from a woman. It's a big part of my life. And it's an organizational issue and it's a diversity issue. And I have been criticized for years that this place was all males. Not intentionally, and I realized soon that my intentions and my perspective don't matter, it's a symbolic gesture, if nothing else. It's very important to have someone in that role that any other person who's feeling left our or held back or disengaged to appropriate their knowledge and wisdom and talk with them and to gain insight on how to become engaged in this society. So that's important.

I'll be giving to each of the managers for their very broad self-development and growth outside of Docuco, but relates to Docuco and relates to their personal life, is a book called *What Your Mother Never Told You and Your Father Didn't Know,* by Dr. Gray. This is the second book after *Men are from Mars, Women are from Venus.* My wife was reading it and I started reading it and it's a fabulous understanding of how different we are and why we're so different and what problems it causes amongst ourselves and then how we might apply our natural state approach to working better with each other. Appreciating the differences and allowing the differences to be retained while being more effective with each other, happier with each other. I think it relates to understanding each other everywhere, at work and elsewhere.

CEFKIN: So you do think men and women are fundamentally different?

M.: They seem to be. I'm not a real great student of it yet, but this book talks about all kinds of things. There are physiological differences like at the base of the brain (this wouldn't surprise you) where the cortex or something connects with the spinal column, there are twice as many cells in a woman's anatomy than a man's. It wouldn't surprise you because women are so smart. The idea that they almost had more connections between the spine and brain, just so interesting to talk about connecting things in a chaotic concept, there's more connections for women.

Voluntarism

M.: The other one of my current ideas is to remind people that this is all voluntary. It's very important for people to realize that this is voluntary. It's very important to recognize that they are not a cog in the machine, they are not owned by this organization. No one owns them. That we are all free, we are voluntarily associating with this group and that at anytime we are free to leave and we should and we will at some point leave this association. One way or the other we will absolutely leave.

And the other thing is, the organization and team are free to dissociate themselves from you. One of the things we're working on is having teams choose their own members.

> A sign of flattening the hierarchy and of shared decision making, having teams hire and fire their own members is considered by many to be one of the aims of workplace empowerment movements. Ultimately, teams themselves should be able to control their own resources, offer up their own evaluations of each other and the team itself, and thus control their own membership. One of the greatest barriers to this approach, however, is that it presumes that the groups who accomplish their work together are in fact at least temporarily fixed and organizationally bounded. Docubis's efforts to identify teams in this way has continually come up against the fact that such working teams are instead dynamic and fluid.

M.: What's happening is, I see a lot of people who are not free, they are showing up at work, they're on this team, they're doing this job, they may even hate it. Imagine if we could just in our little world create an environment where the resources flow to where they are most valued, how happy people would be, how productive they would be, how the other individuals would benefit from that and how the organization would grow and thrive and kick ass in the market place.

Evolve, Volunteer, "Create the Fine Arts and Kill Each Other"

CEFKIN: One of the models that you use is evolution. [Some] say, when evolution is invoked as a reason to make something happen, that once human beings achieved a certain status of being social animals and they use symbolic systems such as language to communicate, that evolution was no longer determining them. And you even pointed out that organizations are our own creation, they're artificial, we made them. So I'm curious about that, how one wants to rely on evolution as a reason for something and yet on the other hand maybe that's just an excuse that we give.

Another model you then shifted to was this notion of voluntarism. That people voluntarily do something. Which is an opposite way of thinking. Evolution says you're determined, the pattern of what's going on in the world out there makes us have to act in certain kinds of ways. A notion of being a volunteer says it's up to our own free will to do as we please. These different reasons are invoked to get at the same thing.

M.: Let me try to answer this question by saying that I'm not a scientist but a philosopher of metaphysics. My focus is on metaphysics, which is my background, not science. (And that is not at all popular, so when people asked me what my major was, it was economics, the other major was philosophy.) So let me give that as my introduction to my answer.

In your conversation about freedom and so on you interjected a concept in evolution that I think shows your prejudice in the word *evolution* that I didn't have. When I say *evolution* I do not think in terms of predeterminism at all. So if that's what evolution means, that's not how I'm using it. If you remove that, then maybe there's not an issue. That it's evolutionary, in other words, it finds itself over time, and in that is free will. In that is the existential plight of man—Sartre and Camus, is man free, and Kierkegaard, if there is a God and he created this and he's the father and he's the director and the rulemaker, are we free and do we do his will?—and all that good stuff. Sartre, I think, was the one who really found the way out of all these things and said that life is meaningless, inherently meaningless. However, man is free. Man is free to do stupid things or anything. That's why we kill each other and hurt each other and we act out, we do things. So the world is meaningless and man is free.

But the exciting thing is that man has certain faculties and man brings meaning to the world. Given those two things—the world is meaningless and man is free—therefore, nihilism, kill yourself. Destroy the world. Burn and pillage. It's ugly. Kill it, kill yourself. That's not necessarily the conclusion from those two ideas, the other conclusion, which is—Nietzsche's *Übermensch,* man is the superman. Man becomes his own god and brings meaning and reality to life. So organizations are evolving as a structure, as a means by which human beings can live their lives and bring meaning and joy. And to the extent that organizations take that away is just not good. Human beings should explore and grow and develop and contribute and learn and weep and so on. They should be human. And so organizations are limiting humans from being humans and that's not a very effective long-term strategy for anything.

Organizations can create their own meaning. But it's very important for people to realize that this meaning that is being created for our organization is not necessarily your meaning for your life. It may play a role. To the extent that it plays a role, it taps into things that are meaningful for you, then we are in alignment with each other. We have something in common.

Alignment is a significant concept in the business world. The organization strives for alignment between strategy and practices, compensation plans and desired business results, expense and growth, and so on. With current attention to the loftier pursuits of visions and missions and purposes, employees will (hopefully) align their vision to that of the organization. Or better yet, their personal vision will *already* be aligned to the organizational one.

M.: So, *evolutionary,* when I use the phrase, is not predeterminism at all.

CEFKIN: Right, and actually and I think your fix on that is quite right. Still, I think evolution does presume, as well as some of the other things you're talking about, that we're starting from somewhere and going somewhere. That there is some sort of universal—

M.: That's a great question.

CEFKIN: Even talking about things in terms of their increasing sophistication, or organizations developing—

M.: Good, that's great.

CEFKIN: So it's that we are starting from somewhere and going somewhere. And I also have a feeling there's a catch to empowerment here, too, because empowerment suggests you are being empowered *to do* something or being empowered *from doing* something. It has a kind of liberation kind of thinking, so there's prior state and an after state.

M.: All I think we're doing is, where we're going is, we're simply exploring the human condition. That's all we're doing. Kurt Vonnegut's book *The Sirens of Titan* is a hilarious, existential, cynical, funny viewpoint of life. There's this whole story about trying to understand why the great wall of China was created and all these things. He goes on and on about the man-years of effort. It all ended up basically as a joke, in a sense. It was all a direct result of a spaceship coming from another galaxy that was sent to send a message to this planet or to another planet. Earth was an imposition on the real purpose and the spaceship got lost or had mechanical problems or something, so all this, all the things, all the human trauma, and all the wars, you know, all this stuff was nothing more than this martian or this space person's attempt to send the message that he could send by his spaceship, which was to say "hi." [*Laughter*] So the horrible joke is on us. We're just pawns in this stupid world that is going nowhere, that is doing nothing, and all it is for one alien in the group to communicate with another one and not even something of substance but rather "hi."

So all we're doing is exploring the human condition. That's all we're doing. It does not have a purpose, it does not have an end point, it is exploring. We are privileged to be alive and we have certain skills and limitations that make us do things. We create fine arts and we kill each other. What we find ourselves in is the twentieth century with certain technology and certain things and organizations, and we can get resources if we do what other people ask us to do, and we can then, in our pure freedom, spend those resources as we wish, including our extremely valuable time to be associated with an organization. It's all very curious.

Toward a Higher-Order Merger

Daily life inside a corporation is punctuated with talk of organizational change. The change that is spoken of is not change for the sake of achieving a new status quo, but change to generate more change. If continuous improvement was the mantra of the quality revolution, continuous change is today's mantra. Out of this has arisen a whole industry of writing and consulting on whether and how such changes can take place in or out of current institutional forms.

Departing from the business concern for generating ongoing innovation and increased productivity, as M. would have it, this change is about creating the dynamic processes of growth, development, evolution, sophistication, connection, and maturity. The metaphorical pathways underlying M.'s thinking suggestively play off each other: in evolution, it is a matter of "finding yourself"; in chaos theory, it is a matter of dumb things finding each other.

One may be left wondering if some of the changes being sought are not incommensurable with one another and with the existing institutional structures out of which such changes must occur. M.'s response is that they are not. Instead he, like many others, looks for a higher-level order, a merged body of selves and organizations, a future of greater unity.

CEFKIN: When I ask a question in bringing together these elements of empowerment, community, and all that in business, you described it in terms of the survival of the organization. Which in itself is interesting, that the purpose is to fulfill the needs of the organization. I imagine, if you had decided to, you could have answered it the opposite way, which is, it's actually fulfilling the needs of individuals.

M.: I think that's where we're heading. I think there is going to be appreciation that the organization is people. The reason that survival of the organization is important is because if it doesn't survive, the people in it don't survive, don't grow, don't thrive. So, the organization is like it's own entity and it has a purpose beyond it's stated mission of producing products or making a profit— to thrive, to grow, and experiment.

Notes
This research was supported by the Institute for Research on Learning. Special thanks go to the members of the research team I worked with—Meredith Aronson,

Libby Bishop, Brigitte Jordan, Nancy Lawrence, Connie Preston, and Lindy Sullivan — as well as to Mazyar Lotfalian and Marc Wilson.

1. The selections presented here were made by the author from a longer interview. The conversation occurred in M.'s office in February 1995.

2. While a popular conception of reengineering is that it is a hard-line, cutthroat set of initiatives driven by desire for profits as against the well-being of employees, the originators of the trend, Michael Hammer and James Champy, envision it quite differently. "Fundamentally, reengineering is about reversing the industrial revolution. Reengineering rejects the assumptions inherent in Adam Smith's industrial paradigm — the division of labor, economies of scale, hierarchical control, and all the other appurtenances of an early-stage developing economy. Reengineering is the search for new models of organizing work. Tradition counts for nothing. Reengineering is a new beginning" (1993, 49). Their vision, too, is of an empowered workforce, cross- and multifunctional teams, and divisional participatory design, and engaged decision making.

3. While organizational restructuring at times does indeed occur, in practice explicit evidence of "empowerment" is embodied in more modest changes — a frontline manager may be granted previously denied signature authority for purchases up to a certain cost, or workers may evidence personal behavioral or attitudinal changes, such as the willingness to question managers.

4. Indeed these empowerment movements need to be correctly historically and structurally situated. Despite their languages of rights and justice, they arose more directly out of trends in business management as top-down initiatives aimed at increased productivity than as bottom-up labor movements. (The ideological and political positioning of individuals toward empowerment, however, are neither singular nor simplistic.) My own estimation at the catalysts of such movements suggests a confluence of a particular range of factors: political rights or identity movements of the 1960s on (empowered work groups mirror social movements for rights and self-determination), self-help, and New Age – oriented trends of the 1970s and 1980s (attention to spirituality and personal growth are embodied in the extremely popular works of business inspirational authors and seminar directors such as Stephen Covey), and the ongoing demands imposed by foreign competition (total quality management sustains the efforts to ward off competition).

5. The notion of self-directed or self-managed work groups follows on the reconceptualization, and often restructuring, of organizations as teams, a move inspired by interests in Japanese styles of management. That the teams are "self-managed" joins together notions. of collaborative decision making, accountability, and local control. Theoretically, self-managed teams have decision-making authority and the right to manage and organize their own work and functioning.

6. The Institute for Research on Learning (IRL), a nonprofit research organization founded in 1987 and supported through public funding and corporate foundation grants and contracts, has been the source for much of Docubis's thinking around learning issues. IRL's social-constructionist view of knowledge and learning is researched in and applied to both school and workplace environments. Researchers come from a variety of disciplines, including anthropology, artificial intelligence, education, and linguistics. Ethnographic methods form the primary basis of research.

7. Peter Senge, most renown for his book *The Fifth Discipline: The Art and Practice of the Learning Organization,* is the founder of the Center for Organizational Learning, a research organization at the Sloan School of Management at the Massachusetts Institute of Technology, a professor of organizational theory and development, and founding partner of the consulting firm Innovation Associates. Senge's five disciplines—systems thinking, personal mastery, mental models, building a shared vision, and team learning—form vital and interrelated elements used to build and/or realize a "learning organization," "an organization that is continually expanding its capacity to create its future" (1990, 14).

8. Margaret Wheatley, a professor at Brigham Young University and the president of the Berkana Institute, a charitable research foundation working on organizational design, was one of the first people to bring ideas developed in chaos theory to thinking on business management and organization. In her 1992 book, *Leadership and the New Science,* Wheatley argues that organizations would be best viewed as self-organizing systems and that it is only through yielding to chaos that true breakthrough thinking can emerge and that people and organizations can be true to their core values.

9. Covey is best known for his acclaimed *The Seven Habits of Highly Effective People* (1989). His work has a strong crossover appeal between business and mainstream readerships: *Seven Habits* was on the *Business Week* and *New York Times* best-seller lists more than five years running. Based in Utah, Covey has an international following, with his books sold in translation in over forty countries (Smith 1994, 118). Businesses are particularly big consumers of Covey's teachings, with many sending their management ranks through intensive training programs with Covey. Covey's philosophy is a blend of middle-class American traditional common sense, Christian virtue, and pragmatic will. The seven habits are: (1) be proactive, (2) begin with the end in mind, (3) put first things first, (4) think win/win, (5) seek first to understand, then to be understood, (6) synergize, and (7) sharpen the saw.

References

Hammer, Michael, and James Champy. 1993. *Reengineering the Corporation: A Manifesto for Business Revolution.* New York: Harper Collins.

Hammonds, Keith, Kevin Kelly, and Karen Thurston. 1994. "The New World of Work." *Business Week,* 17 Oct., 76–87.

Kearns, David, and David Nadler. 1992. *Prophets of the Dark: How Xerox Reinvented Itself and Beat Back the Japanese.* New York: Harper Collins.

Senge, Peter. 1990. *The Fifth Discipline: The Art and Practice of the Learning Organization.* New York: Currency Doubleday.

Smith, Timothy. 1994. "What's So Effective about Stephen Covey?" *Fortune,* 12 Dec., 116–24.

Wheatley, Margaret. 1992. *Leadership and the New Science: Learning about Organization from an Orderly Universe.* San Francisco: Berrett-Koehler.

4

COLOMBO-JAPANESE MIXTURES
AMIDST A CORPORATE REINVENTION

ON FOTO JAPÓN. *This piece presents a thorough examination from several points view of the adoption of an exoticizing creation of culture for a corporation, in this case a retail service corporation of photographic developer stores that has flourished as a chain in Colombia. It is amazing how an experiment so exotic and cultlike has succeeded in conventional business terms. On reflection, the elaborate exoticized work discipline through cultural embodiment that Foto Japon has introduced is an extreme version, employing the metaphors of a "natural" culture "out there" (Japan), of the sort of corporate culture that was being emphasized in the U.S. during the early 1980s. As Newfield and Perin document, more critical versions of culture have since replaced in the U.S. such pure community-building exercises in creating corporate myths. Yet Villaveces and his interlocutors indicate why conditions in contemporary Colombia might continue to be a receptive environment for such an exotic culture as Foto Japon's to work despite the transparency of its ideology, even to its employees.* – G. E. M.

*   *   *

I. Backstage

The history of contemporary Colombia has been imprinted by an ongoing struggle between two deeply rooted trends: on one hand, a rapidly increasing and virulent violence, begun over fifty years ago, that has taken over the cracks of contemporary daily life; on the other, an equally prolonged social quest, initiated countless times by multiple and heterogeneous social actors that convey the need to build collective spaces that seek to enhance a constantly diminished sense of political and social tolerance.

The upsurge of drug money and drug terrorism, together with the more evident incapacity of the Colombian elites to start aggressive political, social, and institutional reforms, has driven the country into a widespread criminality and into a massive disbelief in collective initiatives built on democratic ideals of justice and tolerance. Colombia on the verge of the twenty-first century pictures itself as a nation devoured by the ruling of the free market and the paralegal (outlaw) where uncompassionate individualism seems to be the unifying theme by which the chaotic is interpreted and more dramatically survived.

In the midst of this exhaustion and against this backdrop, private initiatives in the building of profit-generating enterprises have, not surprisingly, been successful. Born over ten years ago, Foto Japón, a 100 percent Colombian business specializing in photographic products and services with over 2,500 employees nationwide and sales of more than $45 million a year, has had to cope with the new challenges of an ever more competitive market. Unexpectedly, Foto Japón today presents itself as a mixture of the crafts of business-as-usual and a pedagogy for building up tolerance among its employees. Its owners, two middle-aged Colombians enamored with everything Japanese have found inspiration in Zen, Shinto, and Samurai philosophy, as well as in popular and traditional Japanese imagery for inventing a quite unique organization where mimicking what is rendered as the best of Japanese culture is a must.

II. Kabuki Theater?

In a shanty part of Bogotá where dust, pollution, and dirt sprout, and among the remains of what used to be a flourishing meat-market spot stands the five-floor building of the central offices of Foto Japón. The building, surrounded by warehouses, small neighborhood liquor stores, and a black market of raw meat and viscera, has the phantasmagoric quality of a ruin among ruins. Inside is a modest and desolate lobby, caught in between two security doors and filled only with a pair of cheap benches, a wooden desk, and a couple of employees dressed in kimonos who welcome and announce the visitors. After passing the second door, a wide staircase leads upstairs through a walking galleria of beautiful Japanese prints and posters from the world's most important museums. On each floor and cutting abruptly the artistic charm, carpets and posted signs remind the visitors to clean their shoes. Arriving at the top floor, one encounters a long white corridor with doors on each side that access either the executives' offices or the company's dining room. It doesn't take long to notice that everyone in the building wears, on top of their everyday garments, a kimono tied with a colored belt, or obi. One soon learns that the color of the obi represents time in the organization and not hierarchy.

The working spaces of Foto Japón are all similar and give the visitor the impression of an office environment with no spatial or hierarchical distinctions. The windows are all covered with a white cloth framed with thin bamboo sticks; the walls, all white, occasionally have a cluster of framed prints of ancient Japanese art; most of the offices have sliding bamboo doors and not much more than what is strictly necessary. The interviews were held in such an environment charged with overwhelmingly Japanese paraphernalia, quite distinct from the one outside, in the old meat market. Occasionally the interview routine was interrupted by a couple of warm invitations to join the executives for lunch. Foto Japón's dining room was not any different from the rest. In between empty white walls, except one that had six Japanese prints nicely arranged, lay a rectangular wooden table with twelve dining places, each with a complete set of bowls of different sizes and painted with Japanese motifs, wooden sticks, sushi, and plenty of tea. Before sitting down I was guided through their daily routine: first we did two minutes of head and neck rotations and limb stretching, then we all sat down and did a three-minute relaxation in which everyone was to clear their mind and rest; finally, I was told, it was prohibited to talk during lunch about anything dealing either with work or unpleasant matters. Before beginning to eat, the employees that are traditionally invited for lunch every day are welcomed and introduced to all. Lunch was served by three Foto Japón employees who had been trained by the main waiter of Hatsuhana, Bogotá's most famous Japanese restaurant. After cleaning ourselves with hot towels we were offered, as expected, a complete Japanese meal.

In such an environment—half familiar, half distinct—my clothing, clearly different from the employees' kimonos, dramatically showed my condition of intruder. Nevertheless, the warmth of my interviewees compensated by far my alien nature. Four key figures from the organization kindly responded to my persistent inquiry: Juan, one of the owners of Foto Japón, a character that could well be the emblematic figure of late twentieth century—entrepreneur, globetrotter, adventurer, mystic, and versed in a wide array of topics; Ignacio, expert in the latest techniques of management, with a broad trajectory in the Colombian business milieu, and a consultant and advisor to the board of Foto Japón at the time of the interview; Margarita, the executive vice president of the organization; and Paola, a member of the division of human resources.[1]

Plunging into the intertextual world of Foto Japón proved to be a constant discovery of different layers and depths that configure a truly postmodern late-century organization where collage, mimic, invention, and business all equally play a role in the creation of recreation of a global and local mix. What follows is a tour of these layers, their specificities, and their resonances with wider contexts.

III. Rituals, Sacralizations, and Pedagogy

In moving beyond the Japanese paraphernalia and digging a bit under the organization's internal structure, a world of rituals and sacralizations that spin around the idea of providing an integrated pedagogy to the workers is uncovered. The rituals, began as mere devices for differentiating the business and its employees from the competition, have become over time important components for identification with the organization and for the promotion of a "Japanese value system" within it. Obi ceremonies and oaths, the Obi Council, the Japanese meals, the Ninja Reports are all parts of a colorful spectrum of symbolic constructions through which respect and reference to the "Japanese value system" is enhanced and performed. As constituent elements of the rituals, two types of sacralizations are performed; each supported by a set of rules or moral and ethical codes, and by a consecrational artifact. These sacralizations operate either toward the outside of the organization or toward its inside. The former ones, condensed in Foto Japón's ten commandments and supported by Neko, a Japanese symbol of wealth and commercial disposition, stress the need to have proper attitudes toward customers and service. The latter ones, embodied in the organization's twelve laws and represented by the image of the mystic monk Daruma, focus on the reigning principles of internal cohesion and behavior.

Foto Japón's rituals and sacralizations operate primordially in the building up of moral subjects out of its employees, moral subjects deeply committed to work, to the organization, to high-quality service, and to family. A pedagogical enterprise seems to be at the backdrop of this mystical halo. The organization is thus converted into a learning site where respect for the other, personal and technical development, and love and admiration for the Japanese are constantly promoted.

Rituals

PAOLA: As soon as a person completes the process of selection and officially enters the organization, and before he is drilled with Foto Japón's philosophy, we ask him to do a Ninja Report. We ask the person to go to one of our selling points and act as a customer. Beforehand he is told what type of treatment he should expect to receive. He must be welcomed, informed about the services, and taken care of while at the store. Afterward we ask him to report on what he saw and how he felt. It is only then that we consider that he is prepared to receive a first drill of Foto Japón's philosophy.

JUAN: We began Japanizing the organization from the outside toward the inside. First it was only cosmetic and later it became the heart and soul of the organization. We started with adopting the kimono, then with introducing the belt or obi, which has different colors, making a parallel with the martial arts: each color representing the status of a person within the organization. Everybody started off with a plain color obi and from there we created the obi upgrade ceremonies. So we had to invent the ceremonies and the oath that accompanies each of them.

After three months in the organization a person upgrades to a white obi. She attends a training course and at the end she receives the corresponding obi. Upon receiving the obi the person recites an oath that says, "I swear to my God and my family Foto Japón that every time I meet a customer less than six feet away from me I'll look straight at his eyes, I'll smile, and welcome him." The first oath serves as a basis for developing an integrated relationship with the customer. Stressing the need to look straight in the eyes of the customer is very important since in our subjugated cultures the natives were not accustomed to look the Spaniards in the eye.

The second oath comes with the upgrading to a yellow obi, after a year with the organization, and it says, "I swear to my God and my family Foto Japón that every morning, after waking up, I'll do ten minutes of physical exercise and twenty sit-ups." What we want with this oath is to allow the person to become aware of their body and especially of their abdomen. The abdomen is the center of everything, if you don't have a good abdomen you'll have problems with your physical and mental equilibrium, therefore you'll be a bad worker and offer bad service.

The third oath comes from upgrading to the orange obi, after three years with the organization. In the ceremony we give the participants the book *How to Gain Friends*. In this case we recreate a Japanese tea ceremony, after which comes the oath. The oath says, "I swear to my God and my family Foto Japón that everyday I'll read ten minutes from the book *How to Gain Friends*." With this we are seeking to help the construction of better relations within work and at the home of the employees.

The fourth oath comes from upgrading to the blue obi, after five years with the organization. For this occasion the ceremony is very simple: we give each participant a package of ramen, an instant Japanese soup, and with it we give them a bowl and hot water. In three minutes the soup is ready and then they drink it. With this ceremony we want to stress the fact that the Japanese invests a very short time in eating, allowing more time for efficient work. In this case the oath is very special; it says, "I swear to my God and my family Foto Japón that for the rest of my life I will use silence as my most refined wisdom, as my most powerful strength, and as my best strategy." We are very inclined to chitchat and if there is one thing that one learns from the Japanese, it is the great importance they give to silence. Silence is a great weapon that stands for its own.

When people reach seven and ten years with the organization we'll invent the oaths for brown and black obis. Maybe we'll also have special ceremonies for each of these occasions.

Sacralizations

JUAN: The commandments were born first, then came the laws. The commandments are the way we synthesized the guidelines of the employee-customer relationship. These commandments must be followed daily by every employee, and every customer has the right to demand their compliance. The

Figure 1. Neko

commandments are: (1) the customer is always right; (2) never argue with the customer; (3) always repeat a job when the customer requires to do so; (4) never leave fingerprints in the negatives or in the prints; (5) ask the customer to check all the work before leaving the store; (6) never give the customer a poor quality job; (7) defend the interests of the customer by suggesting the cheapest ways to have a job done; (8) be always tidily presented (kimono, belt, white gloves, and nametag); (9) always smile and be kind; and (10) maintain a distance with the customer by always using *Sir* or *Madam*. Now each one of these commandments is a need. We must be able to make our employees understand that they have to be on the customer's side. Also each of the commandments is a by-product of experience; nothing came from theory or from projecting an ideal environment, instead they were born from absolutely real situations, from moments of true conflict between the customer and the employee. These are the minimum norms for maintaining good service.

The laws are more like a set of criteria for administrative decision making within the organization. And, like the commandments, they are a by-product of experience, of real situations within our working environment. The first is

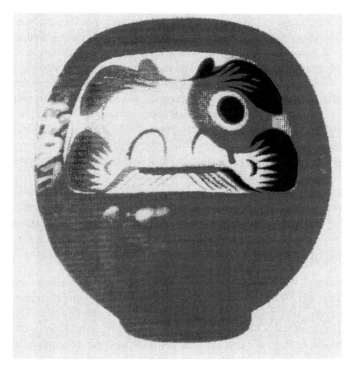

Figure 2. Daruma

the law on *courtesy.* I don't know if you remember a card game called Burro or Tute in which king kills horse, two kills king, and ace kills everything. Well, in a similar way, I think courtesy kills reason, just as reason kills force. The second is the law on *cleanliness;* its purpose is to make people understand the need to be very clean. The third is the law on *order,* which stresses the need to be an organized person. Then comes the law on *honesty;* the law on *logic,* which refers to the need to always think about what one is doing; the law on *justice;* the law on *punctuality;* the law on *formality,* which talks about the need to act according to the circumstances; the law on *distance,* which stresses the need to maintain emotional distance from the working companions; the law on *work,* which deals with the need to be productive; the law on *humbleness,* which deals with equality among all employees; and finally, the bamboo law, which stresses the need of being *flexible* and *noble.*

*

MARGARITA: As part of our philosophy we also have the Daruma and the cat Neko. These two deal more with the mystical aspect of the organization, and both are very important for us. Neko is very dear to us; the Japanese have it in their stores and usually next to the cashier. Neko has her left hand up inviting the customer in. She wears a collar with a rattle through which she protects the place from bad spirits; and she holds a coin in her right hand, symbol of infinite wealth. So Neko represents happiness and wealth. The other symbol is Daruma. He has many stories among the Japanese. One of those stories says that he was a very spiritual and intelligent monk who lived thinking restlessly about everything that surrounded him. He thought and ana- lyzed so much that he ended up turning into stone. Daruma is represented as a blind person and he is used for fulfilling the wish of a person, a family, or an organization: when making a wish one paints an eye on the figure promising that if the wish is granted then the other eye will be painted, so he'll be able to see again. We have him in most of our stores with one eye painted: five years ago the organization made the commitment to win the National Quality Award.[2] When we receive the award we'll paint him the other eye as gratitude.

Pedagogy

MARGARITA: After three years with the organization the person can upgrade to an orange obi. At this point we introduce the personal commitments. To have access to the orange obi the person must have complied with his first personal commitment: for example, a person can promise to stop smoking, and when she does so she can apply to the training course for upgrading her obi. The personal commitments are sent to the Obi Council in a closed enve- lope. The owners, the general managers, and the executive vice president have seats in the Obi Council; its purpose is to impart justice in defense of the em- ployee and to work on the resolution of internal conflicts. For example, if a salesperson feels that she has been wrongly treated by a manager, she can send a letter to the Obi Council saying that she wants to appeal to the council because she feels that an injustice has been committed. So the council works as a mediator between the manager and the salesperson, and the purpose of all this is to begin to build up a learning process among the employees about jus- tice and authority. This process is enhanced through the book *How to Gain Friends,* which we give to the people who upgrade to an orange obi. We con- sider this book a tool of permanent consultation since it has important mes- sages about the individual and his relation with others. The basic points we want to push through the book are the need to avoid criticism, discussions, and bad temper.

    We always try to emphasize that our philosophy must be applied in every- day life: at work, at home. If we are family at work we must be family at home. Many people have come to us saying that they like our philosophy, that it has helped them in their daily lives. What we seek really is to improve our relationships with others as well as to constantly achieve standards toward perfection in ourselves: one can always hope to be better than what one is now. A good example is the oath made when upgrading to a blue obi, the one about silence. We learned about silence by observing the Japanese negotiate: they are extremely diplomatic and by maintaining silence they gain strong and well thought-out positions. From them we have learned to listen, analyze, and then decide what is for our best interest.

*

PAOLA: A year ago there was consensus within the organization about the lack of quality in the products. At that time everybody was talking about quality circles, and someone from Methods and Organization[3] suggested that the only way to win the National Quality Award was to work in teams. She then called a meeting with all the executives of the organization and gave a talk in which she told them the well-known story of the frog: if one puts a frog in water and heats the water steadily, the frog doesn't feel the changes in temperature and ends up dead; instead, if one puts a frog in boiling water, she notices the danger and jumps away. She then said that the organization was like the frog that didn't notice the danger. Nobody reacted to the story! A few days later we decided to call the executives again, but this time we made them build an origami frog. After an hour of work the frog was ready, then we told them to destroy the frog. Everybody complained! Finally we said, "You see, the organization is like an origami. Let me ask you why you want to break it."

JUAN: I believe that the people whom have worked at Foto Japón have lived a quite unique experience. We have managed to offer them a bit of fantasy, of movie, of color; in general terms a positive and enriching experience. We've offered them something more than a salary, we've given them an experience. We've given them something more to talk about, to think. We've given them an environment that contrasts with their own, and part of our idea is to stimulate them to take part of that environment to their personal lives, to their houses, to their rooms. If a person manages to fix his room he manages to fix his house, and he won't be able to fix his room if he hasn't thought about fixing himself. I believe a person from Foto Japón is more open and with a better disposition to listen to what is going on in a model country like Japan. A person more willing to emulate, to feel closer to the model, and to believe that this is a good behavior.

IV. FX

Deep beneath the surface of Foto Japón is a complex intertextual world that unveils the unexpected dynamics of the confluence of local realities and imaginaries with imported hopes, philosophies, and artifacts. The special effects of intertextuality are played out in multiple registers ranging from the origin of

Foto Japón and the demystification of Hollywood's imagery to unconscious Colombian historical legacies that frame the Japanization of the organization in an unforeseen manner: Is Foto Japón a Japanization of Colombia? Or rather is it a Colombianization of Japan? Overall, the bottom line can be summarized in one of Juan's sentences: "We are not *imitating* but *adopting*." A sentence that, following Virilio (1995), questions the very word globalization. Foto Japón is not the intrusion of the global into the local but rather a concatenation of both; Foto Japón is not the colonization of the I from the Other but rather a site for the transformative possibilities of intertextuality and constant representational flux.

Myth of Origin

JUAN: To talk about Foto Japón we have to talk about its history, about how it came to be what it is today, about its virtues and defects. With the coming of computers and electronics the machines were made intelligent. Apparently Kodak, which was the owner of the Colombian photographic market, had been working at that time in the initial phases for developing a minilab; that is, an automated process for developing and printing film. Well then, the invention of those one-hour developing and printing machines made a revolution in the service. In the mind of the customer this was a major change: he could take the film to one place and see how his pictures came out, all in the same day! Two factors were key in imprinting success: not just the velocity of the whole process, but also the surprise of being able to see the photos immediately. It was like magic! In 1982 I saw the machine in a magazine so I decided to search for one. First I went to Los Angeles and couldn't find it, then to Tokyo and couldn't find it. Finally I arrived in Hong Kong and saw the machine just once. Why did this happen?

On one hand, one-hour photography was still a very expensive process and it required high volumes of customers; but on the other hand, the traditional business was deeply rooted everywhere, there were sites for collecting film and sending it elsewhere for developing. It was an easy way of making money: they didn't need technology, they didn't need labs, and they reached good margins of profit. But one has to mention also the type of city Hong Kong is: technology and services are a big thing there, it is like a place where all the commercial phenomena are caricatured. Hong Kong is a place of overwhelming competition and a monstrous commercial density, and this is because the Chinese are the best bargainers in the planet. There is a saying that goes: to beat an Armenian in business you need two Jews, but to beat a Chinese you need two Armenians.

Well, in Hong Kong was where I found the machines I was looking for. I saw them operating and the concept inspired in me much trust. I located the manufacturers: a Japanese enterprise called Noritsu, I contacted them, went back to Japan, bought a machine, took a training course and returned to Colombia. It was then when I started the business that was called Foto Una Hora. I thought it was the most convenient name and it really had no sense calling it otherwise. As soon as we began opening up stores around the city, publicizing the products, and selling, competition popped up. Our competition began using the slogan Foto Una Hora. It was very difficult for us to build up a good will using a generic slogan. It was then when I thought that Foto and Japón are close concepts. Japan is leader in cameras, in massive film processing, in efficiency, speed, quality. So the name was born: Foto Japón.

Bye-Bye Hollywood

JUAN: For many years now I have been deeply impressed by the Japanese. Traveling around the world is like seeing a movie of different cultures, and in my case the most powerful impression came from Japan, and this was because all my Hollywoodesque images of the Japanese came crashing to the ground. Before my trips, for me the Japanese were either a bunch of loud soldiers always defeated by the American, or something similar to the images of *Madame Butterfly:* something very volatile, very romantic, but weak and almost dumb. When I first traveled to Japan, in 1965, I was surprised by the beauty, but above all by the respect for beauty, the respect for nature, the respect for everything that surrounds the individual. A place where the *respect for the form* is extremely marked. The Japanese can teach us so many things: for example, you never see a Japanese dressed inappropriately for an occasion, they have a very profound sense of aesthetics. I think success and aesthetics have something in common. It's amazing to see such a huge human density in which everyone tries their best not to bother the rest; compared to the West, where it's exactly the opposite. We try very hard to be different from the rest whereas the Japanese tries to pass on inadvertently. They have a wise saying that goes: "Every loose nail is exposed to the hammer." I have always admired the Japanese culture, the seriousness of their business, their impact in the markets, their history, and to these one has to add my own readings about Japan, identifying the false images created by the Americans. Historically the Japanese have been admirable, they have always been a great power and that is because of its people, I would dare say solely because of its people.

The Kindergarten of Japanization

When we first established the business, our intention was not to create a philosophy for the organization but just an image.

                                                                    Juan

After starting off with the first Foto Japón, everything was given for us to begin reinforcing the image with a philosophy.

Margarita

A progressive understanding of Japan as Foto Japón's paradigm for cultural and organizational change has led to the need of starting to move from an image toward a philosophy; from an imposition of representations (kimono and obi), to an apparent understanding of cultural change as an exchange achieved through the organization's pedagogy. The movement from image to philosophy in Foto Japón produces a *representational exchange* between sameness and otherness, leaving open the hope and unresolved the question for an integrated *experiential exchange* between sameness and otherness to take place. The paradox that unfolds lies on the inalienable need of first seeking a clear-cut differentiation from the rest so as to be able, later on, to argue for the inevitable need of minimizing the difference—a paradox that seems to be sustained and constantly fed throughout Colombian society.

JUAN: After the name came the Japanization of our stores. The Japanization began with the use of the kimono. It was very convenient because it does not just serve the purpose of strengthening our image but it's also a very flexible garment: all the same size, no buttons, it's comfortable. Everybody liked the idea. Then I began letting the employees know about the Japanese culture and its people. For doing so we used Japanese paintings. Soon everyone accepted the idea that it's not inconvenient to recognize that a good example is worth imitating. What we really try to do is not imitate but adopt Japanese values, so we began building up the bases for our philosophy to which we refer as the three pillars, like a trinity. I don't know why the triangle is a constant in mysticism, in religious thinking. I have been a judicious student of the religious and I feel grateful for everything that can widen my understanding of wisdom. The first two pillars are, on one hand, happiness, because it is the only goal and reason of being; and on the other hand, quality, because it refers directly to the need of always striving to be a better human being, and because it's the only path toward happiness. Happiness is a state of consciousness that one reaches when noticing that one has changed. The third pillar is very Zen, it is the basis of Zen, and that is the present, the now. People mostly think about what they're doing in the present, not what they did in the past or what they'll do in the future. The present is a very difficult thing for our Latin temperament. In our work we don't think about what we're doing and from there the problems of quality arise. The laws and commandments are a development of these three principles. I've found esotericism to be a good venue in which to seek for values, because, sadly, the religious tradition in our schools has been very poor. The Jesuits give enormous importance to the will but their

Figure 3. Cover of an obi upgrade solicitation form.

major problem is management. Poor management made the company [Jesuits] inefficient.

*

MARGARITA: "We still have a lot to learn from and about them [the Japanese]. They are very sensible, very humble, they appreciate the family, they appreciate work, and they are people that are always struggling and working for a common goal. And toward that is where we want to move, we want to have better products, better human qualities. When we are visited by suppliers, by important customers, by people from the banks, they all seem very interested in our philosophy. They all ask, Why the kimono? People always find interesting what is different from them. We consider that differentiating ourselves from the rest is a great advantage that we have. With time the decoration of our stores has changed quite a lot: we have come closer to the Japanese. We now have objects imported by us directly from the East so we are able to give more importance to Japan itself.

*

PAOLA: The first time people go to an obi ceremony we give them a package of Japomicina.[4] Japomicina is simply a pack of sparkies.[5] The box is very nice, it has a prescription written on it saying that the tablets inside make you feel good while at the same time increase the quality of your work. It also says that they are not harmful to your health, that they help you when depressed and have no side effects.

"It's an exclusive product from Foto pón. They are known as motivation tablets and they are a refreshing a sweet way of remembering the im tance of a positive attitude. Each e ployee receives a package of *Japo cina* at every Obi upgrade."—*Gra Revelaciones. Foto Japón.*

JUAN: It's not that in this time we are Japanizing more the organization. Instead it is the result of a process that, as I told you before, began with a makeup then turned into decoration until it reached deeper levels within the organization. And we are still in that process. We are actually enhancing the Japanizing components. It is an *adaptation* and not an *adoption* of the Japanese. Many times I've tried to hire someone from Japan but it doesn't work, maybe because we are walking toward the mountain and not pushing the mountain toward ourselves. We can't push Japan toward us, instead we have to move toward the value model that it offers. I think we are at the kindergarten of Japanization.

Striving for First Grade?

MARGARITA: We are now emphasizing and working more on the philosophy of the organization because in the nineties we've had an accelerated growth: we've opened more stores and hired more people. We have offices in various parts of the country so we have to keep up the diffusion and the rein-

Figure 4. Package of Japomicina

forcement of our philosophy. Nowadays the obi ceremonies are more beauti-ful, the employees have a four-day training course before the ceremony that includes photography courses and a revision of all the details that make the organization. We also have the daily lunch at the main office in which every day six guests are invited to have lunch with the board. We're working in the conversion of the dining room into a Japanese space, we have daily routines before beginning to eat, and the food is very similar to the Japanese. Overall, this is an environment in which people have the chance to feel more like they are in a Japanese surrounding. All this we do because we admire them so much.

*

VILLAVECES-IZQUIERDO: Margarita mentioned to me that a big effort was being made to make the ceremonies more special. All in the mood of a better internalization of the "Japanese" in the people.

PAOLA: That's right! We are trying to work hard on those aspects. People had come to the point of knowing the laws and commandments by heart be-cause at an obi upgrade they would need to know them, so everything re-mained at the written level. We need to correct this, otherwise, people feel that everything is just a lie. I think they need not know everything by heart but they do need to experience the laws and commandments.

Daguerreotype

1. BACKGROUND: CIVIL ETHICS AND MORAL SUBJECTS. In 1880 the Escuela Nacional de Minas (National School of Mining) was funded in Medellín. The inaugurating address stressed the need of transforming the religious enthusiasm so widespread in the Colombian population into a set of professional virtues that would allow for the construction of a moral subject out of the workers. The reigning ethical principles of these professional virtues were to be imagined in a formal and concrete moral behavior detached of any direct relation with religion. Tulio and Pedro Nel Ospina,[6] founders of the Escuela and representatives of a social class that confronted theoretical discussions in the terrain of the practical, saw in the value system of the industrial revolution the set of professional virtues that they sought. "The need to modify the national character by forming a new type of man that, without rejecting his ancestral Hispanic virtues, would have the sense of work and efficiency of the Anglo-Saxon. This was to be the ideal of the newly born Escuela de Minas" (Mayor-Mora 1989, 39). Ethics and utilitarianism were merged in the construction of a moral subject and hence consolidated in the search for these "professional virtues." These abstract postulates were reinforced by the lecture on industrial economy taught during the first years of the Escuela. It was then that the human factor appeared for the first time in Colombia as a constituent element of business management. The human factor was to be appropriated by known rules and methods that incorporated, as novelty, qualities that had a direct relation with the educational backgrounds of the workers. Nevertheless, the novelty of the discourse relied heavily in a conscious return to tradition: "When the first entrepreneurs began to organize their factories they promoted and kept an array of egalitarian values and close personal relationships which have their origin in the eldest histories of Antioquia.[7] Social egalitarianism, the lack of prejudice toward work, and the closeness between owners and workers were all values inherited from the mining, agricultural, and commercial activities of the region, which confronted the rigid hierarchical models of Taylorism. [In these factories] the owner soon became the technical teacher and model of exemplary moral behavior for the workers. It was through the daily activities that he would transmit his disciplinary (and professional) virtues to them" (Mayor-Mora 1989, 271). With the expansion and growth of business came the endangerment of these established links; in order to preserve them, the need to consolidate the figure of the owner as father, judge, counselor, teacher, and friend was understood as the primal factor for maintaining the internal cohesion of the factory, thus keeping alive the ideal of Tulio and Pedro Nel Ospina.

2. MIDDLEGROUND: ALEJANDRO LÓPEZ AND SCIENTIFIC MANAGEMENT. This behavior, rooted in a historical legacy, was taught and enhanced throughout the course of industrial economy. In 1912 this course was offered for the first time in Latin America by Alejandro López[8] at the Escuela Nacional de Minas under the name of scientific management. "The first lessons of industrial economy outlined the new type of capitalist businessman that was required for the country: a man with a rational behavior, with technical capacities, with virtues of character and with a sociological vision of the problems associated with his business. This was the ideal for Alejandro López" (Mayor-Mora 1989, 64). López's vision, according to Alberto Mayor-Mora, was built on the principles of classical economy, in particular the marginalist school of Lis and Marsella, as well as the French sociological school as understood by Tarde.[9] This combination allowed López to argue for a system of values, beliefs and ideals that created a certain degree of social coercion over the individual, a coercion that had an important effect over every economic activity.

3. FOREGROUND: BUSINESS AND MORAL SUBJECTS. López's teachings and insights were soon to be carried to the inner space of the factory, a space not just suited for industrial production but also for personal development: the factory was then understood as a site in which, on the one hand, the search for personal achievement was associated with the search for factory efficiency; and on the other, as a site in which the workers could encounter self-realization and personal compromise. This last task was suited "not just with the determinate actions of the manager, whose paternal image contributed for the workers identification of the factory as a vital space, but also with the collective role played by the Catholic Church in translating to the factories popular and community feelings" (Mayor-Mora 1989, 252). The former actions were accompanied by a severe unfolding of moral control inside and outside the working space in order to avoid any disassociations between labor and family life. This control was aligned with the modes adopted since the turn of the century by the Jesuits to orient the newly born Colombian working class. In 1916 and as enforcement to these processes of identification and moral construction, areas of propaganda were fomented within the factories for the promotion of "good habits and adequate readings" for the workers, without losing sight of the utilitarian goals of ethics: "Multiple acts within work, said López, have their roots in a moral order; an individual who is taming his will and seeking self-control that is, completing his auto-regulation and accumulating force, produces excellent service" (Mayor-Mora 1989, 421). Excellent service and the sense of commitment to the factory were at the bottom line of *living* the morals.

4. THE COMPOSITION: THE RETURN OF THE UNCONSCIOUS. The daguerreotype seems to be a suitable metaphor to talk about the unconscious. Playing with the idea put forward by Benjamin and Freud on the historical affinity between psychoanalysis and photography has provided not only an aesthetic spin in this article through which the connections between the history of a Colombian management school and the case of Foto Japón are traced, but also a haunting

discovery. In an informal gathering with Juan, and after writing up this section of the article, I learned that he was a former student from the Escuela Nacional de Minas. On the question of whether he recalled stories or legacies within the Escuela about its origins or about the figure and teachings of Alejandro López, he responded that he didn't. Nevertheless, the resonances are evident. Juan, without knowing, could have been the best student of Alejandro López, if only López had lived long enough to be his teacher. Furthermore, Juan seems to understand the need to shift from the ethical model of the industrial revolution, suggested by the Escuela's founders as ideal, toward Japan, the emblematic model of the postmodern.

V. Composite Photograph

Francis Galton, an English scientist, explorer, and anthropologist, cousin of Charles Darwin, and creator of the word *eugenics,* invented in 1877 the technique of composite photography. This technique allows for the building up of composites through the manipulation of images. In the 1990s this technique has been extended to digital computer graphics making possible the dynamic transformation of an original image into a set of different ones. Computer composite generated imagery has radically changed the way photographic dynamics is understood.

A similar change has occurred in what we render as history and national and cultural identity. These concepts as traditionally understood have ceased to exist. Instead they have become dynamic composites that play off their transformative possibilities accordingly to contextual settings, situated gazes, and political agendas. Composites as such imply constant ruptures and reconfigurations. Composite history might be a way for opening up wider possibilities for Foucauldian genealogies, as suggested by Juan's and Ignacio's readings below; whereas composite national or cultural identities as sought in Foto Japón might lead the path to a more profound understanding of the way the declaratory and prescriptive functions of identity operate (Burgess 1994). When the status of identity is declared as a lack it calls for the urgency of redefining it, for example, through organizational pedagogical systems. It is then the prescriptive's function to provide a raw model in which to base the pedagogical enterprise. The pitfalls of this diagnosis and its search for solution unfold in Foto Japón's overaestheticization, in the organization's arguments for legitimating the need for a performative cultural translation, and in its own contradictory understanding of tolerance.

Printing Histories: Original and Copy

The evolution of business, of artifacts associated with its cycles of expansion and contraction, of management theory and its conceptual circulation on specific world routes and sites, leave open the possibility of rewriting histories in various different terms. These new genealogies constitute an important asset in the imagination of entrepreneurs and as such, reveal illuminating fault lines and hidden connecting traces that run back and forth from north to south, from east to west, overrunning established historical and spatial boundaries. Where and what makes history? Are there traces that show the dissolution in time and the mixture in space of past events that configure today's beliefs?

JUAN: I don't know if you remember that some time ago the places for developing film were small spaces with a counter and a person that, after receiving the film, would put it away in a drawer. These places were known as Estudios Fotográficos. Then a person from Kodak would pick up the film and send it to the developing facilities in Rochester. After a week you would return to the place and get your pictures in an envelope. That was a photoshop in Colombia years ago. And these places were packed with ads from the four manufacturing houses: Kodak, Fuji, Agfa, and Konica. These four are the only major manufacturers and they represent the countries with most solid technological development. But Kodak won World War II. The bombings in the last days of the war were not to assure a victory, because this was already a fact, but to destroy the great industrial empires of Germany and Japan. If one traces back the market share of the four biggest manufacturers one finds interesting information: in the fifties Kodak had 98 percent of the market; in the sixties it dropped to 65 percent; in the seventies, to 60 percent; and today Kodak holds only 40 percent of the market. What happened?

*

IGNACIO: The concepts of quality management were born in the fifties in the U.S. but curiously enough they weren't applied there, basically because of the industrial and commercial strength that came after the war: Japan and Germany were ruined, and England and France were heavily damaged, but the U.S. was at its best. So they had all the markets at their disposal and no need for implementing new management systems or methods. The concepts of quality management had no resonance in the U.S. but they did have in Japan. All these were spread in Japan at a moment when the Japanese desperately needed improvements in productivity. The latter led them not to limit themselves solely to questions on capital and raw material but also, and most important, to concerns on productivity through employee training and quality control. This didn't happen in the U.S., where quality control came after the production process and not before. In the U.S. the only concern was on producing and any product that didn't meet the standards was simply thrown away. The Japanese couldn't afford the waste, they required a structure, an organization, and maximum productivity.

When the U.S. management gurus arrived in Japan, around 1952, they were welcomed and soon led the way to what is known today as reengineering, quality circles, quality management, and so on. So all these theories born in the U.S. are developed in Japan and later on exported to other countries. This process began in the late sixties, and it has a logic of its own: after the war Japan was looked upon as a country that made poor imitations, that manufactured cheap products, and that was satisfying a market of the unnecessary. Japan was never seen as a potential commercial enemy. It is true that they began imitating: they would purchase an article, dismantle it and try to figure out what kind of improvements could be made, what components could be simplified, what things they could do better and at lower costs, where they could innovate, and by doing this they took the advantage. Forty years ago there was no Japanese organization at the top ten financial institutions in the world; today, nine are Japanese. Photographic technology, watches, cars— Japan is among the best. And all of this has been achieved because they are constantly seeking for better ways to do things. Today the U.S. and Europe are the ones that are imitating Japan's management techniques. It's ironic and anachronistic because these techniques were developed in the U.S., but I guess there are no prophets in their own land.

The Respect for the Form

The Japanese obsession as played out in the organization seems to be caught in the web of portraying a raw model essentially characterized by its respect for the form and guided and motivated by the belief that aesthetics alone leads to success. The intertextual world of Foto Japón is thus the reigning incorporation of the power and performance of constant simulations. The Japanese, first appropriated as a spectacle worth emulating, is reassimilated within the organization also as spectacle, creating what Ignacio acutely identifies as simulated identities, simulated ethics, and simulated cohesion. This endless recycling of images, icons, texts, and styles as mere representational exchange, veils and seduces simultaneously: it veils the organized chaos that lies beneath the well thought-out aestheticization of the organization, at the same time that it provides an exotic halo whose gravitational field seduces even the most stubborn.

PAOLA: People have loved the results of a major ritualization! And they have told me so in various occasions. They don't care about the complications involved in an obi ritual. For example, in the five-day training course for upgrading to an orange obi, people have to be in the Japanese Room[10] from 6:00 to 8:30 in the morning. Among other things they have to do fifty push-ups. Then people feel alive again, motivated, and they feel they're gaining something new. Somebody once asked an employee what had he gained and what had he lost from upgrading his obi; the employee responded, "I couldn't see my family in the mornings for a week, but instead my wife now will never have to iron my old obi again!"

*

VILLAVECES-IZQUIERDO: How do you perceive the adaptation of the "Japanese" within the organization?

IGNACIO: I think that the employees feel a special sympathy for the Japanese because our cultures are very inclined to mythical thinking. People feel as being part of a family but in reality there is no family within the organization, just an appearance. The employee feels he belongs to a family because everybody wears a kimono and uses an obi, but not because there is a real sense of teamwork and common goals. I also believe this schema serves to trick the employee: they are not well paid but they remain in the organization because they feel that eating with sticks once a year with the board or having a blue obi is very important. It's the myth that has been created. What happens is that the laws, commandments, and purposes are very nice on paper, but people at the upper levels of the organization don't practice them. In a similar way, people react with extreme indulgence because everybody applies the laws at their convenience and at the end what is left is a completely organized chaos. Symbolism has been pushed to its limits with the idea that it alone can generate a change in attitude. An employee once told me that he didn't understand why people with blue obis didn't obey such and such laws and nothing happened. This produces negative incentives as a result of adopting a philosophy just in figurative terms.

VILLAVECES-IZQUIERDO: If people feel such incongruencies how do you explain that they feel simultaneously such a fascination toward the organization?

IGNACIO: People feel the incongruencies very clearly, but if you suggested a change, they would revolt. They love what is written! I think this is because most of the people in the organization come from very modest stratas and they find in these symbols something to grab to, even if it's only a simulated identity, or a simulated cohesion.

Cultural Translation

In one conversation with Juan I recall him saying that really it didn't matter if it was Japan, or science fiction, or anything of the kind that was adapted as raw model for building up a moral subject within the organization. In Foto Japón's case, Japan was taken as an ideal value system because chance and an already made model met in Juan's imagination. As such, the raw model adopted within the organization is, as all social constructs are, arbitrary. Its own legitimation comes only from imputing a status of a lack in the formation of a Colombian national and cultural identity, as Juan says. It is then that the Japanese is legitimated as something to be read from the specificity of Foto Japón's gaze, as well as something to be appropriated in the invention of the organization's pedagogy, its ritual, its myths, and its sacralizations—a culture to be consumed.

Ironically, Foto Japón's unfolding of cultural translation has reached the point so familiar in the history of anthropology: the enchantment of simply consuming the Other. Foto Japón embodies an emblematic double bind of postmodernity: while being part of the natural site for promoting consumerism, it has turned also into a site in which the corporate message that "commodities make the man" is actively performed and consumed. An ironic activity of consumption that unfortunately has not made its way to be an ironic mode of self-consciousness. The Japanese, said Ignacio above, began by purchasing articles that they would later dismantle in order to seek possible improvements or components that could be simplified. Indeed, a haunting similitude with the anthropological quest.

JUAN: I have been very impressed by the Japanese culture: the seriousness of their business, the impact of their products in the market, their history. Historically, the Japanese have been admirable, they have always been a major power and this is because of its people, I would even venture to say that solely because of its people. On the other hand, our culture lacks a history of its own, a tradition. With the Spaniards came the end of the native culture, and they didn't leave, as an exchange, much of a culture of their own. Sadly, we have lost our tradition. In the Japanese you see the importance of religious ceremonies, of the visits to the temple, not as a social gathering but as proof of a profound respect for their tradition. We lack that sense of respect, we think, not very convincingly, that we have the most beautiful country, that our people are the best but our pride as a nation is so small.

PAOLA: The Japanese always work in a team, they have a collective consciousness. The collective consciousness is the consciousness of the Spirit. The Spirit only appears as collective, never as individual, that is why they have so many gods. Just take a look at a Shinto temple. One god really doesn't work. Because of our culture and our religion we are individualistic, we work alone, and that is why quality circles can hardly work in this country.

VILLAVECES-IZQUIERDO: Somebody mentioned to me the existence of a high turnover of employees at the lowest levels of the organization.

PAOLA: I think the high turnover of personnel in the organization is due first to the fact that they are required to internalize a set of laws and behavioral standards that are alien to them; and second, because we Colombians don't like order and discipline, and when we feel someone is imposing them on us, we simply leave.

VILLAVECES-IZQUIERDO: In what levels of the organization is this turnover high?

Figure 5. Advertisement from the publicity campaign of
1994. The text reads, "The tree grows as its roots move
deeper. let's give importance to history and tradition."

PAOLA: In the lowest levels, and let me explain you why: in the highest levels of the hierarchy, people have access to a more profound culture, so it is easier for them to assimilate elements from another culture. They can feel themselves as not belonging to it, but surely they can manage to assimilate it. But in the lowest levels, people's own culture has not even been appropriated, and that is because we lack a sense of identification with our own culture. We are not Spaniards or natives, we don't know for sure what we are, and maybe because our identification lies in a mix we are not able to recognize it.

VILLAVECES-IZQUIERDO: How do you translate the "Japanese" to this level of the organization?

PAOLA: Well, I work a lot with group dynamics. I help a person that is very important in the organization, he is like the keeper of the philosophy, like a master. He is in charge of transmitting the philosophy. He keeps things hidden so he is able to create a sense of mystery around the philosophy of the organization. Then people feel attracted to discover the mystery, to penetrate it. So we work together with the people, with theater, with collage, with games through which the employees begin to make sense and internalize the laws and commandments.

VILLAVECES-IZQUIERDO: Let's take the case of the bamboo law and its concept of flexibility. How do you manage its internalization?

PAOLA: We don't achieve that at a first instance. Really what we do is to make the person think about the concept of flexibility. We tell them not to impose on anyone, not to fight positions. Instead, we ask them to identify common goals so it's easier for any type of relationship to work. And we are talking not only about relations with clients, but also family relationships. If you fight a position with your wife, you will never reach an understanding, but if both have a goal as a couple things will surely work out. That is flexibility!

VILLAVECES-IZQUIERDO: Does the increased ritualization of the ceremonies play a role here?

PAOLA: Of course! People are now *living* the laws and commandments and not just repeating them by heart.

What Tolerance Are We Talking About?

Tolerance and its significance have a close connection not just with the way the subject constructs his relation toward difference, but also on how he constructs himself. On the question, How is the Other configured from the I? and How is the Other recognized? it is important to recall how the Colombian self is constructed. The widely accepted belief in the dominant Colombian imagination in a lack of a cultural and national identity, especially in the lower classes, has led to an exacerbated admiration toward the non-Colombian. The lack of cultural and national identity is then substituted with the adoption of external models of identification through which a kind of cultural eugenics is hoped for. Although many of these models call for a profound respect for the Other, their specific Colombian readings and assimilation renders them as new sources for intolerance toward the Colombian: the thirst for differentiation and the fear for Colombianness are rooted in a deep intolerance toward the national Other, while both simultaneously cherish an uncritical fascination and seduction for the non-Colombian.

VILLAVECES-IZQUIERDO: Many of the laws you've invented deal with issues around the creation of tolerance, a key question in contemporary Colombia.

JUAN: It's a difficult question. I have never thought about tolerance, I've thought about courtesy, formality, silence, but that doesn't mean tolerance. Tolerance can mean so many things. For example, it can mean not paying attention to situations that one considers to be wrong; or it can mean knowing how to manage different situations with the clients because we have to be tolerant to all their demands; or it can also mean knowing how to deal with a mistaken behavior inside the organization so it doesn't lead into a conflict. In any case, maybe the way we are stressing the need of courtesy and the avoidance of confrontation has had an effect on the internal well-being of the organization. Maybe then we can say that we are learning to be more tolerant.

*

VILLAVECES-IZQUIERDO: Up to what point does the philosophy of the organization transcend the working environment? I think it's an important question if one considers the wider context in which we are enmeshed.

MARGARITA: People have assimilated everything quite well. Many of them do talk about the benefits that our philosophy has imprinted in their daily relationships with friends and family. Twelve years ago we had serious problems with the employees: they confronted the customers, they fought, and one even ended up in jail. Along the years things have changed radically. Now the people are different, they are more humble and that is because one of the laws is about humbleness. Inside the organization everybody, no matter what their hierarchy is, is called by their first name, without meaning a lack of respect or a questioning of authority. Now we don't have any of those situations of violence in the working environment that we had ten years ago.

*

VILLAVECES-IZQUIERDO: If we contextualize the attempts within the organization in what is Colombia today, one could think that all the effort of "Japanizing" has a purpose of building up a culture of tolerance within the working environment. How do you react to this from your own perspective?

IGNACIO: I believe there is a gap between the paper and the practice. So on many occasions people end up just simulating a behavior. Besides, there are so many other considerations. The way the Japanese work is not simply a management strategy, it is also a deeply rooted philosophy, a religion, a culture, a tradition that cannot be simply transposed from one place to another.

VILLAVECES-IZQUIERDO: Then we would be talking not just about simulated identities, as you mentioned before, but also about simulated ethics.

IGNACIO: Of course! I know many cases within the organization in which violations of ethics are dismissed because of years with the organization. There was a specific case that bothered me quite a lot: a manager of one of the stores was stealing from the organization, he got caught, and it was decided not to fire him because he was a good salesman! For me that has no sense, no logic. I believe that type of tolerance is simply fear. Fear of not putting into practice their own predicament, fear of retaliation, fear of change. I told you before about the existence of an organized chaos within the organization, and this is so because they are afraid to change. They believe that changing rooted attitudes can be traumatic for the individual whom they say they value deeply, but in many ways they really don't value the individual as such. I had the opportunity to participate in one of those training courses for an obi upgrade, and I found that people in the lower levels of the organization are very intelligent, with clear thinking about many things, and then I asked myself why it is, then, that they are treated as children. They don't give people an opportunity to learn, to hold things in their own hands, to have responsibilities, to think and act on their own. They prejudge people without giving them any opportunity for change.

Notes

This article is dedicated to the memory of Ignacio, my father. I am grateful to Rocío Rubio, who not only helped in the transcriptions but gave acute commentaries to sections of the manuscript.

1. All the interviews were conducted in Spanish, and all the translations are my own.

2. The National Quality Award is granted by the government to organizations that comply with defined standards of processes, products, and organizational quality.

3. Methods and Organization is a division in charge of defining employees' functions, job descriptions, and responsibilities.

4. The box of Japomicina has imprinted the following words: "Make your customer feel right by feeling right yourself. Happy, optimist, technical, organized, jovial, kind, positive, risky, novel. Foto Japón always thinks about you and your well-being."

5. Sparkies is a brand of small chocolate pellets.

6. Pedro Nel Ospina was a general from the times of the civil wars of the country. He began the textile industry in Medellín, and was made part of the "Ciudadanos Colombianos" (Colombian citizens), who at the turn of the century actively sought for a new Colombian society. Pedro Nel Ospina was elected president for the period 1922–26. He is considered to be the starter of the process of industrialization in Colombia, as

well as promoter of important changes in part of the public administration, and in the educational and banking systems.

7. Antioquia is a department of Colombia; its capital is Medellín.

8. Alejandro López was one of the first Colombian economists. Trained in Europe during the first decade of the century, López was a key figure in the intellectual and pedagogical movement that led the bourgeoisie toward the modernization of Colombia.

9. F. Lis was a German economist at the turn of the nineteenth century. His perspectives served López to contextualize the economic thinking to a poor and underdeveloped country as Colombia.

A. Marsella was one of the precursors of the marginalist school in economics. His influence over López was important especially in reference to the notions of work, cost control, and management.

Jean-Gabriel Tarde (1843–1904) was a sociologist and criminologist whose theory of social interaction emphasized the individual in an aggregate of persons, which brought him into conflict with Émile Durkheim's theory of society as a collective unity. Tarde held that invention was the source of all progress and that all innovations were imitations that differed in degree and kind. Following Hegel's dialectics, Tarde argued for the oppositional arisals of both varied imitations and the new and the old in culture. As a result, an adaptation would take place, an adaptation that was in itself an invention.

10. Foto Japón's Japanese Room has a large and low rectangular wooden table and zafus (Japanese sitting cushions) arranged throughout the room. The obi upgrading ceremonies are held in this space.

References

Burgess, Peter. 1994. "European Borders: History of Space/Space of History." *Ctheory: Electronic Journal of Theory, Technology and Culture* 17, no. 1–2: 1–9.

Jaramillo-Uribe, Jaime, et al. 1982. *Manual de Historia de Colombia*. Vol. 3. Bogotá: Procultura.

Mayor-Mora, Alberto. 1989. *Etica, Trabajo y Productividad en Antioquia*. Bogotá: Tercer Mundo.

Virilio, Paul. 1995. "Speed and Information: Cyberspace Alarm!" *CTheory: Electronic Journal of Theory, Technology and Culture* 18, no. 3: 1–6.

5

Storying Corporate Futures:
The Shell Scenarios

ON A HUMANIST AT THE HEART OF CORPORATE PLANNING. *This piece comes closest to how academic and corporate discourses are aligned ideologically. What Shell has committed to is very much like academic wisdom about contemporary culture—with the emphasis on the nature of culture as myth and narrative, openness to change, flexibility, and dealing in multiple versions and variations. This is not surprising since Shell has internalized and listens closely to a process of academic consultation, which this piece documents through its rapporteur, Dr. Betty Sue Flowers.*

The function of corporate planning occasions a mode of thoroughgoing culture building within the corporation among Shell managers worldwide, given the importance and mystification (for example, giving the scenarios the status of top-secret documents) the leadership has lent the planning process. Perhaps because this process of working with alternative scenarios is so attractive for critical scholars in the level of reflexive self-questioning and openness about the world it deals with—because it is so "enlightened," in their terms—the extent to which it might still function as a kind of managerial technology, tied in very specific ways to less flexible interests, is overlooked here. – G. E. M.

* * *

> . . . night has fallen,
> and the Barbarians have not come.
> And some of our men, just in from the border,
> say there are no barbarians any longer!
> Now, what is going to happen to us without
> the Barbarians? They were, those people, after all,
> a kind of solution.

> —C. P. Cavafy, quoted on the cover of Shell's
> *Global Scenarios 1992–2020,* edited by Betty S. Flowers

Betty S. Flowers received her Ph.D. in English from the University of London; she is professor of English at the University of Texas. Author of two volumes of poetry, including *Extending the Shade* (1990), she collaborated, in the role of editor, with Bill Moyers on *World of Ideas* (1989), and on the books and public television series *Joseph Campbell and Power of Myth* (1988) and *Healing and the Mind* (1993). Her primary interest is myth. She spends much time in the business world as a consultant, and at the time of our first interview was serving as editor ("midwife," as she terms it) to books on diverse topics: the poetry of Christina Rossetti, the dreams of Vietnam vets, the life and times of a Texas artist, new visions for leadership in America (Jaworski 1996).

In the spring of 1992 Dr. Flowers was asked by a representative from Shell International to serve as editor for myths the company was consciously creating, stories Shell wanted to write about the future, to be backed up by the research data collected from around the world by a team of twenty economists who had been working on this scenario project for three years. She spent four months in England over the summer, working intensively to write and refine these scenarios. They were successfully produced, and were treated as top corporate secrets. Shell disseminated them to its managers worldwide in carefully orchestrated seminars. In early 1995 the Shell management asked Betty Sue to return to London, again in the summer, to produce another round of scenarios; my second interview with her was conducted shortly before she left for that second round.

The point of these scenarios is to teach Shell managers to think mythologically and causally, to see every major local or world event as potentially located in a story, and to make on-the-spot business and policy decisions based on what they know about there that story would lead if allowed to play itself out. Thus these scenarios play an integral role in Shell's futures planning.

Two publications in particular detail the process of scenario building developed by Shell International over the past twenty years—Peter Schwartz's *The Art of the Long View* (see below) and "The Gentle Art of Reperceiving," written for the *Harvard Business Review* by Pierre Wack, retired head of the Business Environment Division of the Royal Dutch/Shell Group Planning Division, and senior lecturer in scenario planning at the Harvard Business School.[1] In cooperation with Edward Newland, Wack developed the Shell system of scenario planning—a process that he sees as one of managerial assumption smashing:

> It is extremely difficult for managers to break out of their worldview while operating within it. When they are committed to a certain way of framing an issue, it is difficult for them to see solutions that lie outside this framework. By presenting other ways of seeing the world, decision scenarios allow managers to break out of a one-eyed view.

> Scenarios give managers something very precious: the ability to re-
> perceive reality. (Wack 1986, 31).

Wack recounts the process through which he came to understand the necessity for the scenarios, so grounded in the "outer space" of the world outside
the corporation—a world of supply and demand, shifting prices, new technologies, competition, business cycles, and so on—to come alive in "inner space,"
the manager's microcosm where choices are played out and judgment is exer-
cised. Three decades ago, in the early days of their work with scenarios, Shell
planners initially developed "first generation" scenarios that simply quantified
alternative outcomes of obvious uncertainties (for example, the price of oil may
be $20 or $40 a barrel in a given year). Managers found such scenarios to be
useless for long-term planning and decision making, as they provided nothing
more than a set of plausible alternatives that included no reason to assume that
one or another would come about, offering no basis on which managers could
exercise their judgment. Such scenarios resembled the straight-line forecasting
that Shell and other companies had engaged in for years, and ultimately rejected as inadequate for the complexities of the contemporary world.

Back at the drawing board, the Shell planners, led by Wack, zeroed in on the
notion that there are forces at work in the world that seem well-nigh inevitable,
unstoppable save by a major miracle or worldwide disaster that would mean
the end of life as we know it. They called such forces *predetermined elements,*
and sought in their futures planning to identify such elements and carry them
through each of the scenarios they developed, sorting them out carefully from
uncertainties. The art of scenario development, they found, revolves around
careful research out in the world to identify the predetermined elements, and
only then to weave stories around the interaction of these predetermined elements with the myriad of uncertainties future-seers must face.

For example, in the early 1970s, a period of recession in the oil industry
because of low prices resulting from an oil surplus after the development of
huge fields in the Middle East, Shell planners began to look at the world from
the point of view of the oilmen of the Middle East whose countries, small and
sparsely populated, did not have the means to absorb all of the wealth flowing
into them from their one valuable resource. That growing surplus of cash would
have to be reinvested, but where? No bank holding, or piece of real estate,
could appreciate in value as fast as the oil in the ground, especially if less oil
were produced in order to keep the price high. Thus the Shell team was able to
predict the emergence of the Organization of Petroleum Exporting Countries
(OPEC) and the rising price of oil as predetermined elements for the 1970s,
forces that would drive the global system. Repercussions of these predetermined elements would of necessity involve shock waves to the economies of
countries dependent on oil imported from the Middle East.

Uncertainties involved various countries' likely attempts at solutions, such as price freezes, or simple inaction, which would result in an energy crisis. So the Shell planners presented to top management, in 1972, a set of scenarios that took these predetermined elements and uncertainties into account. These scenarios varied so sharply from the implicit worldview then prevailing at Shell—explore and drill, build refineries, order tankers, and expand markets—that the planners realized they were unlikely to be taken seriously. So they constructed another set of "challenge scenarios" that postulated a continuation of present trends and business as usual.

These challenges scenarios included "miracles" in exploration and production, such as the discovery of major new fields in non-OPEC nations, willingness on the part of oil producers to deplete their resources at the will of the consumer to keep prices low, and no natural disasters or wars that would generate a need for spare production capacity. The sheer improbability of these events forced the Shell management to realize that their business-as-usual mentality was blinding them to the inevitability of the coming changes. As a result, during the 1970s Shell was better positioned to handle the oil embargo and the dramatic rise in oil prices and in the power of the OPEC cartel than many of its competitors.

In the early 1980s one of the scenarios written by the Shell planners foresaw the likelihood of a rapid and dramatic decrease in the price of oil as the result of the discoveries of new fields outside of the OPEC sphere of influence, in combination with the energy conservation measures increasingly taken by consumers who did not want, after the debacle of the 1970s, to remain overly dependent on imported oil, and who were increasingly aware of the finite nature of "nonrenewable" resources such as oil. Positioning itself accordingly, Shell rose from fourteenth to second place among the oil multinationals during the mid-1980s as prices fell and other companies, heavily overinvested, lost billions.

On Shell's scenario team at the time was Peter Schwartz, brought in because of his years of futures planning at the Stanford Research Institute in California. *The Art of the Long View*, published in 1992, recounts the work of Schwartz and his team at SRI on scenarios building, Schwartz's subsequent tenure at Shell, and his eventual creation of the Global Business Network, a web of individuals and organizations engaged in ongoing information-sharing and scenario-based futures planning. This book in particular shows the ever widening role of scenario-building in the business world, making clear the importance to even small businesses of understanding the forces at work in the global economy.

For example, in the mid-1970s Schwartz was hired by Smith and Hawken, an English company that produces handmade garden tools, to create scenarios that would help them decide whether to undergo the initial capital investment of exporting their tools to the United States. The scenarios had to answer the large question—"Is there a market in the U.S. for handcrafted, high-priced garden tools that last a lifetime?"—along with the myriad small questions that accompanying the large one (should the tools be sold in stores, or by mail-order, or both?). Schwartz and his team at GBN created three alternative scenarios about the future of the U.S. economy. The first, the "official future" scenario, envisioned a world of high economic growth and increasing wealth in which maturing baby boomers made a lot of money and spent a good bit of it on houses. In this world, consumption and materialism were driving forces. The "depression" scenario saw a world marked by a worsening of the severe economic troubles of the 1970s, with low growth, declining prosperity, rising oil prices, and environmental crises. Life would be about surviving in hard times. The third "Social Transformation" scenario imagined a fundamental social change—a shift in values to ecological consciousness involving holistic medicine and natural foods, pursuing inner growth rather than material possessions.

It was clear immediately that the baby boom was a major predetermined element in all three scenarios—a large number of people were coming of age, marrying, and setting up households. Many would garden, as would the parents of the baby boomers, who were approaching retirement. In the official future scenario, people would garden for recreation and for show. They would want expensive tools because they could afford the best. In the depression scenario people would garden for food they might not otherwise be able to afford. They would need sturdy tools that did not require frequent replacement. In the social transformation scenario people would garden as a source of organic food, of contemplation, healing, contact with nature. They would appreciate the value of fine handcrafted wooden tools.

And so Schwartz and his associates were able to assure Smith and Hawken that the U.S. market would be an excellent one for them to enter, no matter which future unfolded. They were also able to show that in the official future scenario, retail space and overhead would be extremely high, and in the depression scenario, the deteriorating of cities could make retailing very problematic. But in all three scenarios it was clear that mail order would do well: it would save time for busy people in the prosperous world, save precious capital in a depression, and work to reach the *Whole Earth Catalogue* community in the social transformation scenario.

Reality as it happened in the 1980s turned out to be a combination of all three scenarios. The yuppies rose to social and financial prominence even as homelessness went large-scale and social problems, especially in the inner cities, increased. The environmental and holistic health movements grew. And Smith and Hawken's mail-order business, in combination with one small retail outlet in northern California, prospered accordingly.

This scenario process represents a fascinating and visionary merging of business and myth, which holds the simultaneous possibilities of foreseeing several possible futures while acting to consciously create one particular future, to choose the story in which one ultimately will live. In late August 1993 I asked Dr. Flowers, who had just returned from a short trip to London doing follow-up work for Shell, for permission to interview her about her role in writing and editing the 1992 Shell scenarios. After receiving Shell's permission to describe the process of creating them, she readily agreed.

The Shell International Futures Scenarios

DAVIS-FLOYD: Betty Sue, I know that you have spent a good bit of your life studying myths and mythology. To begin, can you tell me how you define a myth?

FLOWERS: I think a myth is a story that organizes experience through telling something explicitly about meaning—where we're going, where we came from, or who we are. That's why I say things like "the economic myth," even though economies by definition doesn't have a linear timeline—it's a story without much juicy narrative at all, except for "progress" and "growth."

DAVIS-FLOYD: What is the economic myth?

FLOWERS: It's the myth we're in now. In the West I think we've been shaped in the past by a heroic myth, a religious myth, and a democratic myth; and I think now we're in the economic myth. That myth doesn't have the kind of old fashioned "once upon a time" story we're used to; it doesn't have in Campbellian terms a hero's journey—there's no journey part to it. It has a dynamic and it has implicit values on measurements—number, quantity, growth. It's got an inherent bias toward a series of evolutions that are additive—like we get better and better, we grow more and more. It doesn't tell a very coherent story. But it has a thrust and a power to it. I could be more specific if you ask me what the economic myth says about X or Y or Z.

DAVIS-FLOYD: Well, what would the economic myth say about the directions that American business is taking, for example?

FLOWERS: It would say exactly what American business is doing because they're in touch with it most, which is to downsize in order to economize. The economic myth is very short-term, so it would not talk about investing for long-term growth, but about meeting the next quarter's numbers. It's very present-oriented, which is why it doesn't have a very good narrative story about the past or the future. It's a measuring device for now.

DAVIS-FLOYD: Is that myth articulated differently in Japan?

FLOWERS: No, what Japan has is another myth that's very powerful underlying it—a myth you could call Confucianism—at least the East Asian Center at Harvard tends to talk about it as Confucianism. It's a myth of community based on a kind of onion of enlarging circles, starting with individual

duty and then the family and then the community and then the company
and then the world. This community myth is not incompatible with the economic growth. You can have two myths, but the economic myth tends to take
precedence.

So in this culture, say, we have a light dose of Christian myths still going
on, but when it comes down to the bottom line, it's the economic myth that's
the myth of value. And I think that's true in Japan, too. When people say
that the whole century was one long world war between three ideologies—
fascism, communism, and democracy—and that now democracy has won,
and the century of war is over, I disagree. I don't think democracy has won,
I think it's economics—that's the ideology that has won. So you can have
a very repressive regime, such as in Singapore or China, and still have an
economic, free-market capitalism myth that is the myth of value.

DAVIS-FLOYD: How do you feel about, what is your personal judgment
about the economic myth, about its usefulness?

FLOWERS: Well, there are a lot of limitations. The obvious one is that it
doesn't make any distinctions among goods that are good for us and goods
that aren't, or long-term good versus short-term gain. It has nothing to say
about quality. It has nothing to say about values that might not be economic.
We know how to compete to get the best services in hospitals, but not how to
get every child immunized. What it does is have us set up a society which
seems quite skewed when we look at other values that we might have, like
human life.

Those are some of the down sides, but there are some up sides, which I
think are very hopeful and empowering. One is that it's a universal myth, it's
the first time we've had the potential for a truly global myth, that has within it
enormous capacity for all kinds of things, like the end of war. Now I'm really
being visionary—you know, there is a possibility there, that we will become
so intertwined with each other's business that we're never really fighting
against anyone. It's interesting that the wars now are "ethnic"—many of
them are now fought in the old qualitative terms of the religious myth. Another thing is—and I think this is very much tied with the environmental
movement—the economic myth encourages a systems approach to things, encourages us to look at how one part of the system affects the whole, to look
ecologically at our world. The economic myth has no value placed on saving
nature, I don't mean that, but it does look from the perspective of a total system and how it all interacts. So that, to me, is very hopeful.

DAVIS-FLOYD: How do you see the economic myth reshaping itself in the
immediate future? Do you see any reshaping of it going on?

FLOWERS: Yes, because it's so complex. The heart of its implicit belief system is the notion that numbers have a life of their own, and money has a life
of its own, and that it's best left alone. But we see now such complications

and entanglements with the different monetary systems around the world that there's another way—or theme—that's being superimposed onto that kind of "invisible hand" mentality. This theme is more like a systems approach or more like chaos theory, where you can't predict any individual thing, much as we try, but you can see patterns. You can't predict these patterns, you can only observe them, because structures are so complex. And you can assume that if you influence one side of the pattern, you're influencing it all. So you can't make decisions in a less than global context. Companies are just now beginning to realize that they can't make decisions for themselves or even for their country. They can only make decisions in a global context.

DAVIS-FLOYD: Is that why Shell hired you?

FLOWERS: You could say that that's why Shell does its scenarios. Why they hired me in particular is another, perhaps longer story that has to do with the head of that project seeing the need for this global contextualization and wanting a writer who had a kind of poetic vision, and who perhaps wouldn't be totally seduced by the economists on the team [*Laughs*].

DAVIS-FLOYD: [*Laughing*] What do you mean by "seduced by the economists"?

FLOWERS: Well, lots of people on the team were economists, even though they were from all over the world. There were a couple of historians, and a mathematician, but most of them were economists—and they wanted to talk about things in terms of gross national product (GNP) and arguments about PPP vs. GNP. They wanted to tell a story that didn't have any kind of implicit moral. Even if the moral appeared to emerge naturally they wanted to squelch it.

DAVIS-FLOYD: Tell me the story of all of that from the beginning—of how it was first conceived and how you were brought in and what happened.

FLOWERS: Well, about twenty years ago, Shell started doing scenarios instead of straight-line forecasting. Most companies did straight-line forecasting based on the past. You extrapolate into the future, you know, those graphs?—we did them in high school. And then you would base your planning around that. And you would take it with a slight grain of salt because you knew the future was never what the past was. There were always "contingencies." Well, Shell's planning department started thinking about this, especially given that in the oil business you have to make enormous investments twenty years in advance—you have to build refineries that are not on line for years. So you're really just taking enormous risks with blocks of capital all the time.

And they said, Well, it's actually not only false to have straight-line forecasting, but it's dangerous because you can be lulled into thinking you *do* know the future, that you have the *story* for the future, and that the future is the past, put into the future. So what they decided to do instead was to build self-conscious stories, that is, they would *call* them stories, and to build two of them, equally persuasive, based on the same statistical beginning point and statistically told, that is, told in economic language, for thirty years into the future. They would spend three years putting this together with a team of twenty or so from all over the world, and then they'd spend the next year disseminating them in workshops around the world, so that what you got was a common culture based on not *a* story about the future but *two* stories about the future.

DAVIS-FLOYD: Why two instead of three, or one?

FLOWERS: Well, at times they have had three, I think one year they even had four. The last round of scenarios before the one I worked on had three stories. But it turns out that when you have three stories, people end up choosing "the right one," and they will choose the one in the middle. It's just human nature to want to say, Okay, here are three stories, which is the best? If you have two stories, you don't have a middle to choose from.

DAVIS-FLOYD: So do people usually choose one or the other?

FLOWERS: Oh, they can't help it. The idea is to make them hover, but human nature being such, people tend to pick one over the other just because we don't like ambiguity. We feel like we need to settle on something. One of the stories we told this time was very difficult for the team at first to buy into. They said it was too good to be true, it couldn't really happen this way. But then when we started fiddling with the "real" story, the other story, it turned out so disastrously, so depressing that they began to look at the other story with new eyes, saying, Well, not only might it turn out that way, it had *better* turn out that way.

So for the first time we had a kind of good story/bad story, which they try not to have, but when you take the stories down the line, one ends up with some short-term sacrifices—well, we quit using the term *sacrifice* because the "good story" requires people to take a long-term view of their self-interests and to make decisions based on horizontal linkages that empower poor countries. The other story was more business as usual, but with people pulling back and barricading themselves against change and diversity, and the painfulness of change. The "good story" is extremely painful, very turbulent, but the bad story just kept getting worse.

DAVIS-FLOYD: Are these stories still corporate secrets, or are you able to tell me—?

FLOWERS: They're sort of gradually being leaked out but I can't tell you more than that, nor would you be that interested because, you know, you go into the price of coal in China in 2015 and see what that has to do with cars there and stuff like that. It gets really interesting for certain sectors of the company in terms of detail, working with the little details. People like to take the story, their part of it—like if they're in the chemical division, you take the chemical story and then spin fantasies on that. Well, if it happened this way, what would happen here? and what would happen over there? So part of it is an excuse to sit down and spin the smaller stories that link on to the larger ones.

DAVIS-FLOYD: But it's safe to say overall that the good story has environmental consciousness in it, a sense of the ecosystem and of the interconnectedness of things, and the bad story is more oriented to short-term profit making, exploiting the environment?

FLOWERS: Yes.

DAVIS-FLOYD: Exactly why did Shell want you? What was your role in constructing the stories?

FLOWERS: I wrote them. Which means I would do a draft of several pages every day and have the team tear them apart—they would argue over it, over the story, not so much the writing, but the story. Then I would go back and try to reflect the argument in the next version of the story. These are highly nuanced stories so every word mattered in the summary book. I did two books —the longer book, which was about two hundred pages and is full of tables and figures, and then the summary book, about sixty-five pages. Then I did a video, and then I did a *really* short book to hand out when they were doing presentations at the United Nations, and places like that, which was only maybe ten or fifteen pages.

DAVIS-FLOYD: You talk about the team that helped you. Would you describe the team?

FLOWERS: They were mostly from Shell. There were some outsiders drawn in just for that three-year period, including the head of the scenario process. There was a Canadian physicist, an Argentine economist, an American economist, a Belgian sociologist, an Oxford-trained mathematician, someone who spent the last some-odd years in Venezuela who was a historian, a Scottish economist, someone from Singapore, someone from Africa, someone from Japan, someone from Germany, someone from Australia. They shifted in and out. There were about twenty in all, counting some support people.

DAVIS-FLOYD: So how did this process start? You got a letter or a phone call from Shell?

FLOWERS: Yes, from Joe Jaworski, the head of the scenario process. And he said, I want you to come over to London and write the scenarios. He said, there has to be an editor. And I want you to do a video, and design it.

DAVIS-FLOYD: Did you know this man already?

FLOWERS: I knew him, although not well—we'd only met twice. I had worked with him on a book he is writing, called *Predictable Miracles: The Inner Dimensions of Leadership.*[2] It's about a successful lawyer in Houston who was doing fine until his father, Leon Jaworski, confided in him about Watergate—he was the Watergate prosecutor. And Joe had this incredible sense of anguish about the leadership in this country. And he gave up his very high-powered job as a lawyer—in fact, he helped to build up a firm—he was in the top one percent of litigators in the country. And he gave all that up, sold everything he had. And he ended up going on this amazing journey, this quest for how you could train leaders. He thought through it, and founded the American Leadership Forum for the training of leaders in a different way. Which has had powerful effects in a few selected cities where it exists, but which mostly is a kind of paradigm of what one individual can do who is inspired by a vision and is willing to put a successful career at risk in order to join a larger game that he can't possibly win in the end. And it's from that position, as head of the American Leadership Forum, that Joe was chosen to head the Shell scenario planning process for three years. But the way I had worked on the project before I suppose made him think that I shared a vision about the possibilities for the future that made him trust me as a writer. Because it was such a contentious process, he had to imagine that someone could imagine or see his vision.

DAVIS-FLOYD: What was his vision?

FLOWERS: He very much saw a different—you could say a third—level to these scenarios which, in fact, the team began to see, almost like a far-off, glimmery thing, by the end. Which was, that when you tell stories about the future, even if you're not claiming to forecast, there's some sense that actually the future is the story you *choose*. Now that, that is very uneconomic in its basis. It's not the "invisible hand" working out invisibly, like a machine. It's human beings coming in and saying, I choose scenario A, not scenario B. It's a different emphasis—it puts the human being more in the center, in very nuanced ways, instead of these huge impersonal forces. It's very subtle. But it makes a big difference. Because to tell an economic story in economic language, in which human choice is important, is very difficult.

DAVIS-FLOYD: What was Joe's title at Shell?

FLOWERS: He was the director of scenarios.

DAVIS-FLOYD: So they actually had a position "director of scenarios"?

FLOWERS: Yes!

DAVIS-FLOYD: I mean, that's quite incredible. I don't think most companies have one on staff!

FLOWERS: No! Shell is the only one I know of who does it to such an extent. Now while we were there, and this is kind of interesting—you know, when we began doing sanctions against South Africa all over the world, Shell was one of the companies that decided to stay. They got lots of flack for that. But they decided they would stay and actively try to work in the country for change. They put up big billboards against apartheid, pretty strong stuff. One of the things they did was to do scenarios for South Africa. One of the fun things to do was helping to try to sort out how the workshops to disseminate these scenarios would run. We got to the table amazing people—the Minister

---

The Ostrich Scenario[3]

The Ostrich depicts a government that does not want to face realities. An ostrich supposedly hides its head in the sand when danger threatens. The ostrich does not want to see, and cannot fly away, but has to lift its head in the end.

As a result of the steps taken by the De Klerk government and the outcome of the white referendum, the international community becomes more tolerant toward South Africa, and the National Party in particular. In light of this, the Government hardens its negotiating position. The liberation movements come to be perceived as too radical and lose support internationally, but maintain their bottom line nevertheless. A standoff results and constitutional negotiations break down. The government decides to form a new "moderate alliance" government which is unacceptable to the liberation movements. This results in mass resistance which the State suppressed by force.

Although large scale sanctions are not reimposed, the economy remains in the doldrums because of massive resistance to the new constitution. This resistance leads to escalating repression and violence, and the business climate worsens. This in turn leads to economic stagnation and decline, accompanied by a flight of capital and skills.

The government also fails to deliver on the social front. Resistance and unrest render effective social spending impossible and large outlays are required merely to maintain the status quo. Because the society's major inequalities are not addressed, the vicious cycle continues. Eventually the various parties are forced back to the negotiating table, but under worse social, political, and economic conditions than before.

---

of Finance, and far-right-wing separatists, and African National Congress people, and Inkatta people. What was interesting about the scenarios for South Africa was that the guy who spearheaded them, Adam Kahane, was so inspired by the process and by what it did—the fact that these scenarios generated so many conversations in South Africa that helped people work together better, because the scenarios are so nonthreatening (it's just a story, after all)—he quit his job at Shell and moved to South Africa to do the scenarios full time.

DAVIS-FLOYD: When Shell invited people to the table to discuss the South African scenarios, what did they tell them—did they literally say, We're inviting you to come help us make up stories?

FLOWERS: Yes, about the future. And they made up four stories, and they had very unthreatening names of birds. One was "Icarus" which is a rapid ride and then crash. Another was "Ostrich"—stick your head in the sand, not paying attention, hoping it will all go away. The good one was called "Flight of the Flamingoes." Everyone takes off together, but slowly. The fourth was the "Lame Duck"—this would mean a long and wishy-washy transition. Then if you look at any particular event, and you say, Well, what scenario is this event likely to lead to? people can say Well, I think that would lead to an Ostrich scenario, that belongs to the Ostrich scenario.

It's eye-opening. It allows you to have a very complex story which you can

---

The Lame Duck Scenario

The Lame Duck envisages a formal, protracted transition lasting for most of the coming decade, like a bird with a broken wing that cannot get off the ground, and thus has an extremely uncertain future.

In this scenario, various forces and considerations drive the major parties towards a negotiated settlement. The present government, for example, recognizes the necessity or inevitability of extending full political rights to the disenfranchised, but fears irresponsible government. This fear is shared by some of the major international actors. On the other hand, the liberation movements fear a return to repressive minority rule if they do not make significant compromises. Such considerations lead to a transitional arrangement with a variety of sunset clauses, slowly phasing out elements of the present system, as well as minority vetoes and other checks and balances aimed at preventing "irresponsible" government.

Such a long transition of enforced coalition is likely to incapacitate government because of the probability of lowest-common-denominator decision-making, resulting in indecisive policies. It purports to respond to all, but satisfies none. In consequence, the social and economic crisis is inadequately addressed. Even if the transitional government succeeds in being goal-directed and effective, it will still be incapacitated because of the logic of a long transition. Uncertainty will grow regarding the nature of the government to emerge after the transition.

Regardless of how moderate the declarations of the majority parties in the coalition may be, fears of radical economic policies after the long period of transition will remain. Investors will hold back, and there will be insufficient growth and development. Ironically, the unintended consequence of a long transition is to create uncertainty rather than to enhance confidence in the future.

---

then talk about at a metalevel. See, for example, whenever we talk about health-care reform in the U.S., we always get just totally embroiled in all kinds of arcane discussions—we don't even know if we're using the same terminology. If we're talking about managed care, what does that mean to you, what does that mean to me? We have no way to talk about it except to reinvent the wheel every time we talk, or to have a very low-level discussion, very general.

What stories allow you to do is have a whole, completely fleshed-out story with a level of imagery, like "Flight of the Flamingoes," that encapsulates something about the story that allows you to refer to a much more adumbrated whole, so that you can talk at this level, comparing stories, without getting mired down in the details. But the details are there—which is what Shell calls rich stories. So they have to be rich, much detail, many things all fitting together. We ran the numbers, I don't know how many times, to get it to work out, because you have to tweak this number and then run it through the computer and something else wouldn't work out if you didn't have right numbers—these scenarios are very, very completely worked out.

DAVIS-FLOYD: You went over there to be the editor, to bring all this information together. What kind of facilities did they provide you with?

FLOWERS: A regular office. I was in there alone for ten to twelve hours every day. I mean, it was a real press. The last editor had had to get a private

---

The Icarus Scenario

The third scenario is one of the macro-economic populism—of a popularly elected government which tries to achieve too much too quickly, like the youthful Icarus flying too close to the sun. It has noble origins and good intentions, but pays insufficient attention to economic forces.

The government embarks on a massive spending spree to meet all of the backlogs inherited from the past. It implements food subsidies, price and exchange controls, and institutes other "quick fix" policies. The initial results are spectacular growth, increased living standards, improved social conditions, little or no increase in inflation, and increased political support. But after a year or two the program runs into budgetary, monetary, and balance of payment constraints. The budget deficit well exceeds ten percent. Depreciations, inflation, economic uncertainty, and collapse follow. The country experiences an economic crisis of hitherto unknown proportions which results in social collapse and political chaos.

Perhaps the most sobering aspect of this scenario of boom and bust is that the very people who were supposed to benefit from the program end up being worse off than before. Either the government does a 180-degree about turn (while appealing to the International Monetary Fund and the World Bank for assistance), or it is removed from office. The likely result is an abandonment of the noble intentions that originally prevailed, and a return to authoritarianism—as has been the case in many Latin American countries. Right-wing armies often stage coups under such conditions, claiming a need to restore law and order.

---

office so no one could come lobby him. I mean, he had to get a *secret* office. It was a very pressurized situation.

DAVIS-FLOYD: Why did people lobby the last editor?

FLOWERS: Oh, I got lobbied—all over. Because the way you tell the story influences the way people think about the future. So if you say coal will not do so well because it pollutes, the coal people all over the world will get upset. So every sentence I wrote was faxed around the world to these different interested parties, you know.

DAVIS-FLOYD: And did you get grief if you said something like that?

FLOWERS: Yes. Now, when I say "I," it's the team writing these stories, and figuring out what they would be. When I put them together, I had to make them congruent, and sometimes shape them more than others, but when it came to specific things like coal, or chemicals, where every sentence was run by the people in the field, then one of the technical guys would kind of spearhead what the story would say, and then I would write it.

DAVIS-FLOYD: And what it said was based on the numbers, on all these projections that they were making?

FLOWERS: Well, you start with the story, and then you feed in a number and see how it turns out. If it doesn't turn out the way you have been claiming, you have to change the story slightly. So it's always a dialogue with the numbers.

DAVIS-FLOYD: Because what I don't understand is, if you're not doing

---

The Flight of the Flamingoes

Flamingoes characteristically take off slowly, fly high, and fly together. In this scenario, a decisive politi-cal settlement, followed by good government, creates conditions in which an initially slow but sustain-able economic and social take-off becomes possible. The key to the government's success is its ability to combine strategies that lead to significant improvements in social delivery with policies that create con-fidence in the economy. Access to world markets and relative regional stability facilitate the flamingoes, but South Africa does not receive massive overseas investments or aid on the scale of a Marshall Plan.

The government adopts sound social and economic policies and observes macro-economic constraints. It succeeds in curbing corruption in government and raises efficiency levels. It makes well-targeted so-cial investments which lead to a decrease in violence and give people confidence that many of their social needs will be met in the longer term. Once business is convinced that policies will remain consis-tent in the years ahead, investment grows and employment increases. Initially this growth is slow, be-cause confidence does not return overnight, but over the years higher rates of growth are attained, and an average rate of growth of close to five percent is realized over the period.

The overall income of the upper income groups grows between one and three percent a year, and that of the poorer classes by an average of six to nine percent a year, mainly because of the increase in formal sector employment. From the outset processes are developed which facilitate broad participation, creating the conditions under which it becomes possible to find a sound balance between social recon-struction and sustained economic growth. In spite of conflict between different groups and classes, there is substantial agreement on broad objectives.

Some team members believed that Flight of the Flamingoes could prove to be so appealing that South Africans might choose not to deviate from it, so a set of "Necessary Conditions for Takeoff" were devel-oped. In the political realm, these included: a culture of justice, a break from authoritarianism, a bill of rights, proportional representation, and effective citizen participation. In the economic realm, they in-cluded: a market-oriented (not free-market) economy, monetary and fiscal discipline, increasing foreign exchange earnings by growth in exports and in tourism. Necessary social conditions included: more ef-fective delivery systems for increasingly effective service provision, economic growth and, given the his-tory of apartheid, some degree of redistribution, the curbing of violence, better education and training, improved nutrition and public health. The empowerment of women was seen as a prerequisite for deal-ing with social problems such as rapid growth, educational reconstruction, and the spread of AIDS.

In addition, the scenario team stressed five general points to the South African public about "Flight of the Flamingoes": (1) The scenario is not a blueprint. While team members generally agreed on the broad conditions required for success, they differed substantially on the details. (2) It would be utopian to ex-pect all of the necessary conditions to be fully met. Rather, the team believed that the outcome would depend on the degree of progress toward meeting the conditions. (3) The future is not predetermined. It can be shaped by the decisions and actions of the major players. (4) Various groups, such as the right wing, alienated youth, a corrupt bureaucracy, trade unions, and disinvesting businessmen, each have the power to prevent the flock from becoming airborne. (5) Once airborne, even flamingoes don't always have a smooth flight.

---

straight-line projections from numbers, then how can they be so influential in the story?

FLOWERS: Because they're compelling. Numbers are compelling, psycho-logically compelling. You have to start with real numbers now, because it's

1992, not 2020. So you can't just make up a story like, Suppose that gasoline were so much a gallon—no. You start *here*. And then you have certain things happen that change the price, if you're talking about gasoline. I mean, we had political stories and religious—you have this happen there, and this has this effect. And you have this happen there, and then this happens.

DAVIS-FLOYD: Like for example, you say maybe there's a war in the Middle East, or Bosnia erupts into a larger regional conflict—something like that?

FLOWERS: Yeah, although we tried to keep that to a minimum. We tried not to "cheat" by having a big event that would change it in the direction we wanted it to change. We tried to be as subtle as possible. So if you made a small decision here, you could see the large consequences down the line. So we didn't, we had maybe one big political thing. We flirted with a war over water around Turkey. And we had a few little blowups here and there, but we didn't have a major thing, because that's kind of cheating. I mean, there's a whole sort of culture of telling scenarios, which is to be as conservative as possible, in order to see consequences of actions that in fact you're taking now.

DAVIS-FLOYD: So what kind of big political thing did you pick—a war, a revolution?

FLOWERS: No, not a war or revolution. It had to do with a cabal among suppliers, energy suppliers, in a certain political context to do with the royal family of Saudi Arabia, which we then had to cut out because of its political implications, because of the oil fields. So we toned that down and made it another kind of story that didn't involve political upheaval, but just an oil thing.

DAVIS-FLOYD: Did part of your storytelling involve projecting what would happen in Eastern Europe?

FLOWERS: In one story Eastern Europe becomes Balkanized. In another story, it sort of, you could say it's on the road to being a kind of part of the European Community through a long, complex series of things I can't really go into. But yeah. So in one it's drawn more into the border areas of the European community, and in another, it's like you can see in Yugoslavia.

DAVIS-FLOYD: Did your stories project that the EC would work, would become a viable economic unit?

FLOWERS: Totally different, totally different stories—two very different stories about that.

DAVIS-FLOYD: One story that it does work, the other that it falls apart?

FLOWERS: No, it works in two different ways, that have different economic and social consequences.

DAVIS-FLOYD: Did your scenarios predict, for example, that Japan and Asia would take on greater and greater roles, or that there would be some sort of a balancing between their increasing economic power and the economic clout of the West?

FLOWERS: I think in both stories China particularly takes on more of a role, in different ways—very different ways.

DAVIS-FLOYD: But in both stories, China moves ahead? [*Flowers looks at me as if to say "Don't ask any more."*] Did you have fun while you were doing this?

FLOWERS: Fun—it was exciting to be on such a steep learning curve, so I think I was having fun! but—[*Laughs*]

DAVIS-FLOYD: Was there a lot of deadline pressure?

FLOWERS: Yes, every day.

DAVIS-FLOYD: How long was this process?

FLOWERS: Four months.

DAVIS-FLOYD: And why was there so much pressure every day?

FLOWERS: Well, you had to keep rewriting the thing, and, in terms of printing deadlines, there was a due date on which these things had to be disseminated worldwide, and I had to have these two volumes and a video done, and produced, by that time. You know, the colors right, and the paper right, and all this kind of stuff. And various things happened, along the way—you know, you always get differences of opinion. People would go on vacation and they would be strong people, and while they were gone the story would change, slightly, and they would come back and be upset and lobby to have it changed back, so we were always fighting over the story. And then we drew many more illustrations than we could use, and people would insist on their favorites. They were always changing the numbers, running the numbers again, which would change the illustrations, and change the story. So it was, you know, a kind of battleground, pretty bloody, actually, from time to time.

DAVIS-FLOYD: Did you get emotionally wounded in the process?

FLOWERS: No, I couldn't, because early on I realized that there was a testing process going on. In fact they told me at the very end, at the going-away party, that they tried to break me at the beginning. So I knew that part of the whole ordeal was to be as unflappable as I could be, and still get the job done, and still be passionate enough to write good prose.

DAVIS-FLOYD: Why did they try to break you at the beginning?

FLOWERS: Well, I think there was a number of reasons. One was just to see who I was, because—see, they had been working together for three years, and these things were important to them, and to their careers. And they were a little suspicious at the story the head guy, who was an American, was telling, and they knew that when the crunch time came—there is always a crunch time in these sorts of projects—I'd have to be able to hold up. So I can see why they did it.

DAVIS-FLOYD: So they had been working for three years gathering all this data, then you show up, and did they immediately start feeding you the data?

FLOWERS: Yes. They gave me piles of stuff—*piles*. And then I heard each of them tell the story as they saw it, and they were utterly different.

DAVIS-FLOYD: Sitting around a big table for a day or two?

FLOWERS: No, I went to their offices individually. Eventually we would start meeting together, but there were different factions with different stories so it was quite a political process, learning who had power.

DAVIS-FLOYD: Did you ever go off for a retreat?

FLOWERS: Yes, we all went off for a retreat, to tell the story completely, so that we'd all hear it, and especially so I'd hear it and get it down. But different people told different parts of it, and other people kept quiet when they violently disagreed, and waited till they had a strategic moment to violently disagree.

DAVIS-FLOYD: Were you taking notes during these sessions?

FLOWERS: Oh, yes, madly.

DAVIS-FLOYD: No time for tape-recording because you couldn't transcribe the tapes?

FLOWERS: No, I didn't have time!

DAVIS-FLOYD: High stress, high intensity, exciting—

FLOWERS: Yes, it really was.

DAVIS-FLOYD: Were you in danger of getting addicted to adrenaline during this process?

FLOWERS: No, because it was very wearing, too, and I generally like a little bit more leisure, I think. Although the people were so intelligent, I did get addicted to being around them, because they were so much fun—very high energy and bright.

DAVIS-FLOYD: It *is* addicting to be around intensely intelligent people— you're always stimulated.

FLOWERS: Yes. They complained about everything, from the serial comma to the Cavafy quote I put at the beginning—"There are no more barbarians" —you know, what do we do now that there are no more barbarians? And one of the guys who was in charge of the Iceberg Database—a top-secret database with all kinds of statistics about oil and everything else—complained because I hadn't kept it in the original Greek! So when I was about to leave, he gave me this beautiful thing with a fractal image that he had run off on his computer, and the original Greek of the bits that I had quoted from the Cavafy poem, and I took it outside and was walking down the hall looking at it, because I had just opened it up from my mailbox, and the first person who came down the hall, who was someone who had been in some kind of new heavy motor oil, looked at it and started translating it. You know, looked over my shoulder!

That's just kind of an example of the kind of wit and fun and good education that was so much a part of the people at Shell. They had all lived all over the world, because Shell moves its people every three years to a different country. So they had lived *everywhere,* and the tales were just wild.

DAVIS-FLOYD: How did the team feel about the scenarios once they were finished?

FLOWERS: Well, they were a bit dubious, all the way through. They were dubious about the story we were telling. They were dubious about my being brought in. They were just *dubious.* But since Shell began disseminating the scenarios, the feedback they've gotten, if I can believe what's being reported to me, is that they are the best set that's ever been done there. They've had quite a response, and a lot of extra governmental agencies wanting to have scenario presentations. So I feel good about them.

DAVIS-FLOYD: I get a fairly clear picture of what has happened to these scenarios so far—they are out there in the world being very active. And they're used in seminars all over the place and people react to them, and are using them within Shell—just within Shell?

FLOWERS: Yes, the corporate managers within Shell go through these workshops, that are honed down very tightly, where the scenarios are presented, and then a bunch of events are put up—in fact Shell has kind of patented the process of these workshops—some events are put up, and they are put up in terms of time and area—

DAVIS-FLOYD: You mean real events, events that have happened?

FLOWERS: That have happened and that could happen, according to the scenarios. So you begin to see events now that have happened that could happen in the future that are consonant with the story. Then you begin to see patterns that emerge, and actions that you would take into that kind of future. So there are even more details that participants themselves come up with.

DAVIS-FLOYD: So this process then would make you hyperconscious about—

FLOWERS: Weak signals—*weak signals.* That's their terminology, meaning that you get faint signals of something about an emerging trend, and you learn to be conscious of those, because this process they teach in the seminars through the scenarios attunes you to these weak signals from the environment.

DAVIS-FLOYD: So this is a process of attunement and the idea is that as you become more and more hyperconscious about how different events can lead to alternative futures, you begin to be able to read the future as a text, almost as emergent before it's quite there.

FLOWERS: That's right.

DAVIS-FLOYD: So then you can make your business decisions based on those probabilities that you're seeing emerging.

FLOWERS: Then it gets even more mysterious, because then you begin to

see that the future is what you use to create the present, and that the present
that you then create will create the future that you want. I mean, it's chicken/
egg. It gets very curious. So you see into a future, you see this way and you
see that way, and then you use this future that you'd rather have to create the
present.

DAVIS-FLOYD: So it becomes a very strong cognitive feedback loop.

FLOWERS: Yes. Even though they don't even exist—those futures—it's really fascinating, *really* fascinating talking about them. And over the period of
four months I could see these stories, mere stories, begin to take on life, vitality, depth, in the group, working with the group. So by the end it's not so
much that we were believing them, because they had such power and palpa-
bility—maybe, maybe we were. I'm not sure. They took on a life of their
own, these stories.

DAVIS-FLOYD: I'll bet. What values were stressed in these stories, these
self-consciously created myths?

FLOWERS: In one, the value of individual/group ethnic diversity—"doing
it my way." And in the other, the environmental values of cooperation and a
long-term good future for everyone, because we're all in this together. That's
oversimplifying it a bit, but it would be fair to say that. The first scenario
stressed nationalism, bettering your own group, acting in your own self-
interest. The other one had acting in your self-interest, but your self-interest
was more enlightened, or broader, and included other people than yourself.
So there was much freer access on all sorts of levels—many more horizontal
linkages, much more cooperative interaction.

DAVIS-FLOYD: While the other, "the bad story," is more vertical, more
about one group dominates, that sort of thing?

FLOWERS: Yes.

DAVIS-FLOYD: Was there general agreement among the team over what values would be emergent in each story? When people fought over things, were
values one of the things they fought over?

FLOWERS: Yes, they fought over having any values in there whatsoever besides economic self-interest.

DAVIS-FLOYD: Oh, really? Why?

FLOWERS: Because they're all economists. See, the only way to tell a be-
lievable story is to tell it in economic terms. That's why I went over there—to
learn how to tell a story in economic terms. So this is what I'm saying emerges
from the stories, but that's not the *language* of the stories. The language is
very hard-nosed, about this kind of thing happening with that linkage in order
to predict this result. But that in fact is what drives a different decision about
what you do.

DAVIS-FLOYD: Right. So the value is implicit in your discussion of the linkages, for example, in the good story, or implicit in your projections of what happens with ethnic strife in one's own self-interest in the bad story.

FLOWERS: Yes, it's implicit. Now, I did manage to put in some things, sort of "over their dead bodies." I did talk about fear, in the negative story, and I did talk about a kind of acceptance of change, in the positive story. I did use those psychological terms, you know—in spite of the pain of change, accepting it, and working within it, instead of resisting it. I talked in psychological terms to get the stories going in different directions, as if there's a dividing point—you can either accept these changes, or resist them, and then go back into old ways of doing things. I mean, that's oversimplifying, but it's the best I can do without revealing too much.

DAVIS-FLOYD: Did these economists have any sense of the psychology that goes into making up a human being who will accept change or who will resist change?

FLOWERS: They did in terms of nationalism—fear, and nationalism. That was very strong. And the underlying assumption about people of the economic myth is that we're all motivated by self-interest.

DAVIS-FLOYD: Do you think that's true? Do you think the economic myth is correct when it says that self-interest is the motivating factor?

FLOWERS: It is if we're in that myth! I don't think it's necessarily correct—we have the capacity to be motivated by different things, and have in the past. But we are *in* the economic myth, and so for the most part we are very much influenced by that set of motivations. So if I'm interested in changing the world, I'll work through business, and I'll work through the notion of self-interest. In other words, I wouldn't go out and say, Here's the right thing to do. I would go out and say, Here's the thing to do for your long-term enlightened self-interest.

One of the quotes in the scenarios was by Kaku, who's head of Canon, in Japan, which is a vastly successful company. And he says that the only institution whose self-interest coincides with global self-interest is a multinational corporation. Many corporations are beginning to become conscious of this. This past weekend I was in Boston at a global citizenship conference that was about the interface of education and global business. In the same way that the church influenced education, and then democracy influenced education, and then the state, now it's corporations that are coming in with new ideas about education—all over the country, all over the world, actually. They're becoming very conscious of what they must do to influence schools to produce the kind of people they need *because* of their enlightened self-interest, and, as they see it, the interests of the world.

DAVIS-FLOYD: When you talked about Shell as a largely decentralized corporation, I suddenly realized how powerful the stories must be at the ends of the—you know how if you diagram a corporation you go out to the individual units out there in the field where the action is, where it's most profoundly and immediately happening? If those individuals are the ones that are perceiving trends because of the stories, because of what they've been taught in the seminars, and then acting immediately, what you have overall is a corporate structure that looks very much like an octopus with a brain in each arm.

FLOWERS: Yes.

DAVIS-FLOYD: Instead of a bunch of boxes, like IBM used to look.

FLOWERS: Yes, Shell is very fluid, very decentralized—so they can make quick responses on the ground, like one arm of the octopus reacting to a change. I think that's one reason for their success, and their longevity.

DAVIS-FLOYD: And of course that is very much in keeping with the vision of this director of scenarios that you talked about—his vision for individual choice.

FLOWERS: That's right.

DAVIS-FLOYD: This is very impressive, really. It's not your usual business story. Do you see other companies doing this sort of thing very much? Is Shell really the leader out there? Are there other companies flocking to follow suit?

FLOWERS: There are some who do scenarios—I don't know that they commit as much as Shell commits. I don't see any doing that. I think Shell, because it's been around so long, is able to make decisions in a different way. And because it's so international. They've got so many people all over the world, of different nationalities, so you can't be so boxed into the story of values that, say, the English represent—at any given time in their executive lunchroom where I ate, you could hear all these different languages going on.

DAVIS-FLOYD: So they don't identify themselves with particular countries, not even England and the Netherlands?

FLOWERS: Not really. They really think of themselves as a global corporation. That's their consciousness—it's a global consciousness. And then the reaction to these stories filters back up gradually into the back end of the planning department, so you get the responses to the stories too, gradually.

DAVIS-FLOYD: What does the planning department do with these responses?

FLOWERS: They take them in for the next round of stories.

DAVIS-FLOYD: Why do you think this project matters, in the end? What differences will it make in the course of corporate, human, or planetary history?

FLOWERS: Goodness, who can tell? I'm not into forecasting! [*Laughter*] But I can tell a story.

DAVIS-FLOYD: Tell me your story about the importance of these stories.

FLOWERS: Well, for me they're important in a whole lot of different ways. One way had to do with the whole South Africa thing. I observed what a difference the South African scenarios made. I heard preachers in their sermons referring to these scenarios, and ladies in the boondocks calling in on radio talk shows saying, "I'm afraid we're going in the direction of Ostrich scenario." It was important to see how a language of story could appeal so much, and become a language that all levels of society could enter into for the sake of democratic discussion.

And there are a lot of people now, like the Global Business Network, who are doing scenarios. Almost all of them have come from Shell. They spin off and do their own sorts of things. And you'll see these little things—there was a little book published last year called *The Art of the Long View*—it's all about Shell. This stuff is sort of disseminating now. I saw the scenarios for the California System of Higher Education—four different stories of a possible future. They were done by ex-Shell people. So there are all these little pockets of this stuff that's specifically from Shell.

For me personally, I learned a tremendous amount about working in an economic language, about the power of story, even when it's so narrowly defined that you have to use numbers to tell it. It taught me a lot. So what difference will one individual's learning make for the future? Or many individuals? I don't know. But I do know that we're starting to talk about changing the story of America, and the story of the American dream. If we can go from belief, from holding ideas as beliefs to holding them as stories, then there's a possibility for change at a very profound level. And not the change that comes from somebody from above saying "You *will* do this" in a certain way, because there is more power in disseminating stories than a five-year plan. No central government can be wise enough to give a plan. That's *my* belief. I'm enough in the economic myth to believe that the invisible hand *is* wiser than any particular hand anywhere.

So then the question is, How do we become a community? How do we operate in terms of the large self-interest? Because the economic myth does not allow you to do that. It's wrong to think that the invisible hand is a benevolent hand. It's very effective, it's very powerful, but it's not necessarily benevolent, especially for the powerless. So in this instance I think that stories that have values implicit within them, that are compelling, that become common, are very powerful. They're not directive, they're suggestive.

DAVIS-FLOYD: So, if you wanted to use scenarios to transform health care in the U.S., for example, how would you go about it?

FLOWERS: I would work out three very different scenarios for health care, and then float them around the country, not as plans to be adopted, but as stories, and see how people respond. You know, if you adopt the Canadian system by the year 2000, it'll look like this. But good *and* bad. A scenario has to be perceived as a real story, and not just propaganda: if you adopt managed competition, what happens here and what happens there? And you tell that story. And you disseminate these stories, and then people can talk about the *stories* and not have to stand on positions politically about something. Then you can have a real discussion, and not an argument.

DAVIS-FLOYD: So then when it's time to vote on legislation to create policy they'll have more consciousness about the implications of the vote, rather than getting narrowly trapped into protecting the American Medical Association, or whatever, they'll see it a more systemic way, even.

FLOWERS: Yes, and that allows you to build a coherent policy. As it is now, we're going to have a little bit of this and that, depending on which pressure group is strongest, and when you get a hodgepodge, it can tend not to work, because it's not coherent.

DAVIS-FLOYD: Yes, stories are coherent—they have a beginning, a middle, and an end, things lead to other things, and you can see relation and causation.

FLOWERS: Exactly, that's their power, is the coherence. Not coerciveness, but coherence. It's related, I think, to Wittgenstein saying ethics and aesthetics are one and the same, and I think he was talking about ethics, which is an aesthetics, which has to do with order, and the principle of harmony. Stories have coherence and harmony, and that can actually make things happen in the world, in a way that laws cannot, when you have different ethnic groups and different value systems. So that's how I would have done it, very different from the way they're doing it.

DAVIS-FLOYD: I understand.

FLOWERS: And then, when you talk with someone who is saying By God, we need to have X as our health care system, someone, even a person on the street, can say, Well, you know, that's really a part of "Flight of the Flamingos," that's really a part of that other story—you know, what does that belong to? Because it's always a fight among "goods." So if someone says, We need to have kidney dialysis in every primary school for the people on the block— who's gonna say no? That's a wonderful idea—it's just that it doesn't fit the story of "preventive health care," for example. It's not that it's good or bad, it just doesn't fit. So then you're judging on what fits, and not what's good, because there are too many goods. Too many goods, that's the problem with the economic myth.

DAVIS-FLOYD: So, for example, a kidney dialysis machine on every block wouldn't fit the story of a decentralized, less technological health-care system based on preventive medicine.

FLOWERS: Right. It wouldn't fit that health-care policy. Massive bone marrow transplants in the last year of life for someone dying of leukemia, or some kind of cancer, fits managed competition, but it doesn't fit the preventive story. It doesn't *fit*—you don't have to say it's good or bad. Your grandfather's dying—who's gonna say those transplant are bad? You don't have to argue it on moral grounds, which is what we're continually doing in America. When we argue on moral grounds, we have to make someone wrong. And that's a losing proposition. If you argue on the grounds of fit, then you don't have to be wrong. I think that's why a story has much more power in a diverse society. In a homogeneous society you have the luxury of having beliefs, because everyone believes the same way, and you have a value system and you can make decisions based on values. In a diverse society you do not have the luxury of operating on belief, I don't think, but on coherence.

DAVIS-FLOYD: So of course that's why stories become so important—because they're only stories. But as stories, not only are they coherent, but they focus attention on certain issues without demanding belief.

FLOWERS: Right.

DAVIS-FLOYD: So you can see implications and you're free from all those moral restrictions that make people so livid and rabid and unable to think any more.

FLOWERS: Yes, that's right. It really has to do with the strength we have as a nation, of trying to find the "right." Because we're trying to find out who's right, and there are multiple rights, we're in a kind of gridlock. Whereas if we have coherent stories, we could get out of some of those areas of gridlock without having to make someone wrong. Because when someone is made wrong (and they're not—in most cases, they have a point), they can cry, "Injustice, injustice!" and make a law, and so we have all these ad hoc mutually contradictory bureaucratic things gong on that do not allow us to move forward.

DAVIS-FLOYD: There's a little schema that I find useful for discussing cognitive styles. Stage 1 is either/or, black-or-white, fundamentalist thinking, and stage 4 is highly relational, nonjudgmental, comparative thinking in which the world is replete with options and there is no one reality. Stories are a stage 4 phenomenon, really, when you understand them *as* stories. In stage 1 everybody tells the same story and believes it. But in stage 4, fluid thinking, it's all *just* stories. Stage 4 is more adaptive in conditions of rapid change, so it's a good thing we're becoming a stage 4 society. The problem, of course, is that this stage 4 society is full of stage 1 people, and stage 1 groups. The dynamic that I see is the one between fluidity and fixity—this constant tension between looking at reality as a set of stories, and looking at it as Truth. What's good for the country is the fluidity of the stories, but it's so hard for individuals who deeply *believe* a story to step outside of it and allow it to be fluid.

FLOWERS: That's right. Which is why I've given my life not to preaching any particular story—I don't have any particular thing I'm selling by way of content—but to changing the way we hold stories, as a kind of first step. That to me is a form of literary criticism, and so back to my discipline—it's a way I define myself in relation to my discipline, which nobody else in my discipline gets! I mean, this is truly a discipline of one, in this case. But if someone says, What does all this have to do with you being an English professor? it has *completely* to do with it, through a redefinition of what a literary critic can do if a literary critic is interested in society as well as in criticizing stories.

DAVIS-FLOYD: So your role is one of a culture critic, someone who is able to help people become conscious of the stories that they're telling about themselves and about the world.

FLOWERS: Yes, a culture critic from the perspective of literature, fiction— so it would be closer to a movie reviewer than a sociologist, or pollster. It has different rules to it, which we don't recognize, so it would be very hard for me to have any authority speaking, because the rules of culture critics rest on some kind of evidence that isn't fictional—statistics. We do go with statistics, even though we all know what they may or may not represent.

DAVIS-FLOYD: Movie reviewers, for example, know that the movie could've ended any way that the script writer and the director chose for it to end. So they are completely free to criticize, because there was complete freedom on the part of those creating the movie to make it go any which way. But what *you* know is that, culture-wide, we may actually have the same choices, not quite so freely as in a movie, because we are dealing with large forces, but it's back to the vision of the director of scenarios—there is this powerful role of individual choice. So if we're free to see it as stories, and to see the directions the stories will move us in, we're much freer to make those choices, to come consciously as a culture to where we want to end up.

FLOWERS: Yes.

DAVIS-FLOYD: Do you think that we can do that?

FLOWERS: Well, the South African thing was very hopeful. I didn't go to South Africa to do the workshop—I just helped plan it. But when the head guy came back and was talking about it, it was clear that you could do that, you could tell scenarios in such a way that I wouldn't have to stand on position and argue with you, but could actually yield my position in the interests of the story. I couldn't yield my position per se because then I would be a betrayer. But I could work for a story that *in effect* made me yield in terms of the timing. Like if I'm saying, End apartheid now, I have a very strong moral position, and I can rally the troops behind me. It doesn't matter if ending apartheid tomorrow creates total chaos and, in the end, a fascist government, or whatever. But if I've worked it out, and I see that "End apartheid now" might be "The Flight of Icarus" and that doing this interim thing, and finally having elections in April, is "Flight of the Flamingos," then I can be in coherence with a story in a way that I couldn't, otherwise, without betraying my position.

DAVIS-FLOYD: How did you get interested in myth in the first place?

FLOWERS: There are a lot of ways to tell this story, but if you were going to be psychoanalytical about it, I would say that my parents were very different in how they saw the world. I observed my father making one story about the same event and my mother making another, and that it was her *story* that would cause her grief or discomfort, and that my father's story actually created smooth sailing for him. I realized that the difference lay not in what was happening to them but in something very different in the way that they were thinking about it. And that taught me to be on the alert for the stories people were telling to interpret their experiences.

DAVIS-FLOYD: Were you ever able to actually articulate for yourself what the story was that your father was telling about the world, and the story that your mother was telling?

FLOWERS: No, I was only able to see it in specific instances. I found myself sometimes trying to tell my father's story to my mother so she wouldn't be upset, telling her, I think he things this, or He sees it this way. I just knew that I could change the reality of what happened by changing the story, and that she could.

DAVIS-FLOYD: So then how did you explore that academically?

FLOWERS: Well, there's not really a field called "changing your story" [*Laughs*]—except for psychoanalysis, to some extent, but they're caught up in their own story! So I did read whatever I could about psychoanalysis— more psychoanalysis than psychology, because I wasn't so interested in scientific experiments that count the numbers—how many heads do this, you know, because they're in the economic myth, too, about statistics. We all are. We're statistic crazy because we *believe* them.

But, I was interested in psychoanalysis because it's the theory of story as it relates to the human being. So I read Freud and Jung and Adler—whatever I could get my hands on. It was fascinating to me. It made me look at life differently. But I also felt that their stories were somewhat limiting, that they were caught in a founder story, as many religious groups are—in this case it's a Freudian story—and that the founder story had certain limitations, particularly if you were a woman, and also spiritual limitations. There was not very much room in the myths of psychoanalysis for transcendence or for other experiences that didn't fit that story. So then I began looking around for other ways of telling the story. It seemed as if no one had the whole story in the way that I liked it. I write fiction, too, and poetry, so I thought, Well, what would life look like if I do a different story?

DAVIS-FLOYD: Is that why you picked English as your major rather than psychology, for example?

FLOWERS: Yes, although it would be hard to say I could have articulated that back then. I was very interested in the stories people told about reality. For my Ph.D. I went to the University of London and worked with the British Museum on Robert Browning's influence on contemporary or modern poetry. And I came to realize that to tell a story of influence is to make up lots of stuff. So I was continually having to tell the story in a more muted way because you couldn't say—there are certain stories the academy is allowed to tell, and other stories that it isn't. And part of graduate education is teaching students what stories are permissible in the discipline. And so what I learned in London was what stories were permissible, *how to* tell a story in the discipline of English. But what I found constricting was that "how to tell a story in the discipline of English" did not include how to tell a story that made any difference to what was going on in the world around me, except as it made a difference in individual lives.

But the great cultural stories, which to my mind were the stories of business as it was happening, were not told in literary ways, and it struck me that if I wanted to study the stories that were influencing us now, they were not the stories from religion. Most literature arises from the heroic tradition or the religious tradition—a little bit of it from the democratic tradition, not too much—enough so that it's about salvation in some form or another, even if it's not explicitly Christian or theological. So if you were interested in what was going on in the world, the stories going on in the world, you had to do something else. That's how I got interested in myth theory, if you want to put it that way—learning about and reading about myth, because that seemed to back up and have a more architectural approach that would allow me to look at larger stories.

DAVIS-FLOYD: Who are the storytellers in the business world?

FLOWERS: Well, there is this myth that—it's the *myth,* it's not that they're telling individual stories. There is a myth which you can see in advertising that has to do with the things myths always have to do with—salvation, beauty, power, truth, love—and it has to do with more and better things, and the right way of doing things with things. And so the myth-tellers are the marketing people, you could say. Advertisement tells this story, this myth in which people are embedded. But the measurement of the success of the story is not the applause at the end of the performance or how many people join up with your religion, it has to do with the bottom line. And you can tell a story about your own product that is embedded in the larger story of the culture, and you can tell immediately how effective a storyteller you are by the bottom line.

DAVIS-FLOYD: What happens if people don't like your story? They don't buy the product?

FLOWERS: That's right. Sometimes they buy the product *because* they like your story. I think it's very interesting now to see the battle in Europe, or even here, between Häagen-Dazs and Ben and Jerry's. I mean, basically they both make ice cream. But the Ben and Jerry's story is, We are ecologically sound —we're *really* selling the *environment.* And Häagen-Dazs typically has been selling pleasure. Now it's a toss-up as to whether we're buying the story of pleasure or the environment. I mean, both of them have to do with purchases of certain milk products, but, you know, it's how the marketing *story* goes. And Häagen-Dazs is very consciously trying to change its story because the eighties are over and that self-indulgent pleasure is a little on the wane. See, both of those little submyths are part of a larger myth.

DAVIS-FLOYD: Which is?

FLOWERS: The myth of the power of things—the right thing, the best thing, or more things. See, we're not arguing over whether we should buy ice cream at all, or make it.

DAVIS-FLOYD: Yes, it's fundamentally taken for granted—

FLOWERS: —that we're going to buy *something.*

DAVIS-FLOYD: Yes. When did you first become aware of the role of myths in business? When did you first start looking at how business stories were *stories* that weren't told? I mean, most people don't think of businesses as having stories, much less telling them, or of myth as having any role in business. When did you first start to figure that out, and why?

FLOWERS: I grew up without a TV. Most of my friends in high school did have TV. And I was aware that they saw the world a certain way that had to do with things I wasn't seeing. It wasn't just that they knew things I didn't know, but that they assumed things about—the power of lipstick, or something, that I didn't. Even though I wore lipstick and liked it, it wasn't numinous for me. But it was for them. And it made me very curious. And then I got very interested in ads, in just how ads were constructed. They were by far the most brilliantly produced things on television. Much more thought went into the language of advertising—and I'm interested in language, as a poet—than the language of the scripts, of the shows around the advertising. I became aware that the real story was being told there, in the ads. Some of the ads are brilliant. There are a lot of implicit stories in the ads. And they have to do with happiness, well, with all the things stories have always had to do with, with the "good news."

DAVIS-FLOYD: It's amazing what a profound story you can tell through a series of images that take maybe thirty or forty seconds to watch. If you were to write that out, it would take maybe thirty or forty pages.

FLOWERS: Oh, yes, because imagery—it's the picture worth 10,000 words-type thing. Part of the power of the economic myth is that it's told in numbers, which is a worldwide language, and in imagery, which is also worldwide. We don't need to be impeded by language barriers. We're building a Tower of Babel.

DAVIS-FLOYD: The economic myth is creating a truly transcendent medium of expression.

FLOWERS: Yes, you can show all over the world, even in poor countries, a satisfied person, even with a different ethnic face, getting into a Mercedes with a grin on his face and with his arm around a blonde or something and right there is a whole message about life that's similar to the gospel being spread. It's the good news, and we want it.

DAVIS-FLOYD: Pick some other companies that you've thought about and tell me their stories.

FLOWERS: There's a whole corporate literature that I'm not that familiar with, where they talk about "corporate culture" and "founding stories," like the "IBM Founding Story" and the "Xerox Founding Story," and certainly the "Sam Walton Founding Story." McDonald's has a strong founding story. So there are myths within individual corporations that tell their story. And then there are myths of management that help keep things together, which often have to do with what the mission of the company is, so that they're selling not products but they're selling hope or they're selling truth or they're selling justice—these larger things. So there's that aspect of storytelling in companies.

Now Shell was a different thing because Shell is actually thinking about the future apart from its company, although the company is embedded in it. The job at Shell didn't have to do with talking about the future at Shell, but the future of the world. The way they used "story" was very self-consciously, not just as a marketing thing, but looking at the world in terms of story.

Second Interview

DAVIS-FLOYD: Betty Sue, I've been eager to tell you that since our earlier conversation, whenever I run into anyone from South Africa, I always make a point of asking them about the scenarios, and they all know the stories. They tell me all four stories, and say that clearly "Flight of the Flamingos" was preferable, and that everybody in the country knew the stories, and that those stories made it possible for people to understand that *this* decision leads to "Flight of the Flamingos," and this one leads to "Ostrich," and this one to "Icarus"—so it became not about your group wins versus mine, it became, "This works—this *works!*" So that kind of storied thinking helps me to understand what you mean about creating scenarios for health care rather than arguing over legislation.

FLOWERS: Yes. The practice will change as a consequence of the story changing, rather than the government trying to direct the practice.

DAVIS-FLOYD: How have the scenarios you wrote been received?

FLOWERS: Very well. They've been presented—I should give you the list,

because I don't remember it all off the top of my head. They've been presented to the G7, and the UN, and the European Community, and the French
government here and there, and to different nations around the world, and the
World Bank—just a lot of different places. And I have seen evidence of their
leaking out in various journal articles—in *Foreign Affairs,* for one, and in a
speech I heard given by someone from Washington, who in fact had been in
on the Shell briefings, as I discovered when I talked with the speaker afterward. So the story is getting disseminated, in various forms. And for the very
first time they are using the same story—just tweaking it a bit, for the next
round, and then adding two dimensions on to it—the human dimension, and
technology. So I'm going back this summer, to tweak. But it will be the same
basic story, because the story I wrote has lasted.

DAVIS-FLOYD: Both of the ones you wrote?

FLOWERS: Yes.

DAVIS-FLOYD: Why did they decide to keep the same stories?

FLOWERS: Because they are still alive. See, when a story has power, when it
still explains things that you feel are coming to you from the future, then it's
still useful to tell it. When a story loses power, it doesn't get told any more. So
they still want to tell these stories. And they do it in a storytelling fashion—
it's not like they become any more or less true.

DAVIS-FLOYD: And what kinds of changes does Shell want to make
in them?

FLOWERS: I won't know exactly till I get there—but they want to add two
dimensions, extra bits to them, one on humans—the new relationship of
people to their work. And then another dimension—technology. We dealt
with technology, but they want to do a whole big thing on it. And those are
two areas I'm very interested in, so I'm really eager to go back.

DAVIS-FLOYD: Tell me more about this new relationship between people
and their work.

FLOWERS: Last time I argued strongly for a section on the human being,
which I said would be true for either scenario—that workers were going to
demand more holistic attention, that they weren't going to be machines any
more, that they would look at their jobs as their lives, in a way, and would
be more attracted to what gave them a larger sense of themselves. It's a little
more complicated than that. And we had this story, and it was a huge story,
and we kept trimming it back, because people didn't think it was very important, and finally it was thrown out altogether. And I made a big argument, and
won over the head guy, to keep it in, and we just insisted on it because it is
true to *both* stories, which hadn't happened before.

DAVIS-FLOYD: And why did some people want to throw that out?

FLOWERS: Well, it didn't seem to be as important at the time, as all the economic and military things that were going on in the scenarios. I would say it's still pretty controversial—people will say no, people just work for the money.

DAVIS-FLOYD: Tell me what difference it makes to encode something like that into the scenarios themselves. In other words, you were saying, This is so important that it should be in the story, and they're saying, Well, it may be true but it's not important enough to be in the story? What difference does it make to have it in or out of the story?

FLOWERS: It raises the issue, it raises the question to talk about. The stories are starting places for discussion, really. What they do is throw light on things that managers can look at. If the light isn't thrown on that dimension, then it will not stand out as a subject for discussion. I wanted to see it in the conversation, I wanted it to be talked about.

DAVIS-FLOYD: I've been trying to ask people in the business world if they have heard about the Shell scenarios, but so far I have not encountered anyone who was heard more than a tiny bit about them. Last night I did overhear a conversation between two businessmen at a restaurant, which sounded very intense and very global, so I interrupted them to ask if they had heard of the Shell scenarios, or of scenarios in general. They hadn't, but they asked me what scenarios are. When I explained, they immediately started talking to me about chaos theory, fuzzy sets, and neural network theory.

FLOWERS: Those are the buzz words now, and they are all part of the scenario process.

DAVIS-FLOYD: What have you learned about the scenario-writing process, or about scenarios in general, since you left England?

FLOWERS: Wow. Well, I've learned, for one thing, about how easily companies can believe their own scenarios, which started off as fiction but end up as "fact"—I guess because of the natural human desire to make something that's real—so that by the time you finish with the scenario it is carried around as a prediction, rather than a fiction. Very few companies have the courage that Shell has to claim something as a fiction.

DAVIS-FLOYD: So what makes Shell unique in that regard?

FLOWERS: Well, there were some unique people involved with its founding, as is often the case—when you find something that's really different from the run of the mill there's a human being behind it, in its history. And in this case there was an amazing human being, Pierre Wack, who was a kind of wild man who could be found in his Shell office, in the most sterile building in London, sitting on his floor amidst a haze of *puja* sticks, meditating, to come up with his stories about the future of oil and gas—those are the stories told about him. He would go off on sabbatical, to India or wherever—just disappear for a month at a time, and come back with his head full of ideas. And Shell supported that happening in their midst.

DAVIS-FLOYD: Why?

FLOWERS: For some reason, and I don't know why, they had the instinct that it's good not to get encrusted in one way of thinking about things. And maybe that comes from their multicultural background. You know, it's a very old company, begun over a hundred years ago by a dual team, Dutch and British, so the fact that there are two founders, that from near the beginning, two different cultures have run this company, as they moved their headquarters from The Hague to London every other week—that does something. If you are in constant flux you are reminded again and again that nothing can be depended on to stay. That's a kind of wisdom that we all know intellectually, but very few of us know day by day.

DAVIS-FLOYD: Do you have any concrete information on what differences the stories you wrote for Shell have made in the world to date?

FLOWERS: No, no way, they're too big. There's no way anyone could know that. Which is another interesting thing about Shell, because you could make a case that these have absolutely no influence at all, because there is no way to show it, and yet they continue doing it.

DAVIS-FLOYD: Well, looking at *The Art of the Long View* and "The Gentle Art of Reperceiving" you can clearly see how the scenario helped Shell position itself for the oil price crash in the eighties. And the end of the cold war— one of Shell's scenarios predicted that, so they saw it coming a long way off. But those were dramatic shifts. And in the last two years there hasn't been anything that concrete and dramatic, with that kind of global effect, so the impact of your stories would be harder to assess, right? Because the shifts have been more subtle.

FLOWERS: Yes.

DAVIS-FLOYD: So what are the major things to look for? What could happen, in the scenarios you are going to write this summer, that would be huge and dramatic?

FLOWERS: Probably it would happen on the financial level, the movement of money around the world. Anybody with a huge amount of overhead and a lot of money being moved would have to know *both* fictions, because different things will happen about money in each. If there were to be some kind of global financial crisis—which might be coming—unless you know Shell's books, you wouldn't know what they had done to prepare. I don't know whether it would be obvious, even if they were making tremendous changes. The other place they could be making changes is in the way they run themselves internally. And I won't know that until I get there. And even then I may not know, because that's really subtle.

DAVIS-FLOYD: So let's "scenario" a bit right now. Suppose there *is* a worldwide financial crisis, set off by some trader in Japan, with a snowball effect, in scenario 1. And in scenario 2 everything just kind of keeps rocking along. What could a company like Shell do about it if they wanted to prepare for scenario 1?

FLOWERS: Going back to the real scenarios, a lot of which had to do with communications technology, they would be very wired. They would know, in advance, all kinds of things that were happening, would be tuned in, in touch, to make very quick decisions and increase their speed of implementation.

DAVIS-FLOYD: You mean, to move money here or there, put it in this bank or buy that factory?

FLOWERS: So, if you see these two scenarios, what you might do is say, You know what? We need more computer connections. We need to be more closely connected to the Bank of Tokyo. We need to work out a special deal with them so there is some kind of trigger mechanism whenever any large shift occurs, so we'll *know* if the Japanese do X, Y, or Z with the yen, and then we'll immediately need to flag the bottom-line investment in Singapore. A company could increase its options that way—but, of course, I'm just making this up.

DAVIS-FLOYD: For me, this is part of the process of learning to think in terms of scenarios.

FLOWERS: You wouldn't start by putting it all in gold, because that would be to treat the scenario as true.

DAVIS-FLOYD: And you're hoping that scenario 2 will happen, but because 1 exists, in which there is a crash, you've got to ask yourself how we could respond most effectively in the face of a crash, so then you say, Oh, we don't have enough communications links.

FLOWERS: Right, and we need more flagging mechanisms than we have in place—we should think this through.

DAVIS-FLOYD: So you want to be prepared for scenario 1 while you're hoping for—and trying to create—scenario 2. But in any case, you are ready, whichever way it goes.

FLOWERS: Yes.

DAVIS-FLOYD: What might be another event, besides a worldwide price crash, that would affect your scenarios?

FLOWERS: Well, if there really were a major technological breakthrough in energy.

DAVIS-FLOYD: Like someone coming up with a really cheap and viable alternative energy source that would eventually replace oil altogether.

FLOWERS: Right. It would have a dramatic impact—dramatic. So if you have a scenario that says that in ten years' time it will be economically viable, then what you do is put some of your money in those technologies, maybe establish your own research arm.

DAVIS-FLOYD: So that if there *is* a sudden shift from oil to some other technology, you'll be part of that shift.

FLOWERS: But see, what's important about a story instead of a prediction is that, if I just predict that by 2025 windmills are going to provide the heating and not gas or coal, that won't be enough. Because the thing about a story is that it tells you how we got from here to there, and what if getting from here to there meant passing through Russian gas? (Russia has a whole bunch of gas.) So then the flexible response is not "Let's start building windmills," but "Ah, now let's get heavy into Russian gas and quick out in three years time"—or whatever.

So, the point of a story is that it tells you how you get from A to B, because in the interim you might make very different decisions, even if the outcome is the same. And if you don't get the middle right, by the time windmills are the hot thing, you might be too broke to invest in them. In the scenarios we write at Shell, almost no one disagrees with how we got to the end, if we do our job right. They may disagree about the end itself, but almost no one disagrees with how we got there—and that's what has the influence. And that's why it's not a prediction. It's the story, not the end.

Notes

1. Since these interviews were conducted, a third major publication has come out that also details this process: Joseph Jaworski's *Synchronicity: The Inner Path of Leadership* (1996). See pp. 154–71 for the full text of the two 1992 scenarios, which are entitled "Barricades" and "New Frontiers."

2. The title has since been changed. See footnote 1.

3. Excerpted from "The Mont Fleur Scenarios," *Weekly Mail/Guardian Weekly.* It should be obvious from a quick read-through that none of these scenarios focuses on the divisive issues of black-white antagonism. Rather, they keep their sights on the long-term economic prosperity of the nation as a whole. The word *apartheid,* for example, is only mentioned once. This was intentional, and is one of the great benefits of the scenario process: scenarios shift the focus from specifically opposed political positions to a broader look at what will work—or fail—in the long run.

The creation of these scenarios was sparked in mid-1991 by a request to economist Pieter Le Roux to organize a conference on South Africa's economic future. Feeling the time was right for a different approach, Le Roux put together a multidisciplinary team of twenty-two people—four women and fourteen men—to work on possible scenarios for South Africa. Team members met for the first time at Mont Fleur, near Stellenbasch, in September 1991. Adam Kahane of Shell International in London, a recognized expert in scenario planning, acted as facilitator.

A video, *The Flight of the Flamingos,* describes four scenarios and the process by which they were created. It can be obtained by writing to The Mont Fleur Scenarios, The Institute for Social Development, University of the Western Cape, Private Bag X17, 7535 Bellville, South Africa.

4. The cover page says "Global Scenarios 1992–2020" at the top, and "Confidential" at the bottom. According to the next page, "the cover illustration, a series of fern-like spirals heading off into the distance, is a detail of the Mandelbrot set, named after its discoverer and the father of fractal geometry, Benoit Mandelbrot. Fractal geometry provides a common language to characterize certain complex systems studied in chaos theory. Chaos theory is now being applied in fields as diverse as physics, weather forecasting, economics, cardiology, and traffic planning as a way of dealing with data that cannot be used to predict the long-term future—not because we don't have computers big enough to do the job, but because after a time, small variations in initial conditions (like rounding of decimal places when we calculate with irrational numbers like pi) result in sudden and significant transformations."

References

Flowers, Betty S. 1990. *Extending the Shade.* Austin, Tex. Plain View Press.

———. ed. 1988. *Joseph Campbell and the Power of Myth: Bill Moyers and Joseph Campbell in Conversation.* New York: Doubleday.

———. ed. 1989. *Moyers: A World of Ideas.* New York: Doubleday.

Jaworski, Joseph. 1996. *Synchronicity: The Inner Path of Leadership.* Ed. Betty Sue Flowers. San Francisco: Barrett-Koehler.

Moyers, Bill. 1993. *Healing and the Mind.* Ed. Betty S. Flowers. New York: Doubleday.

Schwartz, Peter. 1991. *The Art of the Long View.* New York: Doubleday.

Wack, Pierre. "The Gentle Art of Reperceiving." *Harvard Business Review,* reprinted as "Strategic Planning in Shell," series no. 1, Shell International Petroleum Company Limited, Group Planning, PL86R21, March 1986.

SPECULATIONS AND RISKS

Gudrun Klein

My sketch is based on interviews with German bankers conducted in Germany in the spring of 1995. With the exception of one person, I had not previously known any of the people I met and talked with, mostly in an office setting. My interest was to find out about their respective self-understanding and their worldviews in the context of their professional lives in a (relatively) large corporation. Before explaining to readers more about the enterprise, I wish to thank my interlocutors for their readiness to take the time and be as open as they were toward an enterprise they did not quite know what to make of initially. While the interviews went smoothly overall, all of them contained moments of bewilderment, occasionally miscommunication, and surprise on both sides. To my own astonishment I noted that often when my interlocutors felt confronted with questions about what they took to be matters of course, they would appeal to either common sense, experience, or an authoritative voice from the history of economics, which to them seemed implicitly universal history or generally sufficient ground to assume such matters to be natural to all human kind. It was through such moments where I saw a common trait in their worldview and differences relating to mine, differences that have to do, for instance, with my understanding of the relative positions we hold within a capitalist society, and the various ways of handling cultural differences otherwise, that I decided to shape the essay in the form it now has. I felt the need to express some detachment without distancing myself from my interlocutors. I took liberty to introduce different voices from the realm of economic theory in response to my interlocutors' consistent appeals to such "common sense." Were I an artist with words I could certainly throw into sharper relief certain issues from the dialogues that I take to be crucial. As it is, I hope the readers will be curious enough to follow the nuances of the various positions, their inherent tensions, contradictions, and coherences. The slight ironic detachment, I trust, will make it easier also to realize that such utterances are but glimpses offered onto a complex web of relationships in which the narrative position is one among others, all embedded in a wider context we keep trying to grasp in our various ways. Were I to do these interviews today, no doubt, the outcome would be different. But I can say that I have, as in previous such endeavors, done all I could to ensure that revisions and translations do not distort the perspective of my respective interlocutors.

Michael Fortun

Steve Shak and I met at the intersection of two corporations. The first, of course, is Genentech, one of the oldest, largest, most innovative, and most profitable of the biotechnology (biopharmaceutical, more properly) companies in the brief history of that industry, and where Shak invented a new molecular therapy for cystic fibrosis. The second was Hampshire College, where I was teaching: a small, innovative, and far from profitable "experimental" educational institution only a few years older than Genentech. Although not technically an alumnus of Hampshire, Shak attended the school when it first opened, in the early 1970s, as part of an arrangement whereby students from other area schools (Shak was at Amherst College) could help jump-start Hampshire while its own enrollment was being built up. Even that brief connection was enough, however, to kick Hampshire's alumni relations and development offices into motion when Shak and his therapeutic substance, Pulmozyme, began making headlines in the business and biotech press. With their help and encouragement Shak came to Hampshire in October 1994 to speak to a class I was teaching on the science, history, and social implications of genetic engineering, and to another class in molecular biology, as well as to deliver a public lecture on his work on cystic fibrosis.

The intersection between Hampshire College and Genentech that brought about my first meeting with Steve Shak is an evocative instance of the trend that is one focus of the interview included here. When I interviewed Shak in his South San Francisco office in March 1995 I wanted to know how scientists in commercial spheres were thinking about the increasing cross traffic, in the life sciences, between those corporate entities called universities and those more strictly called corporations. In the more or less coherent field known as science and technology studies, to which I had come as a historian of science, that question was almost always answered with a lot of hand-wringing, a lot of holier-than-thou posturing, a lot of binarization—and not a lot of ethnographic detail. In this interview I wanted to do something different, detailing how one scientist understood how institutional placement affects the science he can and cannot do. My goal was to provide a sense of how molecular biology is, in fact, practiced, rather than immediately devolving into predictable articulations of when and where biotechnology is good or bad. This approach may provoke some to argue that I have avoided confronting the difficult ethical and social choices that biotechnology poses, and that I present only a "utopian narrative" here. I saw this interview as a welcome opportunity to step outside, even if just for a moment, those "dystopian narratives" about biotechnology with which I am all too familiar. I thought it would make a good experiment to *defer* that narrative for the time being (to take up Val Daniel's ethnographic play on *différance*), and to defer to Shak's different constitution of the world, to develop a more complex and nuanced sense of what that difference was about.

Moreover, the question of academia-industry cross-linkages was only one among many things that interested me. I've also been disciplined to want to know about science as practice, as work: how did Shak get the idea for Pulmozyme? How did he isolate the necessary genetic material? What else had to happen at the laboratory bench? How do you go from test tube to fermentation vat? What other work and skills are involved in managing people in addition to molecules? All of these things tend to get left out in the rush to construct another "Oh my, we're commodifying life!" scenario, and I'm glad to have the space for them here.

I remember standing on one of the hills that Genentech is built on, looking out in amazement at the sprawl of research and production buildings that hadn't existed at all twenty years previously. I know that allegories of autopoietic (self-organizing) systems are perhaps suspiciously attractive in both the life sciences and, to a lesser extent, cultural studies of science, but I nevertheless had this fleeting glimpse of Genentech just kind of assembling itself, a bioindustrial complex evolving from a San Francisco Bay that I saw as a "primordial stew" of venture capital, local scientific talent, pharmaceutical conglomerates, cultural imaginaries, and mighty tiny enzymes. I tried to convey that aesthetic in my introduction, where I "interview" the corporation itself, in many of its different registers. In between the molecular and the molar, the drug and the corporate economy, there's a lot of activity.

6

THE WORLD AS SPECULATION

ON GERMAN LENDING BANKERS. *"Then you get to Germany, where the way in which capital flows is not through public stock markets, the way it is in England and here, but through the banks. The accounting that the public sees in Germany is very obscure, because they want to keep the employees in the dark as much as possible because employees have considerable power. But the banks, which are actually supplying the capital, get whatever information they want. So accounting in Germany is transparent to the banks but opaque to the employees and the public" (Robert Elliott).*

Drawn from Perin's piece (chap. 2 above), Elliott's remark evokes the privileged context of the group of middle managers of a major German bank, interviewed by Gudrun Klein. However, with regard to the relevance of a cultural framework, either as a way to think about their own practices or as a factor in making investment decisions, they remain typically skeptical and fundamentalist. There is a repeated tone of candor about the merciless bottom line in their work. Still, Klein skillfully elicits and displays the traces and moments of hesitation in her interviews, as well as moments of overinsistence and clear contradiction in which there is a legible anxiety regarding such a constitutional performance of the banker's ideological marginalization of the cultural (and thus the moral) in the committed practice of the rational. The mix of purely economic and social considerations in the work of investment bankers is most richly exposed in those passages that deal with risk assessment and investment criteria (particularly the comments of the interlocutors Klein calls Bodo and Christian). In general, Klein's piece can stand as an exemplar of those businesses deeply involved in the instabilities of societies on a global scale, that resolutely resist (with appropriate qualification being part of this rhetoric) engaging in an explicit, operational discourse about cultural differences and values, but can't do so without considerable ambivalence and self-deception. – G. E. M.

* * *

NARRATOR [*to audience*]: Let me introduce the personae of this sketch. They all work at the same German bank, and seem to share a considerable amount of enthusiasm for their work and the institution they work for. They also have in common a certain interest in liberal arts, which they all considered at one time as a professional option. They chose, however, to find a profession they consider immediately relevant, effective, and, (perhaps not so) incidentally, well paid. Most of them see the influence their parents' profession may have had on their own choice of careers. Most have pursued them without manifest detours, if not all with the same clearheadedness they now seem to espouse as a basic shaping value in their lives. All of them concede finding it difficult to match professional demands with concerns which they all conceive of as private in the widest sense. None of them hesitate to call their job the center of their lives, although they all deplore that preponderance and point to the struggle they put up to have a life outside their job. Looking at future developments, none seem concerned that the development of new technology may change banking systematically.

While all enjoy positions within the middle ranks of the bank's hierarchy, they refer to their institution as The Bank. The term connotes all those above them who are perceived as distinctly "other" within the system. What constitutes their corporation as their world with which they identify depends, it seems, entirely on the context in which they are being asked to speak about it. The most stable and common factor is their perception of peer recognition both as part of the competition within the bank's hierarchy and as the only space of well-functioning teamwork. All agree that gender is no issue for them, although they also all verify that women are underrepresented within the hierarchy of the bank. True to their conviction that economy is neutral to such issues as gender, and pragmatic as they all pride themselves to be, they see such inequity as normal since it is pervasive in society at large. Equally normal to them is the belief that human beings are naturally self-serving and that economic activities match such inclinations best in a liberal market system.

THE BANK [*stately*]: The bank fosters the socially oriented liberal market system by its policies; it aims to remain a leading European bank in all important world markets and to serve clients of excellent standing who expect excellence themselves. The bank offers sustained profit as the basis for growth and stability, integrating risks as factors for success in its actions, utilizing sources worldwide, cooperating in alliances to strengthen its powers. The basic power resides in its own members and their creativity. The motto for their modes of action is to create and shape instead of red tape.

BANKERS' CHORUS [*a little weary*]: Sounds good, isn't exactly how it works. You know, the usual theory and practice thing.

ADA [*a middle-aged woman, public-relations specialist in her bank*]:[2] I am responsible for the internal and external public relations and for information. Eighty percent of my work is ghost writing for the leadership, 20 percent goes into presenting materials in our different publications, lectures to guests, etc. I want to inform the general public, the clients of the bank, as well as my colleagues, honestly, comprehensively, and in a readable form about our business, our goals, and about personnel matters. I see it as my function to add to the positive image of the bank inside and outside and to assist in creating a good climate for clients. Not least I try to use the small range of influence offered me to stand in for my own political and ethical positions. On a more personal note: my priorities have to be fitted into a very tight time schedule. I rank family highest, followed by career. I often feel rushed, and cannot always claim that I can handle everything perfectly. In my private life I am interested in things similar to those with which I deal professionally.

Asked about future crises: I see dangers in securing the bank's strength through all kinds of factors, internal and external, for instance, the call for further privatization, or constantly increasing costs, are external pressures, lack of motivation in colleagues and the leaders of the bank, internal ones.

I would hope for less wars, less poverty, less environmental destruction, less crime, more readiness to take responsibility and to invest in social change. But I see little hope for such betterment. As far as the goals of the bank relate to such political and ethical goals, I hope that its activities contribute a little to the improvement of the world.

ADAM [*male philosopher with authoritative voice, cautiously speculating*]: I see a propensity common to all men, namely, the propensity to truck, barter, and exchange one thing for another. Whether this propensity be one of those original principles in human nature of which no further account can be given; or whether, as seems more probable, it be the necessary consequence of the faculties of reason and speech it belongs not to our present subject to inquire.[3]

BODO [*a middle-aged banker, macroeconomist whose function is to rate countries economically and to offer risk assessments to his bank; his area of expertise covers many Asian countries, South and Central American countries, most of the so-called developing countries in Eastern Europe and the Russian Federation, as well as some parts of Africa; speaking with calm conviction*]: Rating decisions are very influential regarding the image countries have for investors generally, not just for the bank establishing the rating.

A VOICE OF ECONOMIC SENSE [*authoritatively*]: Economic man. The name given to the "construct" in economics whereby individuals are assumed to behave as if they maximize *utility,* subject to a set of constraints of which the most obvious is income. Economic man is "rational" if he pursues this objective although he may face obstacles, such as imperfect information, which prevent him actually achieving the goal. Rational man in economics may, however, pursue objectives other than the maximization of utility, in which case he is rational if he pursues that goal in a self-consistent manner.[4]

NARRATOR: Tell me about your criteria of assessment and whether you look more at the country in question or more at the bank's interests.

BODO: A country is reasonable to us when it pursues reasonable economic policies that produce an increased gross national product, trade, or other means of increasing its wealth to enable it to repay what credits/loans have been granted. [*After some reflection, very authoritatively*] Rating is an instrument to assess the bank's risk, not the country's risks. But an economic policy that is reasonable will make a country creditworthy. In that sense it is assessing a country's risks, too. A bank's interests thus are ideally congruent with a country's interests. Normally, it's not ideal, but only because a country's economic policies weren't healthy. If a democracy follows upon a dictatorship and the dictatorship has bled the country, it is a real conflict to deal with such a legacy adequately. [*Quietly, but with conviction*] If I really wanted to see anything from a country's perspective, I would have to use very different norms. But I use the norms of bank business and profit. [*Giving it further thought*] An example would be the question of dictatorship or democracy— for the creditworthiness of a country it may be better to have a dictatorship. It's clear that for the bank it is positive to have strict government, whereas for the country it may be very negative. It is not a contradiction for me, it is simple: I rate the country positively. My private opinion is irrelevant.

A VOICE OF ECONOMIC COMMON SENSE [*matter-of-factly*]: Rationality: behavior by an economic agent (consumer, producer, government, etc.) which is consistent with a set of rules governing preferences.[5]

NARRATOR [*to Bodo*]: Tell me more about how you actually work. Where do you get your information from, what is relevant in your analyses leading to rating and risk assessment.

BODO [*after some deliberation, with firmness*]: I get my information from statistics, the World Bank, IMF, national statistics, published material in newspapers, magazines, etc., but can never really keep up with all material available. I have to focus on certain publications for pragmatic reasons. In my private life I keep up reading other related things, social history and the like. But that I can only use as background.

NARRATOR: Do you ever travel to countries you assess?

BODO [*without hesitation*]: There is no need to travel to countries. Actually, I find it rather distracting and even misleading because you never know what people show you that you cannot put into the right perspective.

[*Enter the bankers' Mephistopheles* KARL *with his notorious friend* FRIEDRICH]

KARL AND FRIEDRICH [*matter-of-factly, but with an underlying warning ur-*

gency]: The need of a constantly expanding market for its products chases the bourgeoisie over the whole surface of the globe. It must nestle everywhere, establish connections everywhere. The bourgeoisie has through its exploitation of the world market given a cosmopolitan character to production and consumption in every country.

It compels all nations, on pain of extinction, to adopt the bourgeois mode of production; it compels them to introduce what it calls civilization into their midst. In a word, it creates a world after its own image.[6]

NARRATOR: What about your competitors in the market?

BODO [*pondering*]: We look at competing banks constantly, it is problematic in the sense that there is a kind of herd instinct: one bank does something, everyone else feels the need to follow suit. An example would be the way we offered credit to developing countries in the seventies, which then led to the financial crisis in the eighties. Mexico is a case in point. Our rating was critical if positive, but we were criticized for not having given a more favorable rating. The crisis has shown that we were right, but it remains difficult to hold such a minority view.

ADAM [*with authoritative clarity*]: We rarely hear, it has been said, of the combinations of masters, though frequently of those of workmen. But whoever imagines, upon this account, that masters rarely combine, is as ignorant of the world as of the subject. Masters are always and everywhere in a sort of tacit but constant and uniform combination.

NARRATOR [*to Bodo*]: But what about the hard data on which you base decisions? One would assume they are indisputable.

BODO [*self-critically aware of a problem, slowly*]: Not even numbers and statistics are indubitable, unambiguous. They have to be interpreted, and thus there is room for disagreement. Unfortunately, there is not one truth; rather, you can dispute everything and judge almost anything positively or negatively. Where the material itself is insufficient, or obviously contradictory, or based on guesswork rather than on fact, this problem becomes even greater. But it is inherent in the rating process as such.

ECONOMIC COMMON SENSE: Positive economics. The part of economic science that concerns itself with statements that are capable of verification by reference to the facts. In principle, all positive statements should be reducible to some form that is testable by reference to empirical evidence.[7]

Normative economics. Economic analysis that provides prescriptions or statements about what should be rather than what is. In effect, normative economics is constructed from positive economics and some judgments about what society's objectives should be (also known as value judgments). Thus we may dispute a statement of normative economics either because we consider the positive analysis to be incorrect or because we disagree with the value judgment involved.[8]

NARRATOR [*to Bodo*]: Where do you see crises in the future?

BODO: The rising unemployment is the biggest one for our economy I can see. [*Visibly resisting addressing global issues that are of less real immediate concern to him and also as being too complex to go into*]

NARRATOR: Do you see a solution?

BODO [*reluctantly*]: Well, the work would need to be distributed more fairly. [*Laughing*] That way, I could also enjoy my private life more, for which I have too little time. [*Ponderingly*] But that's utopian. It's not going to happen, [*slowly*] and I know I'm not willing to sacrifice anything at the moment to make it happen, in this bank, for instance, either. [*Ready to leave the subject*] I am reasonably happy in my job and I have my life outside my job, even if it's limited, but that's what I try to focus on.

[*Enter* Christian, *a young male investment banker who manages investment projects conceived of as economic development projects in Europe generally, but mainly focusing on Eastern Europe and the countries of the Russian Federation. Money for the projects is provided partly by Western political institutions, including governments, partly by private investors. He has learned to analyze processes of investment and economic development and functions as an adviser to interested investors to assess the desirability and realizability of development projects.*]

NARRATOR: What are your criteria for investment decisions?

CHRISTIAN [*friendly, matter-of-factly*]: Economically, certain countries are irrelevant, and our investors as a rule are not interested in them, they focus on other countries. I assume they do so because of the economic and political power of such countries. Also the political structures, the infrastructure, and not least the affinity of cultures may play a role in such decisions.

NARRATOR [*curious*]: Which differences are considered relevant?

CHRISTIAN [*matter-of-factly*]: Well, for example, in Western Europe. The countries of the first European union can be seen as a nucleus, but Portugal and Spain become more important, as does Ireland, because for Germany, at least, there are economic links already, and also because the economic development program of the European Union aims to strengthen structurally weaker countries within the union and thus they become a little more important for investment activities.

NARRATOR: How does that pertain to Eastern European, Slavic, and Turkic countries?

BODO: Within the Russian Federation, the Turkic-speaking countries play no role in our activities. I guess it's not only a question of size, but of history and of the economic and political situation. It is much easier to establish links with the Eastern European countries than with Russia, let alone the Turkic-speaking countries. The latter countries have been shaped much less and much later by the Western European economic and political situation than the former. Let me give you a practical example: the Eastern European countries had such things as trade laws, a constitution, civil rights codes, frames for economy — in other words, things that in Russia, for instance, hardly existed before the revolution and afterward didn't exist because of the system. That makes for a different background of history, economics, politics, and makes a difference in cooperation.

NARRATOR: Would religion account for any differences in this context since you separated the Turkic countries from the others? And what about languages as a barrier or common bond?

CHRISTIAN: To have a common language makes investments easier. The common language in my experience is usually English. In some cases French or German, [*laughingly*] since we, of course, don't speak Slavic language, and Russian isn't popular in Eastern European countries, if we were to try it. In Russia itself I suppose English is also the common foreign language. Turkic countries, I assume, are comparable to Russia with regard to foreign languages, the difference there is simply economic. But Islam makes these countries seem more difficult, no doubt, probably more so than they actually are. And if you hear about political unrest, it adds to a picture that may not be true to reality but is sufficient as a preliminary judgment for decisions, and then you only look at natural resources, minerals, and the like, and you focus, naturally, only on countries where you see the fewest difficulties and the most possibilities.

ECONOMIC COMMON SENSE: Animal spirits. An explanation of *investment* that rejects mathematical models as of little use and instead analyzes investment as deriving from the animal spirits of whims of entrepreneurs. The term was first used by J. M. Keynes.[9]

NARRATOR [*to Christian*]: Could you specify further what makes an economy a "relevant economy"?

CHRISTIAN: First, either the factual or potential size of the market, demand of the products one has to offer, or, in the case of the bank, the demand for products of clients for which either directly or indirectly bank products will also be in demand. The size of the gross national product is decisive here because it tells you what size of trade, and hence profit, is possible. With regard to the Russian Federation, we still only think in terms of potential, not factual markets. It is the future-oriented aspect.

ADAM: Every individual is continually exerting himself to find out the most advantageous employment for whatever capital he can command. It is his own advantage, indeed, and not that of the society, which he has in view. But the study of his own advantage, naturally, or rather necessarily, leads him to prefer that employment which is most advantageous to the society.[10]

NARRATOR: Can you describe your own role in this process?

CHRISTIAN [*after some deliberation*]: The criteria I mentioned are necessary for an economic decision in order to make my endeavors successful. In that sense I set the parameters. In my own area, I have to be responsible for other people's money. Hence the need for even greater care to assure the viability of a project. Were I to invest privately, I could, perhaps, be more lenient, or follow other considerations. As a bank I am obliged to apply strict economic criteria. Political institutions occasionally invest economically in situations not strictly following economic criteria because of, say, political interests. If I advise them, I will point out the strictly economic criteria, but I will not be held entirely responsible for the outcome should the investor insist on giving priority to other criteria.

NARRATOR: Do you consider such decisions as influencing economic affairs in the countries affected?

CHRISTIAN [*very matter-of-factly*]: The decision regarding which countries are at all worthy of economic development considerations is clearly shaped by the instruments we as a bank have available and want to use in a given situation. Inasmuch as our bank is involved in other considerations, such as social and political issues, we keep those criteria in mind as well. We need a clear legal and political frame and stable partners both in the realm of economics, not least banking, and that of politics. It has to be possible to plan two to four years in advance. And while you may not be able to list each country in the world in a neat hierarchy, you see quite easily clusters of countries that fit our interests, and others that don't. For example, Poland, the Czech Republic, and Hungary fulfill such criteria much better than, say, Russia, or the Ukraine, let alone the Turk republics. It is only natural to develop the Central European countries first, before investing elsewhere. The size of Russia and its political weight are criteria for political interests and hence for economic investments, which have to be considered riskier than others elsewhere. By the way, the relative weight seen in different countries can be seen in what kind of representation banks establish there: from absence, to simple offices of representation, to full-size banking service—that's the assessment of viability expressed in concrete visible signs.

NARRATOR: Would you care to give me a brief sketch of the world order according to your criteria?

CHRISTIAN [*laughing incredulously, then, obligingly*]: I focus on those regions in which my local investors are mostly involved. They are concentrated in regions of growth, that is, regions that over a considerable period of time already have and promise to continue to have an increase of economic productivity and therefore are interesting as trade partners. The time frame is anything from now to up to ten years. The turn of the century seems the limit to predict anything economically or politically. That organizes the world, as it were. Southeast Asia, ASEAN countries, Hong Kong, itself difficult to assess after returning to China. Its size and its relative development, Latin America,

North America is not in that sense a developing region, of course. Other markets, like the Near East or South Africa, are relatively small change, so to speak.

NARRATOR: Central Africa, the "rest" of Africa?

CHRISTIAN: As a market, very problematic, too underdeveloped and very likely causally linked with that, politically too complicated. Take Libya or Algeria, or, in black Africa, Nigeria, for example. Even if North Africa is politically a more interesting region, especially for the European Union, I don't see it as a viable market for the next ten years. And I don't see individual investors wanting to take such risks. Unless, of course, they're interested in the natural resources, if you think of oil in Venezuela, or copper in Chile, where firms take risks more readily. But any normal business or entrepreneur will not invest there.

NARRATOR: What about the influence investors have in such countries?

CHRISTIAN: In my assessment they have very little influence, especially politically, but also economically, unless there are a whole lot of investors interacting with each other. I can see investors interested in natural resources exerting political influence to some degree.

NARRATOR: Where does influence begin for you?

CHRISTIAN [*uncertain*]: It depends. You can say everything influences everything. But influence in terms of discernible influence—let's take Zaire and assume a medium-sized firm goes there to invest. The firm hires thirty Zairean workers and produces screws, for example, not for weapons or such things, but simple screws. Let's make it even simpler. Let's take a textile production. Harmless example. T-shirts are being produced by thirty locals under the supervision of one German. This firm is limited in its activities and in its influence. It has effects in the area it works, but that depends itself on the size of the place it works in, what other firms there are, not least what other German or European firms, and on whether local firms interact with it. If it's the only firm of its kind, it may have influence on whether a road will be built to access its buildings. That's the limit of its influence. But it's not an important influence for Zaire as a country.

NARRATOR: What about environmental, social, cultural influence?

CHRISTIAN [*surprised*]: If it pollutes the major river of the area, it has environmental influence, otherwise not. Thirty people make for a relatively small multiplicatory effect, but if you are the only employer there, your influence increases. If you expand your means of diffusion by sending fifty Europeans instead of one, you multiply your influence. I cannot deny that there will always be some influence, but the degree is what counts.

And as for the product, in our example, the screws, you don't have to assume that they are needed in Zaire, but somewhere someone needs screws. Where the demand is doesn't matter.

ECONOMIC COMMON SENSE: Need. It is sometimes argued that individuals will not, in a free market, demand as much of certain commodities as "society" or the "community" deems they should consume. Thus a distinction between the individual's own demand for the product and his or her need is drawn. The need concept may be justified in terms of the good being a merit good, the consumption of which is intrinsically desirable. Demand is want backed by money.[11]

NARRATOR: How do you assess the cultural influence if you have a European boss and African workers?

CHRISTIAN [*reluctant*]: That influence I judge [*hesitating*] to be minimal. I take as an example East Germany. The influence you have on the structure and processes of a firm are minimal if you are alone. You won't change the culture of that firm unless there are more to achieve that than you.

NARRATOR: Do you ever consider issues of investment and influence from the perspective of the country you want to go to?

CHRISTIAN: What do you mean by the perspective of such countries?

NARRATOR: You might actually look at a country not only from the perspective of your economic criteria for development but also from its own concrete situation, culture, etc., in which such criteria might very well be less relevant than they are for you.

CHRISTIAN: I need to differentiate here. As a bank I will always consider net profit, the increase of money, as the first priority. If investors want to prioritize development rather than financial profit, I will assist. The profit in that case might well be political, and thus in the larger sense of that term, there, too, one's own profit is of primary interest. I take this to be absolutely normal. Whoever pays something is interested in the return of such payment. The investor carries the risk of such investment and the profit is the deserved result of such risk taking. Self-interest is self-evidently the first priority of economic activities. I work according to such norms and accept them as given. I identify with them as far as I can. So far, I have not had any problems, but I can see areas where problems might arise for moral reasons.

NARRATOR: If you had to choose between moral and profit, what would you do?

CHRISTIAN [*after some reflection*]: As in my private life, I would be ready to compromise in some areas, and would not compromise my moral attitude in others. Let me give you an example: an investment in Iran is not something I could morally support at this time. Economically, I don't see it as viable. Iran is a country where everyone of political influence has bloody hands and its political system is absolutely beyond my moral value system. Absolutely immoral. That would, therefore, be a limit. Resulting from my moral position, I would not invest any money there, and I foresee such great problems that it wouldn't make sense economically either. I know that people disagree on such an assessment, but for me it would be a decisive moment, jobwise. Libya is another case in point. China is ambivalent. For me, economically and morally, it's complicated, too. Here the question of influence is pertinent, as it was for Eastern Europe, East Germany. The question of realpolitik, influence, and change.

NARRATOR: Have you ever been to China?

CHRISTIAN: No. In all these cases I've given as examples, the issue is one of dictatorship. I see communist regimes as of necessity dictatorships. For moral reasons I am skeptical regarding China because it is a dictatorship. Not every dictatorship is the same. I also have an economic problem. I assume that after Deng's death this dictatorship will gradually end and I foresee similar processes for Russia. As a banker it would be nice to live in a safe world, but [*laughing awkwardly*] it would be boring, too.

NARRATOR: If you could plan the development in China, what would you do?

CHRISTIAN [*repeating the question, a little at a loss*]: That's difficult. I have never thought about that. I have tried to imagine how China will develop, but not how I would like it to develop. To me it's clear that I cannot influence that anyway, so I don't waste thoughts on it. I focus on my expectations of what will happen.

[*Enter* DELTA, *a young female investment banker, Japanese by origin.*]

NARRATOR: Please describe what you do.

DELTA [*with consideration*]: I invest money of investors for them: over the counter, by telephone, computer, stock exchange, speculation, through derivatives, futures, and the like. My investors are private people, as well as institutions like insurance companies. The common goal is to maximize profit and to reduce financial risk.

NARRATOR: Tell me how you understand the market you are working in and with.

DELTA [*reflectively*]: The market is [*long hesitation*] where all money-related activities take place. It is opinions leading to financial transactions. It is many different actors—the investors having money, others needing money. It is people having different reasons for investing or buying money. Many banks with different monies from very different clients, for different reasons want to sell or buy. It is opinion leaders, politicians, and real players, in the narrow sense of the word, with little or no money, who take a loan to invest in futures, for instance, what we call volatility investment. All that is the market.

NARRATOR: Is it a global market?

DELTA: The strongest players (in the more general sense of the word) are located in industrialized nations.

NARRATOR: Please describe more in detail how you understand your job, what you like about it, what you find difficult, if you do.

DELTA: I want to do my job well to earn my own living. I don't see this particular job as a goal of my life, just pragmatically to make a living. It's not my main goal in life to be an investment banker. But I don't know what my real goal in life is. And I don't know how to find out. I have no pressure to change. It's not a job I have illusions about, it's not a job where I feel I contribute to the common good. It's simply a job. But it's my life center, absolutely, [*with felt emphasis*] *absolutely*. I spend all my days in my office and they are long days. I use my free time to do other things. Music, friends, cooking, traveling. [*After a pause, with enthusiasm*] But I enjoy the work because it is free, I can do what I want to do, I can decide myself what to do. Whom I offer something, what I offer to buy or sell are all my ideas. And my relations with clients are my responsibility. I know it's a freedom within parameters others have set. But when you are good, it gets really interesting. It's very changeable, the market changes every moment—weather, political decisions, wars, commentaries—they all influence the market, and it's a never-ending process. The products, too, always change. People get bored and you have to have a sense for what they might like. You have to come up with new things. Also, you constantly interact with a lot of different people. But all like myself, normal people who want to profit from the financial market. And I travel a lot, which I also enjoy. [*After a pause*] I earn a lot of money when I'm good. Hierarchies of age and status matter less than material success, which is acknowledged in good salaries, which, at least in Japan, had not been the case before. It makes for freedom of young people and across genders, although there are more men in the business than women. [*After some more reflection*] Success in my job is not only about money, it's being with people, connected with them, through the telephone, at least, and I know my clients, and they trust me and I trust them—otherwise, it doesn't happen. Trust grows and is established through the bank first. Then I have to work with that. Results and everyday behavior establish continued trust. A relationship is a constant one, not a momentary one. Clients stay for years. If I fail, clients will leave not just me but the bank. That's important [*After some more deliberation*] About the more negative sides: one is always in competition with colleagues. Everyone works for themselves first. We try to act collegially but it's not easy to combine with competition.

NARRATOR: Where do you get your information to act upon?

DELTA: I get information about the world through news, TV, radio; newspapers are too slow. When I come to my office I read financial commentaries on the market. We have colleagues in Japan who contact us about news. I check headlines. I check interest rates, exchange rates, etc.

NARRATOR: When you look at the world, where do you expect crises to arise?

DELTA [*after considerable deliberation*]: For example, take the U.S. deficit.

U.S. people don't save enough. It's not good because money people save becomes a country's material base, its own capital, literally. Germany and Japan
have the highest savings rate and hence a smaller deficit. The U.S. has a huge
deficit and hence is in obligation to others, which is dangerous, at least when
they are demanded to be repaid by the investors or they cannot spend money
where they want to or ought to for the common good. You become ever more
restricted. [*After a pause*] Points of crisis globally can be anywhere. But take
Japan, for instance, which carries almost 20 percent of U.S. debt, of the total
U.S. deficit, Japan has invested 20 percent. Every American would be furious
if they knew that Japan is one of the biggest creditors of the U.S. The Japanese are getting impatient, because what they bought keeps losing value, and
so they buy less. If they were to sell their investment in the U.S. it would be a
huge crisis not only in the U.S. It would, of course, not be in the Japanese
interest either, but it can happen any time. Especially if a war were to occur
that involved both Japan and the U.S. In small measure it's happened already,
when the Japanese sold real estate in New York, prices slumped. People lose
their wealth. [*Reflecting some more*] I don't think that wars between Western
nations are likely, but also not impossible.

NARRATOR: If trade presupposes inequality, and interest is increased where
demand is increased, can you imagine that feelings of envy and hatred may
also be increased?

DELTA: Yes, but we are not like that. For the financial market participants
the market is only numbers. Our attitude is free from emotion, and we've
learned to be objective. I can see that such attitudes can contribute to aggra-
vating differences, imbalances, and the like, but we don't create them. We are
part of the differences, of course. And in that way we are part of the emotional and political issues that may lead to war.

NARRATOR: How do you perceive your own job in all this?

DELTA [*very haltingly*]: I can see that what we do contributes to this state of
affairs. Trade [*long hesitation*] does not contribute to war. It is a truly neutral
world. Feelings are not involved. War happens through feelings like envy, hatred, it happens politically. Okay, if you look at the financial market, it is neutral. But the financial market can be used, abused. [*Pensively*] The financial
market is based on opinions, rather ungraspable guesswork.

ECONOMIC COMMON SENSE: There is currently no universally accepted
theory about expectations.

DELTA: I believe the money market to be neutral because very different
people are active in it, which neutralizes everyone's interests. It's international
and in that sense neutral. But if you want to influence it, you can. African
countries, for instance, are hardly involved at all. And in that sense financial
markets are not neutral. [*Thoughtfully*] People who have a lot of influence are
the industrialized nations. [*Reassuringly*] But we sit in one boat through our

activities, which has lowered the risk of war between us. It seems the only solution—to do business with each other, to make sure that everyone makes some profit in some kind of balance. And I see that there are always some who lose and that it will be a give and take. [*After some deliberation*] Financial markets are profitable mostly to industrialized nations; there's no balance between give and take because industrialized nations can exist without the smaller, less important countries. If in the Middle East there's a crisis, everyone is disturbed; if Yugoslavia goes to ruin, we don't worry as much. It's sad but true and I understand why it is that way.

NARRATOR: What role does language play in this financial world?

DELTA: The business language is English, whether you deal with Germans or Japanese or the U.S. or whatever. We have a very specialized slang. And, in Japan, for instance, it's considered positive if you speak Japanese, but it's not necessary to do business. [*After some consideration*] It makes little difference whether you can speak the client's language or not. That becomes more important only if the client doesn't speak English well enough; if both communicate best in a third language, that's preferable to not speaking the client's language well. And in my experience, management bankers, say, from Germany, have never spoken Japanese well enough to talk with people. Japanese clients will be handled by Japanese bankers, while management is German and the business language is English.

NARRATOR: How do you feel about that?

DELTA: I would find it very good if it were different. I see that it makes a big difference that I speak German well. Before they know I speak German they treat me with little consideration—that's normal, and I see the same in Japan toward foreigners. It's not good, just reality. I'm a practical person and say, if it's not worse, it's harmless. But it can get worse. When people follow stereotypes and don't see the person. [*After more reflection*] The language is my biggest problem. I need more energy to speak German than Japanese, it's more stressful on a less cognitive level. But altogether I feel fine here.

NARRATOR: You mentioned that your job is not your real goal in life, although it plays a central role in it. Do you ask yourself about alternatives? And if so, why and when does it happen?

DELTA: Something is lacking. I think I envy people whose jobs are useful and important, but the transactions don't really help anyone, strictly speaking. You cannot see the product. I cannot see it, taste, it, say it's beautiful. That's a lack. It's like a phantom, a number, nothing visible, tangible. It could be nothing but a game. And I would like something to have more concreteness, I mean, like a painting, where I can say this is beautiful, it has a value. I never know what I sell, the value changes every day, it may not have any value any moment, depending on what happens. You can act to the best of your knowledge and the result may still be bad. You sell something unsafe. It's not predictable, not trustworthy, but people know that about it. It's just part of it that you cannot promise anything. When I've sold something or given advice and have believed in the soundness of my actions, and it fails, I feel that if I could have sold jewelry or a painting, it would have been different.

NARRATOR: The freedom in your job that you enjoy seems paired with an utter dependency on factors you have little influence over.

DELTA: Yes. And in the case of failure, that bothers me. It's like a lottery.

NARRATOR: Let us look at the function of money in Western societies. How do you see it?

DELTA [*very surprised*]: Money? [*Hesitatingly*] Everything is about money.

MEPHISTOPHELES KARL AND FRIEND FRIEDRICH [*with fervor*]: The bourgeoisie has torn away from the family its sentimental veil, and has reduced the family relation to a mere money relation. Constant revolutionizing of production, uninterrupted disturbance of all social conditions, everlasting uncertainty, and agitation distinguish the bourgeois epoch from all earlier ones. All fixed, fast-frozen relations, with their train of ancient and venerable prejudices and opinions, are swept away, all new-formed ones become antiquated before they can ossify. All that is solid melts into air, all that is holy is profaned, and man is at last compelled to face with sober senses his real conditions of life and his relations with his kind.

ECONOMIC COMMON SENSE: Value, theory of. The intrinsic worth of a commodity. If defined in terms of money, value determines the price. Economists have traditionally separated the concepts of use value and value in exchange. Value in use is not an intrinsic quality of a commodity, but its capacity to satisfy human wants. Value in exchange is the worth of commodity in terms of its capacity to be exchanged for another commodity. The exchange ratios of two commodities are the relative prices of those commodities if expressed in terms of a constant money commodity.

In classical economics the existence of use value was a pre-requisite for commodities to have value in exchange. A commodity must possess utility or usefulness in order for it to be produced or exchanged.[12]

NARRATOR: What about interest?

DELTA: Well, you make a profit of something someone lacks. The rate of interest is set by the neediest. If there are a lot of people who have money to spend or invest, interest rates increase. But also if there are a lot of people who need money, the rate increases.

I think that's how it is in life, too. What is exciting in this job, the market is about money, but it's like life itself. People make it, and prices and interest rates are set by people following rules of supply and demand. And relationships have to do with needs, where one gives something another wants or needs.

ECONOMIC COMMON SENSE: Law of demand. The widely accepted view that, other things being equal, more of a good will be bought the lower is its price, and the less will be bought the higher is its price. Strictly, the law states a general expectation and is not a law at all since demand may rise as price increases and it is not always clear what other things are being held equal.[13]

AN ISLAMIC VOICE: Interest, in Islamic understanding, falls under the broader term of usury, and is forbidden. The fair and indisputable basis for making money is that the profit be the result of work. The rate of interest is far from this basis—it (even) destroys it. It is a price in return for no work and it comes through misuse. Therefore, the misuser is paid, which is unreasonable and illogical. It also induces greed for hoarding, which is forbidden and destructive.

The Islamic bank employs commercial funds in projects that give lawful returns; the bank becomes a partner in the ownership of a project, both in profit and loss, and perhaps most importantly links economic development to social development.[14]

NARRATOR [to Delta]: Does what you said mean we have to pay a price for everything we need? Or could we imagine a free exchange?

DELTA [after some deliberation]: I don't know. I don't know. Free exchange usually has a price, too. There's no free lunch, they say. The expectation may be friendship, friendliness, or company. You give your time or energy or whatever.

NARRATOR: So the more you need, the more you have to pay? Is that also a rule of life?

DELTA [without hesitation]: I think so, certainly. You don't pay with money, but with concentration, time, love, you give something. And for a great need, you pay a lot.

NARRATOR: Did you always think of life that way?

DELTA [with great clarity]: No. [Upon some reflection] But by now I find it very convincing. The model is a method of thinking for me by now, which I would apply if I worked in a different job. It's objective to me, it was enlightening for me when I learned about it. We have scientific models explaining how charts develop. Different methods to read charts, and you see different phases.

NARRATOR: Where's the deficit of meaning, the lack you note about your job in all this?

DELTA [uncertain, slowly]: I can assume that it may be a lack I would find everywhere. But I think that the market I deal in is more dependent on greater mechanisms beyond my control than other areas of life.

NARRATOR: What is happening in the financial markets now?

DELTA [after careful consideration]: Investment banking as a business has grown incredibly in the last ten years. As cycles of life are, there will be a decline. Clients and I are aware of that. We are already in a down phase. I hope we will get into an upward move again. At the moment a lot of people are no longer employed. And if that continues, the whole economy will be affected. It should not happen. It's not very pleasant for a lot of people if it happens. And we are all involved.

ERICH [*an elderly male banker, director of a separate sector of the bank, managing building projects; he enjoys the relative freedom of this position because here he can do things more independently than ever before and is only judged by the net financial results of his management and the acquisition of new clients and projects securing such success; he could take the position that he somewhat coquettishly calls marginal thanks to earlier successes in various managerial functions he had in the bank*]: I have fifty people working with me. We have several branches in other parts of Germany. I have chosen the former East German parts because I see good chances for a stable market there for the kind of projects we offer to manage, such as sewage plants, town developments, and the like. On my initiative, we reactivated this branch of activities lately, and I'm pleased to see the success—it's relatively small but steady.

NARRATOR: What fascinated you about this change of career?

ERICH: I was interested in the organization, the management of the people actually guiding the specialists. I had no special knowledge of any of the things related to building projects. And I was clear about my own career opportunities. You don't get too many chances for an interesting change at my age where you gain freedom of decision and can point to the results of the new position as yours.

NARRATOR: How do you decide on expansion of your business?

ERICH [*after some thought*]: I only look at whether prospective projects are financially profitable. If they are, I accept them. But I assess very carefully not to overextend our capacities to manage them well. We have a flat hierarchy in my section, which means we communicate directly with each other. I take that to be essential for good management. So we either have to expand considerably or remain within our present limits. And I tend to believe that it's better to remain smaller in order to be able to guarantee the jobs I'm responsible for. I want to remain a direct partner both to the clients and to my colleagues. That marks quality management for me. And I can only deal with so many people at any given time.

NARRATOR: Within the bank and generally, what do you see as the main problems and challenges?

ERICH: I see the main challenge in retaining highly qualified personnel and being able to finance it and increasing profit. If my section can continue the success we have had so far, I see no basic problems for us. But if we can't we will disappear again. [*After some pause*] I actually see the strength of the bank in its classic fields. I see the main challenges and problems of the bank in the ever fiercer competition. Then in the development to become engaged in all kinds of fields worldwide. I tend to favor specialization, to focus on certain strong areas of activity and am concerned that the bank goes into a different direction.

NARRATOR: Since you chose to be your own boss, and have commented in an aside that you see your bank as not supportive of women in managing positions, could you expand a little on that?

ERICH: I see that the bank is no less friendly to women than the society at large. I also find women reluctant to take it upon themselves to lead.

NARRATOR: You mentioned during our talk that you are married and that you met your wife in the same section of the bank you worked in. Could you expand a little?

ERICH [*very quietly, slowly*]: Well, when it became clear that we wanted to be together, I thought it wasn't good to be in the same section. It so happened that I could make a career move out of my section and soon after we got married. And then she quit. And we had a family. [*After a very long pause*] I now think that was a big mistake. And I know now I am partly responsible. But it was normal. The normal thing to do.

NARRATOR: Is it fair to say that the main focus of your life is your job, your salaried work, and your emotional center is your family and that you do not like the split you experience between them?

ERICH [*very quietly*]: Yes, that's correct. And I don't think it's only personal, I see it everywhere in our society and I don't think it's good.

NARRATOR: If you imagine what the world ought to be like in a hundred years, what would you say?

ERICH [*after a long silence*]: The tension between public and private life would disappear or at least be considerably reduced. We will work from home rather than go to some office far away. [*A long silence again*] I don't think it's good when people focus too much on their own self-realization; too many people have begun to do that and it's not good, to want to have a good life just for yourself, with lots of vacation and the easy life and no children. Somehow that ought to change.

NARRATOR: If you had the power to shape the world to become as you want it, what would you do?

ERICH: I would reduce the tension I talked about. But it's very hard to imagine how. It's a question of consciousness and assumed roles. When I grew up, the woman was at home, the man went to work. In my own family of origin we had the mix of roles at home, mother was the center, business was done from home, the men, father and then son, determined the financial framework; a lot could go together and we were together with different people a lot.

NARRATOR: Again, if you could make the world in your image—

ERICH: Well, there will always have to be a framework. And to reduce the tension between individual, private interests on the one hand, and professional and public on the other, I see as a social issue that needs to be taken care of.

NARRATOR: How do you explain that we have such a problem as a social one?

ERICH [*slowly, clearly trying to make sense*]: I'm sure that somewhere there's a link between how we act economically and live otherwise. When we still were hunters and gatherers, when we weren't working with this strict division of labor, things may have been different. [*After a pause*] Everything that discriminates against family and children needs to be eliminated for the world to become better in my view. I'm convinced we can work very efficiently and still have a better social fabric than we do now. The direction is wrong today.

NARRATOR: Could you imagine transforming something from within where you are now and how you work now? Being pragmatic rather than revolutionary about the changes you envision?

ERICH [*long silence, then, slowly*]: Very difficult. Personally, I would want to quit my job for six months, to rejuvenate, reconsider. But I know full well I will never be let back in again. [*With energy*] And I want to explore something and want to keep the option of returning. [*With clear resignation in his tone*] The problem we have today is that everything is too fixed, that structures are too rigid so that we cannot break away.

NARRATOR: Who says so?

ERICH [*surprised, then conceding*]: Or we believe we cannot break away.

NARRATOR: And why do you believe that?

ERICH: Because [*pause*] I am pretty certain that if I really took a year off, which would be really good for me and very likely also good for my institution, if I came back with new vigor and creativity, I guarantee you that this idea will be met with absolute lack of understanding.

NARRATOR: Why do you "guarantee" that?

ERICH: It is a fact.

NARRATOR: Since you haven't done it, how can it be a fact? If I choose not to believe you, what can you say to support your conviction?

ERICH: I'm simply convinced. I have only answered myself the question "Can I afford to take a leave of absence?" with a no. I would not risk it. It would be too irresponsible.

NARRATOR: Toward whom? Yourself?

ERICH: No, if it were for myself, I would have to do it. For my family it would be good, too, in a way. But the financial part is troubling. It's about material security and a certain standard of living we've all come to accept as normal.

NARRATOR: Looking at this vision of a better world in a hundred years. Is this standard of living part of the vision?

ERICH [*without hesitation*]: No, absolutely not.

NARRATOR: Then, why is it so important now?

ERICH [*with some reluctance*]: It's about the readiness for risk. Risk about the unknown. Too many unknown factors, uncertainties.

NARRATOR: How do you deal with unknown factors in your job?

ERICH: I try to calculate them as best I can.

NARRATOR: In the private part, you think that's not possible?

ERICH: I suppose it must be, too, somehow. It's just that I am perhaps less ready to take risks there.

NARRATOR: What if you called the whole enterprise something different— not breaking out, but something positive. If you made it persuasive as something creative, not loaded with negative values? As you told me you did as a young man reorganizing the course of studies because things had gone stale, or as you "sold" your present enterprise to the bank?

ERICH [*with great hesitation*]: The ones I would have to persuade are so entrenched in the system that they will respond with, "We've never done this, that's not proper, too unconventional, impossible," like an indecent proposal. [*After a long pause*] Perhaps I can run the idea by one of my peers, just to see what happens.

[*Enter another older banker, FRANK, whose responsibility is to look after predominantly institutional clients, such as insurance companies, investment funds, nongovernmental organizations, nonprofit organizations and the like.*]

NARRATOR: Would you describe what is important in your job?

FRANK: My job requires expertise in the markets as well as communication skills on all levels. You have to be really curious, ready to meet many people, to learn a lot, not all of which is immediately relevant for business, but it all feeds into the job.

NARRATOR: What are your criteria for new clients?

FRANK [*after some deliberation*]: First, the economic size of the client, then what services the bank might be able to offer that client, then also to look at a particular type of client and check out that type systematically, region by region. I concentrate on Germany. I look, say, at all insurers; or what is called cross-selling. One of my colleagues will mention a client who has been served by the bank in some area and might be interested in more services.

NARRATOR: How do you find your clients?

FRANK: Well, first, you have connections, links with the press, and as I said before, you have to be ever ready for contacts. But you also have to be ready to inform yourself, say, about legal matters, read the laws and check their implications, which will then open new fields for activities. References, very important. You can say in dealing with clients you have three levels: one directly task oriented, you might say, where you have the data, the management project, etc. The second resides in the actual people, where it clicks between people or it doesn't. If it does, you feel, hey, you could go for a beer together. Happens a lot. Not only over a beer, but around sports, cultural events. We also organize seminars and invite people. Such activities often lead to more private contacts from which business results.

NARRATOR: So you approach individuals in a semiprivate manner and that opens the door to the institutions they work for or represent?

FRANK: Yes. And there we don't separate between private and institutional clients, not least because within the institutions there are all the individuals who also wish to invest as private people, say, and you help them. We communicate with the colleagues who deal with private clients, and that's also how cross-selling can happen. [*After a pause*] I take the most efficient communication to be the face-to-face one. Only when I see and talk with someone can I truly assess who he is and what I might do for him. All indirect modes of communicating are undesirable, really. That may be old-fashioned, but it's my experience, and it works. Younger people with less experience see it differently, I suppose. They use the new media more.

NARRATOR: How do you assess the prospects of your sector within the bank over the next few years?

FRANK: Our particular group of clients is expanding, so I need not worry at present, insurers especially. But population problems will have an effect. And we may have to look at different regions and the various affiliated institutions. But competition is terribly stiff, especially with the local banks of such institutions. That's one reason why it's wise to concentrate on the German-speaking countries which are also Deutschmark markets first, which means focusing on countries like the Netherlands, Switzerland, Austria, parts of Belgium and Italy. But in terms of money management we try to attract money, say, from the Russian Federation countries also. If I had to decide where to remain active, I'd stay in Western Europe because it's the safer market with clearer prospects for success.

NARRATOR: What was your motivation to become a banker?

FRANK: Well, to influence and shape things.

NARRATOR: Do you see crises in a global context and in the time frame of, say, the next ten years?

FRANK [*a little at a loss, repeating the question, then after some reflection*]: I see problems arising from the three monetary zones we are going to get: dollar, ECU, yen, markets will grow together even more; an increase of the divide between poor and rich countries. Europe will have problems not least because of population growth and technological change, as well as the growth of markets. Southeast Asia is going to grow fast as a market; Central America and South America may well become interesting. Politically that will bring about political change.

NARRATOR: Are you saying that political change is preceded by economic change?

FRANK [*without any hesitation, firmly*]: That's always the case.

NARRATOR: How do you see your own role in this scenario?

FRANK [*jokingly*]: My age no longer permits me to contribute to the reduction of the population problem here. Other than that, I hope to assist in educating people. I offer a lot of seminars, for instance, on the ECU. Most people don't realize that it's going to happen. We'll have one currency after the turn of the century because politicians want it and we're getting it even if we don't want it. I think that our economic structures are still way too different to want it. You have to sift things first according to the convergence criteria. And I realize that the economic powers have shown that without economic union, there won't be political union. But we need to make that union possible first. Investors are confused as to what to expect if the monetary union actually happens. I realize that the politicians are serious about a common currency. So I advise my clients to see the change not as another dreaded monetary reform but as a transformation of all currencies into one at a fixed rate following rational criteria. The European Monetary Institute will be a precursor to the European Central Bank and I only see a chance with them deciding whether the criteria of the treaty are realized before effecting the monetary union. If you leave it to the politicians, I'm skeptical.

[*Enter a middle-aged female economic adviser,* GAMMA, *whose job it is to analyze the German market and predict certain parameters for decision-making processes within the bank and in relation to the general public.*]

NARRATOR: Please describe what you do.

GAMMA: I'm in the division dealing with economic theory and communication. I deal with national analyses of money markets, money policies, institutional and legal questions, taxes, and the like. Our prognostic activities usually cover a one to two-year span; occasionally we offer a more general ten-year prognosis. Since all financial markets ar really international, the national market is strongly connected with these global developments. We work together in the divisions, for instance, U.S. decisions I discuss with the expert on the U.S. and work it into our national analyses.

NARRATOR: You work under the rubric of communication. What does that mean?

GAMMA [*laughing*]: I don't really know. [*After some reflection*] What we do we do as a service for the bank as well as for clients. We write for different groups: peers within the bank, clients, the general public. We are meant to contribute to the bank's good public image.

NARRATOR: Which goals of the bank do you find relevant for your work?

GAMMA: The main goal is to sustain the bank, secure employment and the bank's importance. Then to expand the bank, open new fields of business, which competition forces the bank to do. To gain importance. The owners of the bank may have their own ideas, which I am not as aware of.

NARRATOR: Any goals you don't identify with?

GAMMA [*after long consideration*]: I cannot think of anything. I identify mostly with the goal to sustain the bank. How the bank deals with its clients. I can accept the bank's desire to exist and expand and that I contribute to that with my work, but wouldn't necessarily call it identification. Much closer to me is the work I actually do every day. That we do good, competent work and that it is regarded as such by others. I want others to see our work as valuable. If I am in structures with certain norms, I want to be acknowledged. Not least regarding profitability, I want to be acknowledged as someone doing profitable work. For my work I have certain criteria of quality I follow: precision, circumspection, analytic strength, and originality. My work is a product and has a price that it has to be worth. I offer a product and want it demanded. The demand would disappear if my product were a waste, unprofitable. Primarily I want to do something that others need and find valuable. [*After some deliberation*] It is not my first intention to keep my job. If my job were guaranteed, it would not be sufficient if it were wasteful, fake, just there for itself. I would feel less challenged.

NARRATOR: How and where do you obtain relevant information for your work?

GAMMA: Information I gather through monthly data publications by different institutions. The Central Bank, for instance, publishes a lot of what I need for my work. The facts we get through the Reuters' computer service are fastest. An agency whose services the bank pays for. They get the figures from the various institutions, say, the Central Bank has direct connections, certain pages in different news agencies, and they publish them simultaneously in all these agencies. It's very important that they are equally accessible for everyone involved in the market. In earlier times they did it by press conferences and everyone then rushed to the phone.

NARRATOR: What are those data? Who decides which data are relevant to do your work?

GAMMA: The data are strictly defined based on economic theory. What is considered measurable. What is considered necessary for assessment. The practice offers itself for certain data and makes other criteria less relevant.

NARRATOR: Can you say a little more about the relation between theory and practice?

GAMMA: Take, for example, the notion of the necessary amount of money in a market; that is a difficult theoretical and practical question. And also what sector of the financial market belongs in what category within the financial system. The Central Bank discusses such matters with banks and politicians. You need a theoretical concept to know how to direct the money market. If, for instance, you want to keep inflation low, what constitutes a signal for such an agenda? The U.S. Federal Reserve, say, has a different notion of money amount and price development than the German Central Bank. They act differently, and offer a money amount adequate to their different data. But there is often a delayed effect once you take measures to direct the money supply. With practical consequences. Which over time at least lead to a reconsideration of the theoretical assumptions. Or take the assessment on the development of interest rates: it can not for long deviate from the real data of the economy, which are empirical data formulated through theory. But it is true that in shorter terms people who act instantly on published interest rate changes create facts that may lead to changes of the base data. But not for long. [*Ponderingly*] What happens sometimes is not explicable in theoretical terms. I have to assume that the actors in the market who follow certain trends on short terms act rationally. Therefore, I also have to be able to explain their behavior with economic arguments developed from economic theory and empirical facts. [*After some more deliberation*] It is true that in the last two years discrepancies between prediction and what actually happened have been irritatingly consistent and relatively large. The latest explanations are neuronal nets to check what are the most important factors, and they test these links on the basis of certain assumptions of plausibility. Time sequences are fed into the model, and it is assumed that the model then selects the most plausible in a self-regulated fashion. Much like scientists assume our brain works. But it's more about images we have of how the brain works related to the latest in technology. It's the latest fad, as it were. The charts, too, are such models, the fad before this one. People act upon such results, which can diverge rather dramatically from the fundamental data of national economies. [*With tangible skepticism and self-criticism*] It's a service private firms offer to banks and other investors and they create facts of their own, as it were. Journalists and others follow them. We, too, have bought the software and now try to create a new model of our own in collaboration with our division of advisers.

NARRATOR: Expand a little on your choice of career, which, I know from what you have told me, was not easy.

GAMMA: Oh, I was so frustrated when I studied economics, everything was so mathematical, so reduced in its presuppositions, its models; I found it terrible. I wanted to quit and become a journalist. But I never quite made that break either. There was an academic pride in me not to quit, and when I worked for a paper I also realized it wasn't quite as I had hoped it to be. You know, the fast production of texts according to things happening; and the level of writing often wasn't quite to my liking either. So I stayed with macroeconomics.

NARRATOR: How do you see this development today? The motivation to write, to express yourself, which was your basic drive in the choice?

GAMMA: I don't regret having stayed. I learned that there are different ways of expression. When I have to produce something fast for a newspaper, it's not me being expressed, I'm just an automaton processing stuff for others. I have little time to shape something as my own. [*After some reflection, with great emphasis*] In my first job I had the impression I was in the wrong place. I felt incompetent and thus could not see how I could contribute anything and no one bothered to assist me in learning. And I also learned that their statistics were fabricated, and when I complained I was told, "That's the same everywhere." I quit after less than a year although I had no new job. And in my job with the bank I have not found any dubious dealings. I found some space to learn to become competent. The structures and the subject matter in the bank were more familiar to me through my studies, and that's probably why I also felt I had something to contribute. I began to write on things I knew something about. And the people themselves were probably congenial in some ways. That was good. I have accepted the structures and the content matter sufficiently to be okay in that world, to make it my own. I am there to produce a certain value. To achieve certain goals, which I accept even where I haven't defined them.

NARRATOR: Your peers are mostly men. Any observations on the ruling conventions or norms?

GAMMA: The women I see all follow the same norms. And I don't perceive those as masculine. They are norms of efficiency, achievement, success, service.

NARRATOR: Are there qualities and activities which go against these norms?

GAMMA: Yes. To have an opinion on interest rates when the data are confusing. My sense of integrity contradicts the claim that we know when we actually don't. We would write ourselves out of our own jobs if we admitted to not knowing. And for me that can become a loyalty issue, to myself, my colleagues, the institution. Usually, when I write I can bring it together, somehow, give it shape and live with it.

NARRATOR: Where do you see crises arising economically?

GAMMA [*without any hesitation*]: In our national economy I see a huge problem in the development of public debt, [*long pause*] that the redistribution by the state gets out of hand in the international context. I mean, I can see that ever more people have to give ever more of their income to the state, which does all kinds of things with that money. Our rate of private income for public expenditure is almost 50 percent. That is a redistribution, and I see that our high unemployment and the increasing welfare component in our economic system will make for a lot of problems in the foreseeable future. With consequences for competition internationally. Unemployment will rise, and the pressure for more redistribution will increase, which constitutes a vicious circle.

NARRATOR: If you had the power to shape the world, what would you want it to look like?

GAMMA [*long silence*]: I can imagine people acting so responsibly with all resources and that they all can lead a valuable life without wars, without greed. I would wish for that to happen. I believe it has something to do with the structure of desires. Desires as wanting goods, foods, and so forth, re-placed by desires to thrive differently. To develop themselves more, to be pro-ductive in a different way. With the help of religion, I imagine, like in earlier times when they built churches, or through art; getting together to play, to perform. Something within them has to be activated, perhaps, so that they can want a different form of self-realization.

NARRATOR: If you could effect the changes you envision, what would you do?

GAMMA [*slowly, with increasing emphasis, warming to the vision*]: I would assume I had enough money to bring people together who already have achieved a kind of wisdom to go and teach kids in school. Get rid of all the unmotivated educators, not by throwing them out but offering children differ-ent ones so that they could choose. Sports people, artists, I would go out and find the best and ask the best to help me find more. I would have to offer something and make it appealing, not force it upon those whom I would hope to change in their ways. I would buy TV stations and offer alternatives pro-duced by experts. I would see whether there is demand. My hope would be that people would come and change. And if I knew I had done all I could, and people would not change, I would try to find alternatives. But there would be a point where I would accept that someone else would have to try in my stead.

NARRATOR: Do you see any connection between your vision and your ev-eryday reality?

GAMMA: I can only see how I behave, treat myself and others, how I refuse to compete in certain areas, how I consume. I have limited influence and can contribute only in a small way to the changes I envision.

NARRATOR: Does the institution for which you work agree with your vision, or is it contrary to your vision of a better world?

GAMMA [*long silence, with great care*]: My bank is part of this economic and political system that has no desire to change in the way I indicated. Our system is really rather uncreative, an anxiety-driven system, whereas in my mind, too little is being risked, human beings are not challenged enough. I find mostly the politicians not taking the potential of human beings seriously enough, they are treated with too little regard for who they are and who they could be. [*Very pensively and with some hesitation*] My bank is part of that, and I fail to see how else it could be. I cannot imagine how it could be differ-ent. [*Quietly, modestly*] You know, I would find it just wonderful if there were a bigger movement. But within the bank I cannot see it, and I myself don't look for it, either.

NARRATOR: Why not?

GAMMA: Because I am too busy doing other things.

NARRATOR: Is that part of the system?

GAMMA: Yes, and I have accepted that. They don't pay me for realizing my vision and keeping people from doing their job.

NARRATOR: Could you imagine that your own work and that of the institution as a whole might even be working against your own ideals?

GAMMA [*after lengthy deliberation, somewhat pained*]: Oh, yes, if only by using energies, binding activities to certain and not other goals. So that the system can reproduce itself in its dullness, its lack of imagination. I believe [*long pause, and with great hesitation*] that I am not ready to reorganize my life to refocus my own energies toward realizing my vision of a better world. Or you could say I need others to want it with me, and, too, I would have to find it more exciting myself. I am not enough of an idealist to sacrifice all that I have now for something I am not sure I can achieve.

Notes

1. The names of my interlocutors are fictitious, the names of the historical personae are retained.

2. The person agreed to respond in writing only.

3. Smith 1978, 1:5, 6.

4. Pearce 1981, 123.

5. Pearce 1981, 366.

6. Marx 1945, 209.

7. Pearce 1981, 338.

8. Pearce 1981, 311.

9. Pearce 1981, 16.

10. Smith 1978, 4:2, 28.

11. Pearce 1981, 303, 385.

12. Marx 1945, 208, 209.

13. Pearce 1981, 446, 447.

14. Al-Faisal Al-Saud 1982, 129, 136.

References

Al-Faisal Al-Saud, Prince Mohammed. 1982. "Banking and the Islamic Standpoint." In *Islam and Contemporary Society.* London: Longman.

Marx, Karl. 1945. *Selected Works.* London: Lawrence and Wishart.

Pearce, David W. 1981. *The Dictionary of Modern Economics.* Cambridge, Mass.: MIT Press.

Smith, Adam. 1978. *An Inquiry into the Nature and Causes of the Wealth of Nations.* Great Books of the Western World 39. Chicago: Encyclopaedia Britannica.

SIXTY-FIVE ROSES, PULMOZYME, STEVE SHAK, GENENTECH, INC.

ON A SCIENTIST IN BUSINESS. *"Who would have thought that industry, even a small corner of it in a cutting-edge field, located in the atypical San Francisco Bay Area, would be a haven in a heartless world? The contrast with the perpetual petty power plays, seeming insatiable status lust, and insistent incivility of the academy could not have been more unexpected. No paradise to be sure, but nonetheless here was a racially and sexually diverse environment with a group of reflective people, who gave every impression of passionate devotion to their science, who seemed to take an interest in the ethical and social consequences of that science, even without any grants or congressional pressure to do so" (Paul Rabinow, "Reflections on Field-work in Alameda," in* Technoscientific Imaginaries, Late Editions 2).

Michael Fortun's piece takes up the interest in scientists in business contexts that this series has addressed previously in Late Editions 2. Here the concern with cultural issues is more complexly and naturally threaded through the discourse presented than it is explicitly announced as such by a frame such as corporate "culture" or "values." In this account of the simultaneous growth of a successful biotech firm through the personal growth of a scientist, the reader can get an excellent sense of the masking, and even subordination, of the business context to the work of science. Indeed, the question of business values, and of a particular corporate culture, are embedded within ethical issues about science. – G. E. M.

*   *   *

What's the Matter with Kids Today?—Danny Bliss

I imagine myself in second grade—having learned a thing or two, but still relatively clueless—and having to write an essay on my heroes. A good assignment for an eight-year-old nascent anthropologist. My second-grade mind blanks, panics; I decide to cheat. My gaze shifts to the desk in the aisle beside me, where Danny Bliss hunches over his yellow tablet, printing neatly and awkwardly—one line for the small letters, two lines for the capitals—an essay that through some intricate social process would be reprinted in Genentech's 1993 annual report. I copy his paper exactly.

> My heros are Bob Swanson and Herb Boyer. Herb and Bob Started the company Genentech.
> Herb Boyer is tall with curly hair. He is a scientist.
> Bob Swanson is Short with blond hair. And he is a ventuer capitalist.
> Bob and Herb had a conversation in 1976. they decided that they would start a company that would make drugs that would help people.
> Bob and Herb are my heros because they made a drug that saved my dad's life, t-PA.
> In August 1992 my dad had a heart attack on an airplane. They gave him t-PA at the hospital. The t-PA made the blood clot go away.

Later, in her own, much neater printing, the teacher will comment in the upper margins of Danny's paper:

> Danny, I can certainly understand why you chose Bob Swanson and Herb Boyer as your heroes. I think that some of their scientists are heroes too. Good choice!

Although the operations of cultural heredity are a wonder to behold, this piece is not directly about them. The following interview with Dr. Steven Shak attempts to provide a starting point for a different kind of story, certainly not without its heroic elements, but contextualized within the complex practicalities of contemporary research. Nor does this piece concern directly Herb and Bob, or their genetic and professional characteristics so reminiscent of Mendel's pea plants. Herb's and Bob's traces do appear, however, writ large in the form of the biotechnology/pharmaceutical company Genentech, Inc. Nor is this piece about t-PA, although this molecule also figures indirectly in the following narrative at three points. Tissue plasminogen activator (trade name Activase) might have been designed to dissolve blood clots, but through additional strange powers—side effects, we might say—it had an opposite, clogging effect on Genentech's economic and regulatory pathways in the late 1980s. Only additional molecular effects, summoned into existence by other heroes, evoking responses from one of the largest transnational corporations on the globe, would smooth the flows channeled through Genentech.

It's those additional molecular effects, revolving around a new drug for the treatment of cystic fibrosis, that hold this story together and allow those molar effects—"heroes," "scientific research," "the corporation"—to emerge and inhabit our narratives of biotechnology.[1] The story has many subplots, as well as many characters, all of which complicate without necessarily negating the easy identification of good written about by Danny Bliss. With these narrative complexities we can gain a better understanding of the interplay between research and commerce that not only has produced new drugs but also new forms of social organization for "doing" science, and new corporate domains and relationships. Though not yet complete, the story foreshadows the world that kids today will live within, and will need stories to accompany.

What's the Matter with Kids?— CF, Steve Shak

The cover of Genentech's 1993 annual report, in which Danny Bliss's essay appears, shows a four-liter Pyrex beaker filled with rich, red roses (fig. 1). It refers to the mnemonic device that some parents use to help their kids name and pronounce the disease that afflicts them: sixty-five roses, cystic fibrosis. The artistic rendering of this near homonym on the 1993 annual report's cover signifies the importance of one of Genentech's most recent pharmaceutical products, Pulmozyme, both to the health of the corporation and to the health of children and young adults with cystic fibrosis (CF).[2] Cystic fibrosis is the most common genetic disorder among Caucasians, a statistical fact of population genetics which has made CF simultaneously one of the disorders most amenable to genetic analysis, and a disorder with substantial market potential in the U.S. and Western Europe.

This is not to say that the genetics of CF is straightforward, nor is its somatic manifestation. At present, somewhere in the neighborhood of three hundred variants of "the CF gene" have been identified, a fact that has made widespread population screening for the condition practically impossible. And while there is a range of affected organs and symptoms associated with this genetic heterogeneity, the most common is the build-up of a thick mucus in the lungs, making CF individuals subject to frequent and persistent infection, and eventually killing them. The life expectancy for people with CF has been increasing steadily over the last few decades, and has reached an average of thirty years (Tsui 1992). While that progress occurred largely without the aid of pharmaceuticals, it also made CF individuals even more hopeful for new therapies.

If we said that Steven Shak is the person most responsible for the existence of Pulmozyme, most responsible for the presence in the world of a drug helpful to many people with CF, we would not be too far from the truth. Shak is the person most easily associated with the invention of the only new drug therapy for cystic fibrosis to appear in the last thirty years.

Shak is a hybrid figure. The interview tracks his career from his initial training as an M.D., through his university research, to his current position as director of pulmonary research at Genentech. This hybridity is only partially traced through the now common and much commented-upon (discussed later in this preface) movement of scientists from the university to the biotechnology

Cover of the 1993 Genentech Annual Report. Photograph © RJ Muna.

corporation. In the interview that follows, Shak refers frequently to "the team" and to the collective and heterogeneous work necessary to create, test, and sell Pulmozyme—work ranging from Shak's own original research (which would be translated by the popular media into heroic narratives) to experiments performed by a forgotten technician to determine which stopper should be used in the vials of Pulmozyme. Shak's multiple roles extended beyond Genentech; we find him alternately in the role of scientist collaborating with other researchers, M.D. seeing CF patients and monitoring the progress of clinical trials, manager insuring the smooth coordination of tasks, regulatory agent working closely with the U.S. Food and Drug Administration in a newly accelerated approval process, and, inescapably, a media figure who, while not appearing on the cover of *Time* as Genentech founder Herb Boyer did in 1980, has been pictured in the back pages of the *New York Times, Business Week,* and other media outlets—a more minor figure in the modern biopantheon, but a hero of sorts nonetheless.[3]

What's the Matter?—Developing Pulmozyme

Who's the hero of this piece, then? Steven Shak? The Genentech team? Not exactly. Their collective endeavor centers around the production of an enzyme in mass quantities, Pulmozyme, a.k.a. dornase alfa, a.k.a. DNase—the molecule as hero.

Molecules are often accorded heroic status these days, and none more so than deoxyribonucleic acid, DNA. New drug discovery, we often hear, now depends more and more on the mapping and sequencing of human disease genes as a necessary first step. The interesting thing about Shak's invention of DNase is that it didn't depend on knowing the molecular genetics of cystic fibrosis at all; not even one "gene for" CF had been identified when Shak began working on DNase in 1988. For some background on DNase as Shak discusses it in the interview, we would do well to follow *Business Week,* which refers us back through an origin story to the t-PA that dealt life to Danny Bliss's father:

> A pulmonary physician by training, [Shak] left academe for Genentech in 1986, driven by the desire to find treatments using basic science. He came along just as the company was launching t-PA, its best-known drug. That gene-spliced enzyme, which breaks apart the blood clots that cause heart attacks, gave Shak the idea that an enzyme might do the same for CF.
> Once Shak proved in mid-1988 that his enzyme could survive in a spray, his bosses turned him loose to gene-splice a human variety. In theory, it would chew up excess DNA—the main ingredient of sputum lining the lungs of CF patients. After four months of 100-hour

weeks in the lab, Shak had a beaker's worth of his potion and was ready for the test that shook Genentech. He took mucus from a CF patient, cut it in half with a razor, and divided it between two test tubes. He poured saline solution in one, DNase in the other, then turned them upside down. Almost instantly, the sputum in the DNase tube turned to liquid and ran down the side; the gunk in the other stayed put. . . . The results were so dramatic "it didn't take a lot to get the go-ahead to drop everything else I was doing," he recalls. (Hamilton 1993, 66)

The production of drama through science was clearly important at this early stage of the game; a molecule in a test tube can be quite heroic. It is quite another matter to translate that molecular heroism to a molar scale, and produce a drug therapy that is both effective and safe. Shak describes in this interview the ensuing years of collaborative work that went into this effort. After extensive laboratory work and clinical trials, the end result is a drug therapy in which the drama of individual effects. is subsumed within a much broader regime of statistical rationality applied to populations. Cheating once again, I copy from Genentech's "Fact Sheet: Pulmozyme® (Dornase Alfa)" exactly:

Compared to placebo, Pulmozyme®:

- reduced the risk of respiratory tract infections (RTIs) requiring I.V. antibiotics by 27 percent

- improved lung function by 5.8 percent as measured by forced expiratory volume (FEV1)—an improvement maintained over 12 months

- reduced costly hospitalizations (reducing the number of days spent in the hospital and days missed from work and school)

- reduced healthcare utilization and related costs due to decreased days in the hospital and on antibiotic therapy

- improved well-being and quality of life in patients with mild to moderate pulmonary dysfunction

As Shak emphasizes, Pulmozyme is a therapy and not a cure for cystic fibrosis; its effects are distributed and subject to dispersal, best measured in percentage points. Like "sixty-five roses," Pulmozyme does not match "cystic fibrosis" perfectly. That does not make the drug any less welcome or valuable to a great many people. Toward the end of the interview Shak discusses Genentech's latest efforts (along with its subsidiary, GenVec) to develop a cure for CF through gene therapy: a genetic rewriting that would—in the ideal, hoped-for scenario—result in perfect alignment between molecule and disease, disease and name.

What the!?—Genentech, Inc., or Djinn-in-Tactics

What can our second-grade minds read about current changes in the biotechnology industry through the story of Shak and Pulmozyme?

We need to return to Herb and Bob, whose heroic figurations congeal not only in Danny Bliss's classroom, but in art. In a special section called "Science in California," the British science journal *Nature* ran a brief article on Genentech a few years ago under the appropriately mythic title, "Clone your own legend." The article describes a—there's no other word for it—lifelike sculpture in a courtyard outside Shak's office in the new Founders Research Center. (The Founders Research Center is a three-building complex designed to transport its four hundred workers from a past in which "interaction among researchers from various disciplines often required a trek up or down a hill, and usually depended on a planned effort," to a future-present predicated on an "intimate setting where scientists from diverse groups can readily interact" (Genentech 1992, 31).) The bronze sculpture preserves a mythical, albeit quite recent, moment: "They are statues of Bob Swanson and Herb Boyer, at the moment when, over That Beer, they founded Genentech, not even 20 years ago. And as if to votive ikons, their beer mugs are full of money. To a European, it seems hardly seemly that such a memorial could even be considered this side of 1776, let alone 1976, never mind that both protagonists are still alive. Such is the local mythopoeia in compensation for lack of history."[4]

The trope of speed underlying these comments—"Bloody Americans! They live so *fast!* It's certainly uncivilized, and may be irrational"—is certainly pertinent to the current state of the biotech industry and molecular genetic research in its entirety (Fortun, forthcoming). Pulmozyme and Shak operated within this accelerated economy, and here Shak details how it was that (as described in Genentech's annual report): "Pulmozyme went from laboratory to market in less than six years—half the pharmaceutical industry average. This speed is the result of an extraordinary collaboration among Genentech, the Cystic Fibrosis Foundation and cystic fibrosis centers, and the Food and Drug Administration" (Genentech 1993, 12).

To return to Genentech's origin story, after "That Beer," Boyer and Swanson each put up $500 (augmented by start-up funds from the venture capital firm of Kleiner and Perkins), rejected the name Her-Bob, and incorporated as Genentech, Inc., in 1976 (Hall 1987, 84–85; Kenney 1986, 94–95). Genentech was the first major biotechnology company to "go public," and the story of this stock sale has assumed legendary status in the literature on biotechnology: "Genentech's October 14, 1980, public offering of 1 million shares at $35 per share set off a buying frenzy that sent the share price to a peak of $89 before it subsided to $70 at the close of the market day" (Kenney 1986, 156). "Genentech . . . had seen its shares rocket from $35 to $80 on the first day of Wall

Street trading, giving the company a value of several hundred million dollars almost overnight" (Dickson 1984, 80). In Genentech's public origin, cool reasoning and patient laboratory work linked up with the frenzies, rockets, and other rational irrationalities of the market.[5]

The linkage has persisted throughout Genentech's history. Scientists there did early pioneering work in both the cloning (in the case of insulin) and synthesizing (for the brain hormone somatostatin) of human genes. Scientific talent from the University of California at San Francisco was coupled to the talents of multinational firms, beginning with Eli Lilly. "It had been Swanson's plan from the very beginning to hitch Genentech's wagon to a powerful, profitable, and well-regarded pharmaceutical company. Genentech's scientists knew nothing about processing, fermentation, scale-up, testing, shepherding a drug through clinical trials, winning FDA approval, marketing, and sales. Swanson wanted to do his apprenticeship with an established company. When it came to insulin, there were only two U.S. companies as major players in the market, Lilly and Squibb, with the lion's share going to Lilly. Genentech wanted to side with the lions" (Hall 1987, 286).

By the early 1980s Genentech had perfected a strategy that "linked it with a number of companies, yet kept all at arm's length" (Kenney 1986, 161). These companies included Lilly, AB Kabi (a Swedish company that funded the work on human growth hormone), Monsanto (bovine growth hormone), Mitsubishi (t-PA and human serum albumin), and Hoffman-La Roche (interferon). These relationships were not always smooth and uncomplicated: in 1986 Hoffman-LaRoche sued Genentech for infringement on a human growth hormone patent, causing a brief ten-point drop in Genentech's stock (OTA 1989, 55). (This is the same Hoffman-LaRoche that several years later would be buying sixty percent of Genentech's stock.)

By and large, however, this financial strategy worked to make Genentech one of the largest, most securely profitable, and most innovative of the biotechnology companies. It has become so through other strategies as well, both organizational and scientific. Genentech has prospered by creating a research environment well regarded among scientists for its universitylike inculcation of independence and creative exchange, which in turn has been responsible for a diverse line of pharmaceutical products in an industrial field where companies are largely dependent on one or a few marketable substances.

One of these substances, tissue plasminogen activator (Activase), enters the narrative here for the second and third time. The first time was for its corporeal effects—how Activase set Shak's train of thought into motion toward Pulmozyme. Here we are concerned more with its corporate effects—with how Pulmozyme was deployed as an antidote to financial and regulatory crisis.

When Activase was approved by the FDA in 1988, Genentech was pinning its economic future on its success. Genentech, however, "was unable to show that its $2,200-a-dose drug was any more effective than a competing drug sell-ing at one-tenth the price, and sales failed to meet early expectations" (Fischer 1994). One result was bad blood between Genentech and the FDA. Another result, at least in the eyes of some analysts, was a weakened position in the biotech economy, eventually leading to the purchase of 60 percent of Genen-tech by Roche Holdings Ltd., in 1990, for $2.1 billion.[6]

Shak and Pulmozyme did double work in this situation. As he discusses in the interview, one of his tasks was to improve Genentech's relationship with FDA, ushering Pulmozyme through FDA oversight of clinical trials much less adversarially than Genentech with Activase.[7] And Pulmozyme promised as much as $300 million in revenues by 1996. Looking for much-needed research and development funds, Genentech CEO G. Kirk Raab asked Shak to talk about DNase "to a visitor from the Swiss drug giant Roche Holdings Ltd. Shak had no idea how important his talk would be. . . . Today, that visitor, Jurgen Drewes, president of international R&D for Roche, says Shak's enthusiasm for DNase helped bring about the deal. 'If they can [be this creative],' Drews re-calls thinking, 'they are going to make a difference' " (Hamilton 1993, 66).

What did the Roche purchase mean for Genentech and its research climate, as well as for the biotechnology industry writ large? Conflicting statements in the trade literature abound, often within the same article: "No single event could have startled the biotech community as much" (Ratner 1990); "The fo-cus of biotechnology suddenly seemed to shift from South San Francisco to Basel and Nutley, New Jersey, from start-up to staid elder statesmen. . . . we rooted for Genentech to make it on its own, the way the kids from the old neighborhood pull for the block's golden boy to become a star in the world outside—to start for the Yankees or sing at La Scala or win the Nobel Prize or scuff the dust of Mars with his boot" (McCormick 1990). Yet it was the puta-tive logic of this "world outside" that was used to make sense of the deal, to understand how "When It Changed" (as the title of one editorial put it) nothing had really changed at all. "In the context of massive consolidation in the phar-maceutical industry, escalating entry costs, and the supreme importance of a marketing establishment, Genentech's backers have elected to play the drug-making game the way the big boys play" (McCormick 1990).

Another interpretation was proffered by the president of the Industrial Bio-technology Association (the biotech trade group, which has since evolved into the Biotechnology Industry Organization, or BIO), who said the acquisition was not initiated by "pressing economic necessity, but as a matter of corporate planning" (in Gershon 1990b, 681). Under this interpretation, the primary ra-tionale for the deal was the over $400 million in R&D funds that Genentech would receive, and which it sorely needed. More individualized interests were undoubtedly part of the "corporate planning" as well.[8]

One had only to understand "The Logic of Growth," as another opinion in a trade journal was titled, to see how " 'big is better' becomes a true and necessary statement in the pharmaceutical industry." Given Genentech's "rapid and impressive growth," the author asks, "why did its management trade off the company's independence? The suggested answer is a "paradoxical" one: "to preserve the entrepreneurial spirit and the capacity for fast and efficient drug discovery, management chose to sell out to a major player." (Leveque 1990, 776)

This interview should begin to break up such simple "logics," rendering such one-dimensional characterizations of "independence" more complex in the process. *Entrepreneurial spirit* emerges in the interview as an elusive term, hard to define and locate, let alone "preserve," yet somehow operative and begging for further inquiry. There is no simple equation between "selling" and "selling out," but a complex series of moves and trades on a range of levels. And just exactly who is a "major player" in an intricately articulated field in which risk is endemic, molecules realign institutions dedicated to producing more molecules, children play, and scientists retain a firm commitment to ideals of truth and healing?

Narratives of "selling out" and losing "independence" are all too predictable in both academic and public discussions of biotechnology. Like narratives of the scientific hero, they operate on rigid binaries—university research is essentially open, freely communicated, disinterested, and pure, while corporate research is competitive, secretive, subject to skewing, and merely applied. Such oppositions are good mostly for moralistic posturing and sermonizing. Shak's discussion of his motivations for moving to Genentech and the positive capabilities he perceived there both for his own research and for medicine should complicate that story, and keep such thoughtless phrases as "scientists are being lured into industry" from appearing in otherwise thoughtful books on the social dilemmas raised via biotechnology.[9] As should be clear from this interview and other ethnographic work on biotechnology (Rabinow 1995, 1996), scientists can have excellent reasons for working in the private sector, and don't always need to be lured from the presumably more natural habitat of the academy.

As suggested by its name—a condensation of "*gen*etic *en*gineering *tech*nology"—Genentech, Inc. often serves as a synecdoche for the biotechnology industry. It has been used to stand for everything that is wrong or everything that is right about commercial genetic engineering, depending on your perspective. There is no question that biotechnology raises profound questions and challenges for thought, ethics, and democratic politics. To meet those challenges with some degree of subtlety and openness will require that we occasionally defer the certainties of our "logics" and other predictable articulations and look again for difference in the world—which is what I have tried to do here.

In somewhat different terms, if sixty-five roses can remind us simultaneously of cystic fibrosis *and* of the inadequacies of our representational (and interventional) strategies, perhaps we can let "Djinn-in-Tactics" stand in for Genentech, Inc.: close but no cigar, a one-off characterization, a reminder of theoretical and practical work to be done rather than of faithful representation. Djinn-in-Tactics should be a reminder that we need to coin a new idiom, developing language which speaks new tensions, which entangle rather than oppose science and commercial corporations. I'd like Djinn-in-Tactics to mark the seeming macromagic of both therapies and markets as an emergent effect of micropractices, microknowledges, and microevents—molecular forces whose exact operations can simultaneously trouble us, elate us, and elude us. Djinn-in-tactics: a mnemonic to keep the triumphs and inadequacies of our second-grade minds always within the play of inquiry.

FORTUN: Can you tell me the story of your general medical training and interests?

SHAK: Since I was a young kid, I've always been interested in science and math, and intrigued with the idea that we truly can understand the world both by experiment and in terms that are testable. And in terms of pursuing that core interest, I gravitated to the medical field primarily because I enjoy doing science, and this presented itself as an opportunity to do something I loved, and at the same time see it make a big impact on people's lives.

Some people find medical school to be a real drag. I actually enjoyed it immensely. Maybe this was because of some of my past training in college: I tended to educate myself, and I found that in medical school, the way I learned medicine was taking in what was given to me—to a large degree, medical training is a data dump: this is what you need to know; we know it, you don't; here it is, and now we're going to test you to see whether you've learned it. And that approach to education wasn't one that I generally took. I like to go beyond that, and what I found myself doing was doing a lot of learning by actually reading about diseases, by reading current medical journals that were trying to understand something new about a disease. It was both a great way to find out what people really think as of today, and also to learn how questions are being answered in the field, and ultimately, what are the things that we still don't know. And I think I was different than many students in using that tool as a tool to educate myself. I also found that although medical education did in fact involve a data dump, that there was another aspect to it which involved judgment, that involved the fact that in dealing with any medical situation—or even scientific situation—we actually know a lot less than we think we know. We have to make judgments and decisions based on insufficient information, and there's a process for decision making and performing judgments that one has to learn over time, and that really can't be taught in a book. But it's the kind of thing that you can learn by working with other people who have learned that, and by seeing how they approach problems and learning from them how to solve those problems.

FORTUN: Did you find those people at New York University?

SHAK: Oh, yeah. It was a very strong program for clinical training. And although I anticipated that I was likely, in the long run, to have a career doing research in the lab, I also deliberately chose to get a very intensive and extensive clinical training. Again, that might have been a combination of enjoying my clinical experience—seeing patients and being a physician to patients— but also I think it was driven by the knowledge that if what I wanted to do was something very important, then what was going to drive that were the real problems that people had. To the extent that I really understood what those problems were, what people got sick with, what currently could be treated and what couldn't, what the real needs for the future were—I understood that that was going to be critically important to me in the future, in terms of deciding what I should work on.

So I finished medical school at NYU and then went on to do a clinical internship and residency in general medicine, internal medicine, at a very strong clinical place: Bellevue Hospital, in New York. That really did provide me, over that seven-year period, with a very strong background in clinical medicine. From there I went out to the University of California at San Francisco, in 1980. Here I was looking for a fellowship program that truly would provide me with a training in science. I was now almost thirty years old, and really had spent very little time at all in the laboratory. As I look back, I didn't have a lot of personal experience to go on, to say that going into the lab and doing research was something that I wanted to do, but when I looked at fellowship programs, I visited the top pulmonary training programs in the country, I evaluated each one primarily in terms of the research training that I could get, and UCSF was clearly the best from my perspective. Not only because of the quality of the science there, and the size of the program, but there was also a leader there who was committed to science education, a guy named Julius Comroe, who was a giant in the pulmonary field. He set up the program at UCSF, was then in the twilight of his career, but clearly the program there was his program. And to give you some idea, the concept was that you didn't learn how to do research, you didn't learn to teach—that that stuff just didn't come naturally, you needed to be trained. So there were actually courses on the art of speaking, or the art of writing. And I think for science education that's relatively unusual. Most often in science education, those are largely ignored; they figure that just comes naturally and it's not a big deal. I think that presenting your work is as important as the quality of the work that you do.

FORTUN: Do you know what drove Comroe to think these things were important?

SHAK: I think that he knew what was right. And he was right, and I agree with him one hundred percent.

FORTUN: In 1980 molecular biology techniques were relatively new. Did you have a sense that you wanted to learn molecular biology techniques, or was it more general?

SHAK: To be honest, it was very general at that time, because I had little or no experience in the lab. But I had a very fortunate first lab experience. I had a very supportive and very smart mentor, and I also was given a very good initial direction to go in, that proved very fruitful both scientifically as well as great for the development of my own scientific interests and perspectives. From a clinical perspective, I was interested in the process of inflammation or immune responses in the lung. As I thought about almost every lung disease, whether it's asthma, emphysema, chronic obstructive pulmonary disease, sarcoidosis, pneumonia—almost all those diseases involved either a derangement, or an abnormal response, or an excessive response, of the immune system. And if we're going to understand diseases better, we need to understand the mechanisms that are involved. And clearly, in going in the direction of immunology and inflammation, I could perhaps gain insight into some of the mechanisms of these diseases. What was very notable in the case of lung disease—and it's probably true for many other diseases as well—although we know a lot, we still don't know the basic cause of many diseases.

So although I was in a pulmonary program, I did my research training in a rheumatology or arthritis lab that had developed expertise in studying inflammation. So this was a way of getting expertise in a field and then bringing that to the lung. And the area that I was directed into was arachidonic acid metabolites, a new family of molecules called the leukotrienes. These are products of cells that act as immune mediators, as cell-to-cell messengers. And this new class had just been identified structurally in the late 1970s. Activities had been described in the 1950s, and through a really fantastic set of scientific experiments, ultimately leading to the Nobel Prize for Ben Samuelson, the structure of these molecules had been identified. And so I was directed into this area: could I develop techniques in the lab to measure these molecules, and could I then learn about how they might be made, and what activities they might have? This is a classic example in science, I think, where structural identification of an activity or a factor leads to an explosion of knowledge in the field. It occurs all the time, these explosions that are set in motion by the structural identification of what something is.

That turned out to be great for me in terms of my training, because I went into the lab to develop these assays, became very proficient at them, and it was a great opportunity to talk to other people and find out how to do this, and ultimately to work these all out myself. Not only did I have to learn how to measure these new molecules—and I used the classic technique of chromatography, which allows you to separate molecules based on their particular properties. But what's neat in chromatography is that you have molecules flowing out of a column into an ultraviolet detector, and what you see are shadows. You see peaks. You see footprints of the molecules that pass by. To do good science, though, you've got to go beyond those peaks. You actually have to answer the question: now I think that peak that came off was this particular molecule of interest. I think that's the case because if I take that pure molecule and inject it in a separate run, it comes off at exactly the same time. But that's not proof that it is what you think it is. So I also had to develop techniques using mass spectrometry, which is a technique for actually fragmenting a molecule and determining its structure.

I spent three and a half years in the lab, and I had a fairly large number of high-quality publications in the *Journal of Biological Chemistry, Journal of Clinical Investigation,* and others, which basically educated me how to communicate to a scientific audience. I ultimately was able to write a chapter in *Methods in Enzymology,* demonstrating that I really was leading the field in this area. And I think it was something that really reinforced this idea for me, that to understand the world, one had to now go to the molecular level: what was there? How do you know what you think you know? And how do you then study the world at a molecular and cellular level? That's the level one had to work at in order to understand diseases.

FORTUN: These new techniques that you were learning, were you in a one-to-one relationship with somebody, like learning a craft, or were you doing it on your own? How was it that you learned how to do these new things?

SHAK: In general, my approach to doing something new is to first of all read about the method or similar methods in the literature, and to try to pick out from them what the issues are and what the best approach might be. I might also then talk to someone who's done it, to get their advice or input. But ultimately there's no substitute for going in there yourself, and then basically working through it, rediscovering for yourself what works and what doesn't work. Ultimately, that's how you do something new. You need to get the competence yourself, and to convince yourself that you know what you're doing, and that what you're measuring is real. I used that approach in my first lab experience; I don't do it any differently now. But one thing I can say is that now, later in my career, I'm spending less time learning how to do new methods and more time trying to say, with new methods, what important biological questions can we answer? And I think that's just fine. I think you need to know how to develop methods, you need to know how to solve problems if you run into them, but in terms of where I am now, my career is much more focused on just grabbing methods that are available. If it's something that I can't do, I'm not going to reinvent the wheel. I'm going to walk down the hall and find someone else who knows how to do it and who can work with me on a project. And things will go a whole lot faster.

FORTUN: Were you also learning fundamental recombinant-DNA techniques?

SHAK: At this point, I didn't learn anything about molecular biology or cloning. In fact, at this time, in the early 1980s, in medical departments this was still something that only a few groups were practicing. When I started, that wasn't even one of the options of things that I was offered to work on.

FORTUN: How unusual was it that you were trying to learn more about lungs from the arthritis people?

SHAK: I think it was unusual, but I think people thought it was a really good idea. I got support for it right away, there was no question. I think there is a lot of cross-fertilization in science. But it was unusual. I think I was the only fellow in my year that chose that route.

FORTUN: Now I know there has traditionally been strong ties between UCSF and Genentech. Were you aware of that then, and starting to think you might come here?

SHAK: What happened is that after my research training at UCSF, I went back to NYU and took a faculty position there, with a joint appointment in medicine and pharmacology. The goal was to set up an independent research lab, to generate independent research funding, and to pursue the work that I had established in this lab independently.

FORTUN: Were you also teaching?

SHAK: I was teaching, but I was given the opportunity to spend at least 80 percent of my time in research, which is what I knew I needed to get my research career off the ground. My experience there was a good experience, but it was also from there that I made the decision to come to Genentech.

I came to Genentech as a result of seeing an ad in *Science* magazine. There was a position in the molecular biology department for someone with a background in inflammation. I looked at that and I said, "Wow!"—for a couple of reasons. The most immediate one was that I hadn't at that time had any skills in molecular biology, and it was clear in 1985 or 1986 that that was an incredibly powerful tool. And not to possess that tool, if I was committed to a research career over the next twenty or thirty years, was going to be a significant liability. And that presented a problem: how do you go about picking up a new tool when you're now already on the faculty, and where your career is going to be judged by your productivity in your chosen field already. And that's not a trivial problem. So on one hand, this provided an exquisite answer to that challenge: I could come here, and if there was any place to learn how to clone and express genes, this was the place.

The second thing was that I was also very interested and challenged by the

idea of being involved in drug development. And this came out of the following experience. I was working in this field of leukotrienes, these molecules
that are very potent cell messengers, and I had done intensive studies on one
of these particular molecules called leukotriene B_4. The most important question to me, and I think to the field, was, How important is leukotriene B_4?
What role does it play in disease, and will agents that interfere with its function be therapeutically useful? There I was in my lab at NYU, and with all the
training I had, and all the smarts I had, I realized that there was a direct way
to answer that question, and it wasn't what I was capable of doing. I had
learned how to measure this stuff, I had learned how to study how it was
made, I could go into tissues and grind them up and see whether it was there
or not. But all of those things were providing me with indirect information as
to whether it may or may not be important, and if so, where. And I had to
concoct stories, and speculate. I had definitive data, but with regard to what
it meant, the tools I had weren't adequate to answer that question.

Who could answer that question? The tool that one needed was a pharmacologic inhibitor. Who makes pharmacologic inhibitors? Drug companies.
And here I was, in a university, in a unique position of not knowing when
such an inhibitor would be available. Now if an inhibitor was available in
three months, then great: all I have to do is wait three months, and then I can
do the research and answer the questions that I want to answer. But what if it's
three years? What if it's *thirty* years? And what about the fact that I in my
position have no way of knowing whether it's three months, three years, or
thirty years? Which is even worse. So here, at the same time as I thought
about learning this new technology, I also was attracted by the opportunity of
being in the position of driving that process—of not being a passive part of
the process, but actually driving it, defining what reagents, what pharmacologic probe, what question I wanted to answer—getting that reagent and then
going out and doing the experiment.

So I came here. My boss was one of the brightest young molecular biologists here, an absolutely brilliant Ph.D. scientist, Dan Capon. He wanted to
bring me in to do what I wanted to do, I saw that I could come here and do
this, I could come here and spend time learning the technology. And it was
clear, also, that this company, which had developed tremendous expertise in
molecular biology, cloning, and the ability to make recombinant proteins,
now saw for the future that it needed to develop biology inside. It's one thing
to isolate and clone and make a recombinant protein; a second, equally important goal is to understand what it does and how to use it. And for that, a training in cloning isn't going to optimally train someone to approach that problem. And what the company needed to do was to have both biologists and
molecular biologists working together to get the whole job done. So that's
what led me to come here, and I'd say that within four or five months of inter-

viewing I had moved out here with my wife, my three-year-old son and my six-year-old daughter, and I started a new career here.

FORTUN: What position were you hired into? And were you told, Okay, you can spend your time working on *x, y,* and *z?*

SHAK: I was hired as a scientist. When I came here, I just loved that title. I thought that was great, that was super. This is a place that gets a lot done not because it puts an army of people to work on something. When I came, I wasn't given any technical help at all, but I did join a lab that was one of the strongest molecular biology labs here, and I was initially directed to work on a project that was really just getting started, on trying to isolate a novel lymphokine—purifying a protein from a cell supernatant, and then ultimately cloning out that protein and determining its sequence. What I had done before in the lipid field—there really are analogous processes, whether one's dealing with lipids, proteins, or DNA. There are ways of isolating them, there are ways of separating them, and ultimately there are ways of determining the exact structural sequence of what you have. What's so powerful about DNA research is basically two things. One, you can get the precise structural information of what is the DNA sequence extremely rapidly and easily. So I could walk into a lab, and in a day I could get a sequence of five hundred to a thousand base pairs or even more, depending on how hard I want to work. The other thing that's unique about DNA is that once you've got it, you can use various enzymes and cells to make more of it, to replicate it. With proteins and lipids, you start off with little and you end up with less. It really was a great opportunity to work on a great project, but also to learn the technology, how to purify proteins and how to clone genes, that would then allow me to take advantage of my previous training and say: if I now know what medical problems exist, and I now know what this technology can do, and I've also learned a little about the biotechnology business—what makes an idea a good idea as opposed to a bad idea—I can then begin to evaluate some of my own ideas and begin to work on them. And it was after being here about a year or a year and half that, walking down the hall one day, I had the idea that led to the development of Pulmozyme.

FORTUN: You had worked with people with CF previously, right?

SHAK: Yes. But I certainly didn't come here saying I want to find a new treatment for cystic fibrosis. I did come here saying it would be great if I could find a treatment for lung diseases. That's what I know best. But at the time I wasn't focused on CF.

The idea for DNase was generated by asking the following question. From my clinical experience I remembered that patients with lung infections— pneumonia, chronic bronchitis, cystic fibrosis—get into trouble because their airways get filled with these tenacious, viscous secretions that obstruct breathing. And I reasoned that there had to be a molecular explanation, some molecule that causes that stuff to be so thick. If I knew what that stuff was, then maybe I could identify an endogenous enzyme which, when inhaled, would go down and chop it up, and open up the tubes like Drano.

FORTUN: This may be an unanswerable question, but why had no one else thought of that?

SHAK: Actually, as is the case most of the time, it had been thought of previously. In fact, when I followed up that idea right away, I went back to see what had previously been done with regard to understanding what this stuff was made of. And I thought what I would be reading about was mucus glycoproteins: that this stuff was mucus, it can be thick and sticky, and so my first thought was that what I would be working on was some enzyme that breaks down mucus glycoproteins. However, when I went back to the literature that existed, papers that were published in the 1950s, I rediscovered a fact that was known then and had been largely forgotten, which is that when there are lung infections there is a huge amount of white-cell influx that comes in to fight those infections, leading to a tremendous accumulation of white-cell products, including DNA. And the other thing that was unique, I worked in a lab that made up DNA solutions routinely, so I knew immediately that those concentrations were likely to be very thick and to contribute to the physical properties of those secretions. And in fact, thirty years ago it had been suggested that bovine DNase I, a cow enzyme, might be useful. Now that idea never went anywhere because it was quickly discovered that breathing in foreign proteins, like cow proteins, is not a good idea. It's okay to eat cow, it's not good to breathe cow. But here I am at Genentech, here I am with this technology that I now have available. I looked quickly in the Genbank database to see whether human DNase I, a related protein, had ever been sequenced or cloned. And amazingly, it never had. So I now had a project.

And again, one of the great things about this place is that I didn't have to do a whole lot to get the go-ahead to drop everything and work on this.

FORTUN: What did you have to do? Who gives that kind of go-ahead?

SHAK: I just needed to get the go-ahead from two people. I got the go-ahead from, at that time, the head of research, Dave Martin, and he was immediately supportive of my proposal. And I got the go-ahead from Dan Capon, the guy who hired me.

FORTUN: Is this before or after you had done the little test-tube demonstration?

SHAK: This is way before. All I had done at this point is work through the idea. So I did a much more thorough review of the literature, I put together an assessment of what we knew and what we didn't know about the role of DNA, I described what specific experiments I wanted to do. I wanted to clone, express [to get the gene to "turn on" and produce], and make small amounts of human DNase, I wanted to see whether I could see any difference in a test

tube or not. Some of the experiments that had been done in the past with bovine DNase contained proteases, contaminating the DNase, so it was unclear
from the previous literature whether or not pure DNase alone would be
effective.

FORTUN: And this is before the CF gene was isolated. Did you see that as
an advantage, that you didn't even have to worry about what the gene was?

SHAK: What clearly drove it, from my perspective, was the fact that I did
articulate from the very beginning that we should focus on cystic fibrosis.
That came out of my own clinical experience and reflected the fact that individuals with CF have the most urgent form of this problem. They are the ones
who are demanding that we get an answer to this question: Can something
better be done for me? And although there was at that time a large effort trying to identify the gene, it seemed reasonable to me as well as to other people
that the field shouldn't put all its eggs in one basket. We didn't know how long
it would take to identify a gene, we didn't know how long it would take once
the gene was identified that we could capitalize on that with regard to new
therapies, or a cure. And thus it made sense to ask the question: Can we develop something that will make CF kids feel better and do better today? So
that whatever further developments come along down the line, more of them
can benefit.

FORTUN: Did you have direct contact with the other CF researchers?

SHAK: I needed to get advice and input from people in the community who
were good scientists and could be most helpful. We were talking to the CF
Foundation about doing a study on another protein of ours, human growth
hormone. I therefore was able to participate in a meeting where we invited
some of the key advisors to the CF Foundation. I had an opportunity to meet
them and to see who was respected and who wasn't, and I combined that with
a literature review of who was working in the field to identify really one person who I thought would be most helpful. I called up that person in Seattle;
his name was Dr. Arnold Smith. I told him I wanted to tell him about something, under confidentiality at that point. You know, academically, we hadn't
discussed this, this work hadn't been presented. As is the case with early academic research, you do want to maintain confidentiality. And I flew up to Seattle, and at that time I had cloned and expressed human DNase and I had
done the test-tube experiment, and so I went up there and showed him the
results and wanted his frank advice and input.

FORTUN: How does that contract of confidentiality work? Is it a kind of
gentleman's agreement?

SHAK: All these relationships are best worked out in a very specific way. I
had a need for advice and input; if he thought this was interesting, I certainly
would be open in the future to hearing how he thought he might want to do
research, help, continue to advise. I had no idea where this was going to go.

He could easily have said, That's a stupid idea, I think you should drop it. So at that point, the purpose of that visit was to get his advice and input and to find out if he had any further interest in working together. Ultimately it turned out that he thought it was a good idea, and as a result of that initial interaction, we continued to collaborate, and actually his group—there were two phase 1 clinical studies. That's the first stage of testing, and he and his site were one of the first two sites that performed the first studies of DNase in people. And he did a great job, so in this case it actually did work out to be a very productive collaboration for both his group as well as ours.

FORTUN: Does that kind of collaboration work differently, being that you're at Genentech rather than a formal academic? Or is it really that once you're collaborating with other scientists, you're really a scientist, no matter who pays you?

SHAK: From my perspective—and people from academia probably have different perspectives—and I think the case with every collaboration, whether between academia and industry, or within academia or within industry—like marriages, every collaboration is different, just like every marriage is different. There are good ones and there are bad ones. My personal experience is that collaborations are more likely to work in academia. Collaborations work when there are two things: one, a truly important scientific reason to combine forces, mutual interest and complementary skills. That's the most important. If that's not there, nothing is going to make the collaboration work. It will fail. And then the second thing is that the terms be fair and reasonable, that each side feels that based on what they put into it, they get something out of it. So those are the two things you need, and I've had successful collaborations and I've had unsuccessful ones, and that's largely what drives how effective they are.

Let me just say that in terms of what we're trying to do, which is to understand very complicated medical problems and develop new molecular solutions to them, that isn't an effort that any one person alone can do effectively. It does require collaborations, whether they're collaborations within the company, outside the company, with nonprofit organizations. The success of Pulmozyme is due to a successful collaboration among a whole variety of different people, each of whom had a strong reason to work hard and be involved and contribute. Ultimately driven by the needs of the CF kids saying we want something better.

FORTUN: I wanted to go back both to the cloning of DNase and how that was done, and then the assembling of the team.

SHAK: The actual cloning I did with my own hands. I was in the lab from seven in the morning until eleven or twelve at night, daily, for months. But that's something that I had been trained to do here.

FORTUN: Was there a particular cell line that you got it out of?

SHAK: I got it out of a human pancreatic cDNA library which had been prepared here by another scientist four or five years earlier. So I then set out to fish out of that library the human DNase gene, and the strategy that I took was a strategy that was developed here, which was based on the knowledge of the bovine amino acid sequence of DNase I. That protein had been exceptionally well studied by protein biochemists in the 1950s, 1960s, and early 1970s. In fact, the laboratory of Moore and Stein got the Nobel Prize for their work on RNase and DNase proteins, and they had manually sequenced the entire amino acid sequence of bovine DNase in 1973. So that was sitting there in the literature since that time. So really at any point, if someone had wanted to clone out human DNase I, it would have been possible. So with that 1973 published sequence, two probes were designed that would hopefully match, to some degree, two different regions of the human DNase gene. The neat strategy here is that I looked for binding at low stringency of these probes to that cDNA library. I obviously found many clones that lit up at low stringency when I looked at the binding of one probe alone; I found only six clones that lit up with both. And obviously, *I* lit up at that point, because the likelihood that one of those six clones was going to be related to human DNase was high. In fact, one of those six clones was the full-length DNase sequence. Again that's the amazing thing about this technology, that one needs only one copy of that DNase gene in a vial, and that allows for the production of every vial of DNase that we make now and in the future.

FORTUN: But you were still working pretty much by yourself at this point?

SHAK: Yes.

FORTUN: How long did that initial cloning and expression take?

SHAK: About four months.

FORTUN: That's pretty fast.

SHAK: Yes.

FORTUN: One of the press accounts mentions that you then had to go and impress [Genentech CEO G. Kirk] Raab, that this was something to go ahead on. Was that a hard sell?

SHAK: That test-tube result was so dramatic to me, it was so dramatic to everyone who saw it, that it led everyone, including the CEO of the company, to say, Steve, go for it, drop everything and let's see if this is really going to make a difference in people's lives or not.

So then a project team was formed. I had done some of the original work that led to the idea now that we should begin to see whether we could test this in people. And in order to do that, one needs to do a lot of work. I had made small amounts of DNase in little petri dishes; we needed now large amounts of DNase. I had a very impure preparation that I was studying; we needed now to study a very pure preparation. We needed to get this to the lungs, and to come out of a nebulizer as a mist. We needed to make sure the protein would survive that. In order to begin clinical studies, we needed to get information on potential risks. We needed to treat a large number of animals to evaluate its potential safety. We needed to design the clinical trials, and in order to do that we needed an idea of what was likely to be an effective dose. So we needed to do research that would help us understand what the dose might be. I had sequenced one clone initially; we needed to make sure that that was the right clone. We needed to make sure that the protein and DNA from a number of people are identical to the one we chose, and that we didn't make a mistake. All that requires a lot of work, and again, that's what scientists here just do really well.

FORTUN: Did you put the team together yourself?

SHAK: I was given a great opportunity. I was given the opportunity to be project team leader. I hadn't been a project team leader before. I had sat in on some other project teams, so I had an idea of how teams ran and what needed to be done. But clearly this was a fantastic opportunity for me, not only to learn about how to develop a drug, but to be in a position to drive that process. And I think that says a lot about this company, that it thought that it was a good idea to trust a young, inexperienced person with that kind of opportunity. In terms of the other people on the team, they weren't selected by me. Usually what happens is that each of these activities is performed by scientists in individual departments: the cell lines are made by the department of cell genetics. We need to rely on the head of that group to identify the projects currently being worked on, who has time, who could do this job well. And so in terms of who was on the team, that was decided with input from lots of different people, each deciding who made the most sense from their own technical perspective.

It was interesting that as the team was constituted and we had our first meetings, I looked around the room, and I knew that I didn't have a lot of experience, and that that might be a problem. But when I looked around the room I saw that in fact almost everybody on the team was a person who was new, who hadn't had experience developing a protein before. And so one of my first actions as project team leader was to go to the head of project development—and just to give you some flavor of how this place works, it's not a big bureaucratic process. I made an appointment to see him, I saw him two or three days later, I walked into the room and I said, "Rich, I've got a problem. I don't know what I'm doing, and no one else in the room knows either! I think it would be a good idea if there was someone in the room who had been through this before." And Rich said, "You're right," and within a week we had a new member of the team, John O'Connor. And he had been through it before, he was very experienced, and proved very valuable to the team not only because of his own expertise in analytical chemistry, but because he had been through this process before.

FORTUN: What were some of the difficulties that you encountered along the way, in terms of coordinating people, or problems that came up in one section impacting other processes?

SHAK: The teams are the heart and soul of getting things done. You need a good environment, you need good senior management, but ultimately it's at the team level that things happen or don't happen. As the team leader, I did have an opportunity in the lab to work on some of those problems myself. I particularly focused on the issues that I had expertise to address, like trying to get information as to what the appropriate dose might be from *in vitro* experiments. I also worked on sequencing DNase from additional individuals to make sure that it was the right clone. So there were some things that I did, but actually as project team leader, a major goal is to work with the team to make sure there's a focused plan with a clear set of goals and priorities. And then to continue to monitor the progress of the project, to make sure that resources were being deployed to optimally address those goals. And so a lot of that job is anticipating and looking out for problems, and then rolling up your sleeves and fixing them as soon as they come up.

For one group to succeed, it frequently requires work by other groups. For example, the group trying to develop the way to manufacture large amounts of this material, they needed to test various vectors in various expression systems to see which expression system was best at producing large amounts of DNase, and which one produced a molecule which was most natural, most like the DNase that is present in all of our bodies. To do that they needed access to assays that reliably measure the amount of DNase, and they needed someone to purify the protein and analytically determine the structure. Those are efforts that are all going on elsewhere, so for success one needs a very integrated effort, with the success of one group very much dependent on that of other groups.

Problems will always come up, and my goal as project team leader was to put together a team that would ultimately develop not only such a good working relationship, but also an esprit de corps and a confidence, so that whatever problem evolved, or whatever screwed up, we as a team would focus on what we need to do to fix this as opposed to pointing fingers and trying to assess blame. And I'm very proud that the team did develop that esprit, that confidence, so that whatever new problem came up, it was just, Great! Let's go get it! Let's apply science to this problem.

To give you some example of how most problems are not anticipated, everything was looking good, we had a way of making DNase, we had a way of purifying it, the people in the formulation department had figured out what liquid to put it in to keep it stable. All these things have to be figured out anew; every protein is different, and you can't go into a book and read about how you're going to do this. It's extremely empirical and experimental. All

of that had been worked out, it was looking great, we were ready to begin our
human studies. The material was placed in a simple glass vial, and we had
never seen any problem with that. All of a sudden, I get a call from the filling
department that the first fill had been performed, the vials had all been in-
spected, and almost every one had been rejected because when they looked
at them, there were these flakes floating around in them. What I said then is
probably not quotable. So we got together as a team and tried to figure out
what was going on, and what we could do to solve this. Clearly, you can't give
people a product where you've got these flakes floating around. I knew nothing about flakes, I knew nothing about vials. But to give you some idea of this
place and its commitment to excellence at every level, it turned out that in this
company we had an expert on stoppers. And it turned out that when we asked
the question, What did we do differently here? what came out was that we had
changed the stoppers that we were using. And this wasn't even a scientist; it
was a more junior person who was responsible for knowing about stoppers.
Basically, the stopper person said, "I'm sure it's the stopper, what we need to
do now is a series of experiments. Different kinds of stoppers have different
kinds of coatings; it's likely that the coating is interacting with the protein and
somehow caused the flakes. Let's find out what we can do." We set up a series
of experiments to find out what the best stopper is. Those experiments began
within a day or two, and within two or three weeks that problem was solved,
and we had a vial, we had the right stopper, and we were still on track. I think
that gives you some flavor of how problems will arise out of the blue, and
how a good team will have the right people, and give the right people the job
to solve those problems.

FORTUN: But if you were, say, a distant investor in this process, how reliable is the assumption that because you're a smart scientist, you'll be a smart
manager, too?

SHAK: Zero. [*Laughs*] Those are unrelated.

FORTUN: Well, it is quite extraordinary that this team with basically no
experience was put in charge of a drug that by all accounts was given a high
priority within the company. And also in this kind of newly accelerated,
parallel-track process.

SHAK: There were two people on the team—I mentioned John O'Connor,
and also Brian Lawlis, on the process development side, who was very experienced and a very valuable contributor to the process. I just did what seemed
right. I always asked the question, Are we doing what's right? Can we do better? What can we learn from the previous projects that we've done, that would
help us do DNase better?

FORTUN: I'd like to hear about the idea of parallel tracks, which I understand to be a relatively new trend in the biopharmaceutical business. You went
immediately to a high-yield cell line rather than beginning with studies in

low-yield cell lines; you began clinical trials at the same time; you were building a production facility at the same time; you were going through the FDA process at the same time. One analogy in an article I read said that this was comparable to the automobile or electronics industry. I don't know if those kinds of management models were floating around here, or if it was more independent.

SHAK: I think that the strategies were driven from the beginning by two things. One was the urgency of the need of this patient population, and we didn't know from the outset whether DNase would be beneficial and safe or not. Neither did the CF community. We owed it to the CF community, though, to get that answer as soon as possible. If it was safe and effective, then we could get a new and effective treatment to that community earlier rather than later. And it was equally important to learn if it wasn't safe and effective, because then the community could focus its resources on alternative approaches, and I could work on something else. I want to do something that's important; I don't want to spin my wheels, either. And that was captured by the first meeting I had with the CF Foundation, where we told them about this project before we publicly told anyone about this. That was really exciting; it was in December 1989. The CEO of the CF Foundation, Bob Dressing, had a child with cystic fibrosis, so it's clear why he's doing what he does. And he had two responses. One was, Whatever you do, Steve, do it right the first time. And that wasn't a threat. What he was realistically communicating is that this is a community that isn't going to take disappointment very easily. You're not going to want to go to this community and say, We screwed it up this time, we've got to do it again. There was a real need to do it right. So I think the parallel process really came out of us trying every step of the way to answer the question, How can we do this better and how can we do this faster, without compromising one or the other? And when you ask those two questions you end up with parallel development, and you have to go that way.

FORTUN: But at some point you had to sort of gulp and say, Okay, let's build a production facility? So it must have been fairly clear at that point that you had done it right.

SHAK: Actually, I'd give our CEO Kirk Raab a lot of credit. We did have some data that said that it looked like it was working in smaller studies that were short term, but we asked Kirk to okay spending $42 million on a manufacturing plant, without the data that said—and obviously, this is critical— that it was safe when given over a long period of time, and that it was effective over a long period of time. So I give Kirk a lot of credit for taking those risks. But that's also what I've come to see as the nature of this business. We are taking those risks all the time. There might be five to ten projects which enter clinical trials, only one of which ultimately ends up being safe and effective. I don't see that changing in the future. That risk taking, that willingness to go down a number of potentially blind alleys in order to find the really important roads, is something that's just part of our business.

FORTUN: This does happen alongside the t-PA story, and there are interesting parallels. And what I want to get to is your interaction with the FDA, and that seems also to be part of why this was able to go so quickly. Some of the media accounts say that there had been a contentious relationship between Genentech and the FDA, in part because of the t-PA process. Which was not the case with Pulmozyme.

SHAK: Not at all. When I asked the question at the very beginning, What can we do differently and better? certainly what I heard was that we can do better with the FDA. And so we started down that road in a very positive way from the very beginning. I have to say that the FDA is sometimes much maligned in the media, and I think falsely so. A lot of the ways in which they spent time meeting with us, before and after every clinical study we did, providing us with advice and input and direction, isn't something that ever gets publicized, but was invaluable to this process of drug development.

FORTUN: Did David Kessler becoming chair of the FDA also make a difference?

SHAK: My experience doesn't go back very far, but I think this philosophy that the FDA should and can work together with companies was articulated from the highest level.

FORTUN: The FDA did suggest some changes in your clinical trials, right?

SHAK: They suggested important changes in the clinical trials and design, which made the studies better. And I think the CF patients owe them a real debt of gratitude.

FORTUN: You mentioned earlier that there are some things that can't be learned from books, but have to be learned through experience. All of these different kinds of collaborations—within the team, with the FDA—where do people get the social skills for it? It's a new thing that you have to do. You clearly have a real working sense that it's something you have to do, that it's not natural. But how do you prep people to not antagonize the FDA, for example?

SHAK: Well, with regard to the FDA, the amount of preparation that goes into these meetings is really incredible. If you have an opportunity to meet with a lot of smart people for two hours, you want to get as much out of that interaction as possible. And the way to do that is not to go in there and say, What do you think we should do? If you did that, they wouldn't be very helpful at all. That's not the kind of input that they're talking about. But if we did a good job of putting up, as a straw plan, what we thought is the best way of proceeding, those sessions became incredibly productive and useful for getting their feedback and guidance. They had been criticized for being too slow in reviewing drug applications. I'm guessing that what accounts in part for their change in approach was their understanding that many of the times that there were long delays it was because they didn't have input into the study design and into the end points, and therefore when the data was ultimately generated and the reports submitted, they had a very difficult position in making a decision. Because the study wasn't designed to address what they perceived as being needed to show efficacy. So by interacting with us, if the best possible studies are done, it makes their job of evaluating safety and efficacy easier.

FORTUN: One of the things that comes up in these stories, and it's hard to know what to make of it, is that the development of Pulmozyme seems to figure quite significantly in the decision by Roche to purchase 60 percent of Genentech. First of all, what did that look like from your point of view? And second, was it odd to be in these presentations to a major Swiss multinational firm? Both specifically as related to Pulmozyme, but also in terms of the general atmosphere around here. Because you came in, by general accounts, at sort of a low point for Genentech, then there were discussions as to whether Roche was going to buy or not, and what effects that would have.

SHAK: I did present the DNase project to senior management in Roche before they made the decision to buy 60 percent of the company. As to how that influenced their decision or not, there you have to go on what they say, and I think there are some published comments from Jurgen Drewes on his impressions.

Clearly, though, once the deal was done, the question for the DNase team was, Is there a way that this relationship with Roche could be good for or helpful to the DNase project? And in fact, collaboration with Roche on DNase was very important to Pulmozyme development. Not so much in the United States; things were well in place in the U.S., and we had a lot of experience in the United States and understood U.S. regulatory requirements. But we had little experience with regulatory requirements outside the United States, and thus specifically entered into a collaboration with Roche to co-develop DNase for cystic fibrosis and for chronic bronchitis outside the U.S. Early in the project, I never did project that we would get approval outside the United States at any time similar to that as within the U.S. We might have projected that it might occur as long as two years after U.S. approval. I didn't think that was great, if Pulmozyme was safe and effective, that if you had CF and were fortunate enough to be born here that you would have access to it, but if you were born somewhere else you wouldn't. It turns out that with Roche's collaboration we were able to get regulatory approvals almost simultaneously in Europe and the United States. And that was great for DNase, and that was great for people with cystic fibrosis.

FORTUN: So Kirk Raab didn't come to you and say, Steve, you've got to make this presentation and—no pressure—but we think Roche might be interested in buying us?

SHAK: In terms of what Roche was doing and why they were here, I was given no information as to what the nature of that discussion might be.

FORTUN: I ask because the standard academic line on these things, which

I mentioned in my letter to you is becoming very hard to think about and sustain, is that this kind of consolidation of major pharmaceutical companies with not only small biotech firms, but now the "flagship" of the biotech industry—that this kind of consolidation can only be bad, and result in increased control by a few large corporations. It's far too simplistic, it seems to me, but I know that even within Genentech there must have been some sort of discussion about needing the research and development money, and we can do a lot of things with that. And yet also worrying that in some ways—one of the phrases I read was "the stifling embrace of Roche"—that in some way it might affect what people were going to be allowed to work on.

SHAK: I can say that there was no stifling embrace. In areas where it made sense for us to work together, we have worked together and done so productively. And the development of Pulmozyme in Europe is a very good example of that. But there are certainly other areas where we have independent efforts, where working together wouldn't make scientific sense, and we've continued our independent efforts, and we're trying to do the best that we can do for Genentech, in the same way that I'm sure scientists and management at Roche are trying to do the best they can do for Roche.

FORTUN: So there seems to be no kind of visceral change in the place pre-Roche and after Roche? Other than it's maybe easier to get laboratory equipment or easier access to R&D money, the place doesn't feel at all different?

SHAK: I think the interaction thus far has been largely positive, and that we have been and will continue to be, you know, masters of our own destiny. I think that if you don't see yourself as a victim, if you don't see yourself as a pawn of the world around you, you will not be a pawn.

FORTUN: I also wanted to hear a little bit about your current gene therapy work.

SHAK: DNase is not a cure for cystic fibrosis. It is a new and important therapy, but it is not a cure for this disease. And it's certainly my hope, and the hope of all of us who work in the field, that ultimately this disease can be eradicated. Now that the gene that is responsible for the disease is known, it certainly has led to an explosion in new avenues approaching not only treatments but also eventually a cure for this disease. We have been committed to continuing our CF research, in looking at all the possible avenues where additional benefit might be obtained by developing new approaches to treatment. We have focused on gene therapy as the most exciting potential for the future, as have many other groups throughout the world.

The idea is a simple one: if the problem in this disease is an accident in a single gene that leads to a defective protein in the lining cells of the airways of the lung, then a simple solution would be to put the normal gene in, and thereby have the normal protein made. The field right now is working very hard to accomplish the very real challenge of making that simple idea a reality, in terms of something that is feasible, safe, and effective. So we and many other people are working in that area. What we have chosen to do is work primarily by creating a new start-up company called GenVec, that is focusing solely on gene therapy. The strategy is that the development of this new technology will optimally occur in an environment that is focused solely on accomplishing that goal, and on developing that technology. It's been a very exciting year and a half for GenVec and for us. Progress is being made, and the earliest clinical studies in patients with CF are underway, and some data has already been supported.

FORTUN: And what's your relationship to that project? Are you actively involved?

SHAK: Yes, the project is a collaboration between GenVec, ourselves, and Dr. Robert Kristol at Cornell University. There is a research committee composed of GenVec and Genentech representatives that define the research goals and monitor the progress of the project. I'm the lead representative at Genentech, and I've had a tremendous opportunity to help in moving that project forward.

FORTUN: What do you get out of that organization of things as opposed to reformulating a team within Genentech, with the same kind of focus? What can you do there that you couldn't do here?

SHAK: I think that the developments of new technology can sometimes optimally occur in a very small organization, that is focused solely on that problem, isn't distracted by other issues, and probably most importantly, whose future depends on its success. That's not to say that we at Genentech aren't developing new technologies all the time. We are, but in this case, this is a technology that we think is going to need an extensive investment. We in fact have an effort here as well as an effort at GenVec, so I don't want to say that technology development can't happen in a bigger company. In this case, we decided that we want to do everything possible to make it happen, which is to have both an effort on the outside and some effort on the inside as well.

FORTUN: It's interesting, because from the outside the standard line is, GenVec is owned by Genentech is owned by Roche, and it's all one thing. But this story that you tell says that it's very important that there be this small, independent company whose future very much depends on their success. That there's actually a difference within what looks like this unified relationship from outside.

Do you get involved in the question of how much these therapies are going to cost, or is that someone else's problem?

SHAK: The decision of the cost of Pulmozyme was made by another group in the company. Clearly, with regard to the cost, it would have been a disaster if everything had gone well—we could make the drug, it was safe, it was effective—but if we charged so much that it couldn't be available to the patients that needed it. Obviously, from a scientific perspective, we did everything we could to be able to make this protein in as efficient a way as possible. Even with that effort, it's an extraordinarily complex process, and is extremely labor intensive. I'm very happy that ultimately the price of Pulmozyme is actually very reasonable and fairly priced, and is in line with the value that it provides to patients.

FORTUN: What if you didn't think it was fair? Within the company, could you complain to somebody? If you were driven by patient access to this stuff.

SHAK: I guess I'm happy to say that I do work for a company that knows that it's important to be fair and reasonable. And I trusted all along that that kind of approach would be taken, and I wasn't surprised at all. I've heard our CEO make the following comment. He's been asked, wouldn't it be a disaster if someone developed a cure for AIDS and charged a million dollars for it, and no one could afford it? And Kirk Raab's response was, That would be a disaster, I think that's unlikely. I think the more likely disaster is that there wouldn't be any development of a cure for AIDS at all. That is the perspective of Genentech's CEO, and I had no doubt that it would be done right.

As a scientist and as a physician I want to work on a project that will hopefully provide the largest medical impact possible in people's lives. And it's therefore that medical need which drives me in terms of where I focus my research. And clearly there's not a simple formula to define medical need; it's a combination of the severity of the illness, the current availability of therapy, the actual impact on people's lives, and ultimately the number of people that suffer from that condition. With our limited resources we try to focus as much as possible on diseases where there is clearly an important medical need, and where we ultimately deliver a clinically significant medical benefit. Now I happen to think that if we're successful at that, we can make money as well, and we can make money that will help support our effort at continuing to try to revolutionize medical care over the next twenty years. That goal is perfectly consistent with our business, and with the commercial needs of this company and its shareholders, which also exist as well.

FORTUN: Would you have to argue the same thing in a different way if you were asking for research money from the National Institutes of Health?

SHAK: I actually think that it's not very different at the NIH. In any research proposal there are the short-term aims and there are the long-term goals. And many research proposals to NIH focus on long-term goals which have the same kind of goals that I just talked about, which is understanding and eventually treating medically important problems. And I think to some extent the amount of funds that get funneled into certain areas are dependent on the medical need as well.

FORTUN: There are a couple of things about the media representations of you and Pulmozyme that I wanted to ask about. Is it strange to find yourself pictured in the *New York Times,* or is it a charge?

SHAK: There's a reason for the attention. The focus of the attention is on the science that we all did together, and is focused on the impact on cystic fibrosis patients. So to get attention in that context is really fantastic.

FORTUN: There are a couple of phrases in some of the accounts that I wanted to get your reaction to. They talk about the "hands-on culture" at Genentech, or the "entrepreneurial culture." Do those terms make sense to you?

SHAK: Absolutely.

FORTUN: What does an entrepreneurial culture feel like? How do you know it's there? I know that's hard to articulate, but do you have any language for, say, comparing the lab here to one at UCSF?

SHAK [*long pause*]: Actually, I've used the term *entrepreneurial,* but as you ask this question, I find myself asking myself—I'm not sure what I mean when I hear the word or when I use it. As I think about Genentech, what is special about the culture is the commitment to science, the commitment to people, the commitment to trying to do something great and important. And the commitment to rewarding and recognizing people for their contributions. Now I don't think that culture or that spirit is unique to a company. In that context, if that's what I'm calling entrepreneurial, then a research investigator in an academic setting or a research institute can work under the same kinds of conditions and find the same kind of satisfaction.

FORTUN: You also have this very nice quote: "If I'd had this idea in academia, nothing would have happened." So there does also seem to be a difference at the same time.

SHAK: I do think that although there are similarities between academia and industry, there are probably differences in relative strengths and relative weaknesses. Both academia and industry need to be committed to high-quality science, and to scientific investigation, answering questions with hard data. I think a relative strength of industry and a relative weakness of academia, in drug development, is actually enabling, testing, and ultimately performing clinical studies to evaluate new molecular solutions: that is something that a tremendous investment has been made in here at Genentech, to develop an infrastructure to do that as well as anyone in the world. That is not a major goal of academia. Conversely, I would say a relative strength of academia is a long-term commitment to trying to understand diseases at a molecular level, and to basic scientific research. That's not to say Genentech never does, and has no commitment to, basic research, nor do I want to say that academia will never develop a drug. Both of those are untrue. On the other hand, I think that there are relative strengths that each of us possess, and ideally, to the extent that we work together through every stage of development, sick patients are going to be better off.

Our relative strength in drug development stems from not only the resources that we have and the experience that we can bring to bear, but also comes from the fact that that is a process requiring a huge effort. Hundreds of individuals were working on Pulmozyme a year or two ago. Clearly, it is easier for an industry organization to collect and encourage a group of people to work together than it is to do in academia. Although in academia, where scientific collaborations make scientific sense, sometimes that occurs fantastically as well.

Pulmozyme was successful because many, many people, both within the company and outside, felt ownership of the project, and felt that a very important piece of the project was theirs and in their control. The project was big and important enough that it allowed for a lot of people to feel good about the contributions that they could make.

Notes

The author gratefully acknowledges the support of the National Science Foundation (grant no. SBR-9601757), without which this interview and the accompanying research and writing could not have been accomplished.

1. On the differential production of molar and molecular concepts and effects, see Deleuze and Guattari 1987.

2. Kids figure prominently in the annual report itself, with Genentech helping them do what kids do best: play. Danny Bliss is pictured playing baseball with his father. Ten-year-old Christopher Rowe has been sick less often, "and thus able to play outside more often." For eleven-year-old Jolene Ganun, "easier breathing translates into more energy to play" with her dogs Cuddles and Toby. Eighteen-year-old Timothy Arthur now has "more freedom to enjoy his favorite sport" of windsurfing. Each of these individuals has CF, and their enhanced ability to play is due to Pulmozyme. Other conditions and other Genentech therapies are also depicted in similar terms. Three-year-old Jarrett Lamb has chronic granulomatous disease, but with Actimmune therapy "is healthy enough to participate fully in day care center activities." Jaclyn DeLorenzo, photographed in her ballet outfit, "may now have the potential to realize her dream of growing to a normal height" despite her diagnosis with chronic renal insufficiency, with the intervention of Nutropin, one of Genentech's growth hormones. And "thanks to Protropin therapy since infancy" (Genentech's other growth hormone), twelve-year-old Johnny Bland "stands within the normal height range for his age. . . . He is happy about that because when you spend your free time playing ball, bike riding, swimming, and of course, skateboarding with friends your age, height can be an important concern."

3. The media bounces among hero tropes can be quite amusing. The headline of one article employed the phrase "Shak Attack" above a photo of a smiling Shak holding a pipette—a reference to basketball hero Shaquille O'Neal—and in turn a parody of the "Big Mac Attack" of hamburger heroism.

4. Quoted in "Clone your own legend," *Nature* 362: 397.

5. The origins of Genentech also involved a great deal of patient and frenzied legal work. It wasn't simply "market forces" and public demand that sent Genentech's stock prices "skyrocketing," but the combination of those with the concerted promotional actions of lawyers. For a superbly detailed and entertaining account of how the prestigious San Francisco law firm of Pillsbury, Madison, and Sutro managed Genentech's initial stock offering—and the subsequent imbroglio with the U.S. Securities and Exchange Commission over possible inflation of the company's value—see Stewart 1984.

6. In addition to the purchase of this large chunk of Genentech, Roche has made a number of recent deals (most notably the purchase of rights to the polymerase chain reaction (PCR) from Cetus Corporation for $300 million) that have increased its domain in the biotechnology and pharmaceutical industry (Hodgson 1992).

7. Trade commentary attributed Pulmozyme's "relatively quick passage . . . through the FDA and its advisory panels to changes at both Genentech and the FDA," as well as "better cooperation" between the two, particularly in the design of the phase 3 clinical trials. FDA Commissioner David Kessler personally participated in the daylong advisory committee meeting (Potter 1993).

8. The initial agreement included "golden parachutes" for the top six Genentech officials. An "unusually high volume of trading in Genentech securities on the Pacific Stock Exchange just before details of the merger were made public" sparked an SEC investigation into allegations of insider trading (Gershon 1990a). The focus of the investigation was Genentech CEO G. Kirk Raab's wife and members of her family. Some stockholders at the time of the deal felt that Raab had sold them short, and in July 1995 Genentech's board "sent Mr. Raab packing" and announced that he had been borrowing personally from Genentech, and had "sought a $2 million personal-loan guarantee from Roche . . . even as he was negotiating the sale of his company to Roche" ("Down and Out at Genentech," *New York Times,* 16 July 1995, sect. 3, 2).

9. This phrase comes from Holtzman (1989, 121), but the trope is unfortunately typical of how much of the literature in the field of science and technology studies characterizes scientists and their relationship to universities and corporations.

References

Deleuze, Gilles, and Felix Guattari. 1987. *A Thousand Plateaus.* Minneapolis: University of Minnesota Press.

Dickson, David. 1984. *The New Politics of Science.* New York: Pantheon.

Fisher, Lawrence M. 1994. "Rehabilitation of a Biotech Pioneer." *New York Times,* 8 May, C6.

Fortun, Michael. Forthcoming. "Projecting Speed Genomics." *The Practices of Human Genetics.* Sociology of the Sciences Yearbook 19. Ed. Fortun and E. Mendelsohn. Boston: Kluwer.

Genentech, Inc. 1992. "Building the Future." Annual report.

———. 1993. "The Dream Continues." Annual report.

Gershon, Diane. 1990a. "Allegation of Insider Dealing." *Nature* 345 (10 May): 102.

———. 1990b. "Mixed Reactions to Merger." *Nature* 343 (22 Feb.): 681.

Hall, Stephen S. 1987. *Invisible Frontiers: The Race to Synthesize a Human Gene.* Redmond, Wash.: Tempus Books.

Hamilton, Joan O'C. 1993. "A Star Drug Is Born." *Business Week,* 23 Aug., 66.

Hodgson, John. 1992. "An Appetite for Technology: Hoffman-LaRoche." *Bio/Technology* 10 (Aug.): 867–69.

Holtzman, Neil A. 1989. *Proceed with Caution: Predicting Genetic Risks in the Recombinant DNA Era.* Baltimore: Johns Hopkins University Press.

Kenney, Martin. 1986. *Biotechnology: The University-Industrial Complex.* New Haven, Conn.: Yale University Press.

Leveque, Francois. 1990. "The Logic of Growth." *Bio/Technology* 8 (Aug.): 776.

McCormick, Douglas. 1990. "When It Changed." *Bio/Technology* 8 (Mar.): 167.

OTA (Office of Technology Assessment). 1989. *New Developments in Biotechnology 5: Patenting Life.* Washington, D.C.: U.S. Government Printing Office.

Potter, Ray. 1993. "FDA Advisory Panel Okays Genentech's DNase." *Bio/Technology* 11 (Sept.): 972–73.

Rabinow, Paul. 1995. "Reflections on Fieldwork in Alameda." *Technoscientific Imaginaries.* Late Editions 2. Ed. George E. Marcus, 155–76. Chicago: University of Chicago Press.

———. 1996. *Making PCR: A Story of Biotechnology.* Chicago: University of Chicago Press.

Ratner, Mark. 1990. "A New Era for Genentech, and So It Goes." *Bio/Technology* 8 (Mar.): 178.

Stewart, James B. 1984. *The Partners.* New York: Warner Books.

Tsui, Lap-Chee. 1992. "The Spectrum of Cystic Fibrosis Mutations." *Trends in Genetics* 8, no. 11: 392–98.

OPPOSITION, INC.

Michael Fortun and Kim Fortun

Marc Raskin and Dick Barnet founded the Institute for Policy Studies in 1963. In the years following they built an organization that became the preeminent Left think tank in Washington, D.C. Most notably, IPS became a strategic touch point for people working in the civil rights movement and the antiwar movement. IPS also became one of the most referenced icons of the New Left, by those who equated it with Sovietism and every other threat to "American-style democracy." In some ways, McCarthyite iconing of IPS was understandable: since its inception IPS has worked to challenge the ways that politics are "made in America." The goal is "to speak truth to power." The means is an innovative organizational structure, built to provide an institutional space for intellectual work somewhere between the university, government, and social movements.

The interview we include here follows IPS from its origins in Barnet and Raskin's frustrations with the calculative logics and managerial rhetorics of the "national security" establishment, through the challenges posed by the escalation of the war in Vietnam, the creation of a new international economic order, and the rise of the Reagan Right. We wanted to hear about their organizational as well as ideological challenges: how they funded, administered, and strategized their political initiatives, how they justified the hierarchies within which they positioned personnel and projects, and how they retained the organizational stamina to survive for over thirty years.

We came to this interview already entangled in the issues we discussed. For five years during the 1980s Mike worked at IPS, as assistant director of their Washington School, which offered adult-education classes covering themes ranging from health-care reform to Latin American politics and culture. Mike is now working as executive director of the Institute for Science and Interdisciplinary Studies (ISIS), a nonprofit organization working to link the work and concerns of scientists, citizens, and cultural theorists. Much of Mike's vision for ISIS stems from his involvement with IPS; many of the dilemmas described in this interview are now being replayed in his daily efforts. Like IPS, ISIS is working to create an institutional space generative of new roles for intellectuals in politics and of new forms of cultural critique. Kim's interest in the issues thematized in the interview also originated in practical work, some of which is described in Late Editions 2 and 3 (as Kim Laughlin) in articles describing efforts to respond to the Bhopal disaster, in India and internationally. Her interview with Dave Henson in this volume also explores politics as an organizational challenge, but at the grassroots—which compares in useful ways with the focus here on the think tank.

What we found most interesting in our discussion with Raskin and Barnet was, then, more a matter of architecture and location than ideology. In somewhat cruder terms: we were more interested in the tank than in the think. Reviewing the literature on think tanks in preparation for the interview, we were struck by how little attention, relatively speaking, scholars had devoted to the more "everyday," organizational aspects of these nonprofit corporations. Our introduction to the interview shares part of this literature review with readers, raising questions about the links between think tanks, increased flows of information, bureaucratization, and social dissent. We return to the discussion of think tanks in the postscript, their "ambiguous role" in U.S. politics, their ties to farcical games of intellectual hubris, and their importance in a time when anti-intellectualism haunts contemporary society. What exactly is their "ambiguous role," as one analyst phrases it, in the U.S. political landscape? What kind of organizational form can be a "middle space," simultaneously attached to and independent from both government and civil society? What, now, is IPS an icon of, after thirty years of sustained organizational initiative, long after the Vietnam era and the oppositional polarities of the cold war have ceased to configure each and every political enterprise?

Kim Fortun

Dave Henson is a community organizer with experience throughout the United States, Central America, and Eastern Europe. Much of his work is within the environmental justice movement, within politics concerned with pollution, wealth distribution, civil rights, and the limits of liberal democracy. Like many others interviewed for this volume, Henson has developed strategic management techniques responsive to the specific context of the late twentieth century: the end of the cold war, the growth of transnational trade, technological expansion, downsizing of government and changing configurations of civil society. Like many others, Henson has struggled to build organizational forms sensitive to these changes yet grounded in established ideals. Like many others, Henson has learned as much from fiasco as from success.

I first became interested in interviewing Henson after hearing of his involvement in a series of organizational shutdowns, word of which circulated through the coalition I work with in response to the Bhopal disaster. The interview shows why I was impressed that someone had the savvy, nerve, and humility to call a project quits, even though its mission remained important. In working on the issues of "Bhopal" I often found myself, like Henson, within efforts that were simply out of synch with the times. Other efforts were more blatantly problematic: poorly organized, understrategized, and grossly bereft of internal critique. The urgency and obvious significance of the problems addressed legitimated compulsion to act without reflection, explained away failure, and limited all questions about choice of direction. The stories I heard about Dave Henson suggested a different approach.

The interview in this volume spells out Henson's approach. It can be read as an ethnographic glimpse into the worlds of citizen politics, or as a kind of "survivor's guide" to the double binds of grassroots organizing within globalization. Henson can hardly be accused of inaction, nor of the blind rampages of the ideological devotee. Henson is deeply reflective and painfully aware of how ideology veils as much as it uncovers. He is also incredibly persistent at pragmatic tasks, deserving his reputation as someone who can make things happen, keep things going, and, most importantly, knows when to try a different tack.

Henson's changes of direction have not been for lack of loyalty, but were a response to practical contradictions of context and organization. My own experience suggests that it is these contradictions that most need further reflection, combining analytic savvy with deft practical performances. In a world of environmental politics that too often valorizes raw commitment, Henson combines pragmatic finesse, informed judgment, internal critique, and attention to both concepts and context, and articulates a strategic vision worthy of the best corporate or organizational gurus. The portrait Henson provides is refreshing, and might serve others as it has served me, revitalizing a sense that critique and commitment need not be antithetical or even separate projects.

The interview covers a broad spectrum of topics and introduces the reader to many different people, associated with many different institutions, often without comprehensive explanation of who and what is being referenced. In editing the interview I decided to tolerate the ambiguity to preserve the sense of scope and complexity it conveys. I wanted to maintain the sense of constructivism that was so visceral in Henson's way of describing his work. Unlike many who theorize the grassroots from a distance, Henson refuses to essentialize or even stabilize his definition of what the grassroots is and where it should be going. Henson knows that the grassroots cannot be equated with localism, or with any simple definition of community. He does have his own theories about human nature, evolution, and "cyclical remembrance of ourselves as a communal species," garnered through continual, comparative reflection on the projects he has been involved with or heard about. He seems to rely on these theories for coherence, without defaulting on the demand for continual evaluation of context, practical organizational work, and long-term vision. In many ways, his use of theory as a point of reference rather than assertion, and his continual crossing of micro and macro perspectives, is akin to the best of anthropology. Henson illustrates how to read with an eye for critique, asking us to figure with him the narrative calculus of a humane social order, and a role for citizens within it.

Laurel George

The five voices heard in this article belong to artists and administrators affiliated with Movement Research (MR) at various points in the twenty-year history of this New York City-based artist organization. The institutional development of MR serves as a focal point for examining shifts in the business of art conducted by independent choreographers. By tracking the history of this organization and of certain artists' ties to it, we are able to glimpse what impels contemporary artists to build up organizations around themselves. No unified understanding of corporate forms shapes the careers of these artists. Rather, they seem to move between two general orientations to institutions: on the one hand, an impulse to form relatively permanent and stable organizations, and on the other hand, a desire to remain free of specific institutions and their constraints while developing a savvy about how to use external institutions to achieve their goals. The first two voices heard are those of Donna Uchizono and John Jasperse, young choreographers affiliated with MR around the time of these interviews in December 1994. The next two belong to Cynthia Hedstrom and Mary Overlie, who were among the founders of MR in the early 1970s and whom I interviewed jointly in Hedstrom's office at the Performing Garage, a theater in Soho. The final, most extensive interview is with Cathy Edwards, who was MR's codirector at the time of the interview. Conversations with two additional members of the early MR collective, Danny Lepkoff and Wendell Beavers (MR's director from 1981–83), gave a fuller sense of the organization's evolution from a collective to its current, more stratified form.

My association with Movement Research grew out of my work on the artist advisory board of DiverseWorks, a Houston, Texas artist organization and performing arts presenter. In the fall of 1994, a year after joining the artist advisory board of DiverseWorks, I curated a dance series for the organization. The project brought together four choreographers affiliated with Movement Research with four Texas choreographers for performances, workshops, and symposia in Houston, Austin, and New York. The stories of the people I came to know through this project raised questions about how artists both form and move through different institutions as they forge their careers. As these interviews reveal, various institutional and corporate forms alternately shape, impinge upon, and even generate career choices and, sometimes, even the creative choices of artists.

Among the key tropes associated with institutionally determined career choices that surface in the following interviews are: accountability (to funders, organizations, or perceived communities); innovation; organizing and organizations; and flexibility and mobility. Of these, flexibility and mobility most strongly reflect the modus operandi of choreographers working today. As I moved around lower Manhattan during the few days of these interviews in early December 1994, I had the sense that, in a compressed amount of time, I was physically moving in and out of many of the formal and informal institutions these artists daily negotiate in their professional lives. From Hedstrom's bustling office at the Performing Garage to Wendell Beavers's academic office at New York University; from the noisy cafés where I spoke with Edwards and Uchizono to the apartment cum rehearsal studio of Lepkoff and the studio apartment where I interviewed Jasperse, a fluidity of temporal and spatial boundaries and a sense of contingency shaped my meetings with these individuals. This only served to underscore the centrality of contingency and fluidity in their careers. I thank all of my interlocutors for stealing moments for reflection in the midst of the rehearsals, board meetings, photo shoots, classes, and grant writing that form their lives, and for their generosity of spirit in sharing these reflections.

8

Making Space, Speaking Truth:
The Institute for Policy Studies, 1963–1995

> Intellectuals in their diverse academies have been the subject of uto-
> pian speculation since antiquity, and the relationships of learned ad-
> visors have remained central themes in political histories, biogra-
> phies, in books of practical statecraft. Yet modern policy experts and
> their research institutes—no longer fanciful inventions but a funda-
> mental feature of modern political life—have attracted far less atten-
> tion. And their role in American politics is no less ambiguous than
> that of Lagado's grand academy. (Smith 1991, xii)

When Gulliver visits Lagado's grand academy, he laughs. Jonathan Swift's hero
shows little esteem for the experts, bemused by their improbable schemes: ex-
tracting sunbeams from cucumbers, constructing houses from the roof down,
training pigs to plow with their snouts. Gulliver's bemusement is analogous,
perhaps, to contemporary images of the American citizen: disaffected, ironic,
humored rather than awed by expert claims to social solutions. Such black
humor seems driven by myriad factors: material insecurity, widespread disaf-
fection with the institutional forms that are supposed to have sustained modern
democracy, cynicism about knowledge and values. If taken seriously, this dis-
affection prompts more questions than answers, among them, questions about
the purpose and validity of think tanks as institutional forms, and the ways they
claim both legitimacy and social resources.

The questions raised when one thinks about think tanks are noteworthy for
their scope as well as their significance. James Smith's claim that minimal attention has been given to the emergence and growth of think tanks as an organizational phenomenon or social force in U.S. politics is therefore troubling. The
problem, however, goes beyond simple lack of attention, and involves the *kind*
of attention paid as well. Much commentary on think tanks turns around "utopian speculation" (to continue with Smith's terms): unconcerned with the ade-
quacy of our ways of thinking "ideas" and "politics," it presumes that the
relation between the two terms is unproblematic—even when materialized in

institutions that claim immunity from politics while producing the arguments
from which "influence" proceeds. "Utopian speculation" directs our attention
to possible roles for the think tank in building better societies, banking on the
possibility of autonomous thought followed by thoughtful action. It is, then,
utopian on two registers. Idealizing the think tank, it skirts the most basic on-
tological question, What is this? More literally "utopian speculation" is just
that: a theory of no place; all think and no tank.

This interview with Marcus Raskin and Richard Barnet, founders of the Institute for Policy Studies (IPS), takes a different approach, which could be
called topographical reinscription, although ethnographic would do. Focusing
on the kind of social and intellectual *space* that Barnet and Raskin have cleared,
built, and maintained at IPS since 1963, this text offers detailed description of
how thought, social alliances, and organizational practices were conjoined in
purposeful, changing configurations of politics and ideas. While confirming
that IPS deserves its designation as premier think tank of the Left, the text also
shows how IPS departs from conventional models of what think tanks are. In
the process, we hope to show why we have displaced the utopian with the
topographical, working to engage ambiguous questions that resist both ideal-
ization and institutionalization.

A good example of utopian speculation on think tanks can be found in David
Ricci's *The Transformation of American Politics.* Many of his statements and
conclusions—grounded almost exclusively in statistical, political, and textual
analysis—lack any ethnographic complexity or detail. To explain what think
tanks are, why they appeared in the political landscape, and what they are supposed to do, Ricci points to the growth in federal bureaucracies, congressional
staff, and the proliferation of congressional committees and subcommittees (as
well as changes in the seniority structures of these committees). This political
transformation began after World War II but became much more dramatic in
the 1960s and 1970s. These social and political changes fostered the growth of
a "new class" of knowledge workers, professionals who preferred to "regard
themselves as autonomous rather than beholden to traditional authorities," located in the new institutional space of the think tank (Ricci 1993, 31–47).

Ricci's explanation comes down to a simple, aggregative equation: more organizations with more people need more information, advice, and "wisdom"
to understand and manage an increasingly complex society. Thus Ricci can
locate think tanks in a continuous Western historical and philosophical narrative that reaches back to Plato, but found its first full expression in the utopian
"Salomon's house" of Francis Bacon in seventeenth-century England. Three
centuries later and in a vastly changed social space, the utopian holds: "In the
1970's, then, a Salomon's House theme of reaching for truth resonated powerfully in Washington. . . . think tanks grew because their sponsors believed that
people in the city would pay special attention to policy advice tendered by

researchers whose words would seem more valid and more reliable than those of lobbyists, designated representatives, spokespersons, or special pleaders by any other name" (Ricci 1993, 16). In most other analyses as well, think tanks are conceptualized almost solely in these informational terms of providing advice and analyses, and we learn little about the organizational structure and social dynamics of the black boxes themselves.

The interview here loosely tracks the history of IPS, focusing on the political imaginary that informed its founding in 1963, the dramatic changes confronted by the institute with the escalation of the Vietnam War, the problem of defining the role of the institute amidst these changes, and the further changes and challenges brought on by the rise of the Reagan Right. Sidebars provide both elaborations on the interview, drawn from books and articles written by Raskin and Barnet, as well as commentary about IPS from both sympathetic and hostile observers. This elaboration and commentary is intended to provide a sense of the larger space within which IPS has accrued a distinctive identity and sense of its own mission.

In the thirty-five years since Barnet and Raskin left the Kennedy administration, they have negotiated dramatic changes in the context in which they work, but the general mission of IPS has nonetheless remained stable. IPS was formed "to speak truth to power," providing commentary on both foreign and domestic policy that tried to revitalize links between ideas and politics. Raskin and Barnet's experiences within the State Department and the National Security Council made it clear to them that such linkage was not possible within the corridors of power itself. In a series of origin stories, they describe the realization that "managerial terms" and "calculative logic" dictated the language of official politics, even in the Kennedy administration, which prided itself on having intellectuals in positions of power. From the beginning, then, their critique was not so much ideological as discursive and spatial. The goal was to create a space where people could talk differently, acknowledging that the perspectives of embattled civil rights workers, and others "outside," could not be accommodated within the language of "technocratic progressivism."

Today, even after years of FBI harassment, the assassination of colleagues, and continual charges of being antinational, Raskin and Barnet continue to insist that IPS is not "defiant," or even "oppositional." Their goal is to speak from an outside space—an "autonomous space," although that phrase will reveal its own ambiguities over the course of the interview. They acknowledge that this space has to be continually reimagined and recreated: a process of social invention that they believe characterizes democratic governance.

Nonetheless, IPS as an organizational space has provided stability within the necessary flux of oppositional work. Despite being labeled as a dangerous promoter of civil protest, IPS articulated and practiced a critical distance from social movements themselves. Raskin and Barnet describe social movements as important fashions that, more than anything else, need a stable institutional base for reference and regeneration. They perceive intellectual leadership as catalytic, fostering linkages more than specific ideologies. It was the heterogeneity of linkages that IPS was able to build from its space—with social movements, with universities, with members of Congress, with bureaucrats—that constituted its power, and indeed structured it as a "threat" to the establishment, which responded with its own organizational capacity to harass via the FBI and IRS, or with paranoid ideological attacks on IPS as a "communist front organization."

The history of IPS has made Barnet and Raskin keenly aware of spatiation. The terms and tropes of ambiguity and topography circulate continually and productively within their own discourse. This interview can then be read somewhat like a map, drawing lines between ideas and politics, but not without detail on how IPS got there. The challenge is to learn from the hard work, stubbornness, and compromise—and what all these things tell us about how "autonomy" and other utopian qualities are achieved. Barnet and Raskin have indeed strategized a corporation, in the sense of "an association of individuals . . . having a continuous existence independent of the existence of its members, and powers and liabilities distinct from those of its members." Or as Raskin says in the interview, "the question of the Institute" is the question of creating and protecting a space—independent yet linked—so that the movements of the day, "and ones to come in the future, will have a place to be."

K. FORTUN: The world in which IPS works, how has it changed? Is it a different thing to deal with Capitol Hill today than it was thirty years ago?

RASKIN: Historically? When the institute began we had this notion of being independent of power—political power—in order, in the Quaker sense, "to speak truth to power." The interesting thing is that that was predicated on a particular liberal framework: the powerful being prepared to listen; the framework of the corporate-liberal world where people would engage in discussion on specific things, wanting to hear different kinds of ideas. That meant that we would have members of Congress, members of the executive—they would come to seminars for discussion. What was interesting, though, was that within two years that began to change.

BARNET: Marc is right, even from my perspective, coming out of a much less political framework. I really came out of a conservative milieu, not very political. But I was totally influenced by the New Deal. Roosevelt had an importance for me unmatched by any political figure since, even though I was very young. My experience in the government also very much influenced my outlook. I came really knowing almost nothing about how government worked. But with certain expectations of what would be normal and rational. That people talked to each other. That once you got a key to the club, you could enter discussions about national security issues and disarmament that were completely different from what was outside. Outside, that was propaganda; inside, I expected people to be really talking to each other. That couldn't have been farther from the truth. So my question about the bureaucracy, Why were these people, the brightest and the best, so they said, talking this way?

M. FORTUN: In what way were they talking?

BARNET: I remember this discussion with the heads of the disarmament agency about a plan for fairly significant cuts in weapons, for the first time, really, in years. Ever since Dulles fired Stassen, there was an admiral in charge of the military affairs branch, or whatever it was called, leading the discussion. A Cornell professor, Frank Long, was giving a very learned explanation—throw rates, casualties and so forth—a highly technical conversation which implied that if you followed the logic, things would come out a certain way, not building large weapons, and so forth. Then a few people raised questions about things that were not part of the calculation. The admiral got outraged. He stood up and said, "Look, there is always an easy way to minimize casualties. We can *surrender.*" This was before *Doctor Strangelove* came out. But it portended the whole thing. That kind of atmosphere in the government.

RASKIN: Going back to the institute, looking at the history, somewhat in a different way, beyond ourselves. There had been over the course of the twentieth century different moves to try to figure out how to link ideas to politics, outside of the Left view, a usual socialist view of politics, a socialist program. Robert La Follett and his followers had the notion to use ideas in a particular technocratic way for governance, which helped set up the Legislative Research Service, which became the Congressional Research Service. There was a move of Columbia professors in the 1920s to link up to members of Congress, later becoming the Brain Trust for Roosevelt.[1]

BARNET: Then in the thirties, in academia, there was Harold Lasswell, and the whole notion of policy studies and policy sciences.

M. FORTUN: You say you wanted an independent space. Did you not see the university as a possibility?

> Democratic experimentation and participation reflect our commitment to dignity and equality, knowing that this commitment is best maintained by ending organizational tendencies to mystification and selfishness. Some would call this a form of socialism. Perhaps. But it is a very different type of "socialism" than one sees around us. No socialism can be worthy . . . unless it is of the kind which is compatible with individual initiative, liberty, democratic participation, protection of the private space and even anarchism. . . . It must build on what is already there, within us, as Americans and inviolate human beings. It must even build on capitalism, not only in its accomplishments but certain of its sensibilities. . . . State socialism has not found how to separate social service from control and compulsion . . . [and] has been nothing more than the national state's ideological mode to accomplish capital accumulation. . . . Being free of the ideologies of state socialism as they are practiced, except to study them, we are able to promulgate specific ideas and a coherent program which grows out of our own experience, often a local experience which is unreplicable. The relevant political path will vary at each political stage. And emphasis on different projects will vary from place to place for reasons of climate and local culture. (Raskin 1984, 15–17)

RASKIN: No, and the reason touches on what Dick just said: we viewed the universities as absolutely, utterly hooked into the national security state. Except for the smaller colleges, the Quaker colleges, which we called the "Quacker colleges," with which we tried to have links. At the beginning we thought in terms of exchange: we would go to the colleges to give lectures; they would send students to the institute.

M. FORTUN: Why didn't that work?

RASKIN: It did work. It worked very well, but with different schools. The Quakers wouldn't do it because McGeorge Bundy wouldn't support it. They weren't as independent as we thought.

M. FORTUN: How did Bundy tie in?

BARNET: Marc worked for Bundy, so they wanted him to get an endorsement.

RASKIN: They were skittish about where this was going to go. In that sense they were very clever. In any case, universities did have a relationship with the institute. Then the Vietnam War came and students became increasingly outspoken about the war. And the students who came to the institute wouldn't go back to the university.

BARNET: And, also, IPS began to be well known.

RASKIN: There were many costs. Many of which would only show up later on. Trustees had their tax returns audited. For the universities, it was a question of retaining linkage to the Department of Defense.

K. FORTUN: After two years of operation, something changed. Did it have to do with how the "outside intellectual" was perceived? You expected to be listened to, as part of the liberal dream?

RASKIN: Part of it changed; part did not, having something to do with our personal histories in the city. Before starting the institute, I worked on the Hill, before going to the White House, and built up very close relations with members of Congress. Then the Vietnam War happened and a number of these people were influential in opposing the war.

> In 1965 *The Viet-Nam Reader: Articles and Documents on America Foreign Policy and the Viet-Nam sis* was published. Edited by Ras and Bernard Fall, it became a sta reference of the antiwar moveme

BARNET: This was the height of our influence. Not only were members of Congress a lot more liberal, they were also more secure. They came from districts that were secure—California, New York. They were people who cared about issues and politics in the larger sense. As IPS became identified with the early Vietnam criticism, these alliances became more dangerous.

RASKIN: Another factor, the notion of the institute—then, as still—included an open-door policy toward movements. Very quickly, within the first year of the institute we became identified in this way. SNCC [Student Nonviolent Coordinating Committee], through Bob Moses, sent us a number of students who had been fieldworkers in Alabama and Mississippi. And that then began a rather tight linkage with the civil rights movement, and with the Left of the civil rights movement.[2]

M. FORTUN: What were they supposed to get from coming here?

RASKIN: There were two things. The first was rest and recreation, because they had spent a few years—in one case, literally having the hell beat out of them. Charles Sherrod, in Albany, Georgia, would get beaten up virtually every day for six months. And this is in the area where Jimmy Carter was from, when he was a state senator. And it was very harsh stuff. And so this place became, in that sense, a refuge. The second thing was that we had worked out a way in which the various people who came were in a tutorial relationship to one of the fellows at the institute, to work on their ideas of a vision of how to rebuild parts of the South, how to develop communities. And what we did in some cases was develop reading lists with them, and just in that sense have a tutorial to talk through stuff. Also, on the other side of the coin, we obviously helped them with political things. So, for example, we worked on the Mississippi Freedom Democratic Party challenge, all of that stuff.

So very quickly there was an onrush of movements, and that onrush of movements began to define the sorts of people who came to the institute, and also what the agenda of the institute was. Interestingly enough, there were early memoranda that we wrote, which show different stages of the institute, which I think are still very accurate, in terms of the books we would write, the reaching out to the public through shorter articles.

BARNET: Then the next movement that we became involved in was the antiwar movement. And there it was writing and speaking, and being involved in the early teach-ins. And then increasingly getting involved with both activism and writing books and articles. And because we had been involved in it early—I became concerned about it in 1961—we built up a following. And that of course upset a lot of people.

RASKIN: Especially in the FBI.

BARNET: And that's what triggered—the thing that interested the FBI, it's very interesting now, looking at the records: we prided ourselves on the fact that we would have a very catholic group of attendants. So that we had at one seminar the assistant secretary of defense, John McNaughton, one of the leading people

> National security must be based on national power. But the nature of power has changed, while our strategy has not. . . . The revolution in military costs forces difficult choices. In a time of austerity, increasing the military budget while the domestic programs are being slashed raises the issue, not of guns versus butter, but of missiles versus the local police and firefighters. The distortion of priorities has become so acute that as the Administration counsels a massive increase in military spending, essential services in every major American city are being cut. To suggest that the threat of "Finlandization" in Europe is a greater threat to the people of Chicago, Cleveland, Los Angeles or Detroit than the loss of social services, the breakdown of the education system, the rise in crime, the alarming increase in infant mortality, the impending municipal bankruptcies, the failure to invest in appropriate alternative energy systems or to revitalize American industry is to distort the meaning of "strength." (Barnet 1981, 107)

in the planning of the war, a former evidence professor of mine—in fact, I
hoped to get his job—and Charles Sherrod, who—and I remember this very
well—because McNaughton, who was a liberal, was talking about national
security and trying to put the war in the most humane possible terms. And
Sherrod asked him a question. He said, "You're talking about national security.
I don't understand anything you're saying, as it relates to the people in Georgia."
And then he described what it was like, just in security terms, to be living in
Georgia at that time. And for me that was very important, because it made a
connection that we almost never make, and still most people don't make.

M. FORTUN: And what was the FBI's reading of this?

BARNET: That any institute that has a collection of people from Stokely
Carmichael—

RASKIN: He came to that seminar, and Pat Moynihan came to that seminar.

BARNET: It freaked them out. You know, Moynihan, and David Riesman,
and various people—I don't know if they were all at the same seminar, but
they were at many seminars. So the FBI said that this was obviously at the
center of the conspiracy: people who have the ability to draw all these people
together are at the center of this web. And then it escalated, and we just came
across one thing recently where they were requesting $300 a month to spy on
us from across the street, because it looked as if we were probably the center
of the Weathermen, the bombing of the Capitol, and every other thing that
they could think of.

RASKIN: So that goes to another series of questions. One is that during this
period, looking back on it now, there was considerable danger for the people
here at the institute. To read about it in another country, you say, "Oh, these
are really great heroes, and blah blah blah," but we had very little understanding of what that was all about.

BARNET: That's true. We were on the security list.

RASKIN: There's a security index list, which is a first pick-up list.

BARNET: I had a very peculiar tax audit, during the Nixon time. It turned
out it was a little insulting. The guy came to the house, which was not usual,
and I gave him all the papers and he said, "I just don't understand—you don't
have anything."

RASKIN: At the institute, for four or five years, there was a person from the
IRS who sat here looking through the records. And they had somebody in the
office here doing that—somebody on our payroll as well, who was an
informer-agent type who was doing that stuff.[3] So the price as we look back
on it was a very high price. And that goes to several things. Why were people
prepared to pay that price? I think it goes on different levels, and one level is
just pure stubbornness, just, We can face anybody down, and we will.

BARNET: Well, that may be true for you. I would think that for most people,
including me, it's simply a sense that you can't do anything else: that you're
there, you're taking a stand, it's the right stand—

RASKIN: That's what's known as stubbornness [*laughs*]

BARNET: Yeah, it is stubbornness, but subjectively—you made it sound more like defiance.

RASKIN: No, no, no, what I mean is—

BARNET: I think it's more that you can't do anything else, and also—certainly again speaking for myself—I think I'll always have a strong belief that ultimately the system and the people aren't that far gone, and that the risk was—because you know, I took risks. I went to North Vietnam at the beginning of the Nixon administration.[4]

K. FORTUN: It sounds as though when the institute started you had more faith that there was a place for oppositional voices, that wouldn't land you on some security list.

RASKIN: That certainly is true. We didn't see ourselves in that sense as oppositional, in the way that might now be followed. I think that we certainly had the notion that we wanted to be pristine. That is, we wouldn't take government money, because we knew that if you took government money this would taint you, supposedly, and stop you from saying the sorts of things that you wanted to say. So that we understood that in that sense.

BARNET: And also, we thought that the relationship between academics and the government was corrupt. I had personal experience in my job of having a small amount of money to give out, and seeing the pandering of some famous academics for the pittance that we had.

K. FORTUN: So in that first period it sounds as though the main thing you were trying to create was a space where you could talk differently, other than the way you could in a bureaucratic framework.

RASKIN: That's absolutely right.

K. FORTUN: But that that quickly changed.

Dean Rusk, Walt Rostow, William Bundy, Maxwell Taylor, and Robert McNamara are indeed primarily responsible for implicating the rest of us in a moral and political disaster. They have counseled and helped carry out the commission of offenses against the law of nations, against our own constitution, and against elementary morality. For this alone, those of them who are still in office should not serve another day. But it is wildly optimistic to think that the overdue retirement of a group of individuals will in itself produce a change of policy. . . . The roots of the Vietnam failure lie more in the structure and organization of the national security bureaucracy than in the personality of the President or the idiosyncrasies of the particular group of foundation executives, military commanders, Rhodes scholars, and businessmen. . . . The threats which are triggers of national policy are intellectual constructs developed by bureaucracies whose function is to discover and deal with threats. . . . The structure of language itself thus influences bureaucratic choices by reinforcing a particular view of the world political environment. Bureaucratic language is a ready-made instrument for perpetuating error because the realm of discourse is so far removed from the ordinary life experience of the human beings who make up a bureaucracy. (Barnet 1969, 87–89, 112)

BARNET: Well, it didn't change on the domestic policy as quickly. We still, even after the national security connections were cut off, we had health discussions—we had the commissioner of health, we had the commissioner of education, we had a number of things.

RASKIN: A few days after I was indicted,[5] several people from the Bureau of the Budget came to me for advice on the federal budget. So there was in

that sense that kind of trust. But I think in general
your point is right. We attempted to make a space, we
believed that the major questions were moral and political questions, they were not administrative
questions.

What made it clear to me about where we stood—
where I stood in the government: Kennedy was making a speech at Yale, a rather famous speech on economics. And he sent around a thing which said, throw
in some ideas for this speech. So I said that the economics questions were really moral questions and political questions, and you have to look at things in that
way. If you read that speech, it says exactly the reverse: it says that these questions are administrative
and managerial questions, they are not political. So it
was clear the great influence I had.

BARNET: I had the signal the other way. I started
off in a grand office and I gradually got into the
broom closet.

M. FORTUN: Now that we're back to the mundani-
ties of office spaces, you were talking about the relationships with people coming in. I know that, through
stories that I have vague recollections of, there were
tensions about that. So how was it decided who was
going to get office space, who was going to be able to
use the telephone, who was going to have access to
the mimeo machine, because you had to be sort of
careful as to what was coming out of the mimeo machine. So how were those sorts of tensions dealt with
in terms of the civil rights and the antiwar movement?
And also I remember when Orlando and Ronni were
assassinated, that after that there were a number of
people saying it was time for us to rethink our linkages to these kinds of things that put us under direct
bodily threat. And so the two of you always had to
manage this and in some sense be responsible for who
was here and who you were going to link up with.[6]

RASKIN: We were very, very careful. In other
words, the first part of what we said might suggest that we were somewhat
naive about what was going on. We were very, very careful always to stay
within the terms of the tax exemption, within the terms of the law. And in fact
we always had the best conceivable advice on those questions. And we made
clear what was institute business and what was not institute business. And so

President Kennedy took up the two
themes of knowledge and politica
tion when he addressed Yale's gr
ating class of 1962. . . . The cent
domestic issues of the time, said
Kennedy, "relate not to basic clas
of philosophy or ideology but to v
and means of reaching common
goals—to research for sophistica
solutions to complex and obstina
sues." . . . Kennedy stated that th
problems of the 1960s, unlike tho
of the 1930s, posed "subtle challenges for which technical answe
not political answers, must be pr
vided." (Smith 1991, 129).

Some IPS fellows began to objec
the presence of the Chileans in th
institute, identifying in them the c
ject that had attracted violence to
institute for the first time in its fo
teen years of existence. One fello
spoke in anger about the IPS lead
ship having "signed us up for a de
trip without asking." Some of the
same people had risked their live
the civil rights movement in the S
had faced angry White Citizens C
cils, armed Klansmen, and vicious
sheriffs. But even the hateful and
murderous pique of Southern raci
somehow paled before the car bo
ing on Embassy Row. An act of te
ism directed by an actual governm
in power signifies a brutal audaci
that few felt capable of confrontir
(Dinges and Landau 1980, 64)

we had very clear lines on that. The second part of that was that it was obviously individuals, and given the character of the times, the character of the individuals, those people also did other sorts of things.

BARNET: But the difference was that institute money, which includes mimeograph paper, was very carefully monitored, because we knew we could be attacked.

M. FORTUN: And the two of you as codirectors did that monitoring?

RASKIN: Well, that's certainly an overstatement for me, but in fact there was an extraordinary administrative fellow—two of them. One of them was Sue Thrasher, who would give you a much better sense of how that was done.

BARNET: But as far as taking responsibility for it, I certainly saw it as a very important part of my job. I used to be a tax lawyer, and I knew how easy it is to lose these things.

K. FORTUN: Did you get accused of not being committed to the movement, or to radicalism, by spacing the institute apart from movements? I heard those kinds of accusations while I was in India: Left institutions with resources monitored who they shared them with, so they wouldn't get shut down by the government—and were then accused of being Stalinist.

RASKIN: This is an ongoing problem, and it comes in different forms. One form is that we viewed ourselves as not being of the movement, not being part of any particular movement. This became a very big issue here, because my view, and I believe Dick's view as well, was, Look, movements also are fashions, and they can come and go. And so the question of the institute and institutions is that you have to find a way of protecting them, so that in fact those movements, and ones to come in the future, will have a place to be.

BARNET: My view was that the independence of the institute was the most critical factor in the support of movements that we wanted to support. If we were part of the movements, or "serving" the movements, we would be hurting the institute, and ultimately we would be hurting the movement.

K. FORTUN: You wouldn't be sustainably available as a resource across these fashions, across time.

RASKIN: Exactly. You see, there was all sorts of talk about whether the institute should be the staff arm of this and the staff arm of that.

BARNET: It became impossible.

K. FORTUN: But did you have to figure this out by getting a little too involved in something?

BARNET: No, but I remember some of the—at the high point, all kinds of people came to meetings. I can remember all these factions of movements were showing up, and there was a guy who reached out his hand and said

> If this were 1773, and the city were Boston, the Institute would be holding a seminar on British imperialism. There would be tables and charts to show the injustice of the tax on tea. Probably somebody from the Governor's office would be invited. Then independent of the Institute, six or seven of the fellows would go out and dump a shipload of tea into Boston Harbor.—Karl Hess[7]

"May fifth," or something, and I said, "Oh, May seventh"—that's my birthday. And then there were people who wanted to make the institute a "people's embassy," where anybody could sleep here, and so on. So it was clear that the term *movements* covered a lot of stuff.

RASKIN: It also covered, and this is something that we were quite aware of, it also covered people who were informers and FBI agents. So that was very clear, too, that you could pretty well tell that the most cuckoo and extreme positions would invariably be taken by people who were police. So that one of the things that we were very aware of, looking at this politically and intellectually, was that we had to be very careful. We had a kind of a shit detector: be careful of those people who are constantly talking this way, because they're not going to be there the next day, they're not going to be there the next week. And they weren't, and one of the problems now is, they're not. And that's one of the most extraordinary things, about how many people signed a separate peace with the system now.

BARNET: Especially some of the people who were "the most radical." One thing we also found in this recent FBI paper: they had wanted to "penetrate the high command," which was our offices, but they hadn't been able to; they needed more money to do this. But of course our offices were always unlocked, nothing was secret, everything was open; they could have found out anything. But the learning experience of the madness of the bureaucracy was very important in developing our ideas.

K. FORTUN: In those years when you had to take this stand apart from movements, did you arrive at that position intellectually, or did you have to get involved in it and—

BARNET: I did. It never occurred to me that we would be anything else. In the first place, because we made our whole pitch—I mean, the only ideology that we developed in the beginning, and you'll find it in the early papers: there's no word *Left* in them, there's no word *progressive* in them, as far as I remember. We were talking about independence, and we were saying that these were the problems that we were concerned about, and these are the values that we're concerned about.

After the 1960s, when people ref to the Institute for Policy Studies "the only surviving institution of New Left," that description was a slight exaggeration. . . . But the mark also revealed a mispercepti the nature of both IPS and the six revolt. . . . The Institute for Policy Studies provides the perfect insti tional base . . . for radicals to pla roles of "secret agents." . . . Publ they claim to be progressive parti pants in the democratic process. like the leftist progressives of the past, their liberalism and pacifism not political commitments. They a deadly weapons with which to la siege to democracy's defenses, to cripple its resistance to the totali tarian advance. (Horowitz 1987, xi xvii–xviii)[8]

RASKIN: And we're interested in democratization—

BARNET: And we're interested in democratization. And that's what we believed, it was not a put-on.

K. FORTUN: This outside, this critical space: did you see it as a furthering or an enactment of a certain model for the critic?

RASKIN: You speak of a critical space. Our view was, we made the critical space. The institute itself would allow for and encourage the kind of projects and institutions which would develop a series of political spaces within the society, and therefore a different political culture.[9]

BARNET: We wanted the space; we thought it would be possible to have a human and serious relationship with people in government, on a basis of equality, exchanging ideas between two people—especially since this was an administration which prided itself on having intellectuals in positions of power. I don't know of any model. I think the conception was developed out of the pieces. We knew we wanted to have relationships with government, we knew we wanted to have relationships with universities, we knew we wanted to have theory and practice, we wanted to have some social inventions.

K. FORTUN: Were you particularly informed by any sort of ideological lineage—Marx, Dewey?

BARNET: I certainly was not. I had had a course in Marxism at the Russian Research Center, and it certainly wasn't the basis of any ideas that I wanted to pursue.

RASKIN: I came a different route. My view was that the institute should be looked at as a place where Dewey's notions and, adding to that, existential notions of social invention and projects, should come together. So that in fact it was a partial method, that from the inventions and the projects, then, you would begin to see the possibility for what the direction of the society could be. But you know, so much of the 1960s you could view one of two ways. One was to build the new society, which is what I thought we were attempting to do. And the second is a series of Whiggish defenses against problems which seemed to be coming at us extraordinarily fast.

BARNET: For me, I didn't have any grand vision, but it was, really, the sum total of the choices that we made, or the analysis that we made about what were the most important problems and what they were going to be doing to the society.

RASKIN: And what we were presented with by the society.

K. FORTUN: This built-in innovative approach to what the institute was: do you think that has contributed to its sustainability across very different political spaces?

BARNET: Yes, I do, because it also has been widely imitated, and widely imitated mostly now on the Right. I think it was an invention of a new form, but I think it wasn't invented all at once.

RASKIN: But it came very fast. It came as a result of the times, as a result of different movements.

BARNET: Two or three years later, it wasn't exactly what we thought it was going to be when we started.

RASKIN: Just to speak about my own history in some of this, I had seen or believed earlier that there should be a linkage between labor unions and intellectuals, and indeed attempted to do some things with regard to that. Looking back at it, it would have been a terrible mistake, given the situation that labor unions found themselves in over the course of this period, and also the positions they took on the war and so forth. My thought was, believe it or not, that a linkage could be made with the Teamsters because they were outside the framework of the AFL-CIO. Fortunately, God intervened and the guy I was dealing with was killed. But in any case, the notion, then, of independence really did stick, and stuck with us that this was an extraordinarily important thing to look at. And so over a period of time I began looking at issues of reconstruction and social reconstruction as a method. How do you bring about changes in the society? How do ideas work in relation to movements? And so forth. So that was a very strong piece of my theoretical involvement. But we were presented with other things: we were presented with the war, with the national security state—

BARNET: And poverty, and the new awareness of poverty, and getting involved with welfare issues—some of the same issues that are now here.

RASKIN: But also, you see, Dick made major breakthroughs in certain things: in looking at international corporations and the flow of capital in totally different ways that occurred up until the early 1960s. But by the end of the 1960s it was clear that the whole character of capitalism was changing. And so that was a very important intellectual statement.

Let me just make one point on that. All through this, the people who came to the institute as fellows and staff wrote and wrote and wrote. So that it was not only people who had a good feeling about things, but they thought very, very deeply about things. We saw the importance of the institute as funding individuals to write books, articles; to find modes of protection for those people, all that stuff. Which I thought was critical. And the thing that really made it for us, frankly, was that we knew how to beg. That was a central piece of this story.[10]

M. FORTUN: Well, there's a lot of directions to go in. Certainly I'd like to follow up on the begging. But let me also just ask quickly, was the flip side of that, if you have all these people that are connected to other movements, was there ever the feeling, "What is all this writing and writing and writing?"

K. FORTUN: Yeah, did you get accused of being Trots? You know, think about it and never do anything?

RASKIN: No. There was—

BARNET: Yeah, sure. In fact, by funders. We weren't called Trots, but we were called—you know, why are you doing that? I don't want to fund another project, I want to fund a march.

RASKIN: Right, and today, of course, you still hear the same thing. Why are you writing this long book? Why aren't you on television or doing an op-ed? So there's all this fashion bullshit that goes on. But within the institute this became an absolutely critical question, too. Because we attempted, in terms of the people who came to the institute, to have both people who were primarily organizers and people who were book writers. Now the interesting part of this is that the people who were the book writers were also terrific organizers, in fact.

BARNET: And the people who were the organizers are now in the establishment, almost without exception.

RASKIN: That's right.

K. FORTUN: Do you think having writing as such a core part of the institute prevents the hubris, the overconfidence of some leftist programs?

BARNET: A shallowness, I think, because a topic sentence at a rally or even in a *Nation* article is easy to do. But then when you really have to elaborate it and defend it and put it up against other ideas that are thirteen pages later, you really have to think at an entirely different level.

RASKIN: There are two things that movements grow out of—leaving aside personal ambition and so forth. One is very great pain, existential pain. So there's no surplus, there's no possibility of thinking through where that pain takes you, because in a sense, that pain says, "Stop what it is that's going on now, this is just impossible." So, for example, the Vietnam War was a sense of existential pain for large numbers of people. You could write about those things, you could be clear about them, you could move things along in that direction. But once it's the case that you moved away from the immediate pain, you still have to have a program to carry through what you were trying to do: how are you going to defend it, and how would this build something new? Now the Left did not have that, and this is still something that we're attempting to do in our own work.[11]

The other thing is that there were phrases which I am sure were very, very destructive. So for example, the whole notion of leadership was destroyed among people in the movement, in which people were called "ego tripping" if they stepped up in front. I don't know to what extent that really reflected what people attempted to do, to what extent this really was a very clever ruse on the part of the FBI. There's certainly enough evidence to suggest that they were out to destroy leaders, to do everything to entrap people that way.[12] And the same thing was true in attempting to split off intellectuals from movements, and movements from ideas and thought. That's a very important element in this whole struggle. And just as it was the case that they converted to the herd, the thing that was the danger about the institute in people's minds, and perhaps our own feeling of strength, was that we were linking liberals and radicals together. We were connecting people together. And just as in this society, if a leader undertakes to bring together different movements, he or she's in big trouble—personally, physically in trouble.

K. FORTUN: This critique of leadership, whether within the FBI or the movements, where did it come from? It still has broad circulation in India: anyone who takes leadership responsibility is accused of being a Stalinist. There, though, the backdrop is different—at least in part, the accusations are a rebound from earlier faith in the Leninist model, which we don't have here. So where did the squeamishness about leadership in this country's Left come from?

BARNET: I think it came from the analysis of the extent to which the country was hierarchic, and that behind the myths of democracy there was heavy concentration of power in the corporations, in the political parties, and so on. And therefore the organizations that are trying to create a new society have got to have a different conception of leadership—that democracy has to be lived in each moment, and that you cannot create or promote democracy through nondemocratic institutions. So the definition of a democratic institution got stretched and stretched, particularly as movements of inclusion developed. And that's still a problem. And that has been, of course, a theme swirling around the institute ever since, and still is: that you have to have the moral purity and political characteristics of the society that you are trying to bring into being.

M. FORTUN: How did those issues play out within IPS? You two were always "cofounders," "senior fellows." In that sense, you gave this place leadership. And yet, at the time I was here, there was a lot of discussion about democratizing IPS itself—everybody has to have a part in setting the agenda, it can't just be what Marc and Dick want, even though they do raise the money and meet the payroll week after week.

BARNET: What years were you here? I'm trying to remember.

M. FORTUN: 1982 to 1987. You had the program council in that period to decide where to put resources, what projects the institute was going to do, and so on. But even so, the place was always very dependent on your vision of what should be done. The tension between democratization and appreciation of strong leadership always seemed to be a topic of discussion. Usually it seemed it was more of a benevolent, intellectual challenge than a dispute in need of resolution. But I know that wasn't always so.

RASKIN: Let me go back to Dick's point, because I think he was absolutely right. One of the things that I wrote extensively about was notions of nonhierarchy and forms of democracy, and so forth. You'll remember in 1968, the slogans on the walls in Paris: "No class today, no ruling class tomorrow." There was a Deweyan democratic sensibility—they were talking about Maoism, but it's that same sensibility. There's another piece, though, which was very important, and that is the media and television. What happened was

"Participatory democracy" remain the watchword. And the harshest anti-authoritarian demands were placed by many of the new leftist on the often fragile institutions th had helped create, a moral string that frequently caused messy crac ups. The IPS felt the stress of the litical currents it had encouraged. In December 1976, within months Letelier's assassination, the instit financial crisis came to a head. . .

that the media and television made certain people the stars of the movements, which then was very greatly resented by a lot of people in the movements themselves. So that was a piece of it.

Now within the institute I think that our view of leadership—and of course Dick has another view, and we both have a very different view from others— but I saw leadership as a catalytic notion. You put people in motion and you protected them. What you did was say, We're going to protect you, you do the best work that you conceivably can do, and we're going to help in every way we can.

BARNET: I think that's fair. The problem that we had was, at critical points, not exercising the authority that we should have—

RASKIN: It's exactly the reverse of the question.

BARNET: And not—speaking for myself—not out of any suprademocratic ideology, but not wanting to pay the cost of having to struggle. And I think that if one had to point to our failure, perhaps our greatest failure, it was that.

K. FORTUN: The calls, where you weren't as interventionist as you should have been—would it have been on moral grounds, on wasteful expenditure of resources, or what?

BARNET: Mainly on resources. Mainly on acceding to an irrational pressure for increasing expenditures, when I think at least part of us knew better.

K. FORTUN: What function did this program council serve?

BARNET: We didn't have a program council in our time. We had the fellows, it was much smaller. We had the resident fellows.

RASKIN: Actually, it was larger, and by the end, by 1977—

BARNET: But it was the fellows who met and made the decisions, and it certainly wasn't our fiat, at all.[13]

K. FORTUN: If you were going to advise some start-up young group now, what kind of model of decision making would you suggest? Surely they shouldn't just count on the fact that everyone's nice, that good labor relations will follow from being committed.

BARNET: The greatest difference would be a much clearer understanding of the commitments of the fellows to the institution. Which issues, a clearer un-

---

"The problem," said Barnet, "was the infinite expansion of claims on the place. Every subject was valid. There was a kind of pseudo-democracy, an ethos of participation, that excluded establishing priorities." In the name of participation, "an alienation occurred, of the people who were most senior, who had built the institute and raised the money," according to Raskin. . . .

Forced to cope with the shortfall of cash, Barnet and Raskin offered a plan of general cutbacks. The response by eleven of the fellows was to form a union and demand salary increases and absolute democracy in the workplace. Some claimed they were discriminated against because they had written no articles or books. . . . Said Raskin, "People got more and more into constituency organizing without ever figuring out what could be done together. At the institute people were no longer talking the same language. It was a kind of freak-out. It was very hurtful." In the settlement, Barnet and Raskin gave the dissidents $470,000, a third of IPS's endowment, to build their own institute as they wished. Unable to raise more money or even to work together, they soon dispersed.— (Blumenthal 1988, 288–89)

derstanding of how time was spent, and I think more exchange than we had at various points on how the activities of one fit in and supported the activities of others. We carried that much too far. At one point, the autonomy of the fellows was more than it should have been—for the health of the institute.

K. FORTUN: Do you think the institute got spread too thin?

BARNET: Yes. We were trying to do too many things. There was a positive side to that: tremendous energy and excitement, and it gave impetus to a lot of movements. It may well have been the right decision for the society: we were energetic and lucky in getting money, we spread it around, and we spun off a lot of new projects. But the health of the institution probably suffered as a result.

K. FORTUN: Is it even harder now, as opposed to when you started, to keep IPS healthy?

BARNET: It's very different, for several reasons. First, it's different as a result of one of our greatest successes, which is that we helped, by example and sometimes directly by gifts and our own financial support, a lot of other organizations. So that one of our great advantages, from a strictly institutional point of view, was that we had the field pretty much to ourselves when we began. But now there are lots and lots, especially single-issue organizations, which can make a more coherent and more easily understood argument, than an institution that tries to make these connections.

Second, obviously the sea change in the politics of the country, starting with the reaction to the movements.

RASKIN: I would say that the major difference is in philanthropy.

BARNET: I was just going to get to that. We had the experience of somehow finding our way to old-fashioned leftists: that is, people of wealth and knowledge. The people who gave us substantial amounts of money were as intelligent as we were, and as committed politically. Sam Rubin, Jim Warburg, Dan Bernstein, Ed Janss—people like that. They were originals, they were eccentrics.

RASKIN: They owned the money.

BARNET: They owned the money.

RASKIN: They had a vision of what the place was. In that sense, they were typical of philanthropists: people who started with the assumption that you hang in with a place because the place, the institution itself, should exist, and that's what you do. And you support it.

M. FORTUN: And what's the change been?

BARNET: They die, the family hires bureaucrats to run what's left of the money—and the large foundations never supported us. So the bureaucrats come in, and they have no interest in it, and they have all kinds of personal and professional reasons not to give us the money. It's safer to give it to a hospital.

RASKIN: Also, they were in competition intellectually. They were people who said, We never did this work, we never wrote this book. So there was always a sense, from our side and from their side, of not quite liking them, not quite trusting them. What has happened, I think, is the character of how you appeal is different. Before, we didn't have to appeal to those sorts of people.

BARNET: Also, there emerged out of the Vietnam War a much larger group of liberal philanthropists. *These* liberal philanthropists were by and large not interested in ideas. Unlike the conservatives, they did not think that ideas really changed politics. Action did.

K. FORTUN: This gets back to your Kennedy speech, to the rise of administrative-managerial thinking and rhetoric. Was it an unhappy effect of the New Deal, where did it come from, why does it seem to have taken over the world that you work in?

RASKIN: That goes to an old history in this country. You can see it in the struggles between, say, Walter Lippman and John Dewey, at the beginning of the century.

BARNET: A strain of progressivism was always managerial. And one strain of it is "goo-gooism," that government can be better if you just have better managers.

M. FORTUN: There is a long strain, but something else has happened. Doesn't it seem that this managerial attitude really intensified in the midseventies or so?

RASKIN: I think it takes two turns. In the world that we're talking about, the technocratic takes over, because that's the way universities are run, that's the way courses are divided into schools, by the 1970s. But also, now you have a reaction against that from the Right, in effect saying, No, we're going to put money into things that we really care about, in terms of political and social ideas, and we're going to challenge the technocratic structure. And we're challenging it from a rightist perspective. But that rightist perspective is a mask, in my view, for fascism. What they're doing now is not going to change the technocratic structure, they're not going to change the international corporations—they're going to use individualism as a cover story for fascism.[14]

BARNET: For a new form of corporatism.

K. FORTUN: Moralism as a cover story for a new form of interested technocracy?

BARNET: I think that's right. But another factor is

In April 1986, fifteen months into Ronald Reagan's second term, he and other prominent conservatives gathered to celebrate the latest accomplishments of the Heritage Foundation . . . [and] the impending conclusion of a $30 million fundraising campaign. . . . The president commended the foundation's promotion of ideas through seminars, conferences, publications, and "its buttonholing of congressmen—for informational purposes only, of course" (a titter of knowing laughter spread through the ballroom as Reagan acknowledged the fine line between research and advocacy in today's political scene). . . .

As the president reached the end of his speech, he paid homage to paleoconservative Richard Weaver. . . .

the changing consciousness of these liberal philanthropists who grew tired and grew discouraged.
People say, Look, we've given you millions of dollars, and the world is worse than what it was when
we started.

K. FORTUN: But I thought they were committed to
ideals?

RASKIN: No, these are different groups, not the
original funders.

M. FORTUN: Well, that makes sense. For these new
people: you pay the money, you expect an effect.

BARNET: I don't know how many people I've heard
say, If you could just put that on a bumper sticker.

K. FORTUN: But this demand for visible results—

RASKIN: Product.

K. FORTUN: —where did it come from?

BARNET: These people thought that they had won a
great victory: Nixon was out, the war had been won,
it looked as if the boom was going to resume. And the
boom was going to enable the kind of redistribution
which had begun to happen in this country, between
the New Deal and the mid-seventies. In fact, the exact
opposite happened.

K. FORTUN: But what about now, when everything
is horrible? They're still demanding visible results,
aren't they? Now you can hardly say it's easy.

RASKIN: Now another thing has occurred in this
world. Up to a year or two ago, it was emphasis on
product and production, the takeover of a particular
capitalist mentality—which is still there in the universities and institutes. But something else now has
occurred, among exactly those liberal millionaires
who had been committed and very decent in many
ways. They're now saying to themselves, Why
bother? What am I knocking myself out for? Why
don't I just go out and buy myself a yacht? So in a sense they're signing a
separate peace as well.

BARNET: A lot of people are rethinking very basic things. One should not
think that the interest in *The Bell Curve* is only on the Right. Even people
who will totally disagree with its results show all kinds of signs of being influenced by a whole set of ideas on genetics. I think they're saying, Look,
there are no solutions. The situation is objectively getting worse, and all this

---

Weaver, a southerner and a litera
scholar who had taught at the Ur
sity of Chicago, published a book
1948—*Ideas Have Consequence.*
which became a conservative cla
And Reagan knew full well that t
Heritage Foundation had adopted
the book's title as its motto. "It g
back to what Richard Weaver ha
said and what Heritage is all abo
the president reminded them. "Id
do have consequences, rhetoric is
policy, and words are action."
(Smith 1991, 19–20)

"What excites [the *Wall Street J*
nal's David] Brooks is the idea of
'merging an ivory tower life with
life of practical politics; it's a reje
tion of the idea that the best way
inhabit the world of ideas is to be
solitary.' ('I also like the idea of b
ers running the world,' he says w
a laugh.) Like his University of Ch
cago classmate Tod Lindberg,
editorial-page editor of the *Wash.*
ton Times and a former student o
Alan Bloom, . . . Brooks sees the
Great Books as the gateway to pr
cal politics. Twenty years ago the
were boning up on the classics. .
Today they're setting the agenda.
help edit a page that goes out to
million businessmen,' Brooks told
with satisfaction." (Atlas 1995, 62

talk about being nice, and nurture, and so forth, what does that say about a street in which there's no society at all, everybody's killing each other, all the mothers, Rwanda, the Africans, they're all killers. Human nature bears no resemblance to anything John Dewey said it was like.

RASKIN: It bears no resemblance to anything, right? It bears resemblance to the ideas of selfishness and egoism and narcissism and take care of yourself, and that's the way the world is.

BARNET: One by one, live day by day.

RASKIN: Be careful of bureaucracy, because you don't need bureaucracy. If you want to do something, you do it yourself.

K. FORTUN: So what does IPS say to these people?

M. FORTUN: Yeah, now what are you going to do?

RASKIN: Well, I feel very good about what I'm undertaking, and Dick feels very good about his. I'm doing the Paths for the 21st Century project, and rather than talk about that, I'll give you the write up about it.

BARNET: I'm doing a project with my wife on neuroscience and children. It will have political implications; it's not directly an answer to *The Bell Curve,* but it's trying to bring together and popularize some of the very new neuroscience on learning and emotional development. So I'm learning a lot.

M. FORTUN: But as an institutional space, other than maintaining autonomy, have you thought in terms of what's going to have to go on in that space over the next ten, twenty years to deal with this new situation?

RASKIN: There's a very big discussion going on now among the board of trustees, which will go on over the course of this next year. As you can imagine, there are competing views.

M. FORTUN: Can you just quickly lay those out?

RASKIN: Well, I think the first view is that this remains a community of scholars and activists. I think that seems to be—

BARNET: I think the central role of scholarship is the pivotal viewpoint.

Throughout the Cold War, Liberalism and social democracy's defects were hidden in the national agreement to accept the overriding principle of anti-communism as the fundamental evil. But in the post-Cold War and post-modern period, this crutch is no longer present. The role of government is systematically trashed and therefore the issue-specific programs which different administrations since Woodrow Wilson can no longer succeed, whether the Right keeps them as shells and museum pieces or they are retained by a hobbled and intellectually lost Democratic administration at war with itself.

It is time to correct this failure of prevailing political thought and confront the revolution of reaction which goes intellectually unchallenged and without alternatives in any systematic way. As a result, any Liberal political challenge will remain feckless, ungrounded, retaining an issue-specific focus without noting or comprehending that each problem has embedded within it a series of fundamental principles which must be examined both in their specific context and as part of an overarching framework. . . . The participants in the Paths project will be charged with the intellectual responsibility of escaping the boundaries of disaster and failure which framed the Left-Right debate. Calling on leading thinkers in the United States and abroad, the Paths project will examine critically what we have learned from the twentieth century and offer to those in the twenty-first century guideposts, queries, and first principles which will serve as the foundation of social reconstruction. While taking into account the human

K. FORTUN: Are there questions about the nature of the scholarship to be done? Your work on neurosciences is a different type of scholarship.

BARNET: Well, it is and it isn't, and it would take a long time to elaborate.

RASKIN: But your point is important, in terms of some members of the board saying, again, There are people suffering *now*, there's difficulty *now*. Why are you undertaking long-term projects when in fact there is a "nowness thing"? So that discussion is there, and there will always be that pull, because that is the nature of what theory and practice relationships are to each other.

M. FORTUN: The recent reorganizations in politics—the collapse of bipolarism, the declining role of political parties, class complexification, new roles for corporations, including those that mediate our access to information, does this place a renewed importance on empirical work? Do we need to ask where we are before we ask what we should do?

K. FORTUN: There seems to be a double bind in every possibility. Nationalism is said to be part of the problem, but it's also one of the few viable vehicles by which Third World activists can respond to the General Agreement on Trade and Tariffs.

BARNET: One of the concepts we discuss in *Global Dreams*, and that we're going to develop much more, is the notion of the global north and the global south. We have to change the way we think of the map. You have a poverty in the United States and other developed countries which, in certain empirical terms, is as bad as anything you can find elsewhere.

K. FORTUN: So the specifics have to be mapped empirically, before politics can be reconceptualized, and enacted?

BARNET: The same kind of work has to be done with regard to NAFTA. There are a lot of problems with the anti-NAFTA movement.

RASKIN: Which people at IPS—John Cavanagh and Sarah Franklin—have had an important role in building. It turns out to be very complicated—understanding all the interconnections, much less responding to them effectively.

capacity for evil and selfishness, t work of the Paths project builds or the reality of humanity's better sel and those attempts in the twentie century to hold on to the pennant human progress. . . .

The work of the project explore the linked relationship between ca ing, dignity, liberation, decency, cc eration, economic and social justic as these manifestations of empath invariance present themselves in a areas of social life. We expect tha this leap out of pessimism examin by the "invisible college" will gen ate a national and international de bate on root questions raised by t profound transformations which ha occurred in the twentieth century.

Alternatives will emerge from t Paths volumes, films, and study groups. Paths brings together lead scholars and activists, as part of a "invisible college," who will collab rate as catalysts to initiate thinkin and discussion. . . . Through confe ences and through an e-mail netw knowledge workers will trade idea social inventions and projects in preparation of a multi-volume seri under the general heading *Paths for the Twenty-First Century.* (Raskin 1995)

Globalization is not really global. Transnational business activities a concentrated in the industrial worl and in scattered enclaves through the underdeveloped world. Most people are outside the system and the ranks of the window-shoppers and the jobless are growing faster than the global army of the emplo Yet the processes of globalization altering the character of nations

K. FORTUN: Yeah, who's the enemy? The nation-state, the corporation, the new think tanks? Who's office do you march in front of to protest NAFTA, or GATT?

BARNET: This is what we were trying to explicate in *Global Dreams*: how does accountability work in a system of multinational corporations?

RASKIN: One response is taken up by Michael Shuman, who is now the director of the institute. He's very interested in building local communities, and in the devolution of power to local communities. Now I think there are a lot of problems with that, although I believe in it. In the situation we now face, this could go very badly. We don't know the implications of all of this. We could well end up with a constitutional crisis in this country, not knowing the meaning of what the federal government is. If you keep devolving power locally, you end up in dissolution.

BARNET: My own view is that there has to be some devolution, but the devolution that seems most irrational to me is to states. The states are really artificial, historical constructs. These are boundaries which were drawn not with reference to where people lived or real loyalties, but historical circumstances in 1789.

RASKIN: So there are big problems on the table. What's extraordinary is to try to get across the notion that there may be no coherence at this point, there's ambiguity. And it's very, very tough to get people to accept that. Now the question: is there a place where people can think about these things in a "politically relevant" way, outside of the university? That remains to be seen. It's a very, very complicated question; I don't know where it's going to go. I don't know where the money is, in fact; I don't know what the next generation's capacity to raise money is.

BARNET: Or this one's. It's hard to get people to fund ambiguity.

RASKIN: That dog won't hunt.

> everywhere and the quality of life within their borders.
>
> At the same time nationalism is on the rise. The power of national governments over the two most critical functions of the nation-state—security and economic development—have eroded, but the myth of national sovereignty is as strong as ever. The result is the new sort of power vacuum we have described. Yet the gridlock that traps public authority combined with the disclaimer of public responsibility by the private sector guarantees a world economy out of control. Public accountability is the essence of democracy. But the institutions for assuring corporate accountability at the local, national, and international levels are extremely weak. In the absence of public policies developed and enforced at the international level, the sum of individual corporate decisions is . . . determining the character and dimensions of the job market, the quality of the physical environment, and the experience of childhood. (Barnet and Cavanagh 1994, 427)

Postscript

The bad dialectic is that which does not wish to lose its soul in order to save it, which wishes to be dialectical immediately, becomes autonomous, and ends up at cynicism, at formalism, for having eluded its own double meaning or sense. What we call hyperdialectic is, on the contrary, a thought that is capable of reaching truth because it envisages without restriction the plurality of the relationships and what has been called ambiguity. (Merleau-Ponty 1968, 94)

Our preface alluded to the "ambiguous role" played by think tanks in the American political system. The interview ends with a different but related concern with ambiguity, commenting on the practical difficulty of sustaining IPS as an institution when it can't offer straight-line forecasts or easy answers, readable on a bumper sticker. *Ambiguity,* then, is a recurrent term, marking both the context of the contemporary think tank and established ways of understanding how think tanks operate. What is it that drives this recurrence? Why does uncertainty haunt any attempt to link ideas and politics? Why is speaking truth to power so much more complicated than it sounds?

The role played by think tanks in American politics is indeed ambiguous, due in part to residing gaps between ideas and politics. To ask what think tanks are and where they are located in American politics is to ask stubborn questions: what makes the political machine run? How are ideas always already political, carriers of a certain kind of (ambiguous) force? The interview here suggests that such questions are best approached topographically, in terms of institutional spaces. Filling in the gap between ideas and politics is not the intellectual challenge; close ethnographic description of the gap itself *is*—engaging the "space" of the think tank to understand the everyday processes through which new conceptual models are generated, intellectual and political goals are pursued, and collective positioning is funded and mobilized. Who comes in the door? On what terms? Where do they sit, and to whom do they speak? What new linkages do they set up, and how are they sustained? When is it time for people to leave, and where do they go next?

In utopian speculation, think tanks are autonomous—accruing legitimacy through purposeful independence from established power. The space that Barnet and Raskin have been at pains to sustain seems based on different sensibilities of where and how boundaries are drawn and definition achieved. The topographical reinscription of the interview brings the ambiguous nature of autonomy and independence into partial focus. In that space, autonomy becomes a tension requiring ongoing negotiation, the casting and recasting of generative yet risky relations: movements are supported, and kept at arm's length; the establishment is opposed, and invited in.

Another problem is crudely material: acknowledging ambiguity doesn't pay. The problem is evident in a recent year-end fundraising letter, distributed via the technologies of mass-market mailings that the Right has honed so successfully. The image on the envelope conveys well the persistent oppositional logics of justice and politics, with IPS on one side of an unbalanced balance and an undifferentiated array of think tanks on the other. The book is the metonym for the think tank. Ambiguity is the void in the middle, apparently offering no leverage point by which to "restore balance." The letter inside ends by invoking IPS's Other—"unlike the Heritage Foundation, we don't have $22 million from corporations and right-wing industrialists to throw around each year"—identifying in the process the ultimate source of the gravitational force that skews the think tank universe.

In utopian speculation, the think tank—the American Enterprise Institute (AEI), the Brookings Institution, the Hoover Institute, and IPS—came first, a response to the "information glut" from the cold war growth of communications technologies and bureaucracies. The stable identity of the utopian think tank was later complicated by the emergence of so-called advocacy tanks, such as the Heritage Foundation, in the 1970s and 1980s. A topographical approach shows IPS to have "ambiguated" that distinction earlier. IPS never promised neutrality as guarantor of its authority, but nevertheless saw itself as practicing a rigorous empiricism, wedded to moral principles. As Barnet and Raskin tell it, it was in part the success and difference of IPS in working the ambiguous space between theory and advocacy that led to the more conservative think tanks' adoption of a similar approach in a later period.

The periods that Barnet and Raskin describe as the "height of our influence" were periods in which IPS was most successful in drawing diverse actors and ideas into a coherent picture. One result was that IPS was perceived as the "center of the conspiracy," either anti-Vietnam War or anti-America more broadly. The imputed capacity to sway the course of events relied on the unambiguous delineation of a (fictional) plot. By the end of the 1980s, either the world had metamorphosed into something more ambiguous and indeterminate or the "center of the conspiracy" was somewhere else. Even if the Right can, the Left can no longer articulate an unambiguous conspiracy into clear policy narratives and present social dangers. As organizer Dave Henson notes in his interview in this volume, "I think it's a lot easier to pitch the cosmology, or ideology, that the Right's pitching. It's actually comforting for people: God will deal with things. It claims to know the answers. The existentialism of the Left is understandably less popular: it's a relative world and we have to take it in process." In Barnet and Raskin's terms, the think tanks of the Right do not "speak truth to power" but only legitimate, mask, and apologize for the operations of power. Their judgment finds support in Merleau-Ponty's suggestion that the "bad dialectic," the utopian autonomy, escapes its own "double meaning" to become a form of cynicism.

At the end of the interview there are "big problems on the table": the devolution of power, the unaccountability of multinational corporations, and an overall lack of coherence in the political-intellectual landscape. Ambiguity reigns, and it's "very, very tough to get people to accept that"—especially the people who "own the money." Raskin's expression "that dog won't hunt" finds a supplementary articulation within the academy proper. Julia Kristeva's *abject* is "the sign of an impossible ob-ject, boundary and limit"—a boundary that "is above all, ambiguity." The abject evokes horror and a certain edginess of uncertainty; it haunts, rather than hunts. Abject, the ambiguous cannot be "integrated with a system of signs" (in Taylor 1987, 159). Money to fund a march can be integrated into a system of signs—quite literally, if one pictures the placards held aloft at marches and rallies. Money to think the ambiguous cannot be so easily integrated, at least in today's political and funding climate.

But if ambiguity is in fact the "truth" of the situation, how can it be spoken now? What is the idiom in which ambiguity can be made to hunt, and not merely haunt? For now, like Barnet and Raskin, we can only leave such big questions on the table. Part of the answer is surely that there has to be a table for the questions to be placed on, and the table has to be housed. Jonathan Swift has perhaps aptly reminded us that intellectual schemes are often farcical games of hubris. Meanwhile, anti-intellectualism seems to haunt both the enactment and evaluation of contemporary society, suggesting the need for renewed consideration of what intellectual work has to offer, and what institutional forms can best table questions. The challenge, following IPS's own example, would be to produce multiple spaces where ambiguity can be worked rather than avoided, where multiple truths can be addressed to the multiple powers that shape contemporary contexts.

Notes

1. On Roosevelt's "brain trust,' see Smith 1991, 74–77.

2. For further details on SNCC, Bob Moses, Charles Sherrod, the organizing of the Mississippi Freedom Democratic Party, and the events surrounding the 1964 Democratic National Convention in Atlantic City, see Gitlin 1987, 146–62.

3. The IRS conducted an audit of IPS in 1967, after Raskin's indictment as a member of the Boston Five. "By giving a tax exemption to an organization like the Institute for Policy Studies, our government is allowing tax exemption to support revolution," said Sen. Strom Thurmond in 1967 (Dickson 1971, 283). IPS was investigated again beginning in 1970. This kind of veiled operation of power was instituted by the Nixon White House in the summer of 1969, when the IRS established its Activist Organizations Committee (later renamed and further veiled as the Special Services Staff). As a White House memo stated, "What we cannot do in a courtroom via criminal prosecutions to curtail the activities of some of these groups, IRS could do by administrative action. Moreover, valuable intelligence-type information could be turned up by IRS as a result of their field audits" (Lukas 1976, 22).

4. For an example of how such an event appears in the far right-wing imaginary (buttressed by footnotes to FBI documents), see Powell 1987, 37–38.

5. Raskin and Arthur Waskow's "A Call to Resist Illegitimate Authority" was published in the *New York Review of Books* in 1967, with 158 signatures of writers, academics, journalists, and clergy. On this and the resulting trial of other individuals advocating resistance to the draft who became known as the Boston Five (Raskin, Michael Ferber, Mitchell Goodman, Benjamin Spock, and William Sloane Coffin), see Unger and Unger

1988, 324–25, 300. Since one of the themes circulating throughout this interview, and through the history of IPS more generally, concerns the ways in which language and politics become caught in each other, we note that Allen Ginsberg signed the "Call to Resist" while discomfited by its "humorless prose": "You'd be better off telling people to goof off or fuck off from the draft, than all this gobbledygook which takes too long to read" (Unger and Unger 1988, 325).

6. Orlando Letelier was a former minister of defense and ambassador to the U.S. in Salvador Allende's Chilean government. Subsequent to imprisonment in and exile from Chile under the dictatorship of Augusto Pinochet, Letelier became the director of IPS's Transnational Institute, conducting research and organizing programs on human rights and economic policy in Chile. Ronni Karpen Moffitt was a young IPS staffer who worked on fundraising and other projects. On 21 September 1976 agents of the Chilean secret police exploded a car bomb that killed them as they drove to work. IPS, mostly through the efforts of senior fellow Saul Landau, found itself working to solve the case alongside the FBI that had been illegally harassing them for years (Dinges and Landau 1984).

7. The frequent citation of this quote from Karl Hess, a former IPS fellow, in both articles about the institute and in the institute's own literature, signifies its important referential and self-referential function (see Dickson 1971, 276; Friedman 1983, xiv; IPS 1987, 3).

8. The paranoid delusions of former red-diaper baby Horowitz introduce the equally paranoid book by S. Steven Powell (Powell 1987), which, in its obsession for detail and tenuous connections, serves an oddly effective documentary function. If, for example, one was interested in knowing which members of Congress requested the IPS budget studies, one need look no further than appendix 10. Other appendixes display the fantastically reticulated webs of "IPS and the Campaign Against Intelligence Agencies," "IPS and the Media," "IPS and the Campaign Against the Corporation," "IPS and the Peace Movement," and so on. In the early 1980s a previous spate of anticommunist screeds on IPS found their way into *Barron's, Midstream, Forbes,* and the *Congressional Record.* Many of these were inspired by or referred to a novel by Arnaud de Borchgrave and Robert Moss, *The Spike* (1980). In this widely reviewed roman a clef the "Institute for Progressive Reform" was revealed to be "the controlling center for a network of Soviet agents of influence who fanned out into Congress, the media, the academic world, and even the White House" (in Cockburn 1980).

9. Perhaps more than any other think tank, IPS throughout its history has enacted a strategy that might be termed "proliferation of outside spaces." Among the organizations that were direct spin-offs of IPS projects or founded by people who worked at IPS are: East Columbus Citizens Organization (1965); Health-PAC (1967); Cambridge Institute (1969); Bay Area Institute for Public Policy (1969); Center for Black Education (1969); Institute for Southern Studies (1970); Transnational Institute (1973); Conference on Alternative State and Local Policies (1975); Government Accountability Project (1984). IPS fellows and former fellows were also instrumental in the founding of publications such as *Mother Jones, In These Times, Working Papers,* and *Southern Exposure.* For some details on these organizations and the many scholars and activists once and currently associated with them and IPS, see Friedman 1983.

10. The paucity of current and comprehensive budget figures makes it difficult to

compare the monetary scale of think tanks over time. Some figures from 1987, however, allow for some contextualization of IPS within the scope of major Washington, D.C.-based think tanks at that time; our impression from scattered references in the broader literature is that the relative orders of magnitude given here remain largely applicable over much of IPS's history: Brookings Institution, $15.4 million annual operating budget; Heritage Foundation, $14.3 million; Urban Institute, $11.7 million; Center for Strategic and International Studies, $8.6 million; American Enterprise Institute, $7.7 million; Cato Institute, $2.2 million; IPS, $2.1 million (Weaver 1989, 563–78). For a few further comments on money as it was experienced within IPS, see note 13.

11. This distinction between politics driven by immediate pain and politics with a program seems analogous to the difference between activist and organizer made by community organizer Dave Henson. See the interview with Henson, this volume.

12. On the FBI's COINTELPRO activities, see Churchill and Vander Wall 1990.

13. A few words from one of us (M. Fortun): My questions in the interview here stem from my experiences in these organizational experiments in democratic self-governing. I would briefly note a few things: first, ethnographic accounts and analyses of participants' experiences within a think tank's "organizational culture" are a serious lacuna in the literature on think tanks—a hole that we regrettably also leave largely unfilled here. Among other things, such accounts would mention that Barnet, Raskin, and other senior fellows each had to fill in on the switchboard one hour per month during the receptionist's lunch hour, an unquestionably inefficient arrangement but also one with real symbolic effect—an arrangement that was understandably but regrettably discontinued toward the end of my tenure.

Second, while these questions of power, planning, and accountability were always fraught with tensions and inconsistencies, this was precisely an effect of Barnet's and Raskin's (and the IPS staff's as a whole) intellectual and ideological commitment to democratic self-experimentation. Thus while bodies like the program council, general assembly, and staff council that were in effect while I was there (and other internal structures at other times) had their difficulties and limitations, those difficulties and limitations only existed by virtue of the space of that larger commitment. If it is true that, as Barnet is quoted in the accompanying sidebar, the problem in 1976 was a "pseudodemocracy . . . that excluded establishing priorities," such was not my experience on the program council in the mid-1980s, where staff representatives, fellows, and senior fellows had some success in cooperatively establishing the institute's priorities. It's also worth noting that the staff council during the time I was there was given the authority to establish personnel policies related to entry-level salaries, salary review, grievance procedures, vacation and sick leave, and maternity-leave policy.

Finally, to fill in some of the gap from the first point via a theme related to the second: the external awareness of the comparative scarcity of resources between IPS and other think tanks (see note 11) was compounded by a frequent internal anxiety about cash flows and future funding. In my many days working the switchboard, I knew which callers I should patch through to the accountant, and to which callers I should say, "She's not in the office now, can I take a message?" As Raskin notes in the interview above, the fact that he and Barnet "knew how to beg" was indeed a "central piece of this story," and it was largely to their credit that all bills, eventually, did get paid—as did the staff of about forty. And the two times during my tenure there when the alms lagged far enough behind the begging to threaten the biweekly payroll, the senior fellows forewent their paychecks so that staff could be paid.

14. For a more extended and less pointed reading of this "cover story," see the cover story in the *New York Times Magazine* on the new conservative intellectual establishment, excerpted in the sidebar above.

References

Atlas, James. 1995. "The Counter Counterculture." *New York Times Magazine,* 12 Feb., 31–33.

Barnet, Richard. 1969. "The National Security Bureacuracy and Military Intervention." *The New Left.* Ed. Priscilla Long. Boston: Extending Horizons Books.

———. 1981. *Real Security: Restoring American Power in a Dangerous Decade.* New York: Simon and Schuster.

Barnet, Richard, and John Cavanagh. 1994. *Global Dreams: Imperial Corporations and the New World Order.* New York: Simon and Schuster.

Blumenthal, Sidney. 1988. "Left at Sea: The Institute for Policy Studies." *Our Long National Daydream: A Political Pageant of the Reagan Era.* New York: Harper and Row.

Churchill, Ward, and Jim Vander Wall. *The COINTELPRO Papers: Documents from the FBI's Secret Wars Against Domestic Dissent.* Boston: South End Press.

Cockburn, Alexander. 1980. "Apocalypse for Everyone." *New York Review of Books,* 6 Nov., 23.

Dickson, Paul. 1971. *Think Tanks.* New York: Atheneum.

Dinges, John, and Saul Landau. 1980. *Assassination on Embassy Row.* New York: Pantheon.

Friedman, John S., ed. 1983. *First Harvest: The Institute for Policy Studies, 1963–1983.* New York: Grove Press.

Gitlin, Todd. 1987. *The Sixties: Years of Hope, Days of Rage.* New York: Bantam.

Horowitz, David. 1987. Introduction to *Covert Cadre: Inside the Institute for Policy Studies,* by S. Steven Powell. Ottawa, Ill.: Green Hill.

IPS. 1987. "Institute for Policy Studies 25th Anniversary Campaign for the Future." Typescript.

Lukas, J. Anthony. 1976. *Nightmare: The Underside of the Nixon Years.* New York: Viking.

Merleau-Ponty, Maurice. 1968. *The Visible and the Invisible,* trans. Alfonso Lingis. Evanston, Ill.: Northwestern University Press.

Powell, S. Steven. 1987. *Covert Cadre: Inside the Institute for Policy Studies.* Ottawa, Ill.: Green Hill.

Raskin, Marcus. 1984. *The Common Good: Its Politics, Policies, and Philosophy.* New York: Routledge and Kegan Paul.

———. 1995. "Paths for the Twenty-First Century." Typescript.

Raskin, Marcus G., and Bernard Fall, eds. 1965. *The Viet-Nam Reader: Articles and Documents on American Foreign Policy and the Viet-Nam Crisis.* New York: Vintage.

Ricci, David. 1993. *The Transformation of American Politics: The New Washington and the Rise of Think Tanks.* New Haven, Conn.: Yale University Press.

Smith, James Allen. 1991. *The Idea Brokers: Think Tanks and the Rise of the New Policy Elite.* New York: Free Press.

Taylor, Mark C. 1987. *Altarity.* Chicago: University of Chicago Press.

CITIZENS, INC.: BOTTOM-UP ORGANIZING
IN BOTTOM-LINE CONTEXTS

ON AN ORGANIZER. *Dave Henson comes across as the classic sort of populist, social-movement activist in the United States, very different from think tank activists, as in the case of the Institute for Policy Studies in chapter 8, whose fortunes and opportunities have been articulated with those of a state and corporate order. While oppositional, the think tanks have been defined as organizations within that order in complex ways. Henson creates organizations that are the antithesis of the corporate form, lacking the institutional base that IPS's Raskin and Barnet think is necessary. But grassroots movements now confront a complex landscape—where NGOs (nongovernmental organizations) proliferate, with the support of the corporate order itself, which has come to see NGOs as a strategic resource in contemporary realignments of power. Grassroots movements must, then, constantly renegotiate their identities and rhetorics just to keep their place at the table. Henson's account of the United Nations Conference on Environment and Development in Rio de Janeiro provides particularly rich examples.*

This piece in general is Henson's map of the niches that grassroots organizations with traditional populist commitments can now occupy in a vastly changed landscape of corporate forms with explicit and diverse cultural ideologies. None of these corporate forms (whether commercial or nonprofit) are to be trusted, because they involve low levels of democratic participation and because they make it all the more difficult for grassroots articulations to be heard as distinctive and to be supported, even locally. In this regard, the present crisis of representation is a comforting and hopeful circumstance for Henson. – G. E. M.

* * *

What is the difference between a corporate executive and a community organizer? Most obviously, one works long hours for lots of money while the other works long hours for little or none. This difference is significant; it marks variation in the ways people conceive personal motivation, social structure, their own responsibilities and ideals of justice. Differences between leaders in the commercial spheres and leaders of grassroots citizen action should not, however, veil important similarities. Both conceptualize and sustain organizational forms appropriate to their missions and contexts. Both negotiate resource constraints and are expected to produce results, despite numerous barriers. Both respond to dissent within the organizations they lead. Both foster strategic alliance. They learn how to balance long- and short-term goals and when to call a project quits. Both often work at the limits of their imaginative and managerial capacities. Neither will last long if they ignore the pace and direction of social change.

The following interview with Dave Henson explores how these similarities operate in practice. Henson, a respected leader of grassroots citizen action, considers himself both an activist and an organizer; through the latter role he has assumed responsibility not only for issues at hand but also for the broad vision and tactical sensibility that characterizes managerial expertise in other spheres. While committed to radical environmental politics, Henson is no romantic. He is a strategist, keenly aware of connections between macro and micro processes, and of the need for innovative organizational response. In a world of environmental politics that too often valorizes raw commitment, Henson combines pragmatic finesse, informed judgment, internal critique, and attention to both concepts and context, and articulates a strategic vision worthy of the best corporate or organizational gurus.

The environmental justice movement, within which Henson situates himself, is both a supplement and challenge to mainstream American environmentalism. The movement has been built on awareness that communities of people already marginalized by race and economic status have been especially burdened by the health hazards of industrial production. Their concerns are not addressed within conventional conservationists strategies, which many argue "conserve the status quo": saving wildlife to preserve upper-class access to leisure without addressing the uneven distribution of the risks and rewards of industrial production. Since the late 1970s, with citizen action in Love Canal as a landmark case, these communities affected by toxic waste have been increasingly involved in efforts to define and control the risks to which they are exposed. In the process, the discourse of environmentalism has become laden with the concepts and rhetorics of civil liberties, prompting collective action to pursue citizens' rights to know, speak, and decide for themselves. Ironically, the challenges encountered by the environmental justice movement have foregrounded the limits of liberal democracy, eliciting pervasive critique of representational modes of decision making, both in the formal political arena and within oppositional organizations.

Henson's own career has involved continual engagement with these critiques. His first job was as a baseball umpire. Since then he has managed a country store, cooked pizza, roofed houses, and cofounded at least a dozen environmental and peace organizations. Work within these organizations has not been as immune from the racism, sexism, and other egoisms more predictable elsewhere. As this interview makes clear, the role of a community organizer is implicitly entangled, working both within and against established institutions and cultural forms. Henson has had to continually negotiate the tensions, producing, in the process, critically new ideas, social relations, and other modes of change. Highlighting these negotiations through ethnographic questioning allows us to shift our own readings of the grassroots from a natural, spontaneous outcropping to a field of carefully managed practices and cultivated meanings.

The interview is organized around six themes: (1) Henson's definition of his own role as organizer and activist, working within the traditions of the Highlander Center, a "folk" educational institution established in rural Tennessee in the late 1930s that grew to become a major force in Southern labor and civil rights work; (2) his description of the socioeconomic context in which community organizers now must work; (3) his work with the National Toxics Campaign, a premier environmental organization that attempted to link grassroots constituencies nationwide; (4) his involvement with citizen participation at the United Nations Conference on Environment and Development; (5) his experiences with popular education, comparing his work in Central Europe and the United States; and (6) his description of where he thinks we go from here, and how he wants to play a role in getting us there.

I. Organizing Activist Identities

FORTUN: If you were to meet a stranger, how would you describe yourself?

HENSON: I always have trouble with this. In a way, I think about the audience before I answer. If it's a family member or a family friend, it's almost an arbitrary cross-section of where I grew up, a suburb in California. I say I work with the environmental movement and the social justice movement. I think these two concepts are graspable immediately. People often ask me if I work for Greenpeace—that's always interesting, because that's what they see as exciting and radical, if they're supporters or not. It's sort of a cowboy, American ideal.

I say that I have, because I have worked with Greenpeace, then try to spin it out a little more, saying that I work with communities fighting against specific problems in their area—toxic pollution, a corporation wants to put an incinerator in their backyard. We try to develop community-labor alliances because workers and community members are equally affected.

I answer for general folks real generally. I claim participation in a movement; I try to reduce it to environmentalism and social justice. I like to walk away thinking that I've sparked a sense that these two things are related—that the environment is about people, too.

FORTUN: Do you call yourself an activist?

HENSON: Yes, activist, and organizer. I try to put out both those words.

FORTUN: In your mind is there a difference?

HENSON: I think so. An organizer, I think, is more intentional; it's more of an identity. This has been my lexicon. Someone who perceives of themself as an organizer is intentionally involved with strategic planning, has to have a certain detachment in order to be effective. Detached from the issue at hand, seeing the issue in historical context, or the development of issues around that issue, nationally and internationally. Basically, be aware of context. An activist can be that too, but also can be someone out protesting something right up front. The plant behind their house just blew up. They got involved; they're six months into it, and now they're an activist.

I see that we could switch these words around, but I'm interested in the distinction between people, not just those who are victimized being activists because they're called out on specific issues, but—almost—stages of development in self-identity as an activist, into an organizer.

FORTUN: Your definition of an organizer—how does it relate to your notion of an intellectual? Detachment, responsible for an empirical reading of the world.

HENSON: I think that the difference is the grounding in practice—at the start—rather than theory. Sometimes they can both meet in the center. Personally, I clubbed my way through school. Never got a college degree. Went to law school, didn't finish. I like school a lot but, as a student, I was always more of an activist. So I thought I should stop trying to pursue formal education, admitting that what I am best at is organizing. I want to dive into an issue, or a set of issues, helping people figure out what they're doing. Starting from there but still liking to read and discuss with people working at an academic level—to help me understand what I'm doing. These kinds of conversations we are having today.

FORTUN: Do you think progressive academics have something to contribute to the Left project, or do you find yourself more antagonistic? Academics are more part of the problem than any help.

HENSON: I try to experience this, and probably everything, with two heads. One is as organizer-sociologist—the detached analyzer of what's going on in context. The other coming from my personal experience. I value the former much more, because I think anecdotal experience is just that: anecdotal. The people I've met, the processes I've been through, engaging academics and communities, it's given me a lot of experiences. But, nonetheless, it's still anecdotal. I can step back and learn from a lot more people as this organizer-sociologist, and make a better conclusion.

Many people I work with are disdainful of academics because theory and practice are so separated. All it takes is one or two bad experiences for people to classify that way. It's also a stereotype, so it's easy to slip into. Then I know people, like myself, who have reflective discussions about activism, evaluation, strategic thinking separate from the issues you're passionately involved with at the moment. I think that there is a quick understanding that there is a role for academia.

For me, that role is a sense that there are theoretical—no, not theoretical, well-articulated languages to describe what I'm doing and, I know what I'm doing, kind of. But it's only when I stop and think about it, and talk about it, do I actually get fiber on which to identify myself. I think that's critical. When I talk to students, on college campuses, I try to paint a picture of this fiber: What are you as an activist? Because so many people come and go. An organizer for three years, and then leave it. How could that be? Doesn't it become part of your fabric, your identity? And, within that fabric, there are different processes by which we are naming what we are doing. I rely on other people to take the time to do it, this naming.

Yet, I have so many experiences with people who slip over the line. Highlander is a great example. People come to Highlander wanting to write a Ph.D. on popular education or community history. They study what people are doing, get a Ph.D., and the people feel that someone has ripped them off—took up their time without them getting anything out of it. They never saw that person again. Someone who now is a doctor at some university. But, you see something different with the organizer-sociologist head—you can see that person constructing a curriculum for twenty-five years of teaching that's based, in part, on experiences they had at Highlander. Actually, it's really important, for the seven hundred-some-odd individuals who come out of that program. They are going to be important people in society.

FORTUN: While I was working in Bhopal, writing for the movement there, my job was to help produce descriptions of what was going on. And I think my academic training helped me do that. On the other hand, I'm very sympathetic to the critiques of academics that you mentioned. But it bothers me when I encounter anti-intellectualism in the movement here—the sense that scholarly work is not relevant to the Left project. Maybe we need to think more about how scholarly work can circulate in the way you find useful, about ways academics can spread their skills around, just like other resources?

HENSON: A couple of things. I just bought someone's master's thesis, which is supposed to be about different models of grassroots leadership. This guy Tom Shaver, don't know him, a friend of a friend told him to call me because I might be interested. In large part he based his work on Kentuckians for the

Commonwealth, one of the premier grassroots groups who have documented their training processes. They've put out great manuals that I'm using in my training in Central Europe right now. I read a brief description of the thesis, and it appears that he has gone around interviewing a series of people, picking out what's helpful. Looking at their manuals, consolidating, contextualizing. Giving things names. Giving historical relevance. Spitting it back in one hundred and fifty pages. That's something I think I can learn something from. But I'll read it before I recommend it to anyone else. He's made it available, did a mailing to activists. I like that, when someone puts back.

FORTUN: American anti-intellectualism—if knowledge isn't what's privileged, what is? Certain forms of social organization? In my work here I haven't yet understood where notions of community alliance come from: are they brought in from outside, a pragmatic outcome of local work, what? In Texas, for example, there seems to be a very regionally specific sense of civic responsibility, but not through alliance. It's not a collective culture. There are many codes of decency but you wouldn't go to a meeting to enact them. There is almost a sense that if you need other people to help you pull off morality, something is very wrong. So it's not necessarily nefarious.

HENSON: I do think it stems out of the fetish for individuality. It's easily explainable, how it happens. But once seeded, the idea of alliance goes real deep. It's like we know as a species that we are communal, as well as individual. We have to reinvent it constantly. Bring back the communal. Not exclusively. But finding the bounds between our American private space and our communal sense. But you're right. Maybe it's also a class thing. In poorer, or more rural areas, people are much more on their own—rugged individualists. You take care of your own deal. You're neighborly. You kick in when you can. Everybody prides themselves on that: "We're a community that gathers together when there is trouble." Someone dies and everyone brings a ham. But the idea that you would have political alliance, no. Politics is heresy. That you would step out and speak out. People have a sense that they have a right to their rights, but organizing has a bad name. But it only takes a little seed, to get past the first hurdle, then the obvious thing is to get together to figure it out. People first start asking, Who do we call next? Rather than, It's us.

So the next problem is the way liberal democracy deals with complaint. Sure, come on in to the EPA regional office or the corporate public relations office. We'll take care of your concerns. Have a cup of coffee. How's the family? Compromise. It's a beautiful system. Keeps the lid on everything. The machine is a marvel.

But I think the uptake is cyclical. At times, the morphine works, making us forget the next ridge. Highlander's educational programs work directly against this, teaching people to exercise community power, that is called community. It comes and goes as a notion. But there no longer is an eastern excuse; political involvement can't be called pink anymore. So you can actually say that you are a community organization, or alliance, talk about the means of production in various ways—and, its history. That's very exciting. It's a big difference. People don't want to meet with the EPA director, they want to exercise power. Mechanisms of compromise still occur, but with less persistence.

FORTUN: What is it that's cyclical? People's disenchantment with the EPA's cup of coffee?

HENSON: What's cyclical is people remembering that we are a communal species, that alliances give off results. The more power you have in your meeting, before you call in the expert, or the government, the better results you'll get. It's like that movie *The Organizer*. The guy comes into town on a train with a suitcase, an Italian community. He just brings in the seed. Ultimately, the film might have been anticommunist; in any case, people are upset because there is an outrageous situation with a local mill. The organizer moves in, shacks up at someone's house, starts seeding the idea that if we all get together—I think what I'm saying, what's cyclical, is that people remember. It's a deep remembrance. That this stuff works. We don't have to identify with the Wobblies to remember. We're primates. So it's pretty much down there. And people have experience with it. Whether in the PTA or Little League. You have to cross over the big hurdle of embarrassment—I don't know a better word—for getting involved politically. People here are quite civically active. But when it gets political, when you start talking about corporations, it's embarrassing.

FORTUN: If you were talking to people in Texas City, attempting to be a catalyst, to organize, how would you convince them that political participation is important? What do you say when they ask why?

HENSON: It isn't that it's better to participate than not. The function of participation in healthy communities is the question. It's not good or bad, but it's the kind of participation and the level of participation that's in question. Participation for participation's sake is a strange notion.

FORTUN: Are you saying that participation is always, already there, that the choice is one of quality, not quantity?

HENSON: Yeah. Be deliberate about it, be intentional about it. Participation isn't always democratic, and democracy itself can mean different things. Accountability is the key point.

FORTUN: You often use the term *accountability*. Can you define it for me?

HENSON: I mean that in representative democracy, where at one point or another each of us is called to act on behalf of a group—testifying, going to a meeting, taking some action. In economic terms, doing economic activity on behalf of the whole; accountability is a valuation. The plant that's running upstream is accountable to a community in terms of its effects on a community; it's not only accountable to its stockholders: that's what I'm saying is better

democracy. The people who should be involved in a decision about any particular action are those that are affected by the decision. And the activist creating that effect should be accountable to those affected. That's the principle to
start from.

So you set it up by saying, "Wait a minute. You live in this town. That plant
is polluting the river that you live on. What they do, how they do it, what they
produce, how they produce, who benefits from it, who suffers from its side
effects: the people who make those decisions should not be shareholders in
Chicago. It should be the people who are directly affected. And let's sketch
out who those people are: they're the consumers; they're the people who log
the wood that builds the fire to build the material; they're the people who live
downstream; they're the people who work in the factory." Economy ought to
be held accountable to the people in which the economy circulates.

That's the big democracy question: the people ought to be the decision
makers. There's no longer any more room on the planet to exploit and pillage.
Colonists could go into some wilderness with no people and just cut the forest
because the trees would be fine. We all have to manage it together now. We're
all in this together. Nobody's separate from anybody else. And that's the long
term. Then there's the short term: all right, the tannery gets their permit next
Thursday. What are we going to do? Are we going to sit here and talk about
the big picture or are we going to actually do something? We always forgo
the former, the long term, in order to engage now. And what happens is that
after five years of struggle on that incinerator, we win. Or we lose. And either
way, we disappear. Unless Greenpeace sets up an office, or Citizens for a
Better Environment, or the Sierra Club, or somebody with a structure to carry
on something. But it's likely, again, to be staff based, and expert heavy, and
this and that. So I think the other discussion is actually the stuff with which
we reform the terms of our community, the terms of our participation in
community.

Instead of seeing consumers as the primary unit, or parents, which is the
other primary form of engagement, through school and sports and things. And
it's not church, either. But it's equally cosmologically framed. I don't have a
plan or a structure that works, but that's what we need to be doing at every
little place we are.

Real grassroots people get radicalized; we see it in motion at Highlander:
get people around a table for three days to talk about common experiences,
give it time, and the light bulbs go on. I think it's in us to understand that we
all have a common experience. Solidarity is a natural thing. We are all in this
together. Actually, I can take some of your load. I can suffer over here for
your benefit. Because it's in our long term interest. It's like we're genetically
coded to get that, because, otherwise, we'd all be taking each other's food,
and we'd all starve. I think that's the basis, in nature.

In this country, the grassroots haven't built a network with power. It's not like India, where the grassroots actually confront state power. The American party structure won't allow it. It will placate things way before then. It will be made all right enough that it won't be worth your time to spend all of it organizing. So academics, outside organizers, urban people—they have a role as catalyst. We need to bring in the idea of alliance. Get people to remember. Remind people about solidarity. We have a grand tradition of solidarity in this country. You can always bring something out of people's local experience. Bring in Highlander's idea of getting communities to do oral histories. Ask the old people. You'll find amazing stories about how people organized. Create a culture. Remember it. A culture of resistance, and of organizing. A culture of questioning fundamental economic order. Which used to happen in the thirties, the twenties. It was on the national plate for working people. It got truncated entirely after World War II. Not by design, but in a kind of organistic way. Capitalism figured it out that if we call all this communism, link it to Stalin, ride that wave.

II. Discriminating Political-Economic Contexts

FORTUN: This is a good point to define more terms. What's the difference between *the political* and *the civic*?

HENSON: I think it's been defined for us by the post–World War II anticommunist, strategic outlay of American economy. It's like everything else. Was it a decision by some white guys in a back room in Washington? I tend to fall down on saying it's the organism of capitalism. It's an organism. It responds. Not with a brain. You lop off the top and it doesn't matter. It naturally found its way, like a water course, down to thousands of different little acts by individuals. Putting the idea of political activism in the realm of communism. Any critique of the economy: the corporation shouldn't have carte blanche to do whatever it wants, any kind of union organizing. Anything that complains about the system is in the realm of communism. Other than that, you are welcome and encouraged to get involved. Not just the Little League and the garden club, but the local school board and even a development council: taking part in deciding whether a mall should be built on main street. But as soon as you start talking about property rights, about lack of citizen involvement in what's happening economically, and environmentally, it's disallowed, by the organism.

FORTUN: So, the *civic* has disallowed economic assessment?

HENSON: We have a great political democracy in this country. It works. We don't have any form of economic democracy. This argument has been stewing in our movement for a long time. By *political* I mean civic democracy, participation in the details of decisions about the governance of our lives. Even things that are extremely consequential: what our children will be taught, what our individual rights are to speak, act, travel. On the criminal code, the civil code. It's open to discussion and participation. We can write referendums and do amazing things: cut taxes in half, pass environmental laws. But when you approach anything that has to do with the levers of the economy, it's absolutely off-limits. There aren't civic structures built to do that.

FORTUN: Now that the Red threat is gone, is there more space to maneuver?

HENSON: There is more space to maneuver. Very few things these days can be traced to some conference in Geneva; but the end of the cold war, as a construction, I think, interestingly parallels the rise of a grassroots environmental movement that's talking about control of the means of production. It takes alliances like the National Toxics Campaign to actually shift the language, redefine what we are talking about. Communities are starting to organize independently, but with lots of cross-fertilization—that's what makes it a movement, rather than just an odd assortment of events, an aggregation. Basically, people are saying that they want more involvement in the decisions that will affect their lives, their health, their local economy. That plant just can't up and leave. Plant closure laws used to be perceived as socialist-labor versus capitalist-government. Now it's not the labor unions that are at that vanguard, but community organizations—like at Yellow Creek—eastern Kentucky, Appalachia. Screwed over bad in an event that lasted many years. The most unlikely people to start talking about taking control over what's done, asking where the money is going.

FORTUN: At Yellow Creek, citizens won—in court, at least. They got clean drinking water; the tannery was shut down; health monitoring has been funded; culpable individuals were held liable. But Yellow Creek is the exception. What is it that would make it more the rule?

HENSON: The companies can't just leave. That's the first thing. Close the back door. GATT [General Agreement on Trade and Tariffs, now the World Trade Organization (WTO)], it's hard not to see it as a response. The Eastern bloc collapses, opening a space for people to start talking about control over the means of production. Shortly thereafter, just as we're getting a grip on it, GATT takes the back wall out. Paves the exit. The long-standing ways we have been able to organize in the civic sector is to win lawsuits, legislative battles, elections, consumer boycotts. The carpet has been pulled out from underneath us.

FORTUN: Do you think GATT has challenged even the possibility of civic democracy?

HENSON: I think so. Although, I'm looking forward to the first court cases, when Argentina wants to ship DDT up here, or Chile wants to send grapes covered with pesticides banned in California. California says, "No deal"; it's not unloaded. Then Chile takes the United States to Belgium, through GATT.

The court says this is an unfair trade barrier; the United States gets its wrist slapped. But when it's France, it will be a trade war. Then, I can't wait until it hits the California Supreme Court. My hunch is that the California Supreme Court, as conservative as it has become, is going to say that the people of the state of California have a right to decide for themselves: about health effects, economic effects, a whole range of things. Newly protected rights. People are going to go nuts. When the actuality of the worst-case scenario is actually realized. I don't think it will happen. The courts will say to hell with GATT.

FORTUN: What authority will those courts have?

HENSON: The federal government is responsible for enforcing GATT. Even though the shipment went to the port of Oakland, the U.S. government has to answer, not the corporations. The constitution of the state of California grants California the right to say no. Then there will be interesting interstate commerce issues. Then it could go to the U.S. Supreme Court. They will look for the right case. The Court will have to decide whether the states have to abide by the federal government's international contract, a treaty.

FORTUN: The devolution of power to states, playing the contradictions between federal and states' rights, recourse to the local: the Left has both opposed and advocated this for a long time: statist strains have opposed states' rights, but populist strains have opposed centralization, insisting that participatory democracy is only possible when enacted locally. Now there is a new complication: localism is the new agenda of the New Right.

HENSON: It's coincidental, and ironic. What I'm referring to—people-based authority to oppose the unreasonable demands of GATT—will be enhanced by the drift toward federalism. The Left has often sought federal protection, seeing it as a more liberal construct. California may be better off in this than other states. But what happens in Mississippi or Alabama? In the South, it may be the worst consolidation.

FORTUN: Can you trace, historically, how we got tangled in these contradictions?

HENSON: There are two parts of corporate structure. One designates who will make decisions about what is going to be done. The other regards who benefits. Often they're very related, sometimes they're not so related, depending on the shareholder model. Both of them are arcane. They had their place, evolved out of a specific context. They made sense, in an organic way, if you understand the history of North America. Nature provided for that type of economy, where individuals are given the right to get out there and expand and grow and build. It was a natural way to exploit this niche.

FORTUN: You're saying that the corporate model of economic organization had a kind of predictable trajectory in American history and culture?

HENSON: Before the American Revolution, where was capitalism? Capitalism was in its Dickensian phase. Eventually, it was supposed to collapse from internal contradictions tied to the stratification of rich and poor. Marx as an individual, and Marxism as a process, couldn't foresee the incredible developments which would allow the inevitable contradictions to be put off—until now, when the world's smaller again. There's no New World.

FORTUN: Marx regains relevance in the age of GATT?

HENSON: Yeah, I think very much so. Now the true contradictions in what could be predicted in a contained capitalist system are coming out. But the point of all this is that the North American culture fostered the extreme of free enterprise. Regulation was absurd.

It was in the people's interest to subsidize the acquisition of enough capital to build railroads across the country, to bring machinery up to the Northwest and log. It was in the interests of the people that their government would actually assist corporations. Of course, the relations between the government and the corporations become so incestuous that any checks that might have been there were gone. And the economy then controlled politics. So it made a lot of sense, not in terms of right and wrong, but in terms of the way history has evolved in America. It makes sense that the corporation has become incredibly free, self-righteous, able to do whatever they want.

III. Pollutions Within:
Negotiating the National Toxics Campaign

FORTUN: Tell me about the rise, and fall, of the National Toxics Campaign (NTC).

HENSON: The founder was a brilliant guy. But a big lesson: he couldn't get over a founder's syndrome, and being a particular kind of man, in this culture. Not just him, others, too. But he had the vision to see that there were fires out there; communities were bubbling up. Things happening all at once. They seem unrelated. I'm not a naturalist, and think that conditions are behind everything, causing all the bubbling to be happening at once. And that we just jump into the hot spots, issue organizing like we always do. We ask how we can unify. How do we build people power to actually do something very political, very strategic, very radical? We couldn't just walk into communities and start talking. We had to organize. The model was to start a national vehicle for these grassroots groups to have a voice. So much was happening at the national level: Superfund, RCRA [Resource Conservation and Recovery Act]. These grassroots people should have been at the table.

But it all started with the typical line: let's found a national group, not based on community experience. It wasn't the people founding a pyramid, that would result in their projection into national issues. It was a city-based, intellectually influenced group of activists who could see the topography, see what was coming down, conceive of a strategy, figure it out. You can't see that from some county in Georgia facing off a waste management company. In-geniously, the founders of NTC could see that this bubbling was going on—and needed to be interconnected.

At first, NTC was just five people, a board: funders, East Coast philoso-phers and elitists, your typical city organization. And they transformed, through incredible pain and struggle, into an organization with thirty-five people on the board, from all over the country. Crazy, on one hand, economi-cally and logistically. But every person on the board was a grassroots leader. And really was.

But, when you pick people out of some small town in Idaho, or Georgia, and have them fly into Boston for meetings, it screws up their local identity, and group structure. Constructed from the top down, rather than from the bottom up. Because the bottom just can't move in this way. There are barriers which prevent the kind of organizing you see in other countries. Revolutionary movements. People are placated. So the task is to get people to the table, then turn it over to them. Turn over the process, turn over the money. Not without a struggle. And make it multiracial. Make it a majority of people of color. A majority of women. And have an explicit set of discussions about what is be-ing done, about what needs to be done.

With NTC, the founders continued to manipulate things but it got so demo-cratic that the founder no longer had a real role. This never got resolved—reliance on the founder as the visionary. It destroyed the organization. But this model, this vision that never transpired—it was only a third of the way there—was to develop an Oklahoma toxics network, and an Arkansas toxics network, and so on. We had offices in ten states. Real grassroots groups be-coming nationally catalyzed. The Louisiana Environmental Action Network was one that was working on its own. In a congress structure with democratic accountability: we are the representatives of our local groups, sitting around a table. Built-in reporting. And the people aren't staff. They are grassroots people. And their way is paid. They aren't expected to pay.

FORTUN: Paid by whom?

HENSON: Grant raising, by the Veatch Foundation, others. NTC raised a lot of money. People loved this idea. I think it's the right model.

FORTUN: This model that you're talking about. First, it's a representative structure. To what extent is the placating capacity of liberal democracy emer-gent from this representative structure?

HENSON: I've never seen it work, and I've worked with so many organiza-tions. I've tried to be a catalyst, to be an enzyme, to foster a culture that will remember and try to exert democratic control. At Highlander, at NTC, at EPOCHA, at every organization I've worked with. Trying to recreate that. And it's always up against the same kind of barriers. But we've got to start somewhere. We've got to keep popping up, and then, eventually, maybe we can make it happen. I think we've got to keep plowing ahead. That it doesn't matter that it doesn't work. It's the best thing we can do. Then I think, what about other models? NTC kind of started out toward this.

Some people up in Boston have an idea, in a back room, but with an organizing director that was an old Alinskyist. He had this oddball organizing model that did not fit with the grassroots. That's another reason it collapsed. The organizing model was to fly someone down to some town we've never been to and break the balls of the local group, telling them how best to mind their own business. Alinskyan machismo. If they are not with us, they are against us, even if they are our most natural allies in the political spectrum. They're the ones who are the most dangerous, the one's with their own ideas, habits, alliances, complicities. We've got to break them first, reign in their power. Then move forward and take over the state. Have a press conference then fly out, just before the thugs come in to beat up the locals. An exaggerated version, but not far from the truth. The founder of NTC never understood that. He was a cowboy, a macho man. It's a classic thing. People are good on some things, and just miss the boat on others. He was really good at some things. No, I shouldn't credit him with that—grassroots leaders from around the country forced him to cede control of his organization, to embody his own rhetoric: "It's blacks who actually control the organization." Complete bullshit to the very end. "It's actually women." The worse kind of—

FORTUN: patronizing—

HENSON: It was unbelievable. I've never worked with anyone that bad. I'm sure it's rife in military, government, and corporate culture. But here it is in the Left. People from the grassroots seized power from him. They had other business to attend to so it took time. And he went along with it. But when community groups actually controlled the organization, the process by which they could envision and implement strategy was stunted constantly by the peculiarity of them being plucked out of their town and flown into Boston. Personal class issues became important. Where you stay, what you eat. The people left at home are jealous. I think it happened in almost every single community. They were called national leaders, and the founder exploited that—by finding the most victimized women around the country to put on the board. They had lost a child due to chemical exposure and he took them around, got them on the podium with his arm around them, so they could cry. The worst kind of manipulation. Then he would slip them money on the side for the kid's education, because he's got a wife with money. A classic problem, that our labor unions have, and so many Left organizations. But had that not happened I still think there was a barrier to these democratic structures actualizing the vision. Politically. To develop a national organizing strategy based in a grassroots movement. A very good vision. For several reasons. Race—blew it up. Gender politics—exploded. Class politics—fiasco.

We decided to shut down NTC. It was better not happening, although it was a great thing. It was replicating the things we're fighting against. But now there's this huge hole. We're almost worse off than if it never existed. People are scarred; they're burned; they're fried. Nobody is going to fund this kind of thing anymore. For years, we won't be able to have anything national. Not until all those people have disappeared. One of the big costs is that a lot of foundations have gotten very wary. They were infatuated with the grassroots, for awhile.

FORTUN: Tell me more about the after effects.

HENSON: Some of the aftereffects are positive. We learned a lot from the process of quitting, putting together our post mortem. We met five or six times, and it was a majority of people of color. And it was the majority of the board: all the people of color voted to close it, except for two. Most of the white people voted for it to stay open. We decided to write that paper to analyze what had happened, and that's why it has so much on race and gender. But mostly on race because that was the primary experience that people had. And we went through some incredible meetings together. It was one of the most important processes for me, ever.

Here are high-powered people from different organizations around the country getting together for weekends and just plowing through. We broke down the entire organization's history, its organizing model, its structure, its power, everything. And afterward we were drained. It took over a year. We held out for a long time, hoping that we could salvage this incredible multiracial process. In the end we had a great analysis of one of the more recent attempts at multiracial, national revolutionary organizing—within the mainstream culture. And people just wanted to go away and get back to work at home, see what comes up next. There was a sort of sinking feeling that white people and black people, if they're really based in their communities, can't just start working together at the national level. A lot more has to transpire before that.

FORTUN: Are you then saying separate but equal?

HENSON: I would say separate but equal, to a point. I think the obligation for white organizations is to educate themselves and be engaged with issues of white racism, out of necessity to the historical situation and what it's going to take to win in this country, and to make a commitment to engage with groups of color on the terms or the agenda of groups of color. It's a kind of affirmative action approach. Because otherwise the dynamic, in fact, is that the white agenda dominates.

I've convened large gatherings several times, and I'm learning more each time that there's no way to avoid it: when you bring people of such diverse experiences together, there will be culture clashes, since we don't have a common political perception or ideology, a party, or even a language. We can't rely on that to figure out how we're going to proceed during these five days. Thus it ends up operating on surface interactions rather than on the depth of discussion. So events like that, I'm leaning less toward, except when they take advantage of extraordinary opportunities and it's just worth the struggle.

IV. Going Global

FORTUN: The transfer of power to nongovernment organizations (NGOs), which, ironically, includes both corporations and public-sector groups. What's going on here? Is there actual entry into representative processes? Are we pluralizing who participates on the international stage?

HENSON: Our experience at the United Nations Conference on the Environment and Development (UNCED), at Rio, was very instructive on how this plays out. It was the first time the United Nations actually gave certification to NGOs to actually participate; they also began certifying chambers of commerce and industry trade groups. All as nongovernmental organizations. Which gets back to the problem of defining *NGO*. In other countries, *NGO* is a common label, among those who travel in the international circuit of meetings. They talk NGO-speak, learned at all these meetings. Nobody in the United States uses *NGO*; it's not vernacular. United Way uses *NGO* ; Washington uses it, sometimes.

We brought this delegation of sixteen activists down to UNCED in Rio, and had to get into the politics of it. Once before, the Thais organized a People's Forum, under the rubric of the World Bank. It gave us the idea for organizing the People's Forum in New York, before the UNCED meeting. The Thai meeting was an incredible gathering, but all talking NGO-speak, because they had been working on World Bank issues for years. They had adopted the role designated for them by the Bretton Woods institutions. Fighting the World Bank, but in an oppositional role shaped by it. That was the first time I understood that there was a huge NGO sector in Third World countries, made up of groups that are quasi-governmental in their organization, in the number of staff. But it's still the voluntary sector. U.S. groups don't fit into that lexicon. In part, because it's UN-speak, global bureaucracy talk that doesn't affect the United States at all. The United Nations and the Bretton Woods institutions don't affect the United States, but they largely set the social agendas for other peoples' national-level engagement with things.

Grassroots activists have often been called to sit on panels with corporate people, as part of the liberal democratic process. Each testifies, each has a legitimate concern in a democratic process. But it was never such that all were real players versus the government, coming to the table with their own business to deal with. This is what happened at UNCED. And it was outrageous, terribly outrageous. People bought into the process: NGO elites with the nine badges you needed to get past the tanks into the building, where all the heads of state were. The privilege, the buyout, in process, was too much. The heads of groups, lots of lawyers. An occasional grassroots-oriented group. Someone like Vandana Shiva. Progressive agenda, but on their terms.

The rest of the groups were completely marginalized—outside, in the "NGO forum." Forty thousand people. Absolutely no impact. A festival affair. Marginalized because of the organizational construct. People talked about it for days. Realizing that we had bought into the UN's construct of who we are—an advisory arm that sends a couple of representatives: forty thousand of us representing all the peoples of the world. So what did we talk about: how could we have been so stupid, so as not to organize politically, about power?

FORTUN: Could you have seen the sell-out coming?

HENSON: The foundations met well before the possibility of UNCED was ever made public, decided it was going to be important, and that they should put enormous amounts of money toward it. The Ford Foundation was a big one. And some Left foundations. So they decided to organize the U.S. Citizens Network on UNCED. They hired this woman who could be easily controlled by the bureaucrats at the foundations, who had political agendas—of moderation. It's the kind of foundation work that the Right loves to see happening: let's set the agenda of the Left by pouring money into its own Right. It's better than not funding at all, because then the Left is left to its own means—organically, producing what's important. This way, they choose—what to fund, and, thus, what's what.

So this network convened meetings all over the country, brought in the chair of Waste Management, corporate heads from all over the country, heads of NGOs, mainstream environmental groups, science outfits—good people, care about ozone, but talking about the science, not what's behind it all. They did mailings, lots of press coverage, invited lots of people to meetings—including some from grassroots groups. They became the official organ for citizens' participation at UNCED. They became the democratic process, the determination of our common future. And it was outrageous.

In New York, working with the Environmental Democracy Campaign, and Highlander, my job was to keep tabs on these things, which the grassroots don't have the organizational capacity for. NTC and Highlander had set up these international programs, after various members came with us to a conference in Nicaragua. It blew their mind. They began to see how important it is to watch what the World Bank is doing. So we began trying to convene grassroots groups into a People's Forum, based in New York. We had these eight hub groups all over the country that were groups who had the capacity for an extended engagement with UNCED. A well-balanced network geographically: rural, urban, people of color. We tried to instigate this from New York, along with NTC, which was at the peak of its relevance, before it began to collapse. We had a happening national structure that was in direct, hostile confrontation with the U.S. Citizen's Network.

We had a meeting in New York with about two hundred people, and confronted the Citizen's Network—including Gore, who had been ambassador to UNCED, before he was vice president. And we met with the funders, and asked by what authority they had convened this Citizen's Network. And the funders—not the Ford's, the Left among them—they listened, stopped funding the Citizen's Network, and shifted money to the forum. They realized the forum was much more representative, carried a real critique, was much more radical. Made up of people who had no interest in meeting Al Gore.

The people in the Citizen's Network: nice people, but with no political education. We worked with them, but decided that there was no hope in trying to transform the organization; we just needed to take it over. At first the funders said that they shouldn't be dumping more money in a black hole, that early on you could see who was going to convince the United Nations—and it wasn't citizens. But they loved the idea of bringing together key activists from around the country. To miss that opportunity would have been a crime. So it worked out.

The result was our People's Forum, with thousands of people from all over the world, representing NGOs, with funding from the United Nations. All these people flew in, including about 130 grassroots activists from here: each hub selected eight representatives from their region. Fare and other expenses paid. An extraordinary group of people, but not that unlike NTC. Trying to impose a Left democratic structure when there is no culture to back it. But they had more impact than we did in Rio, with all the tank security to keep everyone away.

We went into the United Nations and a lot of the delegates, especially from the Third World countries, were very interested in hearing grassroots critiques. They, too, are afraid that they are getting the short end of the stick. So there are a lot of interesting alliances to be had. But there's also the dictatorships—the Malaysian government was a key leader, meanwhile beating their own activists back home. It was probably most important for these Third World representatives to actually see people of color in the United States. The only people they usually see are lawyers from the Environmental Defense Fund, or Ralph Nader's outfit. Good people doing good work, but coming at things from Washington. All lawyers, almost all white, almost all men. So they met other sorts—colorful characters who gave them a sense that there is a movement in the United States, with issues, with poor people.

We had this one meeting, with about a thousand people. And we hear that the Citizen's Network is also having a meeting. Again, nice people, but the wrong people. The wrong people to be representing anybody. They had this meeting with the UN ambassador to UNCED, a Central American guy who earlier had orchestrated a decade of death-squad activity. A classic guy, just a classic guy. Gore was there. A bunch of delegates from the official U.S. delegation—which included students as well as nongovernmental agencies. This posh reception. We're in our own meeting, railing on this and that. Someone burst in the door and says that *they* are meeting just over there. So people stand up and say, Let's go, let's confront them. I'm the organizer. Thinking, Should, how do we do this? And ended up thinking, Let's just do it.

We get a couple hundred of people in cabs. Met in front of the building. Walk in together. This activist from the Gulf Coast Network, a charismatic Southern, African-American leader, an old CPer, who still carries it with him—an incredible guy. You want him on your side. Richard More, from the Southwest network. A big guy who can just get in your face and exert that authority of a people-of-color group. A bunch of heavies. They're up front, pissed off. Personally, I was just laying back, thinking it was going to be fun to watch.

We storm into this tie and high-heel reception. Bow-tie people serving little hors d'oeuvres. Gore is there. This UN ambassador. Immediately we doubled the size of the room. And it starts to get uncomfortable. Our people are getting their glass of wine, eating the hors d'oeuvres. You could feel something was going to happen.

Next thing I know, they have this ambassador cornered. The CP guy had brought up all these people he could totally control—tenant organizers: really important work, but a party structure. He had these people on hand signals, working this ambassador, backed in a corner. And this guy, all dressed up, getting screamed at about racism, sweating. Gore was over to the side, because no one knew who he was yet. Then they called the police. And we left. But before going, this ambassador had to agree to come to our meeting and spend the whole day. And he came. And people came away different.

It was a high moment for me, too. We came away thinking that we broke their party, business as usual. It was a little thing, it didn't matter, but it did matter. And a bunch of the international people went with us, saw the action. It was worth it, even though, in the end, it blew up. It blew up on race. But it was worth it.

FORTUN: What happened?

HENSON: I liken it to a lynch mob: Stop, we're getting screwed once again, not that we've been anything but screwed, but we're getting screwed again, and we're not going to take it lying down. We're going to call it for what it is and it's racism. And it is racism. No doubt about it. And classism. What hit the wall at the People's Forum was conflict between Appalachian whites, poor farmers from Idaho, and African Americans, mostly from the South. The whites involved were incredible people, even if not totally fluent in race politics, because they aren't around as much in Iowa and Idaho. All of them: aware of race, antiracist in their politics. But the African-American groups came in with a political strategy insisting that we cut everything on race, led by one particular activist whose race line way overshadows his class line. And so he started going after Larry Wilson—white, Appalachian, cowboy hat and boots, an old boy, fifth-generation Wilson from the same holler. The creek floods every year, washes out his house; his Mom's up the hill dying. Incredibly poor.

So the white people in the delegation walked into this hotbed—a highly politicized, stylized attack. They had no idea what they had walked into. It was tragic.

How could it have been avoided? You don't convene a national gathering like this and don't invite the major African-American leaders from the South. Some of them would sabotage it, be there anyway. And it would be a lot worse. I would accuse some of these activists, whom I would rather not name, of movement blackmail. And many others agree. Including other African Americans. But they can't say that with white people around.

It just tears down. If it's not these particular activists, it's someone else. It's not their fault. In fact, the race issue is incredibly deep. It's all about race. The corporations against the people: it could be boiled down to race. But Larry Wilson wants to say that Appalachians are just as poor, and as historically screwed over as blacks. But you can't say that to African Americans working on race issues. And it almost destroyed Larry as a human being. The fallout was really tough. On Highlander. Because it was a Highlander-organized event. This incredible race thing, with people having to choose sides. Really ugly. One delegation from Iowa left, and it was like they were scared. Like they went into the big city and it was just like they would have guessed: they were called racists as soon as they got off the bus.

And I've seen it so many times. At the national level in the United States there's no way around it—race as the primary reality. When people say, This is racism, there's nothing you can say. Because it is. It's all racism. There's nothing you can say. The process blows up. So I think throwing together national multiracial networks is catastrophic from the get-go—until such structural integrity is in place that no individual can pop off like that, just throw a bomb and explode it.

FORTUN: Now tell me about Rio.

HENSON: We took sixteen delegates to Rio. We became important because it was a named grassroots delegation, with a process. The process was really great. We wrote a thick book of community stories, from interviews with a couple hundred organizations. Mostly Southeast, but from all the hub groups. Called them up, got them on the phone. The idea was to get each community to give testimony. Not something off a flier, something fresh. The idea: what is UNCED? Everybody in the Third World knows. Nobody in the United States does. The movement had been co-opted; we only had eight months left. So we asked the groups to have a discussion about what they wanted, out of UNCED. We explained why it was important for them to participate—so we could put together a People's Report, to counteract the official U.S. report.

Every country had to produce an official report, which ended up as incredible whitewashes of problems at the local level. The U.S. report claimed to be an example of how we have solved the problems here. Our report showed it wasn't so. People wrote great stuff. Regardless of what we did with it, it was a great tool for popular education. And many of the participants came to the PreCom. People from all over the country felt like they were part of the process, sending delegates, being represented. And it worked really well. We got a ton of play, as the grassroots delegation, since all the other groups were the ones with money. Not their fault that they had the money, but arbitrary. Arbitrary good people who came home with slides.

Basically, we tried to link up with other grassroots organizations, trying to spend as much time as possible deconstructing the mainstream operations, which were legitimizing the governmental process. Being at the table, when it had been a fraud all along. Bush refused to sign the Global Warming Treaty. Any organization that would stay at the table after that—it would suggest that the official line was right, that they had all their support lined up.

V. Strategizing Knowledge and Authority

FORTUN: Tell me about your work in Central Europe, and how it compares with your work here.

HENSON: One of the biggest challenges in Central Europe is the 100 percent deference to experts. It's the way the culture has worked there: a cult of rationality and science. It applies to everything. One out of every three people is an engineer, as opposed to here, where one out of fifty, at most, goes to college. People will say, I can't answer that question; I'm not an engineer or a medical doctor. They know very much what is going on but they won't even try to say it. We have this here, too, but there is something of an American tradition allowing one to say, I don't need no schooling to know what's happening to me, here and now.

In Central Europe I worked with workshops of about forty people from twenty different grassroots groups from around the country. A five-day workshop addressing a range of things—funding, campaign strategies, how to work with the local government, all of this stuff. Everyone starts out with the sense that they need experts. We try, without being inappropriate, to say that there may be other ways to do this, citing other examples from around the world. We also try to model discussions so that people end up saying what

they don't think they know. But the whole culture is oriented around expertise. So when they go into the city council, or to meet with the corporation,
they are always asked where the doctor is to testify. They're always told,
again and again, You're just a worker.

FORTUN: So you must have to teach some strategic sense about expertise:
it's necessary but it's not necessary. Strategic but part of the problem.

HENSON: Absolutely. We do a lot of work on how to use, contain, and work
with experts—how to make sure experts don't take over your strategic process. Medical doctors can come in with a propensity to urge you to do a
health study that targets urine samples so you can get liver studies because
that's their specialization. We do it with charts, visually, putting medical advice in its place, as part of a strategic plan, in relation to other things, like
grassroots organizing, building alliances with farmers, etc. The advisor is a
part, not the whole.

FORTUN: So in Central Europe knowledge tends to be privileged over social organization? What you know would make up 90 percent of the strategic
pie. How would things cut here?

HENSON: Not 90 percent. One needs knowledge, but with a begrudging attitude. When you've got good experts, you're really proud of them. They're
your ace in the hole, your big cannon to validate your experience. Larry and
Sheila Wilson were here yesterday, from Yellow Creek. Now they're the staff
directors of the environmental health program I've worked with at Highlander.
They just won a lawsuit, after fifteen years in court—an eleven-million-dollar
settlement with this tannery that has destroyed their community. In their own
family, one of their sons, Wade, who is fifteen, is severely altered—his personality and constitution, by the toxins. The number of people who have died
from this is unbelievable. Their daughter has just had her second miscarriage.
This one had no spine; the brain came out of the back of the head. Severe
abnormalities that mimic the abnormalities in the fish and the animals, the
offspring of the sheep and the cows. A personal horror. Just five weeks ago,
she had this abortion—five months into term. They are very poor, an Appalachian holler community. Yet they rose up, with a team of lawyers.

To listen to Larry tell about the case, and what happened in court—during
this fifteen-day trial, after fifteen years of community organizing—it's fascinating. He's constantly bad-mouthing the attorney, but when the attorney
nailed them on something, he was "my attorney, up there fighting for us." But
he was very aware when the attorneys would step over the line and do something without consulting the community. His central pride was that he sat with
the attorneys in the courtroom. When they were questioning somebody, they
would always stop and ask, What else do you got? The community sat behind
and would pass notes.

FORTUN: So do you think of law as an important tool for grassroots work?

HENSON: I think it has always been one of the best tools. Really, there are three tools: people power—boycotts, strikes, organizing people to exert direct power. Legislative—we change the law, we can elect people to change the law. And the third is legal remedy. But I think we've overrelied on suing to get what we want. In California the old-growth issue is a good example. The main strategy for protecting the last five percent of ancient forests in the state, and in the country, has been to file suit. Blocking cutting through suits which have very little to do with the actual issues at hand. The spotted owl, the snake. The way they misfiled this or that. Nickel and diming. A successful strategy for the last ten years, but one that, ultimately, is losing. Because, of course, the corporations tighten up their ship and learn how to circumvent.

In the meantime, we don't have a movement. People in the community value those trees; they would mandate that Pacific Lumber not be able to log the headway. But just a few days ago they announced that the largest privately owned patch of ancient forest is going to be logged. We've failed because we've relied on legal mechanisms. People who understood the issue turned it over to law firms. Fund raising went toward the litigation, rather than building community organization that could transcend the issue—by building a Left movement that has a consciousness and an identity on a variety of issues. They did the exact opposite. They centralized the process in an arcane way, reducing the movement to the staff at a few organizations, reducing relations with the public to a fund-raising appeal. Rather than grassroots organizing. Issue by issue you find this happening.

When you're involved in the issue, it does seem the most prudent thing to do: Look, they are going to cut next Thursday. What are we going to do? Let's file a suit. Get a six-month waiver. Then file again. That's the problem of not having a movement, a party, ultimately, that could have people systemically working on this, finding alternatives that include both political and economic strategy.

FORTUN: This argument is made in the environmental studies literature I teach with: once a movement takes up litigation, participation falters. But a remaining question, Can the law become a reference point for movement building? An example I think of is Institute, West Virginia, where the sister plant to Union Carbide's Bhopal plant is located. A low-income minority community. They are at sea. Outsiders tell them to go knock on doors, but they don't know what to tell people they want them to do. A lawsuit: that could be supported. Otherwise, how do you name a goal, when the problem is so complex, bifurcated, amorphous? It does seem a little much to ask a working mother to take on the chemical industry. Asking them to take on a specific lawsuit, a specific issue, seems more doable.

HENSON: A lawsuit held people together in Yellow Creek for fifteen years. Meanwhile, they also ran for school-board elections, and other things, took

over an incredible Appalachian old-boy power structure—incredibly corrupt—I'll gravel your driveway Thursday if you'll vote for me. That's just the
way it worked. They flipped it on its head. They ran people to take over the
school board, and the water board—which has all the money, because it's all
federal, because there's no local tax base. They focused on the lawsuit. They
met regularly for fifteen years, to talk about the lawsuit. A lot of people stuck
together for a long time to actually build a community power base. It was entirely grassroots; it never got polluted; no one helped them. No one took over
the case. They kept it as a community organization, using direct Highlander
ideology: We're going to keep control of this thing. An almost provincial dis-
dain for academics and other outsiders.

FORTUN: Explain the different ways this could be understood, through the
different approaches of activists and organizers.

HENSON: As an activist, all we do is file suit. Nothing else is possible. My
other head tells me that we have to develop infrastructure to our movement,
so that we have political structures that can ride out the urgency. What's the
goal? To build power. To build community-based power. Democratic power
that people identify with. Not on an issue-to-issue basis but in an ideological
way, a cultural way, a spiritual way. Actually feeling like the future is in transformation, beyond the immediate interest in closing the incinerator. Something indicative of a whole set of problems. This takes political education.
This takes organization. Often outside organization. Methodologically, we are
learning. Popular education. Academics often call it action research. Participatory methods. Transparency. Accountability. Words like that.

FORTUN: Do you think the labor movement is an important forum for this
work?

HENSON: I think the modes of organizing are so fraught with patriarchal
and old structures of organization that I don't know if it can be changed. Yet,
it's absolutely critical that labor keep track of trying to organize, from its
point of view. And I think neighbor-labor strategies are a good idea. It starts
out with the political assumption that labor isn't the movement. There's a
community consciousness that's separate from labor, because labor has often
acted against the interest of the community. And to name that and say it, that
satisfies me. To say labor is labor: self-interested from the get-go, but covering many interests of poor people and working people. It represents families
and to some degree the economic base of communities. But it certainly has
never been able to deal with ecological concerns, because it's structurally and
historically been based on short-term thinking.

FORTUN: What concepts do you rely on for teaching people to think about
ecological concerns?

HENSON: A whole systems approach to organizing—watershed conceptions. In Central Europe, one way I start is by asking people to draw the pic-

ture of the watershed they're in. Everybody in Central Europe is by a river.
There's the mountain towns and the big operations on the river; they've been
there for hundreds of years. And upstream is the same problem: the labor
union has got an interest that's definitely against the people downstream, and
that labor union is very concerned about the environment—regarding the
plant upstream polluting them—and they have even less interest in the labor
union upstream than they do in the environmental problems upstream. And
it's that mode of organizing out of self-interest that's got to be overthrown.
Then the farmers have got to talk to the nurses; the teachers have to talk to
the old folks. Because everybody's part of the same watershed.

FORTUN: How do you explain what a working, democratic society would
look like?

HENSON: I talk, and think, in terms of process, not in terms of point, of result. Because I don't think nature offers results. It's all process. We have to
focus on a result in order to aim ourselves. But I don't expect there is ever any
stasis. It's unnatural. It immediately falls apart because it's not supposed to be;
things aren't supposed to end, they're supposed to keep going, with all the
contradictions. I start there, philosophically. Thus the kind of experiment that
NTC was can be constantly revived in different movements. We learn something. We don't. That's what it's about. Trying to learn from the last mistakes,
adjust to changing conditions, keep doing a couple of principle things: be as
democratic as possible—democracy understood as process, not event—maximum participation, maximum accountability. But you can go too far, where
you don't get anything done.

Many movements have articulated decentralization well, avoiding dictation
en masse. The state socialist experience: a miserable failure. Expecting people
to act in common. Maybe they do in Sweden, where the culture is more homogeneous. I don't mean to generalize. But here, like most places, the experience is entirely different. We're better decentralized, imagined like spokes on
a wheel, where the wheel operates as a structure for us to operate as a whole,
when we choose. That's a North American solution.

China, for example, may be different. I've been reading this autobiography
of Mao and it really reminds of how different cultures can be. They've got
thousands of years of emperors, monarchical structures. People having a designated place in a cosmological order. People act expecting things to be laid
out—whether by Mao or some emperor, it's the same thing. Here, because of
this incredible thing that happened five hundred years ago—a New World—
in terms of European perception. It fundamentally changed our perceptions,
our cultural experience. We've severed the old ties. We're the New World.
It leaves us, as descendants, without any common ideology or cosmology.
That's what we've got to work with. I think it's an opportunity. It has been the
cause of most of our overconsumption problems, our imperialist endeavors,

that kind of detachment. It's allowed capitalism to reach its insane conclusion—fetishizing the individual as consumer. The cosmology of Manifest Destiny, having a separate god you are accountable to—which means we aren't accountable to each other, or to the earth. But at the same time, we aren't shackled, like the Chinese. To stereotype the Chinese, you can't change.

Here we're constantly reinventing whatever we want. That's valuable. And it's not just America. In Brazil, it's the same. The setup, in terms of what's possible, is virtually identical. A lot of other places in the New World. What is suggested is that to change things here we need to allow decentralization, states' rights, community identity. We're best coalescing, finding a common interest, assisting each other. Finding that kind of alliance, rather than a democratic centralist model which lays down the line from up high, asking people to respond.

We need a grassroots-based, decentralized spokes model. Where you have roundtables of representatives and they speak on behalf of others, with empowerment. When they go back to those they represent, they are accountable. Everyone else doesn't just fade away. That's a disaster in the making. We need to enhance those parts of our culture in which representative democracy can work really well. When representatives come back, they not only have to report, but they have to do the will of the group. They are not the leader; they are the representative. A national power structure, which is grassroots based.

Of course, it's rife with contradictions that occur with individuals. Fly somewhere and they become more important. They get interviewed by the newspapers, testify somewhere. But I don't know of a better way. Certainly, in this political context, I can't imagine a party structure like Sandinismo, where, given the historical and cultural traditions there, it made sense to develop a cadre structure, a Marxist, party-discipline structure. Things are laid out by people who can see the whole picture. When you are a foot soldier, you do the work, and if everyone does the work right, you win. If everyone wants to talk about it all the time, you lose.

FORTUN: What cultural context made the cadre model possible?

HENSON: Conditions exacerbated to a point where party discipline was necessary for survival. Those conditions can't happen in this country. We're too rich. Liberal democracy works too well. The wars in Algeria, Vietnam—they all had a party structure. You can't talk about it. You can't know everything. Those models are common. Virtually every modern revolution developed on some kind of Marxist cadre structure. Democratic centralization in one form or another. They were victorious, but they produced disastrous postrevolutionary results. I can't think of any model that actually worked after the victory. The Sandinistas are probably the best example of a total and complete victory. Ninety percent of the population supported. Everybody is happy. All the different parties lined up. But the party structure privileges the strongest party, and we know the problem then.

That can't happen here; conditions won't get to the point where Americans will turn off the TV and go into party discipline. It can't happen, I don't think. Although when you look at the worst-case outcome of GATT, we'll be more balanced with the rest of the world in terms of resource consumption. It's what we should be doing. But it won't be a move toward an equal or better quality of living through less consumption, but a chopping-off-people's-legs kind of approach to lowering them down. The crisis could fuel the kind of discontent that lead to the political movements which the sixties, or the thirties, produced. How to organize them is the question. In this country, the danger is that populism goes Right—with Ross Perot, all the way over to the Christian fanatics—before it can flip over into Hightower, a mirror image of Perot but with a different line. Appealing to "American" sensibilities: anti-government, anticorporate. People are anticorporate pretty easily. Antiright, antileft, oppositional.

VI. Practical Visions

FORTUN: What makes the difference in the direction populism takes?

HENSON: Organizing. The Christian Right has way out-organized us. They have done things that we gave up doing when we went professional. Direct mail was taken up as the only solution; we got totally stuck in that rut. We forgot to actually work with people. Also, I think it's a lot easier to pitch the cosmology, or ideology, that the Right's pitching. It's actually comforting for people: God will deal with things. It claims to know the answers. The existentialism of the Left is understandably less popular: it's a relative world and we have to take it in process.

FORTUN: Nationalist sentiment: is it a problem or a good thing?

HENSON: I think the antidote is solidarity rather than nationalism. Empathy is in there somewhere, too. I think solidarity is almost as easily embodied as nationalism—in individuals who are becoming politically aware through their own victimization, or crisis. The sharp edge can be ugly; it depends on how it's phrased. One response to losing your job is that it's the Mexicans' fault. It's an easy response, which feeds into a world we know about. So there's a Left version of nationalism, a unionism that says that human rights are important, but out of self-interest. In this country, a model of solidarity must go beyond NIMBY—Not in My Backyard—to NOPE, Not on Planet Earth. Understanding the position of everybody. At this point we'll only win if we all win together. If we can only get people to understand that we're getting played off each other—GATT may be the final showdown. Nationalism is the way they want to play it.

Our only hope is international solidarity. And the only way to access that is through people-to-people exchange. As a first step. The results are slow, but it works. Twenty-five people in a room. On Thursday you ask them what they

think of Mexico and you get twenty blatantly racist responses, and five not
comfortable going that far. Bring in two Mexican activists to tell their story
and you have twenty-five people crying in a room together, realizing that the
same son of a bitch who used to manage us is now managing a plant in Juarez.
And here's pictures of my kids, who are sick, too.

Then, it's no longer "the Mexicans." Then the organizer has to tell what it
is instead. People need a political line telling them who's the enemy. A line of
demarcation needs to be drawn. It simplifies, which can be a negative thing,
because it attracts old patterns of small world, small thinking. We need to expand the topography which each individual has in their head. And that's better
done through popular education methodologies. Instead of drawing a line of
demarcation which tells who is really behind it all, it can be drawn out. People
already know. They can say one-eighth of it. Piece together a construct. Tap-
ping what people know from their own experience about how the economy
works. It's not just a boss, it's not just a corporation, it's an economy. And
economy isn't good or bad, it's the way it works. It isn't capitalism or communism—I have a problem with the notion of capitalism. It's economy, the
mechanism of people's economic engagement. It's happening this way; how
can we tinker with the machinery of it to make it more democratic, more accountable, more responsible to people's needs?

FORTUN: Solidarity. Where do the obligations of elites fit in? Those who
aren't suffering, can't claim to be victimized? How do I tell an American professional that victimization in Bhopal is her problem? Does your construct of
solidarity let her off the hook?

HENSON: There's three things. Fairness. What's right, despite my birth luck.
Description that makes the suffering of others part of my own experience.
Understanding that but for the grace of God. . . . Appealing to empathy.

FORTUN: I have been told, by foreigners here, that Americans do seem to
have an extraordinary sense of fairness.

HENSON: I've heard it too, from people from other countries. I think it's because we're largely a classless society. So much more so than the Old World,
East or West. Caste, spiritual determination of worth, no opportunity to change.
Marx pegged the way this worked in Europe. In America, the last ten presi-
dents were actually poor kids. Clinton, look at his background. It's incredible
that ordinary people can reach greatness and power in politics, corporate
structures, entertainment, sports. It happens all the time here. George Bush is
the exception. But he's the standard elsewhere. So people here have a sense
that everybody kind of has a fair crack. Race, of course, suggests something
different. As does gender. But, still, fair play is what people think America is
all about. People should have an equal footing. Not so far as to cut into their
own equal footing, of course.

I think people have a sense that it all comes from the Constitution, that it comes from the culture of the Revolution. You have rights. Personal rights. Your person cannot be violated by the state, or other people. I have a right not to be exploited, beaten. I can say what I want. Amazing. Incredible, revolutionary stuff. And I think it has seeped into the culture.

FORTUN: So a culture of law still circulates?

HENSON: Absolutely.

FORTUN: Where does it come from?

HENSON: Television.

FORTUN: What? How? I don't watch much.

HENSON: I don't watch much either but can presume that shows model every situation that could ever happen; and most people watch six hours a day. Since we don't watch, someone's watching eight hours a day. Out there, there's a rhetoric that says you can make it. Sure there's corruption, and the further out in the hinterland you go, the more likely people won't think it unreasonable. But everybody goes to the movies. Think of them: the boldness with which people perceive their lives, it's incredible. They're having sex, trying to get rich, not barred by anything substantial. And it's always a story about a fight against the machine. It's the classic story. Whether the CIA or somebody else.

FORTUN: So you advocate the export of Hollywood to Central Europe as an organizing tool?

HENSON: No.

FORTUN: Then what are we getting at here?

HENSON: It's not necessarily a positive thing. People come to believe that they get what they get, and that it's me against everyone else. It's a race, a competition. All's fair, if you signed the contract.

FORTUN: So what's the alternative? An ethic of sacrifice, Gandhian aesthetics?

HENSON: Elites may be the way to think about this. They aren't being victimized; they have little interest in the fight; one has to appeal to a general sense of fairness. I think people have a biological predisposition: it's the classic opposition between individuality and communalism. It occurs in nature; it played out most dramatically in our time in the opposition of communism and capitalism, East and West. People have that within them, always struggling to ask how much for themselves, how much for others, knowing that, in the long run, they themselves won't propagate if they are too selfish: everyone will die off because we got overly individual.

The other appeal is to get them involved in the experience of intellectual transformation. I have a belief system, and it includes duty—which is different than doing what's fair. Most people would actually agree: Come on, give it up, you've already got yours, give something to them. The sense that I have a personal responsibility to do the right thing, where does it come from, and how does it work? I have very strong personal convictions, but nonetheless have a hard time feeling that I can convince someone else. An elite that doesn't have a sense of duty, doesn't think he needs one. It's not worth concentrating on. Converting elites can't be a priority.

FORTUN: What's the difference in teaching a sense of duty, and moralism, paternalism?

HENSON: I would never say that we need to have a sense of duty. I think that modeling, being who we are, is as good as we can do. People pick up, learn, or they don't. Creating environments where people can learn from each other. Like Highlander. You can facilitate, catalyze. You can't tell somebody, unless they are asking you to tell them.

FORTUN: Tell me how this place fits in.

HENSON: This is an eighty-acre facility. I had been looking for something like this with a group of people for six years or so. Something like this that was owned by a foundation, that would give us the right terms and we wouldn't have to get a bank loan. What we were looking for was a place with two main parts. One was a place to have an intentional community. I'm a very strong believer that solutions to my own involvement in overconsumption and many other problems is to reclaim community. I think that's the state of nature—much more than the fetishization of individualism that dominates in this country. And sharing resources is a better way of life for me in every way: I eat better; I work less; child rearing is shared; everything is shared. I have way more things: I have five guitars that I can play, instead of just my own. I can leave and my plants are taken care of. And there's a constant process of intentionality: What will we eat? How will we prepare it? What will we buy? What will we build with? We have agendas, and everything gets put on the agenda. I'm more honed and clear, spiritually centered, and productive in a community.

So we wanted a place to put roots down. We had been living in urban communities for a while. We were ready to disengage from the intensity of the city. I feel like I did my time. I spent fifteen years working as an activist in cities, and it was time—not to check out, but to put roots down in a more natural setting, and engage with the city for the rest of my life on different terms. So the first half was to have an intentional community.

The second half was to have a place where we can continue our educational work in the fields that we had been working in. And for us that's been an integration of arts, ecology, politics. It's a question of how humans are going to get by, and how we are going to construct ourselves. Putting root to our activism over the years. How it fits in with what I've learned as an activist and my experience as a grassroots organizer: I think it's particularly important now to have a place in our own minds, in our organizations, and physical places—to reflect. Reflection is always a cyclical part of any organizing. But I think we're in such a state of deconstruction—economically, culturally, everything—it's happening very quickly.

I'm very aware that when you're young, any time or any place in world history, it always seems that the world is always coming apart; your role is to help it out. The sky is always falling. And it's always getting better at the same time, in a weird way. And it's something to be aware of, to avoid the hyperbole of saying that now is the time to organize, or now is the time that we should do this and that. When we step back and look at the arc of history, the waves that go by, the oscillations—this is a particular place on the wave where there is a lot of transformation, but not much clarity. An incredible opportunity to reconstruct.

The pieces are all there. Other times it was much more the time to get out on the street and organize. In my own life I have felt that there have been times when civil disobedience and organizing a movement is most important. And it may also be where I'm at in my life cycle, that I want to take root again. Building from the base.

10

ARTISTS INCORPORATING: BUSINESS SAVVY
MEETS CREATIVE EXPERIMENTATION

ON ARTISTS INCORPORATING. *This piece is remarkable for documenting to what extent artists in their informal associations and minimalist concern with formally organizing themselves as business people have been in fact drawn into rather formal incorporations of themselves, with both subtle and obvious effects on their internal relationships and self-images.* – G. E. M.

* * *

The century-long history of a self-proclaimed artistic avant-garde, both in Europe and in the United States, has been characterized by a stereotype of such artists existing on the outer fringes of their given societies. This stereotype hinges on the assumption that such artists' ability to comment trenchantly on their social circumstances derives from their very distance—philosophical, political, or ethical—from mainstream social and economic structures. If we consider the overarching and defining sociopolitical structure of the contemporary United States to be corporate consumer capitalism, then we must ask to what degree this stereotype holds up.

The "art boom" of the 1980s in the United States offers a vivid example of the intersection of avant-garde sensibilities and mainstream socioeconomic structures. While the eighties witnessed heightened interaction between artistic production and larger markets, comparable connections between art worlds and broad social and political programs have long existed. One of the most convincing studies of such an ideological aggregate is cultural historian Serge Guilbaut's analysis of abstract expressionist painting as the signature artistic genre of the cold-war era in the United States. Guilbaut argues that the widespread success of the New York-based abstract expressionists in the late 1940s and 1950s was a function not only of their innovations of form and style but also of the movement's overall "ideological resonance" with cold-war liberalism (Guilbaut 1983, 2). Guilbaut identifies abstract expressionism as a genre that allowed its practitioners stylistically to break with the past without requiring explicit ideological or social commentary. The very apoliticism of abstract expressionism was in itself a political feature of the work that not only allowed it to be embraced by the mainstream but also to reflect the dominant centrist ideology of the cold-war United States. While Guilbaut concentrates on a specific genre and time period, his study underscores the overall embeddedness of cutting-edge artists within the social, political, and economic climate of the United States.

The visual arts in the United States continue to offer striking and complex examples of avant-garde artists' implication in mainstream social and economic structures. During the art boom of the late 1970s and 1980s consumption-oriented corporate capitalism was strongly reflected in shifts in the production and circulation of contemporary painting and sculpture. During this time certain visual artists were propelled to celebrity status and the prices of their work increased exponentially. This shift in the art world not only mirrored the general sensibility of the corporate world at that moment, but also had direct socioeconomic links that persist to this day, including the development of corporate art collections as an investment strategy. Furthermore, art dealers and certain artists themselves went beyond mere acceptance of consumerism, and began to cultivate key features of consumer culture, most notably celebrity and style. The artists who exemplified a nascent celebrity sensibility marked by an emphasis on style and personality include such colorful eighties figures as Jeff Koons and Julian Schnabel, artists that vigorously asserted their celebrity and squarely placed an emphasis on reputation and aura. Koons, among other lesser-known artists of this period, is known for hiring out the labor necessary to actually produce his work, a feature that links him to contemporary and historical entrepreneurial systems such as the factory and atelier.[1]

Just as the economic boom dominated by corporate culture of the 1980s was reflected in the markets and practices of the visual arts, so has the subsequent financial deflation of the late 1980s and early 1990s had resonances in U.S. art worlds. While many corporate trends do not have exact corollaries within the realm of the arts, what does bear comparison is a general shift in the orientation of artists to the business of producing and circulating their work. Within the corporate workplace, financial crisis has led to the phenomenon of downsizing, which places a premium on flexibility[2] as organizational hierarchies change and corporate personnel are asked to perform a wider variety of functions. During the period of the late 1980s and early 1990s, avant-garde artists have begun to display a style of business acumen characterized by a flexibility of thought and a newly keen awareness of funding resources and structures. Significantly, artists seem to be increasingly attuned to the funding patterns of corporate and private foundations, which differ in structure and philosophy from the public funding sources previously more familiar to them.

Intersections of Corporate Culture and Experimental Dance and Performance

The turn toward commercialism ushered in by the visual arts boom of the 1980s provides an almost transparent example of the ways in which corporate consumerism can generate and shape shifts in art worlds. A different face of corporate involvement in art worlds reveals itself in corporate foundations' support of cutting-edge dance and performance. Anthropologist and choreographer Cynthia Novack's explorations of the dance genre contact improvisation furnish models for examining experimental artists' links to mainstream culture (Novak 1990). Novack identifies the concerns and philosophies of this dance form and treats it as cultural formation with symbolic and sociological connections to popular cultural forms, social and political movements, and overarching cultural values. Importantly, she also identifies a tension between contact improvisation's ideology of experimentation and radical democracy and the desire of some of its practitioners at a certain moment to promote and market the form as a product. Her account of the debates about access and commercialism that occurred in the contact improvisation community in the late 1970s inform my exploration of analogous tensions in the contemporary dance world.

In late 1994 I discussed the concerns of independent artists with seven individuals active in experimental and avant-garde dance and performance in New York City. These individuals shared an affiliation with Movement Research, an organization created in the early 1970s to serve choreographers and dancers who were then exploring and establishing new forms of dance.[3] Over the past twenty years Movement Research has undergone a series of institutional changes illustrative of the changing aesthetic, philosophical, and economic issues facing contemporary independent choreographers. In speaking with four of the early members of Movement Research, two artists currently involved in Movement Research's programs, and the codirector of the organization, it became clear that this small-scale organization acts as a focal point for a range of concerns facing avant-garde artists. The following conversations reveal multiple paradoxes surrounding corporate involvement in an artistic milieu that is both decidedly marginal—due largely to the lack of marketability of its "product"—and constructed as politically oppositional and socially critical by the artists who comprise it. The central paradox is that values and structures of corporate culture shape certain elements of even this decidedly anticommercial and socially critical realm of artistic production. The intersection manifests itself both in the form of corporate foundational support for independent artists (often channeled through small-scale organizations such as Movement Research), and in the increasingly acute business savvy displayed by avant-garde artists in a wide range of circumstances.

The business of art enacted within avant-garde artistic communities differs significantly from the business of large ballet companies or symphonies. Beyond differences in scale and audience, experimental artistic production often relies on intermediary organizations such as Movement Research to channel funding between corporate foundations and independent artists. The flows of resources to avant-garde artists, the products they create, and the evolution of their worldviews constitute a complex and dynamic system. Anthropologist Elizabeth Traube argues that in order to grasp the complexities of cultural products, one must take into account the various stages of their production, circulation, and reception (Traube 1992, 4–5). Tracking such a circuit of production for experimental dance highlights both the moments at which corporate culture limits or restricts certain artists and their aesthetic projects and the moments at which corporate involvement gives rise to changes in artists' genre. Further, it facilitates understanding of the less-direct consequences of corporate involvement in art, such as artists' internalization of business acumen as a valued trait.

A number of direct economic and sociological connections to corporate culture are revealed in the following conversations as choreographers discuss strategies for interacting with foundations and articulate their dilemmas about how to organize their careers. For example, independent choreographers working with very small annual budgets are extremely knowledgeable on topics such as the legal and financial pros and cons of acquiring nonprofit status and the steps necessary to establish a board of directors for their dance company. The less tangible but related cultural connections to corporate culture surface in these interviews in the form of the tone and approach adopted by artists as they discuss the production and dissemination of their work. While these choreographers and their peers function in a noncommercial, nonprofit world, they nevertheless approach their work with flexibility of thought, resourcefulness, and a focus on technology as a way to achieve their goals—all traits associated with the ideal corporate self of the 1990s.[4] In these conversations, contemporary experimental artists seeking funding for their work intermittently reflect worldviews and career strategies strongly shaped by the values of a sector that they have implicitly disavowed by dint of their anticommercial and anticommodity career choice.

The Business Savvy of Contemporary Choreographers: Donna Uchizono

Donna Uchizono exemplifies the current generation of experimental artists who are acutely aware of the intricacies of public and private funding. As she herself describes it, Uchizono's work is characterized by "its wit, speed, and spicy movement." [5] An organizer in the downtown New York dance scene, Uchizono joined forces with choreographer Margarita Guergue in 1989 to begin the Bread to the Bone series at the Knitting Factory (primarily a music venue in downtown Manhattan). Bread to the Bone, directed and curated by Uchizono and Guergue, was meant to unite dancers and musicians in a situation free from the technical worries and production costs of a concert.[6] Conversing with Uchizono, I was struck by her broad knowledge of various foundations' and corporations' funding patterns, and by her ability to conceptualize problems and their potential solutions in terms of institutional structures.

Uchizono and I began by discussing her relationship to Movement Research, but the conversation quickly turned to her own history of grant seeking. Uchizono's narrative was distinguished by her propensity to perceive her personal experience as part of larger funding patterns and models that affect all independent artists in the field of dance and performance.

GEORGE: I have a general question that relates to your use of Movement Research as a fiscal agent. What other similar resources have you taken advantage of to help navigate your way through funding structures? Could you talk a little bit about your development as a choreographer seeking funding from various sources?

UCHIZONO: Well, there are some grants I receive, like National Endowment for the Arts and New York Foundation for the Arts grants, public grants, that don't require me as an artist to be a not-for-profit organization. So those I apply for directly. Now there are organizations that do require that the money be channeled through a 501(c)(3) arts organization, because they can only give money to a not-for-profit organization. Many independent choreographers don't have a board of directors and 501(c)(3) status, a fact that reflects something interesting that's happened in the last ten years of dance history. In fact, I was recently on a panel that was about the changing face of smaller-scale dance companies. One of our most pressing issues was that the resources that used to be available to develop a dance company no longer exist.

In the older model, independent choreographers would start out by asking different dancers to dance for them for a small amount of money. After awhile these choreographers would have their work produced by presenting organizations, usually small downtown theaters. At that point they would be recognized enough to develop a company with a board of directors and not-for-profit status, and able to pay dancers on a regular basis. That kind of support system has totally dropped. More and more, independent choreographers are artistically ready to receive a certain grant, but are not able to receive the grant because they do not exist as a not-for-profit entity.

Uchizono continues to clarify the role that intermediary organizations take in delivering funding to choreographers as she describes how she acted as a catalyst for a partnership between a particular foundation and a number of small-scale dance presenters and service organizations. In her discussion of the role she played in establishing a regranting program by the Joyce Mertz-Gilmore Foundation, she demonstrates the initiative, flexibility of thinking, and resourcefulness that enabled her to shape the existing financial structure to benefit herself and other independent choreographers.

UCHIZONO: Now we independent choreographers without our own companies use dance presenters and service organizations such as Movement Research as fiscal conduits, or fiscal umbrellas, when we apply to foundations and corporations that will only give grants to nonprofit organizations. In return, these organizations take a small percentage, say 5 to 7 percent, of the funds we receive. Lots of organizations do it. Because I'm considered a faculty member of Movement Research, they recently offered to manage the contributions for a benefit of mine. In that case they acted as my fiscal conduit, but what is unique about Movement Research is that they didn't take a percentage of that money. So yes, I use these presenting organizations to access funding.

The other way that I get funding is more indirect, through regranting programs. One of the regranting programs that I helped to set up was through the Joyce Mertz-Gilmore Foundation, which is a great foundation, but is very small, and has a small staff. So I applied for Joyce Mertz one year, and received a grant for my concert at P.S. 122. The next year I applied, they had totally restructured because they were flooded with grant applications. Because they have only three people on their staff, they simply couldn't handle the quantity of grant requests coming in. When I applied they wanted to give me a grant but they had changed their guidelines to reduce the number of incoming applications, saying that you could only get a grant if you had an annual budget of over $75,000, which most independent choreographers don't have. But they felt really bad and asked, How can we address this issue? So I recommended a way that they could give out the money to the artists that they wanted to fund without straining their staff resources. I said, Well, what if you do a regranting program where you give Danspace Project, Movement Research, DTW, P.S. 122, whatever, a chunk of money for their season that they in turn can give to the artists that they present? So I called a few different people like Laurie [Uprichard, at Danspace Project], David White [of DTW],[7] the Kitchen, and then we got this program started and so I'm indirectly getting money from Joyce Mertz through the presenting organization that presents me. In that way, I *do* get funding from presenting organizations.

Uchizono goes on to discuss her own process of deciding whether to become a not-for-profit organization. In her discussion, she refers to the key points of this debate in the experimental arts world at large, and makes clear that the benefits and drawbacks of incorporating are topics not only of informal discussion among artists but also topics for organized seminars and panels.

GEORGE: It's been very interesting to talk to people both formally and informally about the issues surrounding the acquisition of not-for-profit status. I know that many people my age, friends I went to school with, have a sense that you should get 501(c)(3) as soon as you can, and it seems like a burden to have to think about these things while trying to establish yourself as an artist.

UCHIZONO: Everyone has a different opinion on acquiring 501(c)(3) nonprofit status. We at Danspace Project, in the artist advisory meeting, had long discussions about whether independent choreographers should get a 501(c)(3). Ralph Lemon, who *has* a 501(c)(3), was totally against it. He said, "I don't think you should get it. That's my recommendation. If you can use a fiscal conduit, use it for as long as you can." Now there are some large foundations and corporations that will not fund through a fiscal conduit. He said, "But most of us are not at that level where the individual choreographer has to *be* the arts organization." I don't know of that many corporate foundations that won't fund artists through a fiscal conduit. Maybe Philip Morris doesn't. I'm not sure. But most foundations will. The thing about 501(c)(3) is that it takes a lot of work. You have to have a board of directors that is fiscally responsible for this organization. Also, most independent choreographers contract all of their work out, so most of the dancers are considered contract workers, which means they get a 1099 at the end of the year, and no taxes are taken out. Now, if you're a not-for-profit organization, those dancers would definitely be your employees, which means having to get involved with workman's compensation, Social Security, and state and local taxes. And you barely have the ability to pay them anything as it is. So I think that's why most people like myself are wary of taking that step. Sometimes I do wish I had a 501(c)(3), and other times I don't see the need for it.

Now why do you think your friend felt like it was important to get this?

GEORGE: It was one friend, my age, advising someone, about ten years older, who's been working for about fifteen years as an experimental music composer, and getting a fair amount of recognition, playing important venues, but still really struggling financially. And she, the younger friend, said, "You've just got to get your money situation together." I think it was about being professional, being able to approach presenters as a company entity, and lending a sense of legitimacy and clarity to her work.

UCHIZONO: All of those are really, really good reasons to have a 501(c)(3).

GEORGE: But this artist seemed to have a philosophical resistance to it. That why should she have to become a business person, and spend so much of her time doing that when really—

UCHIZONO: She just wants to make her own work.

GEORGE: Exactly, that was the sense I got from their debate.

Tensions Arising from Corporate Involvement in Dance Making: John Jasperse

Uchizono's knowledgeable discussion of the professional issues facing experimental artists provides a sense of the scope and depth of knowledge necessary for an independent artist to survive financially. Her personal career stories exemplify the flexibility and acuteness of business sense possessed by young choreographers working today. While Uchizono's commentary introduces a range of issues facing artists and indicates some of the paradoxes occasioned by corporate involvement in avant-garde art forms, her colleague John Jasperse elaborates some specific paradoxes and problems of corporate involvement in artistic production.

Jasperse is a choreographer active in the downtown Manhattan contemporary dance scene. An extraordinary technical dancer, he has danced with various companies both in the United States and in Europe. In the past several years Jasperse has started to receive National Endowment for the Arts choreography

A scene from John Jasperse's "Excessories" (1995). Photo: Maria Anguera de Sojo.

John Jasperse's "Excessories" (1995). Photo: Maria Anguera de Sojo.

fellowships on a regular basis, and has received a number of private foundation grants. Jasperse's choreography tends to be more technically precise and more abstract than that of his contemporaries. His recent full-evening work, "Excessories" (1995), reveals a new way of working as Jasperse layers more explicit social commentary (in this case about gender personas and personal adornment) over his virtuosic dancing.

Jasperse and I discussed the state of the field of experimental dance, including the problems and tensions that arise when funders and their criteria enter into the creative process. Jasperse sees the trend toward corporate and foundation funders favoring so-called community-based and process-oriented work as causing a shift in the way artists conceive of and produce their work. In addition to showing concern about the aesthetic implications of funding patterns, Jasperse comments on the effect of funders on the definition of the social role of the artist. As he sees it, public and private funders' growing reluctance to give fellowships with no strings attached creates situations in which preconceptions of corporate mentality and avant-garde sensibilities are radically upset. While funders take on the more humanistic mantle of community service, artists are increasingly searching for funding that will enable them to produce a finished work. Many artists understandably fear the imminent demise of fellowships that furnish funding necessary for them to concentrate on their work. As Jasperse describes a number of projects in which he has participated, he acknowledges and questions the effect on his creative process of the "ready-made structures" that result from changes in funders' view of the role and nature of experimental art and independent artists.

GEORGE: The premise of this article is that things are changing dramatically now for artists and you can track a lot of those changes through service organizations and presenters, especially in what they're asking artists to do and what they, in turn, are doing for artists. More and more presenters are acting like service organizations as they administer regranting programs. I think this reflects both economic changes and changes in the perceived social role of the artists. I'm not sure that you can go back to 1963 and claim that the role of the artist is solely to change people's perceptions, which is the sense I got from Wendell [Beavers, an early member of the Movement Research collective]. I understood him to be saying that the truly radical potential of dance is to change the way people see, in a sort of abstract way. That's just not the kind of work that people are making anymore.

JASPERSE: I don't know, I think that depends on the person. I'll give you a perfect example, "furnished/unfurnished" [1993], that table piece of mine, which I feel really good about. I feel like there are certain social things that are happening within that work, but is that really about activism or social consciousness, per se? Is it about making a really overt political statement or is it about precisely dance itself as a political form, about what it means to be dancing? I don't know, maybe that's a much stronger way of being political. To be dancing at all now is such a radical thing, and so, in contrast to what the status quo value system is, maybe it's just inherently a political statement. That's really what I feel. What I'm saying is that that particular piece is not specifically built out of any kind of political content, it's built out of something else, it addresses something else. And I *do* think it's about changing the way people see. I mean, it's this formalist investigation of certain kinds of principles that hopefully resonates on a larger plane.

GEORGE: Well, maybe I overstated it. But I do think there is currently a lot of pressure, and it's difficult to identify exactly where it's coming from, but there's an awful lot of pressure to make work that is much more explicitly—

JASPERSE: —socially relevant.

GEORGE: Yes, both in the content of the work and also in terms of the focus on so-called community work.

JASPERSE: Oh, definitely, completely.

GEORGE: And in a way it's a kind of pseudoradicalism, that pressure to be "political," because it can reflect a very narrow and specific definition of what it means to be politically or socially aware. When granting agencies begin to adjust their funding criteria to encourage art to have some kind of direct, positive social impact, what's at play is the economically powerful defining what constitutes social and political awareness. So I think it can get really convoluted.

JASPERSE: I totally agree. Because what I was trying to get at by describing my piece as formalist investigation is that at this point in time there's something inherently radical about practicing an art form that doesn't exist in a tangible way but is a more experiential thing. As soon as you stop doing it, as soon as you stop dancing, it isn't there anymore. We don't produce a product, really. That's quite a major, major thing. What's more, we're not particularly, solely interested in entertaining people. That seems to me so against current ideas that I think it *is* a big social statement.

I'll give you another example of the problems of defining what it means to be making a social or political statement as an independent choreographer. This friend of mine is doing a big project right now, funded through Creative Time [another New York-based arts service organization] with a school in Brooklyn, and it's all about getting kids involved in dance, and specifically trying to address gay and lesbian youth in this minority community. It's like *the* kind of project that you can imagine getting funded, it's got all the elements. But, again, I feel like unless that's really the focus of what you're doing, it probably won't work to try to fit your work into such a context. I think that has to come from a real organic place for that to work. And I haven't felt like that's happened to me; those possibilities haven't presented themselves.

GEORGE: Well, that's kind of what Donna was saying yesterday, too. We were talking how DiverseWorks is restructuring the way they program their performances and exhibitions. Instead of presenting, say, thirty weekends of performance a year, they're going to be commissioning much more new work and doing long-term residencies where artists would stay in Houston for extended periods of time, and, again, work with different communities. A big impetus for thinking about restructuring has been the prospect of receiving a challenge grant from the National Endowment for the Arts [since awarded to the organization]. So it was, in part, the prospect of that funding that has caused the staff of DiverseWorks to rethink the goals and mission of the organization. That shift in focus is interesting to me because I think it indicates a larger trend on the part of alternative spaces, which are responding to the wishes of funders and passing that on to artists.

JASPERSE: But how do you feel about that?

GEORGE: Well, somewhat differently in the past couple days, talking to you and Donna Uchizono about these things. The idea of artists doing extended residencies and special projects in conjunction with a particular organization sounds like such a good idea—artists will come to a place, spend more time there, and get to make work. But having gone through this recent month-long residency project and hearing you reflect on your experience of it has really given me a different view of it. What I seem to be hearing is that, from an artist's perspective, maybe thirty weekends of work where you bring the artist in, have them perform their work and pay them for that, thank you very much, that that is "cleaner" in a way.

JASPERSE: Well, what's really interesting to me and I've dealt with this time and time again—once the show is done, that's it. I spend a year developing a piece, I perform it three or four times, and basically it totally changes me and everything that I make after it. So it's not like the work is not with me in some way, but largely it gets thrown in the trash can. The moment it's been performed, it's old. Especially in this country, it's just hopeless to get gigs, and part of this is the expense involved if you're talking about moving group work around. What does it mean to spend a year developing something that gets performed four times? I really start to wonder. Clearly it's not a way of working that can be sustained in the current economic situation in the dance world, and yet my work has gotten a lot stronger because I have worked that way. So what's the answer? Is it to continue to work very quickly and make things that are by and large disposable in terms of the product, as I have been doing? Or is it to begin to concentrate on developing processes which bring you into contact with other people, which seems to be a much more appropriate response to the financial situation. I don't know what to say because that's not what I'm doing right now. So I feel really mixed about the whole thing.

Jasperse gives an example of the ways in which the agenda or criteria of an arts funder can cause dilemmas for an artist, and how it is often unclear whether the specifications of a given grant will impinge upon the creative process and product or whether the project will open up new vistas for the artist.

JASPERSE: To take a perfect example, this Mexico project that I'm probably going to do next year with Movement Research, and I'm excited about it, yet James Lo, the composer who I was collaborating with, immediately said, "Well, what are you going to do? What's the point of going to Mexico for two months?" Because I can't bring any dancers or other collaborators with me, so it is a little confusing to me, and I started to be concerned and wanted to be really clear on the goal of this project. What are the expectations, and what can I do that will benefit me as well as be feasible in the context of the situation? And I haven't really found the answers to all of those questions. It's not so clear to me. And yet, it's an exceptional opportunity.

GEORGE: What is the project, exactly?

JASPERSE: Movement Research put together this program; it's a pilot program, funded through the Rockefeller Foundation. It's a residency project where Sondra [Loring, another New York-based independent choreographer] and I are the two artists from New York who would go to Mexico—Monterey and Mexico City, one of us to each—to live for two months and work there. And two Mexican artists, at some other point, would be coming to New York City—all part of the same exchange.

GEORGE: Two months, that's a long time.

JASPERSE: Yes, it's a very long-term project. It clearly needs to be defined well. What exactly are the expectations? Am I supposed to go down and teach class for two months? The money is not what I would want to do that exclusively. If not, what else am I doing with that time? Am I working with people from there? Who are those people? Is it realistic to expect that there's a community of people that I could find to investigate something that would be mutually beneficial? Or are the experience and the aesthetics going to be so divergent that the project will really be about me going in to stimulate a community? Then it's all confusing to me, because I have to ask, is it my priority, or is another one of these ready-made structures that is being presented, but again, do I fit into that structure? And I still need to clarify that.

Mary Overlie and Cynthia Hedstrom

The reflections and positions taken by Uchizono and Jasperse reflect the career-related concerns of contemporary independent choreographers. Their particular assumptions and concerns are characteristic of the 1990s and of the constellation of influences—institutional, economic, political, and historical—on their work. Although their ties to corporate culture are particularly complex and their awareness of certain paradoxes of their working conditions especially astute, the general problem of a corporate mentality impinging on experimental choreography is not at all new. Discussions with founding members of Movement Research revealed that they, too, had a historically resonant awareness of and relationship to the business and economic dimensions of their endeavors. The changes in the experiences and philosophies of artists involved with Movement Research reflect a shifting matrix of relationships between artists, funders, and commercial and corporate sectors. Just as Uchizono and Jasperse are implicated in corporate culture of the nineties both sociologically (through receipt of foundation grants) and culturally (as displayed by the degree and style of their business acumen), so were the founders of Movement Research drawn into the corporate and commercial realities of the seventies.

The following conversation with Mary Overlie and Cynthia Hedstrom revolves around the circumstances of the founding of Movement Research as an institution. Both Overlie and Hedstrom continue to serve on the advisory board of the organization, but have not been active in the governance of the institution for nearly a decade. Hedstrom is the producing director of the Performing Garage, an experimental theater located in the Soho area of Manhattan; Overlie, in New York for an international dance festival at the time of this interview, teaches and practices improvisational dance forms in the Netherlands. As they jointly recall the early days of Movement Research, they offer concrete information about its collective structure, and also convey a sense of the shared adventure of its creation.

GEORGE: I wanted to start with a little bit about each of you in relationship to Movement Research.

OVERLIE: I haven't been working with Movement Research for years and years, but my memories of it are standing on Canal Street, outside of Renee Rockoff's loft in between two parked cars, and I know Danny [Lepkoff] was there, I think you were there, Cynthia. So I just said, "We need to start an organization," and I thought that we could do it as a collective, and sort of make a central location for workshops to advertise themselves, and organize them so that people could come into the city and know where to go. Because it was getting harder to keep track of all the activity happening at that time. People kept coming up to me and asking me where do I study, what's the date of the workshop? I just thought that it needed to happen, and to my total surprise everyone agreed. It sort of started right then, it seemed. We had the first meeting, and just started out from there. That was in 1975.

GEORGE: So the primary impetus was to have a centralized source of information?

HEDSTROM: That's right.

OVERLIE: Yes, it was about gathering information together and providing some support for people giving workshops. But, also, the other idea behind it was somehow to represent the downtown work in a supportive manner. It's always been like that for Movement Research, there's always been this sense of sort of being able to keep it alive. When I left, when I actually disengaged, the next thing I wanted to do was to hire a Madison Avenue advertising team to try to sell postmodern dance like you sell Marlboro cigarettes [*laughs*]. I wanted to do that very much. There's always been that aspect to the organization of trying to bring attention to postmodern dance. Like a kind of real brass tacks support but also an attempt to look toward a future way of keeping the whole scene alive, and keeping the audience coming to see postmodern dance.

Overlie's half-joking desire to hire a marketing firm to sell postmodern dance seems at first to indicate a move toward a more commercial way of viewing the field of dance. However, she quickly reveals that the goal of such an approach would be to increase the visibility of the form and, as she says, "to keep the whole scene alive." Corporate and commercial models are seen as of potential benefit to an entire community of dancers and audiences rather than as ways to build up individual careers or develop a particular organization. For the founders of Movement Research the question of marketability of dance is linked partly to their split from the visual arts that occurred toward the end of the seventies. Dancers and choreographers whose work was presented alongside their peers in the galleries of lower Manhattan witnessed an artistic and economic transition as a number of their peers in the visual arts became increasingly successful through the sale of their work in commercial galleries. Overlie and Hedstrom comment on the lack of marketability of dance and the change in the gallery scene as an impetus for starting Movement Research.

OVERLIE: Another impetus for Movement Research is that in the seventies most of the galleries allowed dance performances because the art scenes were closer at that time because of the Happenings. Most of my early performance experience in New York was in art galleries—John Weber's gallery was an important one, for example. But then the galleries started to pull back, insurance became an issue and I always suspected that it was more about the fact that you couldn't sell this work as a tangible product. They started saying, "Well, we can't insure your safety, we can't give the time over to dance." When they started taking their support out, it further marginalized the scene because we could no longer meet in the galleries and watch each other perform. The galleries had been the central contact point for everybody. And when it started to disappear, people got put on third floors in private lofts, and it was hard to just find people. So another impetus for Movement Research to start was the desire to at least have a flyer to let people know where things were happening.

The Changing Contours of Movement Research:
Cathy Edwards's Organizational History

As Uchizono, Jasperse, Hedstrom, and Overlie relate their experiences of making dance and their efforts to receive funding, they reveal flows and resources and information as well as general worldviews that constitute the cultural circuit of experimental dance in the United States. Cathy Edwards, codirector of Movement Research from 1990 to 1995, is an articulate young arts administrator with an informal yet no-nonsense demeanor that spills over into the personality of the organization. Edwards's lively account of the development of the organization furnishes a whirlwind tour of two decades of the central economic, aesthetic, and social concerns of experimental choreographers, dancers, and performance artists. Her commentary reveals the changing contours of cultural circuit of avant-garde dance and performance and also shows how alternative arts organizations operate as a nexus for art worlds and corporate culture by mediating, reflecting, and shaping trends in corporate involvement in avant-garde art.

Wendell Beavers, an early member of Movement Research and its director from 1981–83, per-
forms his work at the historic Judson Church as part of the Movement Research at the Judson
Church series begun in the early 1990s under the direction of Cathy Edwards and Guy Yarden.
Photo: Anja Hitzenberger.

GEORGE: Why don't we start with you telling me how you see the evolution
of Movement Research.

EDWARDS: My narrative of the story, and it is a bit of a constructed narrative, is that the old artist-run board came to a point where they didn't want to
do everything themselves. So they hired a part-time administrative person,
and that position changed hands several times but never really amounted to
anything. It was a situation where the person worked for four hours a day,
nobody else knew what those four hours were, there was a phone there, probably for the first few years there was no answering machine, then there was
an answering machine, but there was no call waiting, so you could never get
through because the line was always busy. So the organization was sort of im-
penetrable to the people who weren't part of it. It was practically like a service
organization for twenty artists, and they took workshops from each other; it
was really built around the idea of the workshop. And there were some other
great things happening at the same time. There were artist-driven things like
the Studies Project [the brainchild of Mary Overlie], which was curated by
individual artists, and some of them were really fascinating, and there were
a few dance series, one was at the Summer Garden, and that was a really big,
exciting thing. But the core of the organization was postage-stamp-sized, and

this administrative person was paid probably five dollars an hour, and also in kind by being able to take workshops and classes. It was really a nonprofessional situation. And I think that situation lasted until Richard Elovich was hired to be the first executive director, he was probably hired as director, and he turned himself into executive director; the others had all been administrative director or administrator.

Elovich was a pivotal figure for the organization. In addition to moving the organization from a collective structure to a more bureaucratic one, with a board of directors drawn from an entirely new group of people, including administrators and directors of other arts organizations, Elovich gave Movement Research a completely new artistic and political profile.

GEORGE: When was Richard hired?

EDWARDS: Well, I started in 1990, so he was hired in 1987, because he was there for three years when I got there. So from basically 1977 to 1987 it was a postage-stamp-sized little organization. Richard came on and the board had remained basically the same, from my perspective, but they were getting less and less interested in the organization because they had moved on, in some sense. Richard actually was the first person to go in and say, "I am the director of this organization. You, the board, in a sense work for me and my vision, as opposed to me being there to do your mailings." Previously the role of the administrator was to say, "You guys have done the artistic vision part of this puzzle, and I'm doing the manual labor to make that happen." Richard totally switched around that model and began working in the model of David White of Dance Theater Workshop and Mark Russell of P.S. 122 and other Executive Directors and he reshaped the board. He didn't pull in a money board at all, but he pulled in a somewhat high-powered administrative board—Laurie Uprichard [of Danspace Project] joined the board, Bill T. Jones joined the board, Cee Brown from Creative Time and Art Matters joined the board, Jennifer Monson [choreographer] joined the board, and other artists he felt were representative, Yoshiko Chuma, Eiko [of butoh duo Eiko and Koma].

GEORGE: Were these artists you're mentioning people who had taken workshops during the early years?

EDWARDS: These were people who Richard knew personally to some extent. He had directed the Monday-night series at the Poetry Project at Danspace, and he had done a lot of performance art things himself. So he knew people. And I think that someone like Eiko had actually taught an annual workshop at Movement Research for several years until then. And Bill T. Jones, I don't know that he had actually ever done anything at Movement Research except for one very famous Studies Project, he and Steve Paxton. Richard knew Bill T. historically because they were both gay activist figures.

I think they were on a march to Washington and Richard said that they were sitting on the bus together and Richard asked Bill to join the board and Bill agreed to.

Richard embarked on a really ambitious re-envisioning of the organization because the infrastructure of the organization was not up to his vision. That's my reckoning of the situation. He wanted to go on full-time, he wanted to make a reasonable salary, he wanted to have an assistant, an administrative assistant, and interns in the office, he wanted to do a permanent presenting series instead of occasionally, he wanted to do a lot *more* workshops, and he really wanted to introduce performance art. Karen Finley taught a workshop, Reno taught a workshop, there was just a sense of excitement around the program. It wasn't only performance people either, but dance people like Stephen Petronio who were not only doing contact improvisation.

So Richard had this great expansive vision. And he was a real out-there activist, but as the years went on, the financial problems of the organization became more acute. When I came there was a real situation of robbing Peter to pay Paul, where, for example, you get a grant for artists, but you spend it for administrative salaries or overhead, and then when you have to pay the artists six months later you have to dip into something else, and that was a problem. The visibility of the organization rose at the same time that its financial and infrastructure problems also increased. Richard brought the annual budget up to $100,000, which was a big watershed. He was really proud of that, and it was really exciting that Richard had such a great vision of arts in a culture that was really unreceptive at that time. It still is, but I think it felt more exciting, and there were censorship wars and AIDS activism and ACT-Up. There was just so much going on, and he was a real spokesperson for all of that. But, you know, it alienated a lot of the old guard, too. And I think there was also a sense that organizationally we weren't fulfilling our promise to artists, which was also true. Because we weren't paying people on time, we weren't really paying people enough, and the fund-raising was inconsistent. There's this famous story about how Richard hired someone to do part-time development, and the person just forgot about the NEA deadline and missed it for the Services to the Field category, which was where we always used to get three or four thousand dollars. That deadline was totally missed in 1989, I think the year was. Things were just all over the place and then Richard began getting more and more burned out by that, and then he hired me. As soon as he hired me, it was really clear that he wanted to leave because he felt the organization was in fairly capable hands.

So when I got there I really felt like it was an organization with a big vision and a lot of potential that Richard had tapped, but that things were just really chaotic in terms of the running of the programs and in our relationships with artists. I didn't feel like we were actually really serving our community that effectively. So then Guy [Yarden, an experimental music composer and arts administrator] and I officially took over as codirectors.

The aggressive, innovative, and growth-oriented Elovich that Edwards describes epitomizes some of the trends of the art world of New York in the 1980s. Moreover, the rapid expansion of the budget and programs of Movement Research, an accomplishment which caused Elovich himself to "burn out," resonates with corporate economic trends of the Reagan-era United States. Edwards describes the transition from the 1980s to the 1990s as involving streamlining and focusing the goals of Movement Research. Intriguingly, the restructuring of Movement Research that correlated to corporate downsizing coincided with a personal career decision on Edwards's part to eschew the excesses of a very high-budget, high-profile international arts organization for the challenge of running and stabilizing a small-scale arts organization.

GEORGE: How did Richard find you?

EDWARDS: I was working at a really fancy international arts organization, the American Center in Paris, in their New York office, which they had just opened, and it was a really absurd job. All I did was shop for beautiful office furniture and leather couches and Conran's desks, and we had a huge office in the Puck building, and there were only two of us, because the American Center in Paris had this ambitious expansion plan and they had millions and millions of dollars to build a fantastic new building in Paris, and they decided to open the New York office to work with artists from the United States. But then they decided that, well, actually, the building won't be finished for three more years, so starting to work with artists is a little premature, but we hired these two people, I guess they can do fund-raising instead, which neither of us wanted to do. But the one thing that did happen was that my boss was Betsy Gardella, David White's wife, and so she introduced me to people and things, to actual dance and performance that was happening, and I could go to DTW [Dance Theater Workshop]. I didn't even know DTW existed until then.

And so then I heard that Richard and Movement Research were looking for someone, and I called him up and I went over there and talked to him, and he basically said, "If you want the job, it's yours." It was the managing director job. So I just realized that it was a *real* place. I mean, it was depressing, it felt really under siege—the heat never worked there, it was really dark, and Richard was really gloomy. Also, there wasn't a ton of artist traffic. But I still felt like I could see so much potential. I walked in and the Bebe Miller Company was rehearsing in the studio, and it felt like a place where art was actually being made, and I loved the idea that there were dirty dance socks right outside the door to the studio; it just felt so removed from where I had been. So, I said, "Okay, I'll do it." And that's how I ended up there.

Ideological changes accompanied the structural changes of the organization during the late eighties. Elovich brought with him to the organization the passions and sensibilities of identity politics and anticensorship activism. The generational shifts in the organization and its personnel find their most compelling expression in debates over just what constitutes political awareness or engagement. The fall 1991 publication of *Performance Journal,* the third volume of Movement Research's quarterly journal treating issues of concern to the dance and performance community, was instrumental in giving form and expression to these differences. The topic of this issue of *Performance Journal* was "gender performance" and the issue contained articles on topics from gender inequality in modern dance forms to expressions of gay sexuality. In addition, a photo essay on transsexuals by performance artist Annie Sprinkle appeared, alongside an article vehemently (and in sexually explicit language) condemning a Supreme Court ruling restricting publicly-funded clinics from providing information about abortion. The latter article, accompanied by a large photograph of female genitalia, caused Movement Research to be drawn into the arts-censorship and arts-funding debates. The form of political radicalism embraced by the current generation did not in itself generate tension; rather, tension resulted from clashing definitions and perceptions of what it means to be a politicized artist. As Edwards reveals, for a younger generation, politicization often means using art to respond directly and explicitly to events and injustices in the world. For the founding members, politicization generally took the form of using art to change fundamental perceptions and assumptions of artists and audiences. In the conversation that follows, Edwards touches on myriad changes in the philosophical, political, and economic concerns and assumptions of independent artists.

GEORGE: Do you think under Richard there was a rift in terms of the organization's connection to its own history?

EDWARDS: In a sense, yes. I mean, the history was still reflected in the organization, but he maintained a lot of the workshop teachers, I think, for purely financial reasons, because he knew that those workshops would make some money, 30 percent of which would go back into the organization. But, the context in which those workshops existed was an organization that was becoming really radicalized, and those artists teaching workshops weren't welcome in the rest of the organization. They wouldn't feel comfortable in the Studies Projects, which were about issues of censorship or HIV, for example. I think the breaking point, when the older group of artists finally rebelled, was the publication of *Performance Journal* number 3. They came to me and Guy and said, "Let's separate the calendar of workshops offered by Movement Research from the journal. The calendar and the journal are not reflective of each other. We feel uncomfortable being in that environment." It's not an ongoing battle anymore, but it really *was* for a year. And *we* felt like it was really important to keep the two integrated and to both provide increasingly political workshops to match a more political profile of the organization. Not that we have a single political stance, but one thing is that we really do feel grounded in contemporary culture, not in the culture of the 1970s. And it is politicized in certain ways that those artists in the seventies weren't politicized, and they haven't changed. I mean, they have their houses in the country. A lot of those people moved up to Vermont in the eighties; some have moved to upstate New York. They want to keep things the ways they were. They bought their loft spaces or they did whatever they did. I'm not saying they were rich and successful, but they were able to remove themselves to some extent, and the rest of us, the younger people, like Donna Uchizono and John Jasperse, don't want to, they're part of this particular mix, we don't want to step away, it's what makes art interesting to us, is that it's reflective of a particular culture. But anyway, on the other hand, I think we've also toned down the journal a lot from *Performance Journal* number 3, I hope not in a substantial ideological way, but I think we've broadened it, deepened it, and made it more interesting than this sort of in-your-face statement, which that was a little bit.

GEORGE: Whose idea was *Performance Journal* number 3?

EDWARDS: That was Richard. Richard kicked off so many things, I really feel like the vision has shifted now. Richard was bored with artists and dance when he left. He didn't enjoy working with choreographers, and he didn't enjoy working with the old guard. People didn't really feel a connection with him or the office. They came in and they did their workshop and just left. It was all disjointed. But I think that the difference in vision that Guy and I have added is that we actually really do care, and we want to make relevant things happen. And we take pride in the fact that we are so rooted in the dance community, that's really important to us.

GEORGE: One thing that's really interesting to me is the connection to Judson Church, a space which links Movement Research to an earlier moment in recent dance history. How do you see your connection to Judson and the postmodern dance movement that has become synonymous with that space?

EDWARDS: In one way, it's simply that Judson was willing and interested in supporting whomever asked. I think that's what happened for those artists in the sixties, and what happened in the nineties when we just went back to the church and just asked. I think, in another sense, it was our feeling like we want to shamelessly capitalize on the Judson legacy and get a lot of visibility from doing that, and it was irrelevant how consciously we worked with that or didn't work with that. To be honest, Guy and I used to joke that we were sort of happily exploiting Judson, which I think was actually fine and great, there was nothing negative about it. I mean, all these young people really wanted to do things there, see it, and feel like, "I performed in the same place as the founders of postmodern dance." But no, I don't think there was necessarily an organic connection. I mean, the work that they were doing back then, I feel like it was all about abstraction. Even though it was also incredibly pedestrian, I think of it as fitting in with the visual art of the time. And now I feel like a lot of dance is both about really politicized identity stuff, or it's about really beautiful dance movement, neither of which was happening back then.[8] Ideally, I think that what's happening at Judson now, and what happened back then reflects the artistic sensibility of a certain era. And those sensibilities are different.

GEORGE: I think Movement Research having its Monday-night series at Judson is great; even though the contemporary work is very different, the history of Judson is very powerful.

EDWARDS: Another thing I want to say about Judson is that Movement Research benefited from Judson in a big way, but on the other hand, the Judson name was so big that I think it has actually overshadowed Movement Research this time around. So many people, in their biographical materials, will say, "I was presented at the Judson Church," and Movement Research isn't mentioned anywhere in there. At the beginning of the Judson series we looked around and thought, Nobody in this room knows who Movement Research is, they're just here because they're at the Judson Church. And we've tried to do a lot of educating about that. But it's funny, it has brought a lot of people to us, but it's also "Judson," and Movement Research will always be the smaller part of that. Also, the Judson Church is a political space, it really is. So it's nice to be situated in that context.

GEORGE: I think no matter how apolitical the work from the seventies may appear by nineties standards, they really felt that the new ground they were forging artistically was politically relevant. Wendell Beavers was saying that the Movement Research collective was even more radical than identity politics because they were breaking down people's whole ways of seeing.

EDWARDS: Yes, definitely. I see it as a continuum. In no way do I denigrate what's come before us. I think it's our burden to live up to a lot of the research and development that happened before us. But, still there are clashes. I still remember this one conversation Guy and I had with Simone Forti and Steve Paxton after *Performance Journal* number 3. They said, "We want to go out to lunch with you and express some of our concerns and thoughts," and they really took us to task on a lot of things. We were flabbergasted, because we thought of those two, especially Steve Paxton, as having the most out-there, in-your-face, political, disruptive sensibility to the status quo of the sixties. But they said, "This journal is all about sex, it's all sexual identity, sexual identity, can't anybody talk about anything more than their genitals?" That was really the sense that we were getting from them. We were just so surprised that these people, of all people, couldn't understand the relevance, even if for no reason at all beyond confronting propriety or the status quo. We were really surprised that they were so unwilling to see that in an art context.

GEORGE: So you were surprised by the force of their reaction?

EDWARDS: I was shocked. I feel like Simone and Steve actually really listened to us, which was great, but I don't feel like they agreed, underneath it all. We had this fantastic conversation; I wish *that* had been tape-recorded for all time, because it was really intense. There was Simone, Steve, Cathy, and Guy, this major difference in generations, but all having had responsibility for the organization at one point. And they said, "You know, we don't think the workshops should be seen in the context of the *Performance Journal.*" They brought that up, saying, "We're not interested in this. Why is it so important? Why is it so relevant? There are other things really worth thinking about." And we just tried to say to them, "Isn't that what people were telling you in the sixties?" It was just so weird. But, in the end, I just love the fact that they cared so much to say anything. I thought that was pretty great.

Postscript

During the time that has elapsed since these conversations took place, the National Endowment for the Arts (NEA) has suffered a 40 percent reduction in funds and a nearly 50 percent reduction in staff. Although none of the artists or administrators I talked with would claim that the NEA is the sole determinant of any one artist's or arts organization's financial stability, all would agree that policy decisions and funding available from the NEA have a major impact on independent artists and alternative arts organizations. The recent announcements by the NEA that their regranting programs have been abolished and the more devastating news that fellowships to individual artists will be discontinued in all disciplines except for literature beginning with the 1996 fiscal year signals the advent of a new era for avant-garde artists and alternative arts organizations. Independent artists such as Uchizono and Jasperse typify the kind of recipient most likely to benefit from fellowships and regranting programs.

It is no coincidence those artists most likely to create controversial work will be the most deeply affected by the NEA cuts. Fellowships and regranting programs have both presented problems for the NEA in terms of "accountability." That is, the no-strings-attached nature of a fellowship and the transfer of decision-making power to an intermediary body that occurs in regranting programs represent a gap between the final artistic product and the NEA's imprimatur. This gap becomes a problem for the federal agency when their funds end up financing a controversial project. As entrepreneurialism and downsizing migrated to avant-garde art worlds from the corporate sector in the 1980s and early 1990s, respectively, so is the notion of accountability, a buzzword of contemporary corporate management philosophy, currently seeping into the sphere of experimental artistic production.

The demise of a number of NEA programs will force independent artists and arts organizations to strengthen their ties to private-sector funders. Over the past two or three years, the NEA itself has strengthened *its* connections with the private sector (and with other federal agencies) as it has begun increasingly to focus on forging partnerships as a way to keep the arts alive. Partnerships reflect the NEA's interpretation of the rhetoric of privatization. Accountability, privatization, and partnerships dominate the models available to independent artists and arts organizations as we move toward the twenty-first century. As with earlier paradigms such as entrepreneurialism, flexibility, and downsizing, these newer models are sure to resonate within art worlds and even to change their contours, but need not, as is understandably feared at the moment, dominate or destroy this intellectually and creatively vital sphere. Perhaps, ironically, the very adaptability of avant-garde artists to mainstream cultural and socioeconomic changes and trends, and *not* their ability to stand completely outside of the mainstream, will prove to be the key to survival.

Notes

1. Even the more "outsider" artists from this era, such as Jean-Michel Basquiat and Keith Haring, courted celebrity in their own way. The original sense of immediacy and oppositionality in their work (as epitomized by their ties to graffiti art) was transformed into a kind of consumerist-inflected disposability. Basquiat would paint on nightclub walls lending the venue a hip cachet, and Haring's symbols and graphics turned up everywhere from political-slogan T-shirts to, more recently, Honda ads.

2. Although I hadn't read anthropologist Emily Martin's *Flexible Bodies* at the time I was writing this article, its publication sparked a good deal of discussion in my immediate academic community. The notion of flexibility as characteristic of a moment in the recent history of the United States is certainly related to that interest in and discussion of Martin's book.

3. In addition to the five individuals whose voices are represented here, two other early members of Movement Research, Danny Lepkoff and Wendell Beavers, talked with me at length about the organization. Lepkoff, a founding member of Movement Research, was also an important figure in the contact improvisation movement in the 1970s. Beavers, currently associate director of New York University's Experimental Theater Wing, was the director of Movement Research from 1981 to 1983. Thanks are also due to Audrey Kindred, who took over as acting director of Movement Research in 1995, for loaning the photograph of Wendell Beavers.

4. Traube's work is the inspiration for identifying manifestations of the ideal corporate self in unlikely places. In *Dreaming Identities,* her study of Reagan-era Hollywood movies, she argues that the style of the heroes in four particular movies that present images of success and mobility (including the hit *Ferris Bueller's Day Off*) reflects and reaffirms the 1980s notion of the ideal corporate self, which she characterizes as "a cool, breezy, highly verbal, yet distinctly boyish style of rebellious independence" (1992, 68).

5. Donna Uchizono, personal communication, Sept.1995.

6. Cultural historian Sally Banes cited Bread to the Bone as exemplary of the trend toward a pared-down mode of operating that distinguishes the experimental dance scene of the 1990s from the growth period of the 1980s (1994, 346–47).

7. Uchizono later pointed out that Dance Theater Workshop already had been engaged in a regranting program with Joyce Mertz-Gilmore Foundation, but that her initiative sparked a meeting that resulted in the expansion of the regranting program to include more organizations, thereby benefiting more choreographers.

8. Movement Research founding member Cynthia Hedstrom read the transcript of my interview with Cathy Edwards and noted a number of misperceptions and rifts across generations. She eloquently responded to my conversation with Edwards by writing (in a 15 October 1995 personal communication): "and what does building a house in Vermont have to do with not being politicized; it might mean becoming more politicized—it is a really strangely damning connection to make. The perception that there was not 'politicized' or 'really beautiful dance movement' happening in the 1970s is very strange and sad to me. Perhaps [the misperceptions] are the tragic reality of dance—that once performed, it is gone. One can not really know it without having seen it."

References

Banes, Sally. 1994. *Writing Dancing in the Age of Postmodernism.* Middletown, Conn.: Wesleyan University Press.

Beavers, Wendell. 1993. "On Movement Research." *Performance Journal,* no. 6 (Spring-Summer 1993): 2.

Guilbaut, Serge. 1983. *How New York Stole the Idea of Modern Art: Abstract Expressionism, Freedom, and the Cold War.* Trans. Arthur Goldhammer. Chicago: University of Chicago Press.

Novack, Cynthia J. 1990. *Sharing the Dance: Contact Improvisation and American Culture.* Madison: University of Wisconsin Press.

Traube, Elizabeth G. 1992. *Dreaming Identities: Class, Gender, and Generation in 1980s Hollywood Movies.* Boulder, Colo.: Westview Press.

Contributors

Melissa Cefkin is a research scientist at the Institute for Research on Learning.

Robbie Davis-Floyd is a research fellow in the Department of Anthropology at the University of Texas, Austin, and a research associate in the Department of Anthropology at Rice University.

Kim Fortun teaches in the Department of Science and Technology Studies at Rensselaer Polytechnic Institute.

Michael Fortun is a historian of science and executive director of the Institute for Science and Interdisciplinary Studies at Hampshire College, Amherst, Massachusetts.

Laurel George is a graduate student in the Department of Anthropology at Rice University.

Gudrun Klein is a research associate in the Department of Anthropology at Rice University.

George E. Marcus is professor and chair in the Department of Anthropology at Rice University.

Christopher J. Newfield teaches in the Department of English at the University of California, Santa Barbara.

Constance Perin is a visiting scholar at the Program in Science, Technology, and Society at the Massachusetts Institute of Technology.

Santiago Villaveces-Izquierdo is a graduate student in the Department of Anthropology at Rice University.

INDEX